In accordance with the latest syllabus prescribed by the council for the Indian Certificate of Secondary Education Examination, New Delhi.

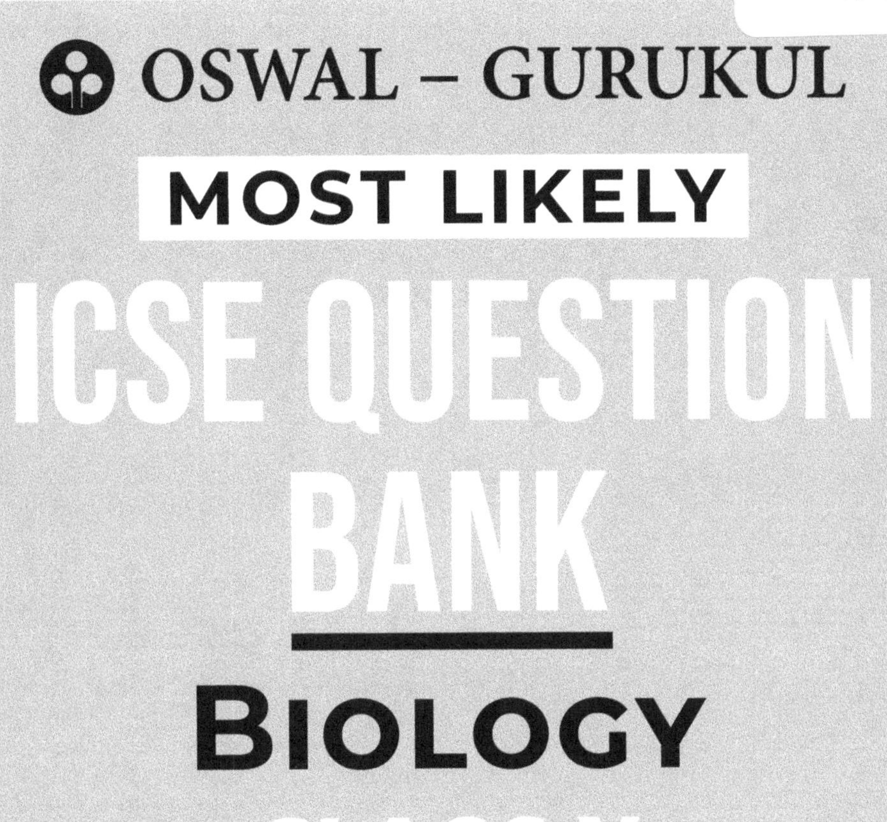

By

PANEL OF AUTHORS

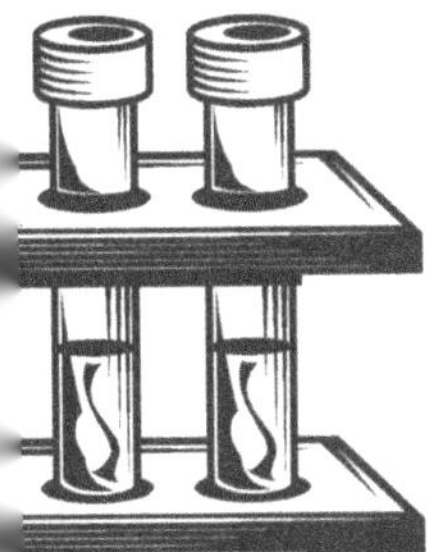

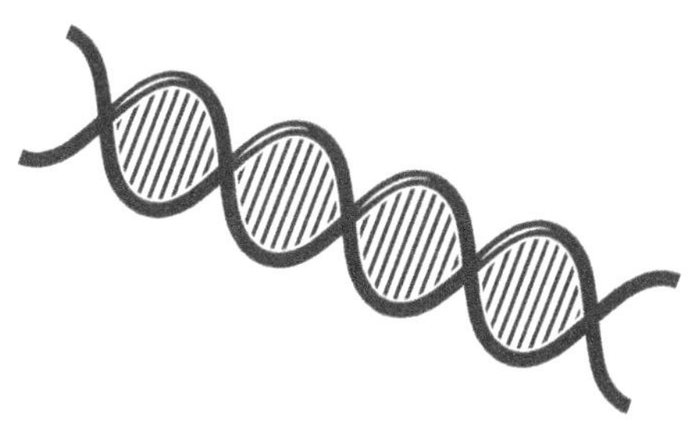

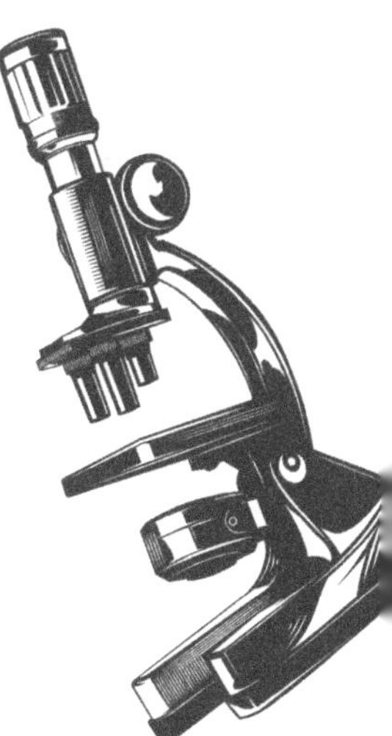

DISCLAIMER

With the ambition of providing standard academic resources, we have exercised extreme care in publishing the content. In case of any discrepancies in the matter, we request readers to excuse the unintentional lapse and not hold us liable for the same. Suggestions are always welcome.

EDITION : 2022

ISBN : 978-93-92563-78-2

PRICE : ₹ 299.00

PRINTED AT :

PUBLISHED BY

OSWAL PUBLISHERS

Head Office : 1/12, Sahitya Kunj, M.G. Road, Agra – 282 002

Phone : (0562) 2527771-4

Whatsapp : +91 74550 77222

E-mail : info@oswalpublishers.in

Website : www.oswalpublishers.com

The cover of this book has been designed using resources from Freepik.com

PREFACE

It is a matter of immense pride for us to present our 'MOST LIKELY ICSE QUESTION BANK' series, especially prepared for students appearing for Board examinations in the oncoming year.

This book is a perfect capsule for building self-confidence during exam. preparation. Based on chunking strategy, the 'Categorywise–Chapterwise' format with its exhaustive set of questions allow the students to cover every category in a chapterwise manner.

Covering easy categories first boosts student's self-esteem and the ascending score braces them to take up challenging categories without fear. This prepares the student to see the exam paper as achievable at all times.

With its simple language and style, it is a one-stop solution for smart study. We are confident that the book will enable the candidates to develop a better understanding of the curriculum and help them organize their learning process. This book shall definitely prove to be a fruitful tool for the students and encourage them towards scholastic excellence.

Constructive suggestions for further improvement of the book are always welcome.

Note: Questions marked with '*' are frequently asked in previous years board examinations.

—Publisher

LET'S GO ORGANIC

 Growing microgreens can be a good, easy and economical way for a student to start practicing plantation at home.

 You can spread a mixture of coco-peat and fertile topsoil or a stack of moist tissue papers over it. Remember to keep the tissue paper moist till the seeds start germinating.

 Microgreens are highly nutritious plants that are harvested after the sprout-stage and just before the maturity phase.

 Cover the box with newspaper and keep it in a place where there is no direct sunlight.

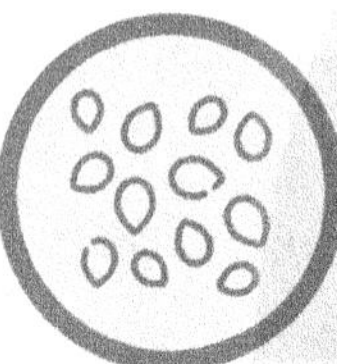 Microgreens may include mustard, coriander, basil seeds, dried peas, beans, broccoli, radish, spinach, beetroot, cauliflower and others.

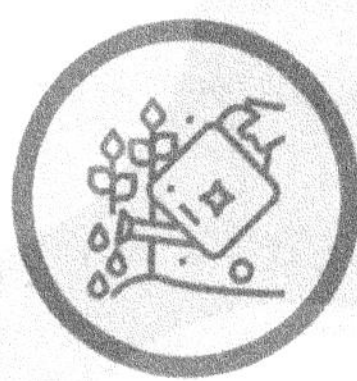 Spray water twice a day atleast.

 It is more convenient to start growing microgreens that require low maintenance like mustard, coriander, peas, basil and others.

 On third and fourth day, once the leaves start to appear, start exposing the germinating microgreens to indirect sunlight.

 Start with finding a flat tray or a shoe-box or any tetra-pack carton.

 You can try to expose them to direct sunlight for not more than 4 hours.

 Make holes in the box for easy drainage of water.

 By ninth or tenth day, your microgreens will be ready, harvest them!

 Spread two inches of soil in the box. You can get ready-made soil from the garden or nursery. Sprinkle your desired seeds over the soil.

 Microgreens can be eaten with sandwiches, wraps, salads, smoothies, juices or as garnishers on pizza, soup and curries.

CONTENTS

Note: Questions marked with '*' are frequently asked in previous years board examinations.

SUGGESTIONS FOR STUDENTS

1. Read the scope and syllabus prescribed for ICSE Biology.

2. Revise the topics repeatedly for better understanding of concepts.

3. Prepare a list of abbreviations you come across the syllabus, absorb them mentally.

4. Learn the keywords/biological terms/ technical terms /definitions with conceptual clarity.

5. Practise drawing neat and labelled diagrams.

6. Give importance to biological and technical terms.

7. Revise previous years question papers.

8. Make the best use of the 15 minutes reading time to understand and assimilate the questions.

9. Read the rubric attentively and choose the questions as per the rubrics, plan and organize your thoughts accordingly to give your best.

10. Follow carefully the instructions given for each question.

11. Attempt only the number of questions asked for in the question paper.

12. Select the four questions you know the best in Section II.

13. Write the correct question number before answering.

14. Be methodical and organised while answering.

15. Practise writing the overall balanced equation for Photosynthesis.

16. Revise your answers thoroughly after completion so as to eliminate errors or terms/words missed out.

17. Do not separate the subsections of the question.

18. Write in a neat and legible handwriting.

19. Be confident and rely only on yourself.

20. Do not attempt more questions than asked for in the question paper.

Word of Advice

Chapter 1. Cell Division

Topics Found difficult By Students
- Difference between Plant cell and Animal cell.
- Stages of Mitosis, number of chromosomes in daughter cells as a result of Mitosis and Meiosis.
- Nuclear changes in Mitosis.

1. Majority of students could identify the stages in the *mitotic cell division* correctly but could not give a valid reason.
2. Many students did not draw the correct *diagram of Telophase. Daughter nuclei with nuclear membrane were not shown.* Some students labelled *nuclear membrane* as *cell membrane.*
3. Majority of the students were unsure of *the difference between plant and animal cell.*
4. A few students were unable to give *the pattern of arrangement of Chromosomes,* in the cell division stages.
5. A few students did not keep the chromosome number constant in Anaphase diagram.
6. Most students were unsure of *the sequence of mitotic stages.* Many of them did not draw the required number of chromosomes.
7. Many students could not spell *Mitosis* and *Meiosis* correctly.
8. Many students were confused in *Anaphase* and 'Metaphase' stage.
9. Many students were confused in the number of daughter cells and chromosome number.
10. Some of the students were not aware about *the difference between chromosome and chromatid.*

Chapter 2. Fundamentals of Genetics

Topics Found difficult By Students
- Diagram of duplicated chromosome.
- Number of Chromosomes in somatic cells and gametes.
- Nucleosome and Nucleotide.
- Mendel's Laws, Monohybrid ratios of F_1 and F_2 generation.
- Genetic diseases and Mutations.

1. Some students wrote *Homozygous* instead of *Homologous chromosomes.*
2. Most students could not relate the term *genetic disease.*
3. Some students wrote *Dioxyribo nucleic acid,* instead of *Deoxyribo nucleic acid*
4. A few used a criss-cross method to answer, instead of Punette square when clearly mentioned in question.
5. Few students confused dihybrid cross with Monohybrid cross.
6. A few wrote *Thiamine and Adenosine, instead of Thymine and Adenine* while naming nitrogenous bases of DNA.
7. Some students mentioned *covalent bonding,* instead of *hydrogen bonding between bases.*
8. Majority of the students could not write the *possible combinations of the gametes* that can be obtained if two F_1 hybrid plants are crossed.
9. A few students wrote only the generic name of the plant which Mendel used for his experiments.
10. Some students confused between *nucleosome* and *nucleotide.*
11. Most students could not spell *Guanine* correctly.
12. Instead of writing nucleotides, some of the students specified the components of nucleotides and lost marks.
13. Most students were unsure of *the inheritance of sex linked diseases* and their answers were vague.
14. The majority of the students were unable to differentiate between *Phenotype* and *Genotype* and between F_1 and F_2 generation and hence could not write the correct answer.

15. Most of the students were confused with *the three laws of Mendel* and were unable to write the correct one as per the question.
16. Most of the students wrote just 'X' and 'Y' as sex chromosomes in males and females.
17. Some of the students missed out the word *'sudden'* in the definition of *Mutation*.
18. Some of the students did not mention *the concept of a pair of contrasting characters.*

Chapter 3. Absorption by Roots

1. Some students could not explain *plasmolysis/exosmosis* using technical terms.
2. Few students wrote *imbibition* instead of *endosmosis*, for absorption by roots.
3. A few students wrote *semi permeable membrane for cell wall.*
4. Most students wrote the definitions of active transport and diffusion instead of their significance in plants.
5. Withdrawal of cell membrane from cell wall was not shown as the students failed to understand the concept of *Plasmolysis.*
6. Few of the students who were unsure of the concepts wrote diffusion or osmosis instead of Active transport.
7. Some of the students wrote *particles for molecules* in the difference between the *diffusion* and *osmosis.*
8. There was general confusion between *Turgor and Wall pressure.*
9. Some of the students wrote incorrect answers like 'cell organelles' instead of 'cell contents'.
10. Some of the students did not understand the meaning of technical terms and hence wrote *'high concentration, low concentration or same concentration of solution'.*
11. Some of the students were not clear about the reason for the size of potato cube being the same. They were not aware about the *concept of osmosis.*
12. Some students did not mention the *role of semipermeable membrane.*
13. Some of the students wrote *more permeable/less permeable* instead of writing technical terms in the definitions or the scientific terms.

Chapter 4. Transpiration

Topics Found difficult By Students
 ➢ Diagram of Stomatal apparatus.
 ➢ Tonicity of solutions and their effect on cells.
 ➢ Plasmolysed cell – Labelling and causes.
 ➢ Definition of Turgor Pressure
 ➢ Identifying experiments associated with Transpiration from those of Photosynthesis.

1. Most of the students wrote that transpiration occurs in soil, which is incorrect.
2. Most of the students failed to mention the *intensity of external factors which will accelerate the process.*
3. Most students did not draw epidermal cells surrounding the guard cells, in the *diagram of a stomatal apparatus.*
4. Few students could not recognise the *experiment set ups related to the photosynthesis and transpiration.*
5. Many students wrote common words like *Swells* and *Shrinks* instead of *Turgid* and *Flaccid* respectively.
6. Many students wrote the explanation in terms of transpiration instead of hypertonic medium and ex-osmosis in response to the statement: *Plants growing in fertilised soil are often found to wilt if the soil is not adequately watered.*
7. Some students wrote *Absorption* instead of *Transpiration.*
8. Majority of the students could not relate bright sunlight to loss in weight of the plant due to increased transpiration.
9. Some students were confused between 'endosmosis' and 'exosmosis'.
10. Majority of the students mentioned the process instead of the state of cell in case of plasmolysis.
11. Many students were unsure of the part of the cell which is selectively permeable.
12. Many students did not mention the term *deplasmolysis'* for the recovery of the cell.
13. Few students spelt *"Potometer"* as *"Photometer".*
14. Some of the students were unsure of the content and the corresponding physiological experiments they identified the process as Photosynthesis instead of Transpiration.

15. Most of the students did not know the *significance of the air bubble in the experiment*. They were vague in their answers and mentioned that it demonstrates transpiration.
16. Most of the students did not mention that the prevention of water loss is from the soil.
17. Majority of the students were unaware that even *the stems of plants can transpire.*

Chapter 5. Photosynthesis

Topics Found difficult By Students
  ➢ Factors affecting Photosynthesis.
  ➢ Definition of Photophosphorylation.
  ➢ Interdependence of Photosynthesis and Respiration.
  ➢ Experiments on Photosynthesis and significance of Photosynthesis.
  ➢ Various steps involved in starch test while testing a lead for starch and their importance.
  ➢ Significance of destarching before beginning an experiment on photosynthesis.

1. Most students did not name the factor studied in *the experiment for sunlight in photosynthesis*. They wrote the process instead of the factor.
2. Many students could not give a clear explanation of the *starch test*. They did not specify the colour change in the covered and uncovered parts of the experimental leaf.
3. A few balanced the *photosynthesis equation* by taking $6H_2O$ instead of $12H_2O$.
4. Most students drew an incorrect diagram of *an experimental setup to show oxygen is released during photosynthesis*, using a mouse and bell jar instead of taking a Hydrilla plant submerged in water.
5. Some students did not know *the usage of methylated spirit in the starch test*. Most of students wrote *'iodine'* instead of *'alcohol'* for solvent in starch test.
6. Majority of the students mention that *de-starching takes place in plant instead of leaves.*
7. Majority of the students did not mention the **parts of leaf** which give positive and negative test for starch.
8. A few students did not draw a *double membrane for chloroplast.*
9. Most students were unable to expand the abbreviation *NADP.*
10. Some of the students did not mention that *oxygen is released during Photosynthesis.*
11. Most of the students were unaware of the *reaction of sodium bicarbonate in water to increase carbon dioxide.*
12. Students failed to mention *the significance of sunlight and chlorophyll for Photosynthesis to convert ADP to ATP.*
13. Most of the students were confused in the experiments related to *respiration and photosynthesis* in plants.
14. Some of the students failed to mention the raw materials or the end products at the end of the process.
15. Majority of the students were confused and wrote that both plant and snail evolved bubbles. They could not relate photosynthesis to respiration.
16. Few of the students did not mention the factors affecting the photosynthesis process such as sunlight and chlorophyll.
17. Many students were unaware about *the steps involved in starch test.*

Chapter 6. Chemical Coordination in Plants

Topics Found difficult By Students
  ➢ Difference between Stimulus and Tropic movement.

1. Most students could not spell *Abscisic acid*, correctly.
2. Some students spelt *Indole* as *'Indone'*, while expanding IAA and did not mention the *number '3'. (Indole 3-Acetic Acid)*
3. Some students could not label the diagram showing experimental set up to *demonstrate tropic movement in germinating seeds*. They labelled the parts as, root and shoot.

4. Some students could not differentiate between *thigmotropism* and *nastic movements* correctly.

5. A few students were unable to give a clear differentiation between the '*Positive*' and '*Negative*' tropic *movements* in plants.

6. Most students wrote the *tropic movements* instead of the *stimuli*, for the germinating of seeds.

Chapter 7. The Circulatory System

Topics Found difficult By Students
> Internal structure of heart, valves and blood vessels associated with heart, left and right side of heart.
> Functions of WBCs.
> Efficiency of RBCs in transporting Oxygen to tissues.
> Compounds formed by CO_2 and CO with haemoglobin. Effect of CO poisoning.
> Difference between carbamino-haemoglobin and Carboxyhaemoglobin.
> Blood vessels supplying the organs and the kind of blood they carry.
> Structural differences between artery and vein.
> Importance of Hepatic portal vein.

1. Most students wrote *carboxyhaemoglobin* instead of *carbaminohaemoglobin*.
2. *Supply of oxygen to tissues being cut off*, was not mentioned while explaining *the effect of CO inhalation*.
3. Some students wrote *vein*, instead of *artery*, for *measuring pulse rate*.
4. Majority of students are unaware of the fact that *sperms form are of two types: X- and Y- chromosome containing sperms*.
5. Most students could not explain the *function of coronary artery* correctly and not specify *oxygenated blood*.
6. Some students got confused between *Hepatic artery* and *Hepatic vein*.
7. Majority of the students were confused with the oxygen content in *pulmonary artery* and *pulmonary vein*.
8. Many students wrote the *location of the pulmonary semilunar valve* in between right and left ventricle.
9. A few students named the soluble protein found in plasma which forms insoluble threads during clotting of blood as *Fibrin* instead of *Fibrinogen*.
10. Many students could not write the correct *sequence for the process of clotting of blood*.
11. A number of students were vague in writing the *source of antibody*. They wrote 'WBC' instead of '*lymphocytes*'.
12. Many students did not write the *reason for thickening of the right ventricle* correctly.
13. Many of students could not give a reason for diagram of *diastolic phase of circulation*.
14. Several errors were noticed in drawing the *cross section of an artery and a vein, their labelling and the size of lumen*.
15. A lot of confusion prevailed among the students regarding *the valves in the heart* and *the sound produced during their closure*. Most mentioned only one valve for each sound and lost marks.
16. The majority of the students were confused with the right and left side of the heart.
17. Most of the students were unaware of the *structure of arteries*. They could not relate the thickness of walls and the narrow lumen to flow of blood.
18. Students were not able to identify the blood vessels correctly while some of the students identified the blood vessels as blood cells.
19. Some of the students did not mention the *exact shape of RBCs* while differentiating between the *RBCs* and *WBCs* some of the students drew nucleus in *RBCs* as they were not sure that they are *enucleated*.
20. Most of the students failed to mention the *closure of both cuspid valves*.
21. Most of the students labelled *Pulmonary artery* as *Aorta* and vice versa.
22. Most of the students did not relate the *Pulse* to *heart beat*.
23. A few candidates misspelt '*Aorta* as '*Arota*'.
24. Most of the students did not know the importance of the terms *oxygenated* and *deoxygenated blood* while answering *the function of Hepatic artery and Inferior Venacava*.
25. Most of the students were unaware of *the importance of Hepatic Portal Vein*.

Chapter 8. The Excretory System

Topics Found difficult By Students
- Structure and Significance of Nephron and the reason for ultrafiltration in Urine formation.
- Drawing and labelling Malpighian capsule.

1. Majority of students named *Excretory system/Urinary system* as 'Urinogenital system'
2. Some students could not mention the *main nitrogenous waste present in urine.*
3. A few students could not show a clear differentiation between renal cortex and medulla.
4. Majority of the students, instead of writing *Urochrome*, wrote *Bilirubin* for the *colour of urine.*
5. A few students were confused between *renal artery* and *renal vein.*
6. Some students confused between the terms *Homeostasis* and *Osmoregulation.*
7. Few students wrote kidney instead of liver, as organ which produce urea.
8. Many students did not relate *the concept of sweat formation to urine output.*
10. Some of the candidates were unsure of the parts of the kidney and hence could not explain the stripped appearance of medulla.
11. Some of the students wrote *neuron* for *nephron.*
12. Majority of the students drew the diagram of the entire *nephron* instead of just the *Malpighian capsule.* Some were unaware of the difference in *diameter of the Afferent and Efferent arteriole.*
13. Most of the candidates related selective reabsorption to kidney instead of nephrons.
14. Some of the students wrote *collecting tubule* instead of 'Collecting duct'.

Chapter 9. The Nervous System and Sense Organs

Topics Found difficult By Students
- Parts of brain and their functions.
- Placement of Cytons and Axons in brain and spinal cord.
- Medulla Oblongata from spinal cord.
- Number of spinal and cranial nerves.
- Reflex arc and the neurons associated with it.
- Parts of eyeball and their functions.
- Layers of eyeball and their associated structures.
- Accommodation and Adaptation of eye.
- Functions of Rods and Cones in Retina.
- Reasons for myopia and hypermetropia and their correction.
- Parts of ear and their functions.
- Parts of Membranous labyrinth.

1. Most students could not spell *Choroid, cerebellum* correctly.
2. Few students wrote *Choroid as part of eye donated from a clinically dead person.*
3. Few students did not know the *number of Cranial and Spinal Nerves.*
4. Many students could not explain the *location of Corpus callosum* and wrote vague answers such as, in the brain, in the cerebrum.
5. Majority of the students confused with *the functions of cerebellum and medulla oblongata.*
6. Most students were unsure of the *placement of cytons and axons in brain and spinal cord.*
7. Many students did not mention *the role of rhodopsin for adaptation of eye.*
8. Many students confused between *choroid* and *sclera.*
9. Many students were unsure of *the location of aqueous humour.*
10. Many students were confused with *the location of the three meninges.*

11. The students were unaware of the *fluid surrounding the organ of Corti.*
12. Many students were unsure of the layer of eyeball which forms the Iris.
13. Majority of the students, instead of writing upper outer corner of the eye, wrote above the eye, while mentioning the location of *lacrimal gland.*
14. Majority of the students did not know the difference between *synapse* and *synaptic cleft, nerve* and *neuron.*
15. Some students labelled *neuron* as *nerve.*
16. Many students wrote *the location of grey and white matter instead of Cytons and Axons.*
17. Some were confused with *the function of Saccules.*
18. A few mentioned myelin sheath as '*around the neuron*' instead of '*it surrounds the axon of neuron*'
19. A few labelled the '*spinal cord*' as '*medulla oblongata*'.
20. Most students were confused with *the arrangement of neurons in the cerebrum and the spinal cord.*
21. *The concept of Membranous Labyrinth* was not clear among the students. Most of them, did not draw the three semi-circular canals and the cochlea. Many students drew all the parts of the ear.
22. Some of the students were confused with the parts responsible for *static* and *dynamic balance* of the body. Some of the students wrote *Perilymph* instead of *Endolymph* for the fluid in the middle chamber of Cochlea. Some of them lost marks for writing Cochlea instead of organ of corti for sensory cells for hearing.
23. Most of the students gave the incomplete explanation for the *Reflex action definition.* Enough stress was not laid on important words like involuntary, automatic and quick actions.
24. Some of the students failed to give the complete explanation regarding focal length of lens and distance of objects.
25. Some of the students got confused between the terms "*Cornea*" and "*Conjunctiva*".
26. Some of the students were unsure of the concept and wrote "*hyperopia*" instead of "*Presbyopia*".
27. Most of the students related *the function of ear ossicles* to sound waves and not sound vibrations.
28. Some of the candidates misspelt the names of *pigments.*
30. Some of the students did not describe *the shape of eye lens in near and distant vision* correctly.
31. Most of the students were unaware of the *specific functions of corpus callosum* and wrote incorrect answers like 'joins cerebrum'.
32. Some of the students mentioned '*Synaptic cleft*' instead of '*Synapse*'.
33. Some of the students mentioned '*dorsal root*' instead of *Dorsal Root Ganglion.*
35. Some of the students made labelling errors especially with Cyton and Axon and labelled one for the other. A few did not draw dendrites and Axon endings for the neuron.

Chapter 10. The Endocrine System

> *Topics Found difficult By Students*
> ➢ Disorders in human body due to Hyposecretion and Hypersecretion of hormones.

1. Few students expand TSH as *Thyroxine Stimulating Hormone,* instead of *Thyroid Stimulating Hormone.*
2. A large number of students could not give the *exact location of the endocrine glands.*
3. Many students were uncertain of the *hormones secreted by the two lobes of the Pituitary gland.*
4. A few students wrote *insulin* instead of *glucose* present in the blood in *Diabetes mellitus.*
5. Some students wrote the names of the structure instead of writing the names of the organ, secreting hormones.
6. Many students spelt *Oxytocin* incorrectly.
7. A few wrote *calcium* instead of *Iodine* for *Thyroid gland.*
8. Majority of them were confused between *Cretinism* and *Myxoedema.*
9. Most students did not write '*Overgrowth or over secretion of cortisones*' as the reason for facial hairs in women.
10. Some students wrote *Calcitonin* but gave the function of *Thyroxine.*
11. Some students were not specific in answers and just wrote Beta cells instead of mentioning pancreas as well.
12. Most of the students did not mention the term Endocrine glands in the explanation when the definition of the hormone was asked.
13. Some of the candidates were unsure of the *hormone* and the related disorder.

14. Majority of the students explained the term '*Hormone*' correctly but were unable to give the role of Tropic hormones in the human body.

Chapter 11. The Reproductive System

Topics Found difficult By Students
- Parts and function of male and female reproductive system in human.
- Exact location of accessory glands of male reproductive system.
- Chromosomes in sperm.
- Internal structure of testis.
- Fertilization, Implantation, Gestation and Menstrual cycle in female reproductive system.

1. Some students spelt *Umbilical cord* as '*Ambilical cord*', and *Amniotic fluid* as '*Amnion fluid*'.
2. Many students could not explain the *location of testis* and wrote vague answers such as, outside the abdomen instead of Scrotum.
3. A few wrote the *function of testis instead of seminal vesicles*.
4. A few students did not mention the word female or male while identifying the reproductive system.
5. Majority of the students confused between the labelling of *Vagina* and *Cervix*.
6. Majority of the students were unable to specify the *exact location of Epididymis*.
7. A few students were unsure of *the sequence of fertilisation*.
8. Some students were unable to explain *implantation*.
9. Some students were unable to show a clear differentiation of the three *parts of the sperm*.
11. Most students were unable to give *the exact location of the prostate gland*.
12. Many students could not relate temperature regulation, storage and maturation of sperms to the functions of *scrotum* and *epididymis*.
13. Most students did not mention about the *level of progesterone* which increases to stop the *menstrual cycle*.
14. Some of the students were confused with the location of *Placenta* and *Amniotic fluid*.
15. Some of the students get confused between the terms "*Menarche*" and "*Menopause*".
16. Some of the students misspelt as '*Prostrate*' instead of *Prostate* gland.
17. Some of the students get confused between the terms "*Tubectomy*" and "*Vasectomy*"

Chapter 12. Human Population

Topics Found difficult By Students
- Birth rate, Death rate, Growth rate.
- Distinguishing reasons for population explosion in India and in the world.

1. Most students could not differentiate between *Birth rate*, *Death rate* and *Growth Rate of population*.
2. A few students wrote incorrect explanation for the statement: *All the food chains begin with green plants.*
3. Many students defined '*demography* 'correctly but the definition of '*population density*' was incomplete.
4. Few of the students were not familiar with the term *population density* and hence wrote *census* instead of it.
5. Student did not stress on keywords like – *live*, *number* and *year* and mistook the term *Natality* for *Death rate*.

Chapter 13. Human Evolution

Topics Found difficult By Students
- Discoveries of Watson, and Crick, Lamarck and Darwin.
- Organism for industrial melanism.

1. Most students could not differentiate between the theories of *Mendel, Darwin* and *Lamarck.*
2. Most students could not write the *common name or scientific name of the organism.*

Chapter 14. Pollution

> ***Topics Found difficult By Students***
> - Acid rain and its effect on environment.
> - Biodegradable and Non-biodegradable wastes.
> - Greenhouse gases and gases causing depletion of ozone layer.

1. Some students wrote 'CO_2' as *ozone depleting gas,* instead of *CFCs.*
2. Most of the students could not explain the term *pollutant.* '*Causes Pollution*' was the vague answer written by many students.
3. A few wrote '*vehicular emissions*' instead of '*refrigeration equipment*' as a source of CFCs.
4. Most students were confused whether *DDT* was an *antiseptic* or a *disinfectant.*
5. Many of the students were confused with the gases of Acid rain and the Greenhouse effect.

Miscellaneous :
1. Biological abbreviations and expansions.
2. Identifying the odd term and mentioning the category of the rest.
3. Arrangement of terms in logical sequence.
4. Stating the exact location of structures/organs in the body of plants and animals.
5. Explanations of biological terms.
6. Giving appropriate reasons for biological statements.

❑

Chapter at a Glance | Set 1 |

Chapter 1. Cell Division

- **Cell Cycle :** The orderly sequence of events by which the cell duplicates its contents and divides into two is called cell cycle.

  Cell division was first studied by Prevost and Dumas (1824 A.D.) in the zygote of a frog and details were studied by Nageli (1846 A.D.)

  Types of Cell Division : Cell division is of three types :
  (i) Amitosis or direct cell division
  (ii) Mitosis or indirect cell division

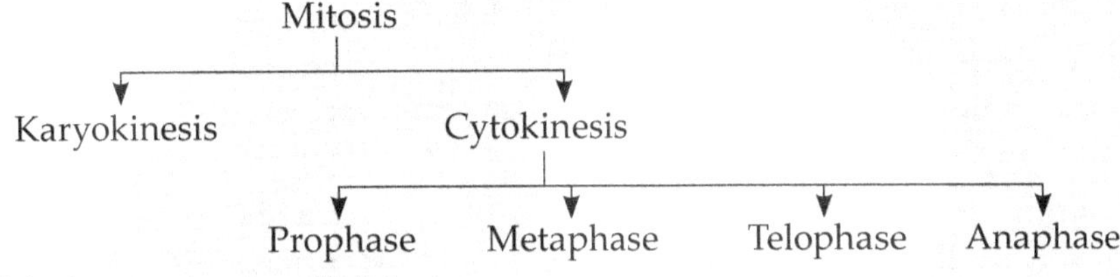

  (iii) Meiosis or reduction division

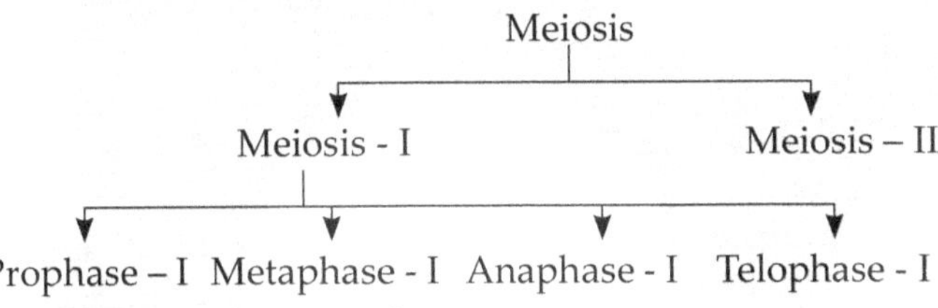

  Chromosomes : They are of two types

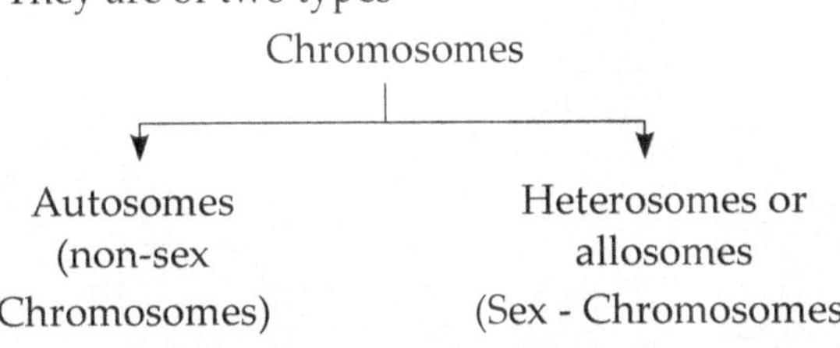

Chapter 2. Fundamentals of Genetics

- Genetics is the science of study of heredity and variations from one generation to the next.
- The phenomenon of passing of characters from parents to progeny through successive generations is called heredity.
- The differences found in the offsprings of the same parents and in the individuals of the same species are referred to as variations.
- Genes are the specific parts of a chromosome (DNA segment) which determine the hereditary characteristics.
- **Chromosomal Theory of Inheritance :** It was propounded independently by Sutton and Boveri in 1902.
- **Mendelian genetics :** Gregor Johann Mendel (1866); the 'Father of Genetics' gave the very basic ideas of genetics based upon his long term studies on pea plants (Pisum sativum).

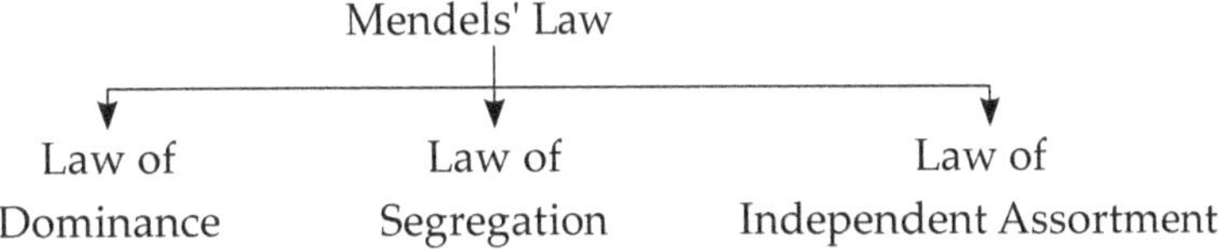

➤ **Phenotype :** The characters which are visible from the outside and they are genetically controlled form the phenotype.

➤ **Genotype :** The combination of genes in an organism which cannot be seen from outside form the genotype.

➤ **Determinattion of sex :** Sex-chromosomes determine the sex of the individual. They are either X- or Y-chromosomes. A male has XY (heterozygous) chromosomes while a female has XX (homozygous) chromosomes. So the sex of a baby depends upon the type of sperm cell that fertilizes the egg. That is male determines the sex of the child in Humans.

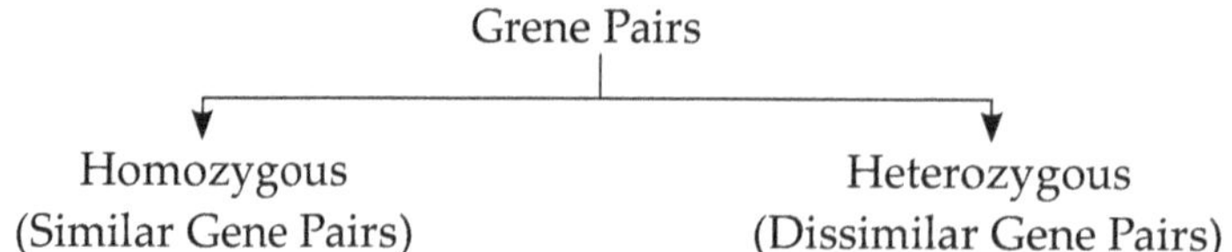

➤ **Genetic Diseases :** Genetic disorders are mostly related to X-chromosome since it is common to both male and female.

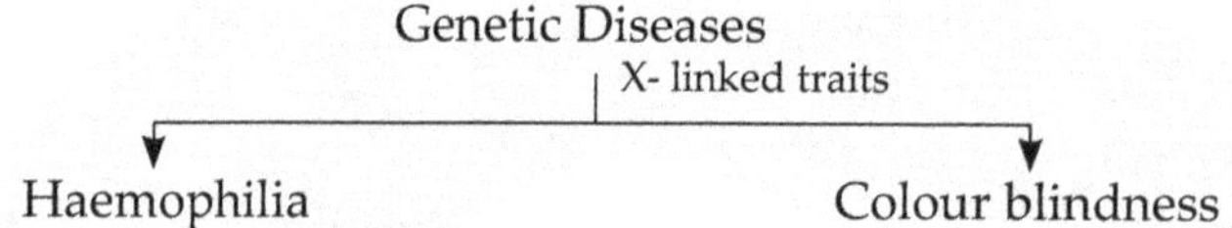

➤ Any Sudden change brought about through external or internal factors in the genetic composition is known as mutation. It can be artificially induced by X-rays, radiation, high temperature, etc. Mutation can play an important role in speciation and evolution.

➤ Some genes, of a particular chromosome are linked together and they are inherited together from generation to generation. This, phenomenon is called linkage. Linkage of a particular set of genes may not be permanent.

➤ Interchange of parts of chromatid of a pair of chromosomes is known as crossing-over. Temperature, X-rays and radiation treatment greatly influence the frequency of crossing-over

Chapter 3. Absorption by Roots

➤ Water is a universal solvent needed for all the important life activities. Land plants absorb water from the soil by root hairs. These are unicellular outgrowth of roots.

Absorption by roots

Roots absorb water and minerals from the soil.

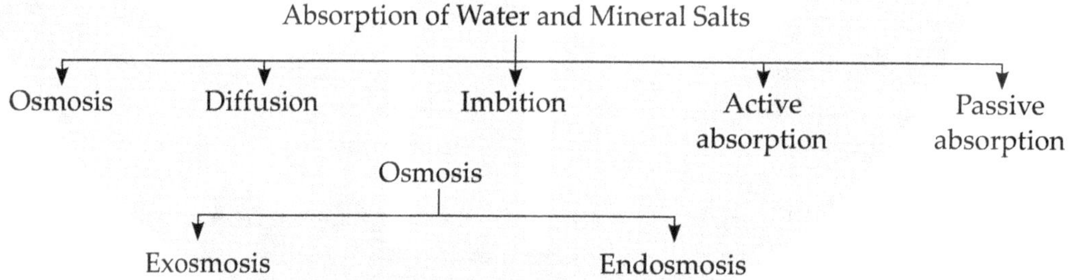

➤ **Active Transport :** Active transport is the passage of a substance (salt or ion) from its lower to higher concentration (opposite to what happens in diffusion), using energy from the cell, through a living cell membrane.

➤ **Passive Transport :** Passive transport is nothing different from diffusion but just explaining its meaning. 'Passive' refers to requiring no input of energy. There is a free movement of molecules from their higher concentration to their lower concentration.

Significances :

  (i) Osmosis : Absorb water from the soil by transpiration.

   Regulates opening and closing of stomata.

  (ii) Imbibition : Helps in the uptake of soil water by the root hairs.

   Helps in the ascent of sap.

  (iii) Turgidity : Brings about movement of water.

   Essential for initial growth.

   Provides rigidity.

Chapter 4. Transpiration

➢ **Transpiration :** Loss of water in the form of water vapour from aerial parts of the plants through stomata, lenticel or cuticle is known as transpiration.

Types of transpiration :

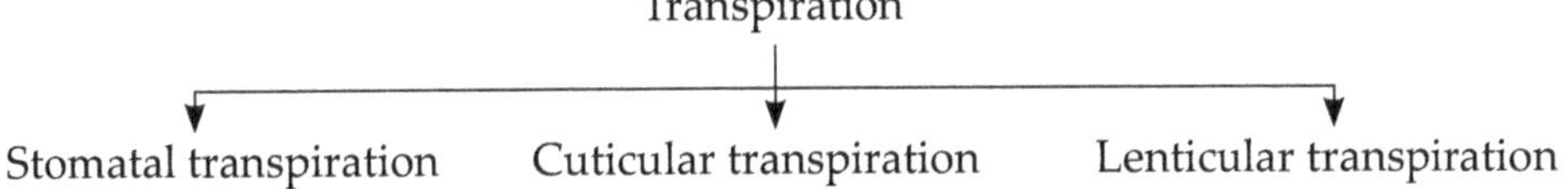

➢ Potometer is used for measuring the rate of transpiration in plants. The potometer uses only very small volumes of water. Therefore, changes in temperature produce almost negligible contractions and expansions which do not significantly affect the results of the experiment.

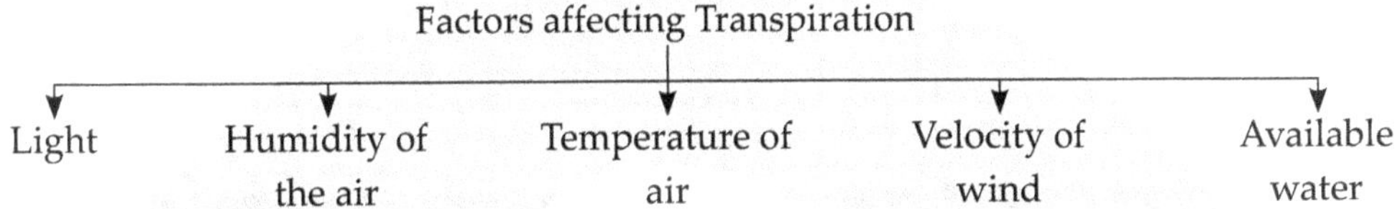

➢ Guttation is the exudation of drops of Xylem sap on the tips or edges of leaves of some vascular plants, such as grasses, and a number of Fungi.

➢ Bleeding is the flow of the plant sap due to injury. The oozing liquid may contain sugars and amino acids.

Chapter 5. Photosynthesis

➢ Photosynthesis is a photochemical process by which green plants manufacture complex molecules of food (carbohydrates) with the help of chlorophyll and solar energy, from simple inorganic compounds, such as carbon dioxide and water and release oxygen to the atmosphere.

The general equation of photosynthesis is

$$6CO_2 + 12H_2O \xrightarrow[\text{Chlorophyll}]{\text{Sunlight}} C_6H_{12}O_6 + 6H_2O + 6O_2\uparrow$$

Photosynthesis

Light reactions (Takes place in Grana)

Dark reactions (Takes place in Stroma)

Factors affecting Photosynthesis :

Factors affecting Photosynthesis

Light   Carbon dioxide   Temperature   Water

Chapter 6. Chemical Coordination in Plants

➢ The changes in the external or internal environment of an organism in known as stimuli and the resulting actions or movements caused by the stimuli are called respones.

➢ The term Hormone was first used by William Bayliss and Ernest Starling in 1902.

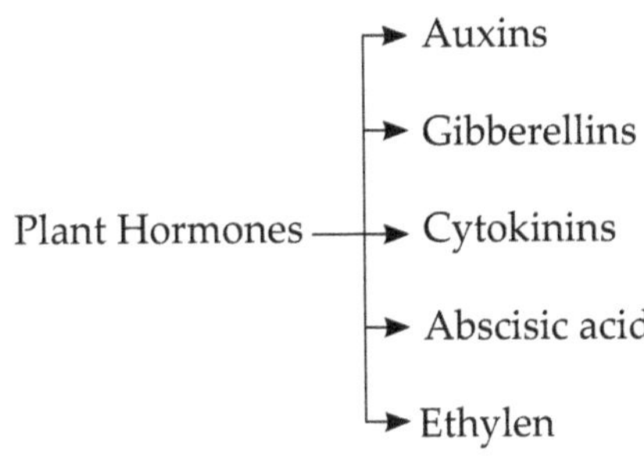

S. No.	Hormone	Discovered By
1.	Auxins	F.W. Went in 1928
2.	Gibberellins	Teijiro yabuta in 1935
3.	Cytokinins	Skoog and Miller in 1950s.
4.	Abscisic acid	Cornfortt and his associates in 1965.
5.	Ethylen	R. Gane in 1934.

➢ Plant hormones and their functions at a glance

Plant hormone	Site of synthesis	Functions
1. Auxins	Synthesized primarily in shoot spical meristems and young leaves.	Promote cell elongation. Suppress the growth of lateral buds. Delay fall of leaves. Induce formation of parthenocarpic fruits.
2. Gibberellins	Synthesized primarily in the meristems of apical buds and roots.	Help in stem-elongation. Break dormancy of seeds and buds. Delay senescence. Induce parthenocarpy.
3. Cytokinins	Systhesized primarily in roots and transported to other organs.	Stimulate cell-division and cell enlargement. Prevent ageing of plant parts. Inhibit apical dominance.
4. Ethylene	Synthesized in senescent leaves and flowers, germinating seeds and ripening fruits.	Induces fruit ripening. Promotes senescence.
5. Abscisic acid	Synthesized in green fruits and seeds at the beginning of the wintering period.	Induces dormancy of buds and seeds. Inhibits seed-germination and development. Stimulates closing of stomata.

➢ Trophic movements in Plants

Phototropism	Movement towards light
Geotropism	Movement towards earths' gravity.
Hydrotropism	Movement towards water or moisture.
Thigmotropism	Movement towards touch stimulus.
Chemotropism	Movement towards chemicals.

Movement	Root	Shoot
Phototropism	–ve	+ve
Geotropism	+ve	–ve
Hydrotropism	+ve	–ve
Thigmotropism	–ve	+ve
Chemotropism	–	–

Chapter 7. The Circulatory System

➢ A system which transports food, water, electrolytes, enzymes, hormones, antibodies and respiratory gases to or away from the body tissues is called the circulatory system.

➢ **Main Components :** Blood and lymph tissues, heart and blood vessels. (Arteries, veins, capillaries, lymphatic ducts, etc.).

➢ **Types of Circulatory System :** Two types of circulatory systems are found in animals :

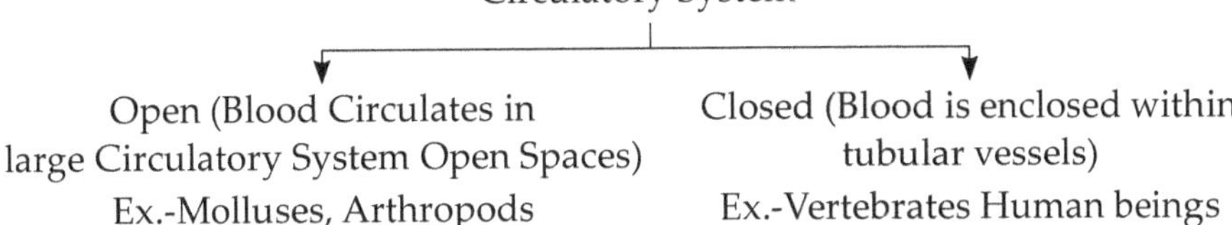

➢ William Harvey (1628) was the first who discovered the function of the heart and the circulation of blood.

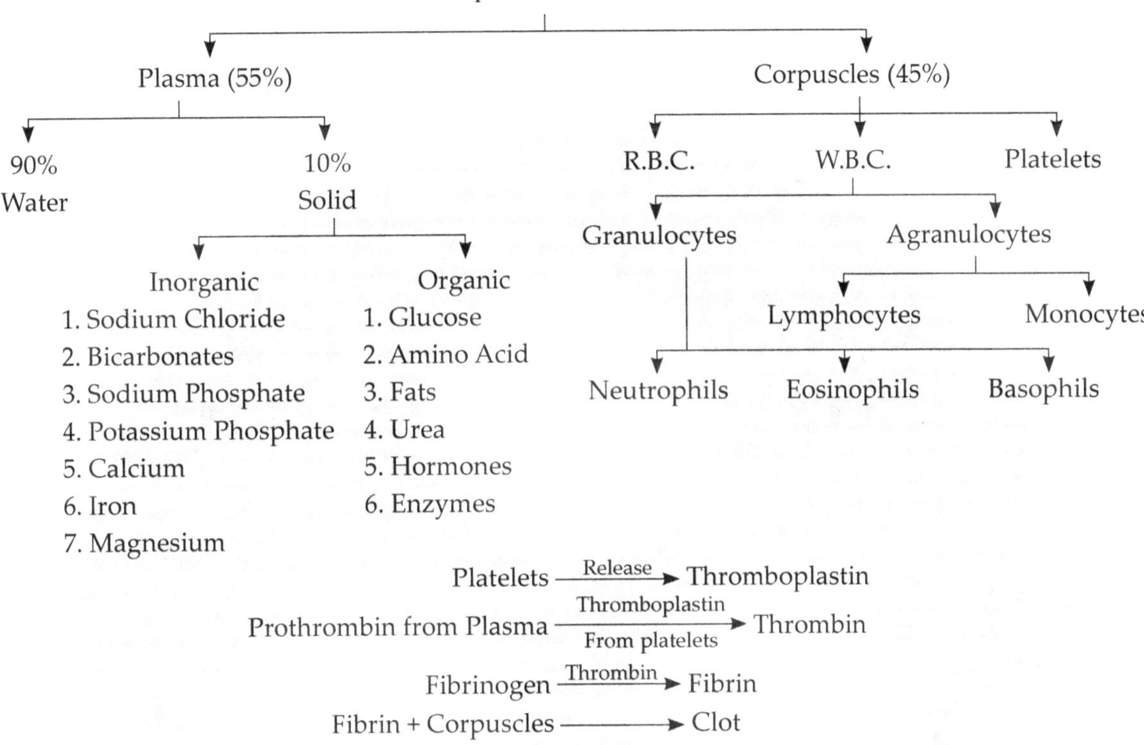

$$\text{Platelets} \xrightarrow{\text{Release}} \text{Thromboplastin}$$
$$\text{Prothrombin from Plasma} \xrightarrow[\text{From platelets}]{\text{Thromboplastin}} \text{Thrombin}$$
$$\text{Fibrinogen} \xrightarrow{\text{Thrombin}} \text{Fibrin}$$
$$\text{Fibrin + Corpuscles} \longrightarrow \text{Clot}$$

➢ Ca^{++} is necessary for blood clotting.

➢ **Blood Groups :** There are four types of blood groups in human beings. These are A, B, AB and O.

Antigen and Antibody in different Blood Groups

Blood Group	Antigen on RBC	Antibody in Plasma
A	A	Antibody B
B	B	Antibody A
AB	AB	None
O	None	Antibody-A and Antibody-B

➢ **Rh Factor :** It was discovered by Landsteiner (1940) in Rhesus monkey. The persons bearing this factor are Rh^{+ve} and persons who do not possess this factor are Rh^{-ve}.

➢ **Blood Pressure :** The pressure exerted by blood on the walls of blood vessels is known as blood pressure.

1. The normal blood pressure in the man is 120/80.
2. The pulse rate of a man at rest is about 72 beats per minute.
3. The time of the cardiac cycle is 0·8 seconds.

Disorders of Circulatory System

➢ **Hypertension :** Resting arterial pressure over a prolonged period of time.

➢ **Heart block :** Impulses are interrupted at any point of the heart.

➢ **Haemorrhage :** Excessive loss of blood.

➢ **Coronary thrombosis :** It is a kind of heart attack in which the clot is formed in the coronary artery which supply blood to the heart muscles.

Chapter 8. The Excretory System

- The elimination of harmful and unwanted waste products derived from the organism during its own metabolism is known as excretion.
- The excretory organs include kidneys, lungs, skin, intestine and liver.
- **Mechanism of Urine formation :** Urine is formed by the kidneys in the following three steps :
  - **(i) Ultrafiltration :** Formation of a protein free filtrate from the plasma into the Bowman's capsule through the glomerulus.
  - **(ii) Selective Reabsorption :** Some filtered materials are reabsorbed in the renal tubules.
  - **(iii) Secretion :** Collection of urine by the Pelvis from the tubules.
- **Disorders of the Kidney :**
  - **(i) Uremia :** (Nephritis) Due to malfunctioning of kidney, urea level in blood increases.
  - **(ii) Stone formation :** Due to precipitation of uric acid or accumulation of oxalate crystals, stones are formed in kidney.
  - **(iii) Diuresis :** The formation of excessive urine.
- **Renal Dialysis :** Renal dialysis is a device to treat kidney failure.

Chapter 9. The Nervous System and Sense Organs

-
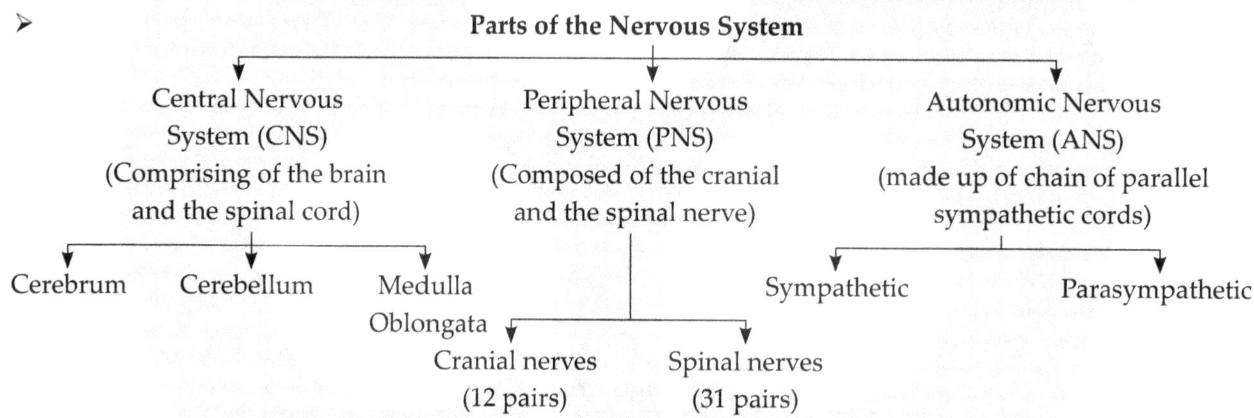

- **Neuron :** It is the functional unit of the nervous system. Each neuron consists of a cell body with cytoplasm, nucleus, nucleolus, mitochondria, Nissl's granules, golgi structure and thin processes or dendrites originating from dendrons a relatively long extension or axon originates from the cell body.

Types of Neuron

Sensory	Motor	Interneuron or Synapse
Carry impulse from sensory organs to CNS	Carry impulse from CNS to effector organs	Connects different neurons

- **The Brain :** In proportion to the size of the body, the human brain is the largest among all animals. The brain is a very delicate organ well- protected inside the brain box (cranium) of the skull.
- The brain is protected by three meninges-outermost duramater, middle arachnoid and the inner vascular piamater. The cranial bones give extra protection to it.

It has three parts :

Part of the brain	Function
1. Fore Brain : Cerebrum	Intelligence, voluntary actions, memory, sensation, etc.
Hypothalamus	Control of body temperature, emotions, appetite, etc.
Pituitary gland	A number of functions are performed through hormones secreted by this gland.
2. Mid Brain : Optic nerves	Vision and movement of eye balls.

3. Hind Brain : Cerebellum	Muscular co-ordination and balancing of body.
Medulla Oblongata Pons	Involuntary actions of several internal organs. It carries impluse from one hemisphere of the cerebellum to other.

➤ There are 12 pairs of cranial nerves arising from the pons, medulla and the diencephalon (between mid brain and cerebrum).

➤ The spinal cord transmits impulses from the periphery to the brain and vice–versa. It controls spinal reflexes routed along the reflex arc.

➤ There are 31 pairs of spinal nerves in humans, which emerge from the spinal cord at regular intervals as dorsal and ventral roots.

A reflex is an unconscious, unlearnt sudden response to a stimulus.

➤ **Reflex action :** is the involuntary automatic and often unconscious action or response brought about by stimulus received by different nerve endings or receptors. The reflex arc is the nerve chain between a receptor and an effector organ.

Types of Reflexes

Simple Reflexes   Conditioned Reflexes

➤ The sense organs (Receptors)

Kinds of Receptors	
1. Light Receptors or Photoreceptors	The eyes that are responding to light and capable to form images.
2. Heat Receptors	These receptors are capable of responding to changes in temperature rather than to heat and cold, e.g., skin.
3. Mechano-Receptors	These are sensitive to mechanical stimulations like touch, pressure, pain and vibrations producing sound.
4. Chemical Receptors	They have the ability to detect chemical changes in the environment and is a general property of protoplasm. Flavour of food, taste, smell etc. are detected by these receptors when their vapours or liquid forms come in contact with them.
5. Proprioceptors	These receptors, located in the muscles, tendons and joints of the bones, are sensitive to changes in the tension of the muscle or tendon and initiate impulses to the brain which are responsible for our awareness of the position and movement of the various parts of the body.

Chapter 10. The Endocrine System

➤ The branch of biology which deals with the study of endocrine glands, hormones and their effects is known as endocrinology.

➤ **Summary of some major Endocrine Glands**

Gland	Location	Secretion	Function	Hypo-secretion Under secretion	Hyper- secretion over secretion
1. Thyroid	On the either side of the root of trachea. They are joined by a narrow Isthmus	1. Thyroxin	It regulates the basal metabolism *i.e.,* the rate of cellular oxidation resulting in heat production.	Simple Goitre enlargement of thyroid cretinism. Dwarfism and mental retardation, myxedema swelling on face and hands, sluggishness	Exophthalmic goitre, protruding eyes, increased meta-bolism shortness of breathe, restlessness
		2. Calcitonin	Regulates calcium and phosphate levels in the blood	Tetany	
2. Adrenal gland	Situated on upper pole of each kidney				

Gland	Location	Secretion	Function	Hyposecretion	Hypersecretion
(i) Adrenal medulla (Central Medulla)		Adrenalin or (Epinephrine) or (Emergency hormone)	Heart beats faster. It constricts blood vessels		
		(i) It constricts the arterioles of digestive system. (ii) Constricts the arterioles of the skin.			Prolonged fight or flight symptoms which wears down the individual.
(ii) Adrenal cortex		Cortisone	Regulates metabolism helps body to adjust the stress.	Prepuberty males develop female secondary sex characteristics and *vice-versa*	In adults results acute change in secondary sex characteristics in young ones causes adrenal virilism.
Pancreas (i) Duct gland	Slightly below the stomach	Pancreatic juice (Exocrine gland)	Poured in the duodenum for digestion		
(ii) Ductless gland Islet of Langerhans (Endocrine gland)		(i) Insulin (from Beta cells)		Diabetes (Diabetes mellitus)	Insulin shock.
		(ii) Glucagon (alpha cells)	Raises blood sugar level		
		(iii) Somato - trophin (delta cells.)	Inhibits secretion of insulin and glucagon.		
Gonads					
(i) Testis (Male)	In the scrotum of males.	Testosterone and androsterone	Development of primary and secondary sex characteristics in males influences sexual instincts and reflexes.		
(ii) Ovary (female)	In the pelvic cavity .	(i) Oestrogens	Development of primary and secondary sex. Characteristics in female.		
		(ii) Progesterone	Prepares the uterus for the implan- tation, retention and growth of the foetus.		
		(iii) Relaxin	Helps to dilate the cervix towards the end of pregnancy to enable child birth.		

> **Hormones of Pituitary Gland :**

Gland	Location	Secretion	Function	Hyposecretion	Hypersecretion
1. Pituitary gland (master gland)	Attached to the hypothalamus of the brain.				
(i) Anterior lobe		1. Human growth hormones (HGH)	Stimulates general body growth	In childhood dwarfism	In childhood gigantisms in adult Acromegaly.

		2. Trophic hormones	Stimulate certain other endocrine gland		
		(i) Thyroid stimulating hormone (TSH)	Control the activities of thyroid.		
		(ii) Adrenocorticotrophic hormones (ACTH)	Stimulate adrenal cortex.		
		(iii) Gonadotrophic hormones	Stimulate testes and ovaries to produce gametes.		
		(iv) Luteinizing hormone (LH)	Stimulate the formation of corpus luteum to produce female hormone progesterone, and testes to produce male hormone.		
		3. Prolactin	Promotes lactation (milk formation and secretion)		
(ii) Posterior lobe		1. Vasopressin	Increases reabsorption of water from kidney tubules	Diabetes insipidus (Water diabetes)	
		2. Oxytocin	Stimulates the muscles of the uterus to contract during labour.		

Hormones are the chemical messengers as they function at a site for away from its place of origin.

- **Islet of Langerhans :** It is the group of polyhedral cells in the pancreas having endocrine functions.

  Epinephrine is called emergency hormone

- **Hormone**   **Full name**

  STH   Somatotrophic hormone

  ACTH   Adrenocortico trophic hormone

  ADH   Antidiuretic hormone

  GTH   Gonadotrophic hormone

  FSH   Follicle stimulating hormone

  LH   Luteinizing hormone.

- Pituitary gland is also known as master gland or Hypophysis.

- Castration is the process of removal of testis or ovary from the animals.

- **Endocrine Gland :** Gland that secretes hormones into the blood stream in order to regulate life processes are known as endocrine gland. In humans the main endocrine glands are the pituitary, thyroid, adrenal, pancreas and gonads.

Chapter 11. The Reproductive System

- Reproductive system is the system of organs which takes part in reproduction, i.e., multiplication of the individual.

- **Reproduction :** It is the ability of living organism to produce new living organisms, similar to themselves.

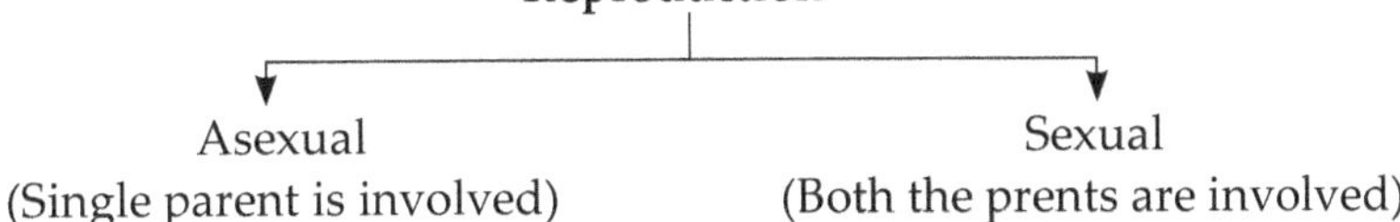

Reproductive Organs

Male Reproductive System

Testes (one pair)	Ducts	Accessory glands	Supportive Structure Penis
Produces sperms and hormones	Stores or transports the sperm to the exterior	Add secretions to the sperm constituting part of the semen	Transfers the sperm into the female body
(a) Seminiferous tubule (Produces sperms)	(a) Ducts of testes	(a) Seminal vesicle	
	(b) Epididymis	(b) Prostate gland	
	(c) Vas deferens	(c) Cowper's gland	
(b) Interstitial tissue (Secretes hormones)	(d) Ejaculatory duct		

➢ **Spermatogenesis :** The process of transformation of male germ cells, spermatogonia, into spermatozoa is called spermatogenesis.

Female Reproductive System

Ovaries (One pair)	Oviduct (One pair)	Uterus	Vagina	External organs
Produce ova and hormones	Transports ova to uterus	Protects and nourishes the developing embryo	Receives the sperms	Vulva

➢ **Fertilization :** The process of union of two dissimilar gametes, i.e., male and female gametes is called fertilization.

➢ **Gestation** Period is the period between conception and birth, i.e., the full term of development of the embryo in the uterus.

➢ **Implantation** is the attachment of mammalian blastocyst to the wall of uterus prior to further development, placenta formation, etc.

➢ **Menarche** is the first menses that occurs and it signals the onset of puberty in females.

➢ **Menopause** is the cessation of menstrual cycle women usually experience it around the age of 45 to 50 years.

➢ **Menstrual** Cycle is the series of changes in the endometrium of non-pregnant females that prepares the lining of the uterus to receive a fertilized egg.

➢ **Ogenesis** is the process of transformation of female germ cells, oogonia, into ova is termed as oogenesis.

➢ **Ovulation** is the release of ovum or oocyte from the mature follicle.

➢ **Puberty** is one at which reproductive system becomes functional in human beings. The males attain puberty at the age of 13 to 14 years, while females attain it at the age of 10-12 years.

➢ **Placenta** is the organ that attaches the developing foetus to the uterus. It links the blood supply of the foetus to the blood supply of the mother allowing the exchange of nutrients, wastes and gases.

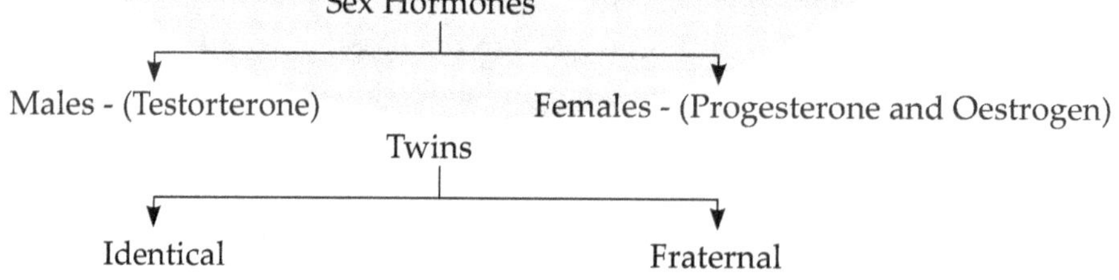

Sex Hormones

Males - (Testorterone)   Females - (Progesterone and Oestrogen)

Twins

Identical   Fraternal

Chapter 12. Human Population

➢ Population is defined as the total number of individuals of a species present in a geographically localized area.

➢ The scientific study of human population is termed as demography.

➢ The rapid increase in population is termed as population explosion.

➢ When the population growth rate is higher than the national income, the per capita income tends to decline. This condition is called overpopulation.

➢ The physiological capacity of a population to produce offsprings is known as biotic potential.

Factors Responsible for Population Explosion in India

| Illiteracy | Traditional beliefs | Mortality rate | Economic reasons | Religious and social customs | Desire for a male child | Lack of recreation |

Problems posed by the Increase in Population

| Food | Land | Forests | Water | Energy | Mineral resources |

➢ Rising Population (Pressure on Natural Resources) : In the context of rising human population the six main resources under pressure are as follows :

(i) Food, (ii) Water, (iii) Land, (iv) Energy, (v) Forests, (vi) Minerals.

With the rise in population, their production falls far short of the demand.

Methods to Control Population

| Natural Methods | Surgical Methods Leading to Sterilization (Tubectomy and Vasectomy) | Use of Contraceptives | Use of pills and drugs |

➢ **Census :** It is the counting of existing population at a fixed time as regards name, age, sex, occupation, date of birth, matrimonial status, number of dependents in a family, race, religion, language, education, residence etc. In India, a census is carried once in every 10 years.

$$\text{Birth Rate} = \frac{\text{No. of live births in a year}}{\text{Population in the middle of that year}} \times 1000$$

$$\text{Fertility rate} = \frac{\text{No. of live births in a year}}{\text{No. of women aged 15 to 45 in the year}} \times 1000$$

$$\text{Infant Mortality Rate} = \frac{\text{No. of babies less than 1 year old in a given year}}{\text{No. of babies born in that year}} \times 1000$$

$$\text{Death Rate} = \frac{\text{No. of deaths in a year}}{\text{Total population in the middle of the year}} \times 1000$$

Chapter 13. Human Evolution

➢ Evolution is the process of change in all forms of life in the generations. These differences accumulate over generations, resulting in changes within the population and genetics defines as the properties and features of the organism w.r.t. genes; therefore, the researchers have been put forward various theories on the origin of life. These are summarized below:

Origin of Life

	Name of Theory	Who and When	Objective
(i)	Theory of Special creation	By Father Suarez	'God' the supreme power has created the earth, water, sun, moon and above all; Adam and Eve, the first man and woman on the earth.
(ii)	Theory of spontaneous generation (Abiogenesis)	Van Helmont.	Living creatures could arise from the non-living matter due to the influence of heat and moistures.
(iii)	Theory of Biogenesis	Rudolf Virchow, 1858	This theory demonstrated that life originates from pre-existing life.

(iv) Modern Theory of the origin of life or Oparin- Haldane theory of the origin of life	Russian scientist A.I.Oparin (1923) and England born Indian scientist J.B.S. Haldane (1928).	The natural process by which life has arisen from non-living matter, such as simple organic compounds.
(v) Origin of Eukaryotes 1. Evolutionary theory. 2. Symbiotic theory.	Theory supporter Raff and Mahler (1972); Vzzell and Spolstary (1974). Theory Proposer Wallin (1920); Supporter Mangulis (1970).	This theory explains the origin of eukaryotic.

Some Important Theories

	Theory	Who ND When	Objective
(i)	Darwinism theory	English naturalist Charles Darwin (1809-1882)	Species of an organism arise and develop through the natural selection inherited variations that increase the individual's ability to compete, survive, and reproduce.
(ii)	Modern synthetic theory of evolution	Charles Darwin (1744–1829)	Genetic changes occurring in the population that leads to the formation of new species. It also describes the genetic population or Mendelian population, gene pool and gene frequency.
(iii)	Hardy- Weinberg's Principle	Hardy Weinberg	Genetic variation in a population will remain constant from one generation to the next in the absence of disturbing factors.
(iv)	Embryological evidence- 1. Theory of recapitulation	Ernst Haeckel in 1866,	The theory describes that before they are born, organisms pass through developmental stages that look like adult animals of other species, in roughly the same order that these other species split off during evolution.
(v)	Lamarck's theory	de Monet Lamarck in the year 1744-1829	That all the physical changes occurring in an individual during its lifetime are inherited by its offspring. E.g. evaluation of the long neck of a giraffe, the resistance of mosquitoes to DDT and resistance of bacteria to antibiotics.

Evidence of Evolution

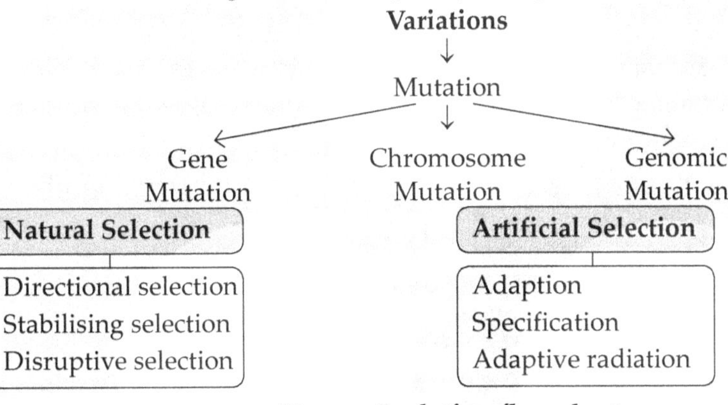

Homologous structures
Some structure, different function;
e.g. wing of bat, flipper of whole, arm of human.

Vestigial Structures
Structures which once had a function, but no longer
do; e.g. vestigial hind limbs of modern wholes.

Fossils
Provide a visual record
of how organisms change over time.

Evidence of Evolution

Analogous structures
Unrelated organisms, similar physical
structures; e.g. wing of bat, wing of bird,
wing of butterfly.

Embryology
Similarities in the early development of
vertebrate embryos; e.g. early embryonic
development of humons and monkeys.

Molecular biology
Number of difference in amino acid sequence;
e.g. sequence of human hemoglobin identical
to chimpanzee while less closely related
primates have greater differences.

What is Evolution?
Change in allele frequency of a species over time.

Variations

Mutation

| Gene Mutation | Chromosome Mutation | Genomic Mutation |

Natural Selection

Directional selection
Stabilising selection
Disruptive selection

Artificial Selection

Adaption
Specification
Adaptive radiation

Human Evolution flow chart

Dryopithecus-Apes
(20yrs million yrs)
↓
Ramapithecus
(14-15 million yrs)
↓
Australopithecus africanus
(5million years)
A.robustus
A.boisei
↓
Homo habilis
(2 million years)
↓
Homo erectus
(1.7 million years)
Homo sapiens neanderthalenis
(100,000 years, 1.5- 116M, 1300-1600 c.c.)

$\downarrow$

Homo sapiens fossils (Cro-Magnon)

(48000 Years ago)

$\downarrow$

Homo sapiens

(25000 years)

Chapter 14. Pollution

> Pollution may be defined as "an undesirable change in the physical, chemical or biological characteristics of the air, water and land that can be harmful for health, survival or activities of human or other living organisms."

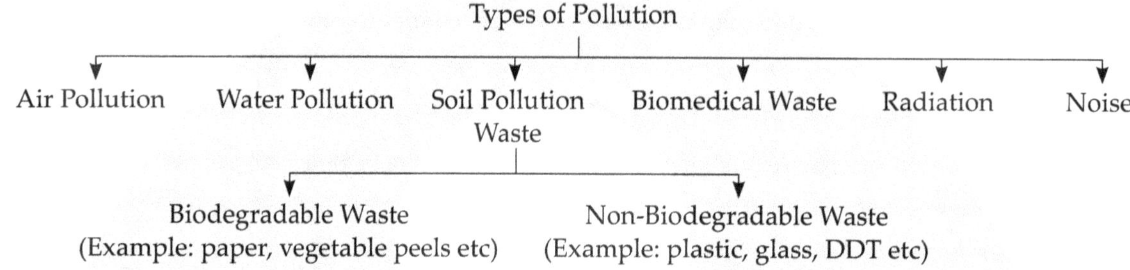

> **Acid Rain :** Due to industrialization there is lot of emission of CO_2, and sulphur dioxide (SO_2) and oxides of nitrogen which get dissolved in the rain drops falling on earth as rain.

> **Greenhouse effect and Global Warming :** Carbon dioxide gas is released into the atmosphere in a large quantity. Excessive release of carbon-dioxide leads to greenhouse effect that increases the average temperature of earth. It is also referred to as the global warming.

> **Ozone Layer Depletion :** Ozone is an allotropic form of oxygen. It prevents the harmful type of ultra violet rays coming down from the sun. Certain gaseous compounds such as CFCs (chlorofluorocarbons) are chemicals which are widely used in a variety of household goods like refrigerators, spray can etc.

> **Vehicular Standards :** Certain norms have been laid down under the titles Euro/Bharat norms which are applicable to all automobiles, on the levels of emissions given out-stricter control in most large cities. Government of India has adopted auto fuel policy to effectively cut down sulphur and nitrogen oxides in the automobile exhausts.

> **Swachh Bharat Abhiyan (Clean India Movement) :** The Swachh Bharat Abhiyan is significant cleanliness compaign started by the Government of India. It was officially launched on 2nd October 2014 with a dream of clean and hygienic India. It emphasized upon people to neither User, nor let others litter. Millions of people from different sections of the society came forward and joined this mass movement of cleanliness. Following are some objectives of the campaign :

> to clean the streets, roads and infrastructure of the country's cities and towns.

> to eliminate open defecation through the construction of individual, cluster and community toilets. The goal is to make an Open Defecation Free (ODF) India by constructing toilets in rural India.

> to establish an accountable mechanism of monitoring latrine use.

> to achieve efficient solid and liquid waste management systems.

❑

Chapter 1. Cell Division

1. The process by which a cell divides into two identical daughter cells.
2. The type of cell division found in unicellular organisms where cytoplasm divides without spindle formation.
3. The two kinds of cell division found in living organisms.
4. The cells in which mitosis occurs.
5. The process by which there is replacement of dead cells.
6. The kind of division normally seen at the tip of root and shoot system.
7. The stage in which microtubles form a bipolar spindle.
8. The structure responsible for initiating cell division in animal cells.
9. The part of the cell associated with heredity.
10. Process by which gametes are produced.
11. The process responsible for variation.
12. The kind of division that takes place in the reproductive tissues.
13. The longest phase of a normal cell cycle.
14. The stage when chromosomes arrange at the equator.
15. The stage in which separation of sister chromatids takes place.
16. The stage in meiosis in which the crossing-over takes place.
17. The point at which the duplicated chromosomes are joined.
18. Name the stage during which nuclear membrane and nucleoli reappear.
19. 'V' shaped chromosome having the centromere at the centre.
20. Process of division of cytoplasm of a parent cell.
21. Result of uncontrolled cell division.
22. The repeating components of each DNA strand lengthwise.
23. Chemical bond which joins the complementary nitrogenous bases.

Ans. 1. Cell division	7. Metaphase	13. Prophase	19. Metacentric
2. Amitosis	8. Centrioles	14. Metaphase	20. Cytokinesis
3. Mitosis, Meiosis	9. Chromosome	15. Anaphase	21. Cancer
4. Somatic cells	10. Meiosis	16. Pachytene	22. Nucleotides
5. Mitosis	11. Crossing-over	17. Centromere	23. Hydrogen bond
6. Mitosis	12. Meiosis	18. Telophase-II	

Chapter 2. Fundamentals of Genetics

1. The study of heredity and variation.
2. Cells having a single set of chromosomes.
3. The genetic composition of an organism.

4. Number of pairs of chromosomes present in human gametes.

5. The diploid number for cell of man.

6. Chromatids where recombination of characters occurs.

7. A specific part of chromosome that determines hereditary characteristics.

8. The pattern of arrangement of genes along a chromosome.

9. Pair of genes responsible for a particular characteristic.

10. The type of gene which, in the presence of a contrasting allele, is not expressed.

11. A pair of corresponding chromosomes of the same shape and size and derived one from each parent.*

Ans. 1. Genetics

2. Haploid

3. Genotype

4. 23 Pair of chromosomes

5. 46 chromosomes

6. Non-sister chromatids

7. Gene

8. Linear

9. Alleles

10. Recessive gene

11. Homologous chromosomes

Chapter 3. Absorption by Roots

1. The part of the plant which absorbs water from the soil.

2. The kind of cells that constitute the cortex of a root.

3. The pressure through which water can rise upto some feet.

4. Root hairs are the extension of which cells?

5. The movement of a liquid through a selectively permeable membrane.

6. The process by which water enters the root hair cell.

7. The process by which raisins swell up when placed in a beaker of water.

8. The membrane which allows water molecules to pass through, but not solute molecules.

9. The inward movement of solvent molecules through the plasma membrane of a cell.

10. The solution outside the cell having lower solute concentration than the fluids inside the cell.

11. The process by which wilting and drooping of leaves occurs.

12. The condition in which the contents of a cell exert pressure against the cell wall, making it distended.

13. Condition of cell in which the cell contents are shrunken.

14. Movement of ions from the region of lower concentration to higher concentration by using energy (ATP).

15. Name the process by which intact plants lose water in the form of droplets.

16. The phenomenon by which living or dead plant cells absorb water by surface attraction.

Ans. 1. Root hairs

2. Parenchyma

3. Root pressure

4. Epidermal Cells

5. Osmosis

6. Osmosis

7. Osmosis

8. Semi permeable membrane

9. Endosmosis

10. Hypotonic solution

11. Transpiration

12. Turgidity

13. Plasmolysed

14. Active transport

15. Guttation

16. Imbibition

Chapter 4. Transpiration

1. The process of loss of water in the form of water vapour through the stomata.

2. Season in which transpiration rate is the highest.

3. Minute openings present on the surface of the stems and twigs for transpiration.

4. In potometer experiment, transpiration in experimental plant occurs through this part of plant.

5. Plants in which lenticular transpiration occurs.

---

* Frequently asked previous years Board Exam Questions.

   6. A plant having sunken stomata.

   7. The waxy protective covering present on the leaf epidermis meant to reduce transpiration rate.

   8. The structures through which guttation occurs.

   9. Exudation of plant sap from the ruptured or cut surfaces of the plant due to root pressure.

   10. A substance which causes partial closure of stomata.

   11. The plant in which stomata are totally absent.

   12. An apparatus that measures the rate of water uptake in a cut shoot due to transpiration.

Ans.
1. Transpiration
2. Summer
3. Lenticels
4. Stomata
5. Woody trees
6. Xerophyte
7. Cuticle
8. Hydathodes
9. Bleeding
10. Anti-transpirant
11. Hydrilla
12. Ganong's potometer

Chapter 5. Photosynthesis

   1. The process by which plants prepare their food.

   2. The principal site in a green leaf for photosynthesis.

   3. Name the source of oxygen given out by plants in photosynthesis.

   4. Colour of light in which maximum photosynthesis takes place.

   5. The immediate product of photosynthesis.

   6. The form in which carbohydrates are stored in plant cells.

   7. The chemical substance which is used to test the presence of starch in the cell of a leaf.

   8. The part of the chloroplast where the dark reaction of photosynthesis takes place.

   9. The different products of photosynthesis.

   10. A plant that does not perform photosynthesis.

   11. The form of energy into which the radiant energy gets converted during the process of photosynthesis.

Ans.
1. Photosynthesis
2. Chloroplast
3. Water
4. Red
5. Glucose
6. Starch
7. Iodine
8. Stroma
9. Glucose, water and oxygen
10. Pitcher plant
11. Chemical energy

Chapter 6. Chemical Coordination in Plants

   1. A permanent or irreversible increase in the dry weight, size, mass or volume of a cell, organ or organism.

   2. The optimum temperature required for the growth of plants.

   3. The gas which helps in building up of carbohydrates in plants.

   4. A plant that exhibits strong apical dominance.

   5. A plant that exhibits weak apical dominance.

   6. The auxin that is used to prevent the premature fruit fall of apples.

   7. The auxin that is used to enhance the sweetness of the fruits.

   8. The plant hormone that leads to an elongation of the internodes.

   9. Basic hormones that stimulate cell division.

   10. The only gaseous hormone in the plant system.

   11. The hormone that nullifies the geotropic effect.

   12. The alternative name of ABA.

Ans.
1. Growth
2. Between 20°C-30°C
3. Carbon dioxide
4. Sunflower
5. Tomato
6. 2, 4-D

7. IBA
8. Gibberellin
9. Cytokinins
10. Ethylene
11. Ethylene
12. Dormin

Chapter 7. The Circulatory System

1. Number of chambers present in the human heart.
2. Name the muscles which make up the wall of the heart.
3. The protective layer which surrounds the heart.
4. The blood vessel leaving the left ventricle of the mammalian heart.
5. The valve present between the left atrium and the left ventricle.
6. The blood vessel supplying blood to the kidney.
7. The blood vessel that begins and ends in capillaries.
8. The blood vessels which have valves in them.
9. The fine blood vessels in the tissues through which exchange of materials occurs.
10. Name the metallic element present in red blood cells.
11. The number of RBCs in an adult male.
12. The instrument by which RBCs are counted.
13. Unstable compound formed when oxygen binds to haemoglobin.
14. The enzyme which converts fibrinogen to fibrin.
15. The blood plasma from which fibrinogen has been removed.
16. The cells which protect the human body from invading bacteria.
17. The mineral element essential for the clotting of the blood.
18. The fluid found between the membranes of the heart.
19. The smallest blood vessel formed by the union of capillaries.
20. Phase of the cardiac cycle in which the ventricles get filled with blood from atrium.
21. Vein which starts from an organ and ends in another organ besides heart.
22. The compound formed when haemoglobin combines with carbon dioxide in blood.*

Ans.
1. Four
2. Cardiac muscles
3. Pericardium
4. Dorsal aorta
5. Bicuspid valve
6. Renal artery
7. Hepatic portal vein
8. Veins
9. Capillaries
10. Iron
11. $5,000,000/mm^3$
12. Haemocytometer
13. Oxyhaemoglobin
14. Thrombin
15. Serum
16. WBCs
17. Calcium
18. Pericardial fluid
19. Venule
20. Diastole
21. Hepatic portal vein
22. Carbamino- haemoglobin/ $HbCO_2$

Chapter 8. The Excretory System

1. Major excretory organ of man.
2. The organ which produces urea.
3. Name the primary function of sweat glands.
4. The structural and functional unit of kidney.
5. Inner region of kidney which is light in colour and subdivided into conical renal pyramids.
6. The inner concave margin of kidney.
7. The term used for Bowman's capsule and glomerulus together.

*** Frequently asked previous years Board Exam Questions.**

8. The branch of renal artery which enters into Bowman's capsule.

9. The blood vessel which brings pure blood to the kidneys.

10. The process by which the unwanted nitrogenous wastes are eliminated from the body.

11. The muscle which controls urination.

12. Process of excreting urine from the urinary bladder.

13. A product which is excreted by the liver.

14. The gas excreted by the lungs.

15. The substance that is found in excess in the urine of a diabetic patient.

16. The part of the kidney tubules where the term urine is first used for the fluid in it.

17. The vein in which the urea concentration is maximum.

18. The hormone that regulates the reabsorption of water from the kidney tubules.

19. Name three substances that are reabsorbed from the renal tubules by the secondary capillaries.

Ans.

1. Kidneys	7. Renal corpuscle	13. Bile pigments
2. Liver	8. Afferent arteriole	14. Carbon dioxide
3. Thermoregulation	9. Renal artery	15. Glucose
4. Nephrons	10. Excretion	16. Renal tubule
5. Medulla	11. Sphincter muscle	17. Hepatic vein
6. Hilus	12. Micturition	

18. Vasopressin or Antidiuretic Hormone [ADH].

19. Glucose, amino acid, and some salts of sodium and potassium.

Chapter 9. The Nervous System and Sense Organs

1. Unit of nervous system.

2. The fluid that is present inside and outside the brain.

3. The types of neurons present in cell bodies of the dorsal root ganglion of the spinal cord.

4. The chemical messenger by the help of which the nerve impulse travels from one neuron to the other.

5. The part of the central nervous system in which the gray matter is located on the outer side and the white matter on the inner side.

6. Name the bony box in which the brain is located.

7. The protective membranes around the brain.

8. The scientist, who conducted the experiment on a dog to show conditioned reflex.

9. The two types of nervous system.

10. Name the nerve which transmits messages from the ear to the brain.

11. Spontaneous and automatic response to a stimulus without the involvement of brain.

12. Type of reflex which develops due to some past experience and training.

13. Nerves which carry messages from CNS to the effector organ.

14. The pigmented circular area seen in the eye.

15. The most sensitive region of the retina.

16. The innermost layer of the eye.

17. The contraction of which muscles helps in alteration of focal length of the eye lens.

18. The area where the image is formed but not seen by our eye.

19. The region in the eye where the rods and cones are located.

20. The part of the eye that is responsible for change in the size of the pupil.

21. Fluid present in the posterior chamber of the eye.

22. The defect of the human eye caused due to the uneven surface of the cornea.

23. The type of lens used for correcting myopia.

24. The inability of eye to distinguish between certain colours.

25. A condition during which the person feels difficulty in seeing in dim light.

26. Name the photoreceptors found in the retina of the eye.

27. The layer of eye ball that forms the transparent cornea.

28. The ear ossicle which is in contact with the oval window of the inner ear.

29. Name the three ear ossicles of the ear.

30. The biological term used collectively for the three small bones present in middle ear.

31. Name the part of the ear associated with (i) static balance, (ii) hearing, (iii) dynamic balance.

32. The layer of eyeball that provides nourishment to the eye.

Ans. 1. Neuron

2. Cerebrospinal fluid

3. Sensory

4. Acetylcholine

5. Brain

6. Cranium

7. Meninges

8. Ivan Pavlov

9. (i) Central nervous system, (ii) Peripheral nervous system.

10. Auditory nerve

11. Reflex action

12. Conditioned reflex

13. Motor nerves

14. Iris

15. Yellow spot

16. Retina

17. Ciliary muscles

18. Blind spot

19. Retina

20. Iris

21. Vitreous humour

22. Astigmatism

23. Biconcave

24. Colour blindness

25. Night blindness

26. Rod cells and cone cells

27. Sclera

28. Stapes

29. Three ear ossicles are : (i) Malleus (hammer), (ii) Incus (anvil) , (iii) Stapes (Stirrup).

30. Malleus, incus, stapes are collectively called ear ossicles.

31. (i) Utriculus and Sacculus, (ii) Cochlea, (iii) Semi circular canals.

32. (i) Choroid layer

Chapter 10. The Endocrine System

1. The gland which behaves both as an exocrine as well as an endocrine gland.

2. The hormone secreted by the parathyroid gland.

3. Hormone secreted by β-cells of Islets of Langerhans.

4. Disease caused by the deficiency of insulin.

5. The hormone produced by the thyroid gland.

6. Disorder caused by excess secretion of thyroxine hormone.

7. The hormone produced by adrenal medulla.

8. The hormone that increases the blood pressure.

9. The hormone which abnormally increases the urine formation.

10. The hormone which requires iodide for its secretion.

11. The master gland of the body, which controls the activity of other endocrine glands.

12. Hormone that controls reabsorption of water from kidney tubules.

13. Hormone secreted by corpus luteum.

14. Name the hormone secreted by alpha cells of Islets of Langerhans.

15. Gland which regulates the normal growth of an individual.

Ans. 1. Pancreas

2. Parathormone

3. Insulin

4. Diabetes mellitus

5. Thyroxine

6. Exophthalmic goitre

7. Adrenaline

8. Aldosterone

9. Antidiuretic hormone (ADH)

10. Thyroxine
11. Pituitary

12. ADH or Vasopressin
13. Progesterone

14. Glucagon
15. Pituitary gland.

Chapter 11. The Reproductive System

1. The type of reproduction found in amoeba.
2. The age or period when the reproductive organs become fully operational.
3. The term used when beard and moustache appear, harshening of voice, broadening of shoulders etc., take place in males.
4. The basic unit of the testes.
5. The male copulatory organ in human.
6. The male gamete (male reproductive cells) of mammals.
7. The tubular knot fitting like a cap on the upper surface of the testes.
8. The site of production of sperms in man.
9. The structure in which testes are present in man.
10. The accessory gland in human males whose secretion activates the sperms.
11. Muscular extension of cauda epididymis.
12. The hormone that stimulates development of secondary sexual characters in males.
13. The cells of the testes that produce male hormones.
14. The female copulatory organ in human.
15. A temporary mechanical and physiological connection between foetal and maternal tissue for nutrition, respiration and excretion etc. of the foetus.
16. The structure formed after release of ovum from follicle.
17. The term used for mature follicle.
18. A cellular sac containing maturing egg.
19. The onset of menstruation in a young girl at about the age of 13 years.
20. Sloughing of uterine wall during menstrual flow.
21. The term used when menstruation in females stop at the age of 45-50 years.
22. A hollow pear shaped muscular organ that holds, nourishes and protects the foetus.
23. The process of attachment of fertilized ovum to uterine wall.
24. What protects the embryo inside the uterus from jerks or mechanical shocks?
25. The hormone that stimulates contraction of uterus during child-birth.
26. Gestation period of human beings.
27. Surgical operation of fallopian tube in females for family planning.
28. What does these abbreviations stand for?
    LH, FSH, IUD.
29. A female gonad responsible for the production of ova.
30. The structure which connects the placenta and the foetus.*

Ans.
1. Binary fission
2. Puberty
3. Puberty
4. Seminiferous tubule
5. Penis
6. Spermatozoa
7. Epididymis
8. Testes
9. Scrotum

10. Prostate gland
11. Vas deferens
12. Testosterone
13. Leydig cells/Interstitial cells.
14. Vagina
15. Placenta
16. Corpus luteum
17. Graafian follicle
18. Graafian follicle

19. Menarche
20. Menstruation or menses
21. Menopause
22. Uterus
23. Implantation
24. Amniotic fluid
25. Oxytocin
26. 280 days
27. Tubectomy

28. (i) LH : Luteinizing hormone.   (ii) FSH : Follicle stimulating hormone.
    (iii) IUD : Intra-uterine device.
29. Ovary
30. Umbilical cord

---

* Frequently asked previous years Board Exam Questions.

Chapter 12. Human Population

1. A group of organisms of the same species that live in a geographically localized area.
2. The measurement of a population in relation to per unit area at a given time.
3. Branch of science that deals with changes occur in population due to alteration in mortality, sex ratio and age groups.
4. Another term for birth rate.
5. The addition of new individuals to the population from other localities.
6. Number of deaths per 1000 living people in a year.
7. Number of children born per 1000 living persons in a year.
8. The cutting and ligation of vas deferens in males.
9. Number of females per 1000 males.
10. Name any two non-renewable resources of energy.
11. Name any two renewable resources of energy.
12. Expand MTP.

Ans.
1. Population
2. Population density
3. Population dynamics
4. Natality
5. Immigration
6. Mortality
7. Natality
8. Vasectomy
9. Sex ratio
10. (i) Minerals, (ii) Fossil fuels
11. (i) Solar Energy, (ii) Geothermal energy
12. Medical Termination of Pregnancy

Chapter 13. Human Evolution

1. The first person to coin the term "Evolution".
2. The first tool maker on earth.
3. The person who explained the mechanism of organic evolution.
4. The term used for constant struggle or competition for the limiting factors such as food and space.
5. Any evidence that favours Darwinism.
6. An example of a life form that has remained unchanged for a hundred millions of years.
7. The book published by Darwin.

Ans.
1. Herbert Spencer
2. *Homo habilis*
3. Jean Baptiste de Lamarck
4. Struggle for existence
5. Artificial Selection
6. *Selaginella*
7. Origin of species

Chapter 14. Pollution

1. Name three greenhouse gases.
2. The gas present in large amount in upper part of stratosphere.
3. Number of oxygen atoms in ozone.
4. The gas that leads to the reduction of oxygen in the atmosphere.
5. The gases which mainly contribute to acid rain.
6. The category of sewage treatment which involves physical methods to remove larger, undissolved and suspended particles from sewage.
7. Name three monuments affected by acid rain.
8. Name three types of industrial pollutants.

9. The fuel used in vehicle that reduces pollution.
10. Name two chemical fertilizers.
11. Name one non-biodegradable pollutant.
12. A bio-fertilizer.
13. What acts as a storage reservoir for water and other plant nutrients?
14. A free living bacteria which helps in nitrogen fixation.
15. Waste materials which can be broken down to non-poisonous substances in nature.
16. A symbiotic bacteria.
17. Bacteria that break down dead organisms to liberate nitrogen.
18. List the three major sources of water pollution.
19. A national level campaign that aims to clean the streets, roads and infrastructure throughout length and breadth of the country.
20. One gaseous compound which depletes the ozone layer.*

Ans.
1. Carbon dioxide, Methane, Nitrogen oxide
2. Ozone
3. Three
4. Carbon monoxide
5. Sulphur dioxide, oxides of Nitrogen (NO_2)
6. Primary treatment
7. Parthenon of Athens, Taj Mahal of Agra, Parliament building of Ottawa.
8. (i) Chemicals, (ii) Smokes and ash, (iii) Heat.
9. CNG
10. (i) Urea, (ii) Ammonium Sulphate
11. DDT
12. *Anabaena/Rhizobium*
13. Soil
14. *Azotobacter*
15. Biodegradable waste
16. *Rhizobium*
17. Nitrifying bacteria
18. (i) Human waste, (ii) Industrial waste, (iii) Chemical runoff.
19. Swachh Bharat Abhiyan.
20. CFCs [Chlorofluorocarbons] or CCl_4

*** Frequently asked previous years Board Exam Questions.**

Give appropriate terms for the following :

Chapter 1. Cell Division

1. The stage in mitosis when the nucleolus starts disappearing.
2. The stage at which spindle fibres begin to be formed.
3. The shortest phase of mitosis.
4. The stage when sister chromatids separate from their paired positions.
5. The period between two successive mitotic divisions.
6. Point at which two sister chromatids are held together.
7. The stage at which chromosomes reach the opposite poles.
8. The process of cytoplasmic division.
9. The process of division of nucleus.
10. The type of Cytokinesis in which the cell plate begins in the centre and moves towards the wall.
11. The phase of the cell cycle during which the cell grows.
12. The phase of the cell cycle in which DNA replication takes place.
13. Type of cell division which brings about vegetative growth.
14. The longest phase of a normal cell cycle.
15. The stage at which progressive condensation and coiling of chromatin fibres take place.
16. The stage at which synapsis in chromosomes takes place to form bivalents.
17. The stage at which formation of chiasmata occurs.
18. Stage of meiosis during which crossing over takes place.
19. The stage of meiosis at which there are two cells, each with sister chromatids aligned at the equator.
20. The phase usually skipped in meiosis.
21. The phase of meiosis at which homologous chromosomes are separated.
22. The process during which the meiosis occurs in human beings.
23. Period between Meiosis-I and Meiosis-II.

Ans.
1. Prophase
2. Late Prophase or early Metaphase

3. Anaphase	10. Centrifugal cytokinesis	17. Pachytene
4. Anaphase	11. G_1 phase	18. Prophase I
5. Interphase	12. S phase	19. Metaphase II
6. Centromere	13. Mitosis	20. Telophase I
7. Telophase	14. Interphase	21. Anaphase II
8. Cytokinesis	15. Leptotene	22. Gamete formation
9. Karyokinesis	16. Zygotene	23. Interkinesis

Chapter 2. Fundamentals of Genetics

1. Transmission of characters through generations.
2. Differences occurring within offsprings of the same progeny.

3. Cell organelle which is directly involved in genetics.

4. Structure that transmits characteristics from parents to offspring.

5. A virus with DNA as hereditary material.

6. The hereditary unit, which is responsible for inheritance.

7. Cell which determines the sex of a baby.

8. An individual having similar pair of genes.

9. An individual having dissimilar pair of genes.

10. Twins born from a single egg fertilized by a single sperm.

11. Twins which develop from a separate egg and each egg is fertilized by its own sperm cell.

12. Genetic disease in which a person cannot distinguish red and green colour.

Ans.
1. Heredity
2. Variation
3. Nucleus
4. Genes
5. Retro virus e.g. HIV
6. Genes
7. Sperm cell
8. Homozygous
9. Heterozygous
10. Identical or monozygotic twins
11. Non-identical or fraternal twins
12. Colour blindness

Chapter 3. Absorption by Roots

1. Phenomenon of absorption of water by surface attraction.

2. Solutions which have the same osmotic pressure.

3. A solution whose concentration is equal to the cell sap.

4. A solution whose concentration is greater than that of the cell sap.

5. The pressure which is responsible for the movement of water molecules across the cortical cells of the root.

6. The condition in which the water from a cell is completely removed due to exosmosis and no more shrinkage is possible.

7. A cell in a fully expanded condition.

8. The pressure exerted by cell contents on a plant cell wall.

9. Condition of a cell, when placed in a hypotonic solution.

10. Tissue which transports manufactured food from leaves to other parts of the plant.

11. The tissue responsible for the ascent of sap in plants.

12. Tissue which transports water from the soil to other parts of plants.

13. Pressure developed in the roots due to the inflow of water, brought about by the alternate turgidity and flaccidity of the cells of the cortex and root hair cells.

14. Drooping of leaves due to loss of turgidity.

15. Water together with mineral salts that gets absorbed by the roots.

16. Mutual force of attraction between the water molecules that binds them together.

Ans.
1. Imbibition
2. Isotonic solutions
3. Isotonic solution
4. Hypertonic solution
5. Osmotic pressure
6. Plasmolysis
7. Turgid
8. Turgor pressure
9. Turgid
10. Phloem
11. Xylem
12. Xylem
13. Root pressure
14. Wilting
15. Sap
16. Cohesive force

Chapter 4. Transpiration

1. Loss of water from the aerial parts of a plant.
2. Opening found on the under surface of leaf.
3. The kidney-shaped cells present on stomata.
4. Tissue that transports water to all parts of the plant.
5. The substances which reduce the rate of transpiration.
6. The apparatus used to compare the rate of transpiration in a plant.
7. The process by which excess of water is forced out directly from the tips of veins in the leaf.
8. Process of exudation of cell sap or watery solution from injured parts of a plant.
9. Type of transpiration that takes place directly from the surface of the leaf.
10. Type of transpiration that takes place from the minute openings on the surface of the old stems.

Ans.
1. Transpiration
2. Stomata
3. Guard cells
4. Xylem
5. Anti-transpirants
6. Potometer
7. Guttation
8. Bleeding
9. Cuticular transpiration
10. Lenticular transpiration

Chapter 5. Photosynthesis

1. Process responsible for the conversion of solar energy to chemical energy in order to sustain life on this earth.
2. Structure where photophosphorylation takes place.
3. Form of energy which is converted into chemical energy during photosynthesis.
4. Organisms which cannot prepare their own food by photosynthesis.
5. Breaking down of water molecule into its constituent components using light.
6. Tissue that transports manufactured starch from the leaves to all parts of the plant.
7. The part of the chloroplast where the dark reaction of photosynthesis takes place.
8. Name the experiment to demonstrate the importance of light for photosynthesis.
9. A high energy reduced compound formed in the light reaction.
10. The site of light reaction in the cell of a leaf.
11. The green colouring pigment of the plants.
12. The energy currency of the cell.

Ans.
1. Photosynthesis
2. Chloroplast
3. Radiant energy
4. Heterotrophs
5. Photolysis
6. Phloem
7. Stroma
8. Light screen experiment
9. NADPH
10. Grana
11. Chlorophyll
12. ATP

Chapter 6. Chemical Coordination in Plants

1. The chemical substances released by the plants that help in creating responses to stimuli.
2. The chemical substances that affect the growth and development in the plant's body.
3. Plant hormones that have a negative effect on growth.
4. The rapid increase in the internodal length in rosette plants.
5. The tropic movement of plant in response to stimulus of light.
6. The tropic movement of plant in response to the stimulus of earth's gravity.
7. The tropic movement of plant in response to stimulus of water.

8. The tropic movement in response to stimulus of touch.

9. The tropic movement in response to some chemical.

Ans. 1. Hormones

2. Plant hormones or phytohormones

3. Growth inhibitors

4. Bolting

5. Phototropism

6. Geotropism

7. Hydrotropism

8. Thigmotropism

9. Chemotropism

Chapter 7. The Circulatory System

1. The study of blood vascular system including arteries, veins and heart.

2. An unstable bright red compound formed between haemoglobin and oxygen to carry oxygen to the body cells.

3. An artery which carries deoxygenated blood.

4. Vein in the human body which carries oxygenated blood.

5. A fluid that transports fatty acids and glycerols.

6. The phase of cardiac cycle in which the auricles contract.

7. The respiratory pigment contained in human blood.

8. The blood vessel that supplies oxygenated blood to the liver.

9. An instrument which is used to check heart beats.

10. The soluble protein present in blood plasma responsible for blood clotting.

11. The process by which leucocytes engulf and destroy bacteria.

12. Passage out of WBCs through the walls of the capillaries into the tissue.

13. The phase of the cardiac cycle in which the ventricles get filled with blood from atrium.

14. The valve present between the chambers on the right side of the human heart.

Ans. 1. Angiology

2. Oxyhaemoglobin

3. Pulmonary artery

4. Pulmonary vein

5. Lymph

6. Atrial systole

7. Haemoglobin

8. Hepatic artery

9. Stethoscope

10. Fibrinogen

11. Phagocytosis

12. Diapedesis

13. Ventricular diastole

14. Tricuspid valve

Chapter 8. The Excretory System

1. The organ which filters out urea and uric acid from the blood stream.

2. The organ which helps in the excretion of carbon dioxide from the body.

3. The organ in which urine is stored before its elimination from the body.

4. The organ that is concerned with maintaining water balance in the body.

5. The waste product excreted by the liver.

6. The pigments produced by the breakdown of haemoglobin in liver.

7. The tube joining the kidney to the urinary bladder.

8. The outer part of the kidney containing the Bowman's capsule.

9. Cluster of fine blood capillaries found in each Bowman's capsule.

10. The hormone that helps to increase the reabsorption of water from the kidney tubules.

11. The process by which kidneys regulate the water content of the body.

12. Thin membranous sac serving as the reservoir of urine.

13. Process of removing excretory products from the body by artificial means.

Ans. 1. Kidney   4. Kidney   7. Ureter

      2. Lungs   5. Urea   8. Cortex

      3. Urinary bladder   6. Bilirubin   9. Glomerulus

      10. Vasopressin or Antidiuretic Hormone [ADH]

      11. Osmoregulation   12. Urinary bladder   13. Dialysis

Chapter 9. The Nervous System and Sense Organs

1. Short, thread like branches arising from the cell body of a neuron.
2. The neurons which conduct impulses from the central nervous system to the organs.
3. The junction between the two nerve cells.
4. System that comprises both spinal cord and brain.
5. The seat of intelligence and memory in the brain.
6. The part of human brain that controls body temperature.
7. The structure which joins the two cerebral hemispheres in man.
8. Response to a stimulus without the intervention of the will of an animal.
9. Colourless fluid found in brain and spinal cord.
10. Nerve that transfers impulses from ear to brain.
11. The part of the central nervous system in which the gray matter is located on the outer side and the white matter on the inner side.
12. The part of the eye which is responsible for its shape.
13. The part of the eye that prevents the eyeball from collapsing.
14. The most sensitive region of the retina.
15. The cells on the retina that are sensitive to colour.
16. The part of the retina on which an image is focused for the clearest vision.
17. Ability of eye to adjust its focal length in order to obtain a clear vision of objects at different distances.
18. A defect in the eye due to which some part of the object is seen clearly while other seem blurred.
19. An eye defect due to which two eyes somewhat converge leading to what is called cross eye.
20. The nutritive layer of the eye which also prevents the reflection of light.
21. The fluid which conveys the vibrations of sound in the cochlea and semicircular canals.
22. Technical term for the structure found in the inner ear.
23. The receptors which help in the sensation of taste.

Ans. 1. Dendrites   9. Cerebrospinal fluid   17. Accommodation of eye

      2. Motor neurons   10. Auditory nerve   18. Astigmatism

      3. Synapse   11. Brain   19. Squint

      4. Central nervous system   12. Sclera   20. Choroid

      5. Cerebrum   13. Vitreous humour   21. Endolymph

      6. Hypothalamus   14. Fovea centralis or macula   22. Membranous labryinth

      7. Corpus callosum   15. Cones   23. Sensory papillae

      8. Reflex action   16. Yellow spot

Chapter 10. The Endocrine System

1. Chemical substances that control the growth and development in animals.
2. The condition caused due to hyposecretion of thyroxine in adults.

3. The condition which results in the abnormally long bones, long lower jaw bone due to hyper secretion of pituitary hormone.

4. The cells of islets of langerhans in pancreas which secrete insulin.

5. The hormone which maintains glucose level in the blood.

6. Hormone which controls the development of male secondary sexual characters.

7. The structure which controls the master gland.

Ans.
1. Hormones
2. Myxoedema
3. Acromegaly
4. β cell
5. Insulin
6. Androgens (Testosterone)
7. Hypothalamus

Chapter 11. The Reproductive System

1. The process of fusion of ovum and sperm.

2. Name the male gamete of a mammal.

3. Gland in male reproductive system where maturation of sperms takes placce.

4. The male androgen producing cells of mammals.

5. Term used for the production and maturation of sperms in the testes.

6. The canal through which the testes descend into the scrotum just before birth of a human male child.

7. The place where fertilization occurs in the female reproductive system.

8. Name the tube that leads from the ovary to the uterus.

9. Term used for the production and maturation of eggs in the ovaries.

10. The connective tissue that surrounding the ovary.

11. The monthly discharge of blood and disintegrated tissues in a human female.

12. The onset of reproductive phase in a young female.

13. Rupture of the follicle and release of the ovum from the ovary.

14. Term used for the arrest of reproductive capacity in females.

15. The part in the uterus which is concerned with the supply of nutrition from the mother to the foetus.

16. Membrane that surrounds the foetus and secretes a protective fluid.

17. The fluid surrounding the developing embryo.

18. The period of intrauterine development of the embryo.

19. Structure which connects the placenta with the foetus.

20. A method of contraception in which the sperm duct is cut and ligated.

21. The phase in the menstrual cycle in which the remnant of follicle in the ovary turns to corpus luteum.

22. The expulsion of the foetus from the body of the mother.

23. The twins developed when two eggs are released from ovaries at a time and both get fertilized.

24. The twins developed when a single fertilized egg gets split and separated into two parts during the early stages of division.

Ans.
1. Fertilization
2. Sperm
3. Testes (Epididymis)
4. Interstitial cells
5. Spermatogenesis
6. Inguinal canal
7. Fallopian tube
8. Fallopian tube
9. Oogenesis
10. Tunica albuginea
11. Menstruation
12. Menarche
13. Ovulation
14. Menopause
15. Placenta
16. Amnion
17. Amniotic fluid
18. Gestation period
19. Umbilical cord
20. Vasectomy
21. Luteal phase
22. Parturition
23. Fraternal twins
24. Identical twins

Chapter 12. Human Population

1. A statistical study of human population of a region.
2. The number of individuals belonging to different age groups.
3. The comparative number of males and females in a population.
4. The rapid increase in population.
5. The technical term used for the difference between birth rate and death rate in population.
6. The zoological name of man.
7. The size of the population in relation to unit area at given instant of time.
8. The surgical removal of testes.
9. The methods to prevent union of sperms with the ovum.
10. Act of migrating out from a population or area to join another one in a new locality.

Ans.
1. Demography
2. Age ratio
3. Sex ratio
4. Population explosion
5. Growth rate of population
6. *Homo sapiens*
7. Population density
8. Castration
9. Contraception
10. Emigration

Chapter 13. Human Evolution

1. A long process of change that occurs in population of organisms.
2. The branch of science that deals with the history and evolution of organisms.
3. Differences among the individual of same species.
4. The organs that were completely developed and functional in the ancestors but are in a reduced, non-functional form in the current species.

Ans.
1. Biological evolution
2. Evolutionary biology
3. Variations
4. Vestigial organs

Chapter 14. Pollution

1. A natural phenomenon that becomes harmful due to pollution.
2. The chemical element which caused the minimata disease in Japan.
3. The pollution chiefly due to use of pesticides in agriculture.
4. The bio-indicator of pollution.
5. Bacteria which break down dead organisms to liberate nitrogen.
6. The chemicals that lead to the formation of ozone holes.
7. A free living, nitrogen fixing blue-green alga.
8. Term used for an average increase in the temperature of the atmosphere near the Earth's surface.
9. The waste materials which cannot be broken down into non-poisonous or harmless substances in nature.
10. A combination of smoke and fog.

Ans.
1. Greenhouse effect
2. Mercury
3. Soil pollution
4. Lichens
5. Denitrifying bacteria
6. Chlorofluorocarbons (CFCs)
7. *Anabaena*
8. Global warming
9. Non-biodegradable waste
10. Smog

Fill in the Blanks | Set **4** |

Complete the following sentences with appropriate words :

Chapter 1. Cell Division

1. The type of cell division that occurs in apical meristem of plants is ....
2. .... means splitting of nucleus during the cell division.
3. The period of time between Meiosis-I and Meiosis-II is called ....
4. Colchicine arrests cell division at ....
5. .... is the point at which sister chromatids are held together.
6. The spindle fibres are made of ....
7. The pairing of homologous chromosomes is called ....
8. Chromosomes are .... material.
9. Polytene chromosomes are found in .... of fly larvae.
10. Mitosis occurs in our .... cells.
11. Meiosis occurs only in .... cells.
12. During the pairing of chromosomes in meiosis, the .... chromosomes come to lie side by side.

Ans.

1. Mitosis	4. Metaphase	7. Synapsis	10. Somatic
2. Karyokinesis	5. Centromere	8. Hereditary	11. Gametic
3. Interkinesis	6. Microtubules	9. Salivary glands	12. Homologous

Chapter 2. Fundamentals of Genetics

1. The chromosomal theory of inheritance was proposed by .... and .... in 1902.
2. The term Genetics was introduced by .... in 1906.
3. .... is the hereditary unit.
4. In mammals, the female is homozygous while the male is ....
5. A chromosome is composed of DNA and ....
6. .... is the Father of Genetics.
7. The number of chromosomes in human is ....
8. The physical expression of genes is called ....
9. The small differences among individuals are called ....
10. The dissimilar pairs of genes present in an individual are known as ....
11. .... chromosomes do not take part in sex determination.
12. .... are the alternative forms of a genes producing different effects.
13. .... is the ratio of dihybrid cross.
14. .... gene is the gene whose expression is suppressed by a dominant gene.
15. After .... the diploid number of chromosomes are restored.
16. Phenotype is the observable characteristics which is .... controlled.

Ans. 1. Sutton, Boveri   2. William Bateson   3. Gene

4. Heterozygous
5. Proteins
6. Gregor Johann Mendel
7. 46
8. Phenotype
9. Variations
10. Heterozygous
11. Autosomal
12. Alleles
13. 9 : 3 : 3 : 1
14. Recessive
15. Fertilization
16. Genetically

Chapter 3. Absorption by Roots

1. Osmosis is the diffusion of .... molecules from the region of their .... concentration to the region of .... concentration through a semi-permeable memberane.

2. Diffusion is the movement of molecules from a region of their .... concentration to the region of their .... concentration.

3. .... serves as a medium for the transport of inorganic salts and food molecules in the plant.

4. The pressure by which the .... molecules tend to cross the semi-permeable membrane is called osmotic pressure.

5. When there is no movement of water in the cell from the outside medium, the medium is considered to be .... to cell sap.

6. A plasmolysed cell has .... protoplast.

7. Raisin swells up when kept in a .... solution.

8. Water and mineral salts absorbed by root is known as ....

9. The condition opposite to turgid is ....

10. Plants get wilted if .... is removed from the plant.

11. The pressure develops in the cortical cells of roots which forces a part of the water upward is known as ....

12. Wilting and drooping of leaves is due to loss of ....

13. Active transport is in a direction .... to that of diffusion.

14. Wooden doors swell up in rainy season due to ....

15. .... is the phenomenon of contraction of the cytoplasm from the cell wall.

Ans.
1. Water, higher, lower
2. higher, lower
3. Water
4. Water
5. Isotonic
6. shrunken
7. Hypotonic
8. sap
9. Flaccid
10. Xylem
11. Root pressure
12. turgidity
13. opposite
14. imbibition
15. Plasmolysis

Chapter 4. Transpiration

1. Plants become cool as a result of ....

2. Transpiration is the loss of water in the form of .... from the leaves of the plant.

3. Transpiration normally takes place in the presence of ....

4. 95% of the total transpiration takes place through ....

5. In Nerium, the stomata are present in ....

6. Openings found on the under surface of the leaf are ....

7. The leaves of the .... plants have cuticular wax.

8. Guttation takes place generally at ....

9. Transpiration helps in creating .... force and in eliminating excess ....

10. Closing of .... and shedding of leaves reduce ....

Ans.
1. Transpiration
2. Water vapour
3. sunlight

Fill in the Blanks

4. Stomata	7. Xerophytic	10. stomata, transpiration
5. Sunken pits	8. night	
6. stomata	9. Suction, water	

Chapter 5. Photosynthesis

1. A light induced reaction which leads to splitting of water is called .... of water.
2. One of the products of .... of water is oxygen.
3. .... are regarded as complete photosynthetic units of plants.
4. ADP stands for ....
5. .... molecules of chlorophyll make one quantasome.
6. Carbon dioxide enters the leaf through ....
7. Xanthophyll is .... coloured pigment.
8. The conversion of physical energy of light into chemical energy by the chloroplast is called ....
9. A dark reaction is a .... reaction.
10. A light reaction is a .... reaction.
11. ....$+ 12H_2O \xrightarrow[\text{Chlorophyll}]{\text{Light energy}} C_6H_{12}O_6 + ...+.....................$
12. $4OH \longrightarrow$ ....
13. Stroma is the ground substance present in ....
14. In the flowering plants, food is transported in the form of ....
15. The chemical substance used to test the presence of starch in the cell of a leaf is ....
16. Complete the following paragraph by filling in the blanks (i) to (v) with appropriate words :*

   To test a leaf for starch, the leaf is boiled in water to (i) .... It is then boiled in Methylated spirit to (ii) .... The leaf is dipped in warm water to soften it. It is placed in a petri dish, and (iii) .... solution is added. The region of the leaf which contains starch, turns (iv) .... and the region which does not contain starch, turns (v) ....

Ans.

1. Photolysis	8. Photophosphorylation	15. Iodine
2. Photolysis	9. Thermochemical	16. (i) Kill the cells
3. Chloroplasts	10. Photochemical	(ii) Remove chlorophyll
4. Adenosine diphosphate	11. $6CO_2, 6H_2O, 6O_2\uparrow$	(iii) Iodine
5. 230	12. $2H_2O + O_2$	(iv) Blue-black
6. Stomata	13. Chloroplast	(v) Yellowish Brown
7. Yellow	14. Sucrose	

Chapter 6. Chemical Coordination in Plants

1. External actions that create responses in the living beings are called ....
2. .... is a growth inhibitor.
3. Phytohormones can either act .... or .... with one another.
4. .... is the main naturally occurring auxin found in all plants and natural fungi.
5. In plants, the auxins are usually synthesized in the .... tissues.
6. The secondary growth of the stem and the differentiation of the Xylem and Phloem tissues are mainly controlled by ....
7. Gibberellin was named by .... and.............
8. The first Cytokinin was discovered by .... and ....

---

* Frequently asked previous years Board Exam Questions.

9. .... is most widely used for the artificial ripening of fruits.

10. Abscisic acid was discovered by ....

11. Abscisic acid is formed from ....

12. Stems show .... phototropism, while roots show .... phototropism.

Ans. 1. Stimuli

    2. Abscisic acid

    3. Synergistically, antagonistically

    4. Indole acetic acid

    5. Meristematic

    6. Auxins

    7. Yabuta, T. Hayashi

    8. Miller, Skoog

    9. Ethepon

    10. Frederick T. Addicott

    11. Mevalonic acid

    12. Positive, negative

Chapter 7. The Circulatory System

1. .... is the iron-containing protein that gives red colour to blood.

2. The .... is the most powerful organ in the circulatory system.

3. The average heart rate is .... beats per minute in human being.

4. .... is a disorder in which person's blood is not able to clot properly.

5. The erythrocytes contain an iron-rich pigment called ....

6. The capillaries have no ....

7. The .... have thin and less muscular .... and have .... to prevent the back flow of blood.

8. When oxygen is in fairly high concentration, the haemoglobin quickly combines with it and forms an unstable compound known as ....

9. The element required for blood clotting is ....

10. .... are responsible for clotting of blood.

11. The three distinct types of blood vessels are .... , ... and ....

12. The site of production of WBCs is ....

13. The .... is referred to as the graveyard of red blood corpuscles and the .... is referred to as the cradle of red blood corpuscles.

14. The red blood corpuscles are .... shaped cells without ....

15. The fluid in the space between the tissue cell is called ....

16. The foundations of physiology were laid by the physician ....

17. Beside food, oxygen and waste materials, circulatory system transports .... to various parts of the body.

18. .... are the blood vessels which usually carry oxygenated blood.

19. The chamber of heart which pumps blood into aorta is ....

20. Arteries are .... walled and the veins are .... walled vessels.

21. The blood vessel which transports blood from heart to an organ is ....

22. The sequence of one systole followed by one diastole is termed as the ....

23. The membranous covering of the heart is ....

24. The heart is made up of special muscles known as .... muscles.

25. All arteries except .... carry oxygenated blood.

26. The blood vessel leaving the left ventricle of the mammalian heart is the ....

27. The blood vessel that begins and ends in capillaries is the ....

Ans. 1. Haemoglobin

    2. Heart

    3. 72

    4. Haemophilia

    5. Haemoglobin

    6. Muscles

    7. Veins, walls , valves

    8. Oxyhaemoglobin

    9. Calcium

10. Thrombocytes
11. Arteries, veins, capillaries
12. Red bone marrow
13. Spleen, Bone Marrow
14. Biconcave disc, nucleus
15. Tissue fluid/interstitial fluid

16. William Harvey
17. Hormones
18. Arteries
19. Left ventricle
20. thick, thin
21. Artery

22. Cardiac cycle
23. Pericardium
24. Cardiac
25. Pulmonary artery
26. Aorta
27. Hepatic portal vein

Chapter 8. The Excretory System

1. The process of removing the metabolic waste from the body is known as ....
2. Human kidney is made up of ....
3. .... is the functional unit of kidney.
4. The sum of all the chemical reactions taking place in the cell is known as ....
5. The process of releasing urine is called ....
6. The U-shaped portion of a nephron located in the medulla region is called ....
7. The knot of blood vessels inside the Bowman's capsule is ....
8. The tube which transports urine from kidney to urinary bladder is ....
9. .... supplies blood to kidney.
10. The human liver converts ammonia into ....
11. Besides excretion, the kidneys also carry out the important function of ....
12. Automatic self-regulation of salt and water within the body is known as ....
13. The outer surface of the kidney is ....while the inner surface is .... in shape.
14. Urine is collected in the ....
15. Sweat formed in the sweat glands passes into the sweat duct which opens to the outside at the surface of the skin by means of ....

Ans.
1. Excretion
2. Nephrons
3. Nephron
4. Metabolism
5. Micturition

6. Loop of Henle
7. Glomerulus
8. Ureter
9. Renal artery
10. Urea

11. Osmoregulation
12. Homeostasis
13. Convex, concave
14. Urinary bladder
15. Sweat pore

Chapter 9. The Nervous System and Sense Organs

1. .... is the structural and functional unit of nervous system.
2. A bundle of axons enclosed in a tubular sheath is called a ....
3. .... is the largest part of the brain.
4. Cerebrum is the site of ....
5. The part of brain where the respiratory center is located is ....
6. The medulla oblongata is also known as the ....
7. A nerve chain between a receptor and an effector organ in a reflex action is called............. .
8. The part of the central nervous system which responds to the reflex action is...........
9. Inability of an eye to focus on nearby objects due to loss of elasticity of the lens with age is called ....
10. Hypermetropia can be corrected using a ....
11. Optic nerve is a type of .... nerve, whereas spinal nerves are .... nerves.
12. .... is the organ of balance and hearing in the body.

13. Tympanic chamber is filled with .... fluid.

Ans. 1. Neuron
2. Nerve
3. Cerebrum
4. Memory/thinking
5. Medulla Oblongata
6. Spinal bulb
7. Reflex arc
8. Spinal cord
9. Presbyopia
10. Biconvex lens
11. Sensory, mixed
12. Ear
13. Perilymph

Chapter 10. The Endocrine System

1. .... is called father of endocrinology.

2. Nervous system and .... are very closely related.

3. The glands with ducts are called ....

4. A hormone which influences the ossification of bones is ....

5. The activities of the thyroid gland are controlled by............... secreted by the .... gland.

6. A disease caused in children due to under secretion of thyroxine is ....

7. In adults, deficiency in secretion of thyroid hormone causes a disease called ....

8. Lack of iodine in diet causes ....

9. The endocrine part of the pancreas is ....

10. .... is a disease caused by hypoparathyroidism.

11. Insulin makes the liver turn blood sugar into ....

Ans. 1. Thomas Addison
2. Endocrine system
3. Exocrine/ducted glands
4. Parathormone
5.   Thyroid stimulating hormone, pituitary
6. Cretinism
7. Myxoedema
8. Goitre
9. Islet of Langerhans
10. Tetany
11. Glycogen

Chapter 11. The Reproductive System

1. The sperms in a human male are produced in ....

2. .... hormone is secreted by the interstitial cells.

3. The surgical sterilization in male is known as ....

4. .... hormone plays a key role in the development of male reproductive tissues such as the testis and prostate.

5. The female equivalent of penis is the ....

6. .... hormone plays a central role in reproduction in females.

7. The process of releasing of egg from the ovary is called ....

8. One egg is normally released from ovary in the human females after.................. days.

9. Fertilization of human egg by the sperm normally occurs in the ....

10. The process of attachment of the blastocyst to the wall of uterus is known as ....

11. .... produces Human Chorionic Gonadotropin (HCG) and protects the embryo.

12. The umbilical cord connects .... and ....

13. The embryo inside the uterus is protected from jerks or mechanical shocks by.................

14. Placenta is .... permeable.

15. Human gestation period is about ....

16. .... is the innermost membrane that closely covers the embryo when first formed.

17. The period of complete development of the foetus till birth is termed as ....
18. A hormone secreted in a female to facilitate parturition is ....
19. The expulsion of the foetus from the body of the mother in a human female is called ....
20. Complete the following by filling in the blanks 1 to 5 with appropriate words :

The human female gonads are ovaries. A maturing egg in the ovary is present in a sac of cells called ....(i). As the egg grows larger, the follicle enlarges and gets filled with a fluid and is now called the ....(ii) follicle. The process of releasing the egg from the ovary is called ....(iii). The ovum is picked up by the oviduct funnel and fertilization takes place in the ....(iv). In about a week, the blastocyst gets fixed in the endometrium of the uterus and this process is called ....(v).

Ans.

1. Testes	9. Oviduct (fallopian tube)	17. Gestation
2. Testosterone	10. Implantation	18. Relaxin
3. Vasectomy	11. Placenta	19. Parturition
4. Testosterone	12. Foetus, placenta	20. (i) Follicle
5. Clitoris	13. Amniotic fluid	(ii) Graafian
6. Progesterone	14. Selectively	(iii) Ovulation
7. Ovulation	15. 280 days	(iv) Oviduct (fallopian tube)
8. 28	16. Amnion	(v) Implantation

Chapter 12. Human Population

1. World population in 1994 was ....
2. Total population in India in 1999 was ....
3. A rapid increase in population over a relatively short period is known as ....
4. Another term for birth rate is ....
5. Population increases in .... ratio while food production increases in arithmetic ratio.
6. Minerals are .... resources of energy.
7. The sign of family planning in India is ....
8. Pregnancy can be avoided by using ....

Ans.

1. 5·6 billion	4. Natality	7. Inverted Red triangle
2. 103 million	5. geometric	8. Contraceptive pills
3. Population explosion	6. Non-conventional	

Chapter 13. Human Evolution

1. Evolution does not change any ...., rather it represents genetic change in a ....
2. .... is a branch of science that deals with the history and evolution of organisms, particularly the origin and descent of species, as well as their changes over time.
3. The .... is considered to be the "Age of man".
4. The scientific name to human as *Homo sapiens* was given by ....
5. Lamarck published his principles in the book, ...
6. The principle of inheritance of acquired characters was seriously criticized by .... in ....
7. The formation of new species is the backbone of ....

Ans.

1. Individual, generation	4. Carl Linnaeus	7. Evolution
2. Evolutionary biology	5. Philosophie Zoologique	
3. Holocene epoch	6. August Weismann, 1892	

Chapter 14. Pollution

1. Global warming is caused due to .... concentration of CO_2 in air.
2. Burning of coal and diesel releases ....

3. Petrol engine gives off gaseous oxides of …………..

4. Acid rain is caused by oxides of …………..

5. The ………… is the layer of the atmosphere that contains the protective ozone layer.

6. Chemicals intended to kill insects and other organisms that damage crops are called …………

7. Rain that is more acidic than normal is called …………..

8. The release of hot water into rivers causes …………..

9. Sewage is the source of pollution of …………

10. Drinking polluted water causes diseases like ………… and …………

11. Noise pollution causes ………… and …………

12. ………… are man-made compounds that have been widely used as refrigerants and in spray propellants and foam blowing.

13. Emission norms were first introduced in India in ………… to regulate the levels of pollution.

14. ………… is planting of trees of a single type or different types on all private lands for the benefit of the society.

Ans.

1. increased	8. Thermal pollution
2. SO_2	9. Fresh water
3. Nitrogen	10. Cholera, dysentery
4. Sulphur and nitrogen	11. Hearing impairment, hypertension
5. Stratosphere	12. Chlorofluorocarbons
6. Pesticides	13. 1991
7. Acid rain	14. Social forestry

True and False

Mention, if the following statements are True or False. If false, rewrite the wrong statement in its correct form :

Chapter 1. Cell Division

1. Somatic cells of a multicellular organisms arise from a single cell by mitosis.
2. Mitosis results in four daughter cells.
3. Mitosis keeps the chromosome number constant through the generations.
4. Germ cells divide meiotically to produce gametes.
5. The alkaloid colchicine inhibits formation of mitotic spindle.
6. Asexual reproduction is accomplished through mitosis.
7. Chromosomes other than sex-chromosomes are Autosomes.
8. Cytokinesis takes place through cleavage furrow in animal cells.
9. Chromosomes are arranged in the form of chromatids at the equator in prophase.
10. Chromosomes are the thickest and shortest in telophase.
11. Meiosis is also called heterotypic division.
12. Prophase of meiosis-I has five sub-stages.
13. Meiosis leads to recombination of characters.
14. Lysosome is a part of the cell in which chromosomes are present.
15. Centromere is the organelle of the cell that initiates cell division.
16. Mitosis is the type of cell division occuring in the cells of injured parts of the body.
17. Chromosomes other than the pair of sex chromosomes are called Alleles.

Ans. 1. True.

2. False, Meiosis results in four daughter cells.

3. False, meiosis keeps the chromosome number constant through the generations.

4. True	6. True	8. True
5. True	7. True	

9. False, chromosomes are arranged in the form of chromatids at the equator in metaphase.

10. False, chromosomes are thickest and shortest in metaphase.

11. True	12. True	13. True

14. False, Nucleus is a part of the cell in which chromosomes are present.

15. True	16. True

17. False, chromosomes other than the pair of sex chromosomes are called autosomes.

Chapter 2. Fundamentals of Genetics

1. Mendel experimented with plants of *Oryza sativa*.
2. DNA has a double helical structure.
3. Genes are responsible for genetic characters.
4. Linkage is a permanent feature of few genes.
5. Mutation can be brought about artificially.

6. A female is responsible for the sex of the progeny.

7. Most genetic diseases in man are recessive in character.

8. Male acts as carrier for colour blindness.

9. Females are more affected by sex-linked genetic disorders.

10. Colour blindness is a Y-linked disorder.

11. *Haemophilia* exhibits X-linked inheritance.

12. A colour blind male cannot distinguish any colour.

13. Cancer is a genetic disorder.

Ans. 1. False, Mendel experimented with plants of *Pisum sativum*.

2. True   3. True   4. True   5. True

6. False, male is responsible for the sex of the progeny.

7. True

8. False, female acts as carrier for colour blindness.

9. False, males are more affected by sex linked genetic disorders.

10. False, colour blindness is a X-linked character.

11. True

12. False, a colourblind male cannot distinguish red and green colour.

13. True

Chapter 3. Absorption by Roots

1. Xylem is the water conducting tissue in plants.

2. Osmosis is defined as the movement of water from a concentrated sugar solution to a dilute sugar solution.

3. The plasma membrane permits the passage of all solutes and water.

4. During exosmosis, water moves from inside the cell to the outside of the cell.

5. Plasmolysis makes the cell turgid.

6. Cells that have lost their water content are said to be deplasmolysed.

7. Flaccidity is the reverse of turgidity.

Ans. 1. True

2. False, osmosis is defined as the movement of water from a dilute sugar solution to a concentrated sugar solution through a semi-permeable membrane.

3. False, plasma membrane permits the passage of certain substances.

4. True

5. False, Plasmolysis makes the cell flaccid.

6. False, the cells that have lost their water content are said to be plasmolysed.

7. True

Chapter 4. Transpiration

1. Transpiration is a physiological process.

2. Root hairs are the extensions of the outer epidermal cells of the root.

3. More transpiration occurs from the upper surface of a leaf.

4. Transpiration takes place only in green plants.

5. The pH of the guard cells increases during day time.

6. Evaporation is a physiological process.

7. The wall of the guard cells towards the stroma is thin.

8. Low humidity in the atmosphere results in decrease in the rate of transpiration.

9. Calcium chloride paper is used to demonstrate transpiration.

10. Moist cobalt chloride paper is blue in colour.

11. A controlled experiment is one in which two different experiments are set up.

12. Transpiration results in loss in weight of plant.

13. Guttation occurs through stomata.

14. Potometer is an instrument used for measuring the rate of transpiration.

Ans. 1. True

2. True

3. False, more transpiration occurs from the lower surface of a leaf.

4. False, transpiration takes place in green plants and in some non-green plants also.

5. True

6. False, evaporation is a physical process.

7. False, the wall of the guard cells towards the stoma is thick.

8. False, high humidity in the atmosphere results in decrease in the rate of transpiration.

9. False, cobalt chloride paper is used to demonstrate transpiration.

10. False, moist cobalt chloride paper is pink in colour.

11. False, a controlled experiment is one in which two identical experiments are set up.

12. True

13. False, guttation occurs through hydathodes.

14. True

Chapter 5. Photosynthesis

1. Photosynthesis occurs only in plants.

2. Too much light destroys chlorophyll.

3. The unit of light absorbed by the chlorophyll during photosynthesis is the proton.

4. The process of photosynthesis takes place in the dark.

5. Carbon dioxide is the life supporting gas produced due to photosynthesis.

6. Photolysis of water means the breaking up of water molecules into its components.

7. Radiant energy is converted into chemical energy by photosynthesis.

8. Leaves are broad and flat to increase the surface area for photosynthesis.

9. The raw materials for photosynthesis include water and CO_2.

10. Photosynthesis results in loss of dry weight of the plant.

11. Land plants obtain their CO_2 from atmosphere.

12. Photosynthesis occurs in all the cells of a plant.

13. No transpiration occurs during photosynthesis.

14. A variegated leaf (one that has green as well as white patches) will Photosynthesize only in the green areas.

15. The dark reaction of Photosynthesis is light independent.

16. All the starch produced in a leaf remains stored in it for 2-3 weeks before it is used by other parts of plant.

17. Photosynthesis can also occur in artificial light such as that of a 100 watt electric lamp.

18. In an experiment of Photosynthesis, KOH crystals were used to absorb CO_2.

19. Out of nine types of chlorophyll, chlorophyll 'a' and 'b' are most abundant.

20. The rate of Photosynthesis continues to raise as long as the intensity of light rises.

21. If you immerse an intact leaf of a plant in ice cold water, it will continue to photosynthesize in bright sunshine.

22. Photolysis is the process of splitting of water molecules in the presence of grana and temperature.

Ans. 1. False, Photosynthesis occurs in all green plants, algae and some micro-organisms.

2. True

3. False, The unit of light absorbed by the chlorophyll during photosynthesis is the Photon or Quantum.

4. False, it takes place in the presence of sunlight.

5. False, oxygen is the life supporting gas produced due to photosynthesis.

6. True   7. True   8. True   9. True

10. False, photosynthesis results in gain of dry weight of the plant.

11. True

12. False, respiration occurs in all the cells of a plant.

13. False, transpiration occurs along with photosynthesis.

14. True.   15. True

16. False, it remains stored in it for 24 to 48 hours.

17. True   18. True   19. True

20. False, the rate of photosynthesis can increase only upto a certain limit as after that it gets stabilized.

21. False, ice cold water will hamper the photosynthesis process as temperature has a direct influence on this process.

22. False, photolysis is the process of splitting of water molecules in the presence of grana and light.

Chapter 6. Chemical Coordination in Plants

1. Growth is internal in all living beings.

2. Chemotropism stands for the phenomenon of movement of plant towards light.

3. The first group of phytohormones to be identified are gibberellins.

4. Auxin promotes cell division.

5. The presence of high concentration of auxins promotes root growth.

6. Gibberellins play no role in overcoming dormancy.

7. Cytokinins promote cell division only in meristematic cells.

8. Ethylene promotes the growth of the lateral buds.

Ans. 1. True

2. False, it is the phenomenon of movement of plant towards chemicals or nutrients.

3. False, auxins were the first hormones to be identified as phytohormones.

4. True

5. False, they promote root growth at extremely low concentrations.

6. False, they help to overcome dormancy.

7. False, they promote cell division even in non-meristematic cells.

8. False, Ethylene inhibits the growth of lateral buds.

Chapter 7. The Circulatory System

1. Serum is a blood plasma not having clotting properties.

2. WBC contains Haemoglobin.

3. RBCs are of several kinds whereas WBCs are of one kind.

4. Leucocytes show amoeboid movement.

5. The average life of red blood cells in our body is about 120 hours.

6. The heart of a normal human adult beats more than one lakh times per day.

7. Blood group AB is a universal donor.

8. The walls of auricles are thicker than those of ventricles.

Ans. 1. True

    2. False, RBC contains Haemoglobin.

    3. False, RBCs are of one kind whereas WBCs are of several kinds.

    4. True

    5. False, the average life of a red blood cell in our body is about 120 days.

    6. True

    7. False, blood group O is a universal donor.

    8. False, the walls of auricles are thinner than those of ventricles.

Chapter 8. The Excretory System

1. Sometimes urine may contain certain excess vitamins.

2. Harmful ammonium compounds formed during the metabolism in the cells are broken down to form urea in the kidney.

3. Urine leaves the urinary bladder of a female by means of the uterus.

4. Urethra carries urine from the kidney to the urinary bladder.

5. Glomerular filtration is influenced by the hydrostatic pressure in the glomerulus.

6. Glomerular filtrate consists of many substances such as water, salts, glucose and white blood corpuscles.

7. Diuretic increases the production of urine.

8. The kidney is composed of number of neurons.*

Ans. 1. True

    2. False, harmful ammonium compounds formed during the metabolism in the cells are broken down to form urea in the liver.

    3. False, urine leaves the urinary bladder of a female by means of the urethra.

    4. False, ureters carry urine from the kidney to the urinary bladder.

    5. True   6. True   7. True

    8. False, The kidney is composed of number of **Nephrons** Uriniferous tubules.

Chapter 9. The Nervous System and Sense Organs

1. A nerve impulse passes from one neuron to another across a synapse.

2. Sensory nerves and Motor nerves constitute the central nervous system.

3. Cranium is a portion of the brain.

4. There are 12 pairs of spinal nerves present in human body.

5. The nerve impulse in the eye is generated due to the chemical changes brought about in the sensitive cells (rods and cones) by the light energy of the image.

6. Reflex action involves brain.

7. A reflex action is a spontaneous, voluntary response to a stimulus.

8. Reflex action is a unit of nervous action.

9. Cones are the receptor cells in the retina of the eye that are sensitive to dim light.

10. Rods are responsible for vision in the dark.

11. The least distance of distinct vision for the human eye is 25 cm.

12. Hypermetropia is a defect of the eye caused due to the elongation of eyeball.

13. Dilation of pupil is brought about by the sympathetic nervous system.*

*** Frequently asked previous years Board Exam Questions.**

14. Cochlea is a part of ear concerned with the sense of balance.

15. Deafness is caused due to the rupturing of the pinna.

16. The part of ear associated with dynamic balance is the cochlea.

17. Maintaining balance of the body and coordinating muscular activities is carried out by the cerebrum.*

18. The part of the eye which can be donated from a clinically dead person is the Retina.*

Ans. 1. True

    2. False, sensory nerves and motor nerves constitute the peripheral nervous system.

    3. False, cranium is a bony box that encloses brain.

    4. False, there are 31 pairs of spinal nerves present in human body.

    5. True

    6. False, reflex action involves spinal cord.

    7. False, a reflex action is a spontaneous, involuntary response to a stimulus.

    8. True

    9. False, cones are the receptor cells in the retina of the eye that are sensitive to bright light.

    10. True

    11. True

    12. False, myopia is a defect of the eye caused due to the elongation of eyeball.

    13. True

    14. False, cochlea is a part of ear concerned with the sense of hearing.

    15. False, deafness is caused due to the rupturing of the eardrum.

    16. False, the part of ear associated with dynamic balance is the semicircular canal.

    17. False, maintaining balance of the body and coordinating muscular activities is carried out by the **Cerebellum.**

    18. False, the part of the eye which can be donated from a clinically dead person is the **Cornea.**

Chapter 10. The Endocrine System

1. Hormones are produced by endocrine glands.

2. Hormones are chemically protein.

3. The Pituitary gland is both exocrine and endocrine in function.

4. The alpha cells of the pancreas secrete insulin.

5. Adrenal gland is called Master gland.

6. Calcium is the main element of thyroxine.

7. Adrenal cortex produces emergency hormone adrenaline.

8. Hypersecretion of adrenal cortex is responsible for *Cushing's syndrome.*

9. The two kinds of diabetes (Diabetes mellitus and Diabetes insipidus) are related to two different hormones.

10. Thyroxine regulates basal metabolic rate (BMR).

11. Rickets is caused due to deficiency of iodine.

12. Glucagon converts glucose into glycogen in the liver.

Ans. 1. True

    2. False, hormones may be protein, amine or steroid.

    3. False, the pancreas is both exocrine and endocrine in function.

    4. False, the beta cells of the pancreas secrete insulin.

    5. False, pituitary gland is called master gland.

6. False, iodine is the main element of thyroxine.

7. False, adrenal medulla produces emergency hormone adrenaline.

8. True

9. True

10. True

11. False, goitre is caused due to deficiency of iodine.

12. False, glucagon converts glycogen into glucose in the liver.

Chapter 11. The Reproductive System

1. Sperm is a single cell.

2. Sperm is highly motile male gamete.

3. Vas deferens transports sperms into urethra.

4. Cowper's gland opens into the urethra.

5. Tubectomy involves the cutting and tying of the vas deferens in male.

6. Women after the age of 45 years normally, cannot produce children.

7. The cilia lining of the oviduct funnel push the released ovum into the uterus.

8. Menarche is the stoppage of menstruation.

9. Uterus is also known as birth canal.

10. Process of fusion of the sperm nucleus and the egg nucleus is termed as implantation.

11. Zygote is formed due to fusion of male and female gametes.

12. Fertilization is the product of egg nucleus and sperm nucleus.

13. Nutrition and oxygen diffuse from mother's blood into foetus's blood through amnion.

14. Pregnancy in women can be prevented by the method of vasectomy.

15. The protective sac which develops around the developing embryo is called the Pericardium.*

Ans. 1. True　　　　2. True　　　　3. True　　　　4. True

5. False, vasectomy involves the cutting and tying of the vas deferens in male.

6. True

7. False, cilia lining of the oviduct funnel push the released ovum into the oviduct.

8. False, menarche is the onset of menstruation.

9. False, uterus is also known as the womb./vagina is also known as birth canal.

10. False, process of fusion of the sperm nucleus and egg nucleus is termed as fertilization.

11. True

12. False, fertilization is the process of fusion of egg nucleus and sperm nucleus.

13. False, nutrition and oxygen diffuse from mother's blood into foetus's blood through placenta.

14. False, pregnancy in women can be prevented by the method of tubectomy.

15. False, the protective sac which develops around the developing embryo is called the **Amnion.**

Chapter 12. Human Population

1. The present human population is about more than 7 billion.

2. Birth rate is the number of live births per 1000 of population per year.

3. Growth rate of a population is the difference between the birth rate and death rate.

4. The sign of family planning and welfare in India is an inverted blue triangle.

5. Urbanization is the process of growing urban population.

---

* Frequently asked previous years Board Exam Questions.

6. Mortality is the number of deaths per thousand of the population per decade.

7. The full form of IUD is intrauterine device.

Ans. 1. True   2. True   3. True

    4. False, the sign of family planning and welfare in India is an inverted red triangle.

    5. True

    6. False, mortality is the number of deaths per thousand of population per year.

    7. True

Chapter 13. Human Evolution

1. Humans and the great apes of Africa, that is, chimpanzees and gorillas, share a common ancestor.

2. *Homo sapiens* is the only living hominid.

3. Vestigial organs are not present in the human body as they are highly advanced.

4. Lamarck published his principles in the book called "The Origin of species".

5. The traits acquired by the organism during his lifetime due to changes in environmental conditions are called acquired traits.

6. Darwin explained the inheritance of vestigial organs.

7. Natural selection is the only cause of evolution.

8. The theory of Inheritance of Acquired characters was proposed by Watson and Crick.*

Ans. 1. True

    2. True

    3. False, vestigial organs may be present in the human body but they are not functional.

    4. False, Lamarck published his principles in the book called 'Philosophic Zoologique'.

    5. True

    6. False, Darwin could not explain the inheritance of the vestigial organs.

    7. False, Natural selection is the main cause of evolution but not the only cause of evolution.

    8. False, the theory of Inheritance of Acquired characters was proposed by **Lamarck.**

Chapter 14. Pollution

1. The average home creates more pollution than does the average number of cars.

2. Sources of groundwater pollution include leaking sewer lines, landfills, fertilizers and sludge.

3. The only health effect of ground-level ozone pollution is coughing.

4. Ozone in the troposphere is a harmful pollutant.

5. Indoor pollution is 10 times more toxic than outdoor pollution.

6. Benzene, chloroform and vinyl chloride are known as inorganic pollutants.

7. When air is polluted, you can always see and smell it.

8. Acid precipitation is created by reactions in the atmosphere, and can fall many miles from where pollution originated.

9. High amount of CO_2 in the air causes difficulty in breathing.

10. Emission standards specify the maximum output of pollutants from petrol, diesel or gas driven engines.

Ans. 1. True   2. True

    3. False, it can also affect our lungs, it can make it harder to breathe and make asthma worse.

    4. True   5. True

    6. False, these are organic pollutants.

    7. False, some pollutants are odourless and colourless (such as ozone).

    8. True   9. True   10. True

State the Location | Set **6** |

Chapter 1. Cell Division

Name	Location
Asters	Around the centriole at each pole.
Cell plate	In the centre of the plant cell.
Chromosomes	In the nucleus of plant and animal cell.
Polytene chromosome	In the salivary glands of *Drosophila melanogaster*.

Chapter 4. Transpiration

Name	Location
Stomata	In the epidermis of green, aerial parts of plants, especially the leaves.
Lenticels	On the bark of woody plants.
Cuticle	On the outer surface of the primary organs of all vascular land plants.
Hydathodes	On the edges and tips of leaves of many plants.
Guard cells	Leaf epidermis.

Chapter 5. Photosynthesis

Name	Location
Thylakoid	Chloroplast and cyanobacteria
Stomata	Mostly on the under-surface of plant leaves.
Chlorophyll	On the walls of thylakoids.
Stroma	In the inner portion of chloroplast.

Chapter 7. The Circulatory System

Name	Location
Sino-auricular node	In the wall (myocardium) of the right atrium of the heart.
Bicuspid valve	Between the left atrium and left ventricle of the heart.
Pulmonary vein	Arises from lungs and pours blood into the left auricle.
Semilunar valves	Located in the arteries.
Bundle of His	In the interventricular septum.
Spleen	Above the stomach in the left upper quadrant of the abdomen.
Hepatic portal vein	Between alimentary canal and liver.

Chapter 8. The Excretory System

Name	Location
Kidneys	Along the posterior abdominal wall on either side of the vertebral column.
Medulla of kidney	In the cortex of kidney or in the inner lighter region of kidney.
Urinary bladder	It lies in the pelvic region of the abdomen.

Chapter 9. The Nervous System and Sense Organs

Name	Location
Node of Ranvier	Between the axon of medullated neurons.
Corpus callosum	Near the centre of brain.
Meninges	Covering of brain and spinal cord.
Cerebellum	In the hind brain.
Ganglia	On each side of the spinal cord.
Lacrimal gland	Above the lateral end of the eye.
Iris	In the eye behind the cornea.
Yellow spot	Near the centre of the retina.
Organ of Corti	In the cochlea of ear.
Pinnae	Side of the head, face.
Eustachian tube	Between the middle ear and pharynx.
Semicircular canals	In the internal ear.
Incus	Incus is the middle bone of the three bones of ear ossicles which is connected to Malleus on one end and Stapes on other end and is present in the middle ear of human beings.*

Chapter 10. The Enocrine System

Name	Location
Thyroid	At the base of the larynx.
Adrenal gland	At the top of each kidney.
Pancreas	Between the stomach and the duodenum.
Prostate gland	At the base of urinary bladder.
Pituitary gland	At the base of brain.

*** Frequently asked previous years Board Exam Questions.**

Chapter 11. The Reproductive System

Name	Location
Seminal vesicle	At the posterior end of vas deferens between urinary bladder and rectum in male.*
Prostate gland	At the base of urinary bladder surrounding the urethra.
Cowper's glands	About 4-5 cm below the prostate gland.
Ovary	In the upper pelvic cavity one on each side of uterus.
Uterus	Above and behind the urinary bladder in the abdominal cavity.
Bartholin's glands	On the sides of vaginal orifice in female.
Amnion	Amnion is a sac which develops around the embryo inside uterus of human females.
Testis	Testes are located in thin walled sac like structure called Scrotal sac.*
Amniotic fluid	Thigmotropism is the growth movement of plants in response to touch stimulus. **Example-** The tendrils of *Cuscuta* coil around a support in response to touch.*

State the Function | Set **7** |

Write the functional activity of the following structures :

Chapter 1. Cell Division

Name	Function
Chromosome	Heredity, *i.e.,* transmission of characters from parents to offspring.
Spindle fibres	Helps to divide the chromosome equally in the daughter cells from the parent cell.
Chiasmata	Crossing-over, in which genetic material is exchanged between non-sister chromatids.
Colchicine	It inhibits the formation of mitotic spindle or microtubule.

Chapter 2. Fundamentals of Genetics

Name	Function
DNA	Controls biosynthetic processes of cell.
Chromosomes	Carries genes which carry information to be transfered to the offsprings from the parents.
Genes	Carries parental characters to offspring.
Autosomes	Responsible for physical character of progeny.
Heterosomes	Sex determination.

Chapter 4. Transpiration

Name	Function
Stomata	(a) Loss of water vapours due to transpiration. (b) Gaseous exchange.
Lenticels	They help in gaseous exchange in woody parts of the plant and some amount of water is lost by transpiration.
Cuticle	It protects the surface of leaves, stem etc., and reduces water loss.
Hydathodes	Plants secrete excess of water through hydathodes when atmosphere is very humid and transpiration process cannot occur.
Guard cells	Regulate the rate of transpiration by opening and closing of stomata.
Leaf spines	Reduces the surface area for transpiration.

Chapter 5. Photosynthesis

Name	Function
Granum	Light reaction of photosynthesis.

Stroma	Dark reaction of photosynthesis.
Chloroplasts	Conduct photosynthesis by trapping solar energy.
Thylakoids	Help in photosynthesis and contain chlorophyll pigment.
Guard cells	Control the opening and closing of stomata.

Chapter 6. Chemical Coordination in Plants

Name	Function
Cytokinins	Cytokinins stimulate plant growth by cell division and cell enlargement. They inhibit apical dominance, prevents ageing, breaks seed dormancy, delays senescence.*

Chapter 7. The Circulatory System

Name	Function
RBC	To transport oxygen to the body cells.
WBC	To fight against micro-organism by producing antibodies.
Platelets	Helps in bloods clotting.
Thrombocytes	Helps in clotting of blood.
Haemoglobin	It helps to carry O_2 from respiratory organs to all parts of the body.
Vitamin K	Helps in clotting of blood.
Semilunar valves	They prevent the back flow of blood from the pulmonary artery and aorta into the heart.
Bundle of His	They carry the wave of excitation from atrio-ventricular node to the ventricles.
Bicuspid valve	It prevents the back flow of blood from the left ventricle into the right.
Pericardium	It protects the heart.
Tricuspid valve	It prevents the back flow of blood from the right ventricle into the right auricle.
Chordae tendineae	To keep the cuspid valves in position.
Vena cava	To carry deoxygenated blood from the body parts to the right auricle of the heart.
Pulmonary artery	It transports deoxygenated blood to the lungs.
Pulmonary vein	Brings oxygenated blood from lungs to the heart for circulation throughout the body.
Coronary artery	It carries blood to the muscles of heart.
Lymph	(a) It transports fatty acids and glycerol. (b) It also protects the body against micro-organisms.

Chapter 8. The Excretory System

Name	Function
Sweat glands	Excretion by eliminating extra water and salts.
Kidney	Excretion of waste materials from the body.
Nephron	To regulate the concentration of water and other soluble substances by reabsorption.
Bowman's capsule	Ultrafiltration.
Glomerulus	Filtration of blood.
Henle's loop	Reabsorption of water from glomerular filtrate.

* Frequently asked previous years Board Exam Questions.

Renal artery	To supply oxygenated blood to the kidneys.
Renal vein	To collect deoxygenated blood from the kidneys.
Iliac artery	To supply blood to pelvic region.
Iliac vein	To collect blood from pelvic region.
Vasopressin	Regulates the concentration of urine by water reabsorption.
Aldosterone	Na^+ and K^+ reabsorption./ Regulates sodium and potassium level in the body.
Ureter	Transfer of urine from kidneys to the urinary bladder.
Bladder	Storage of urine.
Urethra	Passage for urine and semen (in case of males).
Bladder sphincter	Regulates micturition.
Adrenal gland	Secretion of hormones.

Chapter 9. The Nervous System and Sense Organs

Name	Function
Myelin sheath	The myelin sheath provides insulation to axon and prevents indiscriminate distribution and leakage of nerve impulse.
Cerebrum	Cerebrum is concerned with a number of senses like sight, hearing, taste, etc. The motor areas in the cortex give rise to voluntary movements such as speech, locomotion, etc. Other areas of the cerebrum are responsible for memory, intelligence, learning, emotions etc.
Cerebellum	Cerebellum of the brain regulates and co-ordinates muscular contractions and skeletal movements. It is also concerned with balance.
Medulla oblongata	Medulla oblongata is concerned with certain vital activities such as respiratory movements, heart beat and the dilation of blood vessels.
Hypothalamus	The hypothalamus of the mid-brain regulates the body temperature, smooth muscles activity, water balance, appetite, blood pressure and the metabolism of fats and carbohydrates.
Cerebrospinal fluid	Cerebrospinal fluid offers protection to the brain and spinal cord by acting as a cushion to absorb shocks. It also supplies nourishment to the brain tissue.
Acetylcholine	It helps in the transmission of the nerve impulse from one neuron to other neuron under enzymatic reactions.
Cornea	It covers and protects the iris and allows the entry of light rays into the eye.
Iris	It controls the size and diameter of the pupil, according to the intensity of illumination.
Aqueous humour	It allows light rays to pass into the eye, prevents their refraction and dispersion and keeps the lens moist.
Choroid	Choroid layer with many capillaries forms the nutritive layer of the retina and absorbs light rays to avoid reflection.
Cochlea	It is the organ of hearing.
Visual purple	It has vitamin A derivative that helps the eyes to see in dim light.
Conjunctiva	It supplies nourishment to eye and prevents infection. It covers the cornea and lines inside of the eyelid.
Vitreous humour	It maintains the shape of eyeball.
Suspensory ligaments	They are fibres which hold the lens in position.
Yellow spot	Yellow spot is the place of best vision of the normal eye. This spot contains the maximum number of sensory cells, particularly cones.
Ear drum	It vibrates according to the sound waves and transmits them across the middle ear.

State the Function

Ear ossicles	Ear ossicles amplify the vibrations of the ear drum and transmit them to the delicate membrane stretched along the oval window.
Semicircular canals	They are concerned with maintaining equilibrium and posture of the body.
Endolymph	It transmits vibrations to the hair cells of the inner ear to produce acoustic perception.
Eustachian tube	It equalizes air pressure on the ear drum from inside.
Tears	Tears clean the front surface of our eye by removing dust particles and the enzyme lysozyme present in tears, kills the germs.*

Chapter 10. The Endocrine System

Name	Function
Thyroxine	It increases rate of metabolism and maintains energy balance in the body.
Insulin	It converts glucose into glycogen, decreasing blood sugar level.
Testosterone	Development of primary and secondary sexual characters in males.
Oestrogen	Development of primary and secondary sexual characters in females.
Progesterone	It maintains normal course of pregnancy.
Relaxin	It loosens the pelvic ligaments and softens the cervix of uterus during childbirth.
Oxytocin	It stimulates uterine contractions during childbirth and causes ejection of milk from mammary glands.

Chapter 11. The Reproductive System

Name	Function
Testis	The main function of testis is the formation of spermatozoa and testosterone hormone.
Seminiferous tubules	Production of sperms.
Seminal vesicles	Their secretion provides energy for the sperms and neutralizes the acidic medium in the urethra and female tract.
Seminal fluid	It provides nutrition to the spermatozoa and lubricates the reproductive passage so that sperms transfer efficiently.
Prostate gland	It secretes alkaline fluid into the semen. This fluid neutralizes acidity of urine in the urinogential canal. Urine sample.
Cowper's gland	Its secretion lubricates the end of penis during copulation and neutralizes the acidic environment of the urethra.
Inguinal canal	It acts as a pathway by which testes descend down from the abdominal wall to the external genitalia (scrotum) and vas deferens.
Urethra	It acts as common passage for urine and spermatic fluid (semen).
Ovary	Its main function is the formation of ovum and reproductive hormones.
Fallopian tubes	To carry ovum from ovary to the uterus.
Graafian follicle	Its main function is to allow the oocyte to grow to full maturity and release of mature ovum. It also forms Corpus Luteum which promotes and maintains implantation of the embryo.
Uterus	It holds, protects and nourishes the foetus by its placenta.
Amnion	It protects the foetus and secretes a shock absorbing fluid—amniotic fluid.
Placenta	Its main function is the exchange of materials between mother and the foetus (such as nutrients, respiratory gases and waste products).

Choose the Odd One Out |Set **8**|

Mark the odd one out and write the category to which the others belong for the following questions:

Chapter 1. Cell Division

1. Amitosis, Mitosis, Meiosis, Cell cycle.
2. Prophase, Meiosis, Anaphase, Telophase.
3. Zygotene, Pachytene, Diplotene, Telophase.

Ans. 1. Odd : Cell cycle   Category : Type of cell division

     2. Odd : Meiosis   Category : Stages of Mitosis

     3. Odd : Telophase   Category : Substages of Prophase-I

Chapter 2. Fundamentals of Genetics

1. Genes, Chromosomes, Alleles, Ovule.
2. Seed shape, Seed color, Flower position, Inflorescence.
3. Law of dominance, Law of segregation, Law of independent assortment, Blackman's law of limiting factor.
4. Haemophilia, Colour blindness, Night blindness, Albinism.

Ans. 1. Odd : Ovule   Category : Terms related to genetics

     2. Odd : Inflorescence   Category : Features controlled by genes

     3. Odd : Blackman's law of limiting factor   Category : Laws given by Mendel

     4. Odd : Night blindness   Category : Hereditary diseases

Chapter 3. Absorption by Roots

1. Diffusion, Imbibition, Osmosis, Oxidation.

Ans. 1. Odd : Oxidation   Category : Plant processes

Chapter 4. Transpiration

1. Transpiration, Photosynthesis, Phagocytosis, Guttation.
2. Cuticular transpiration, Lenticular transpiration, Stomatal transpiration, Guttation.
3. Stomata, Cuticle, Lenticels, Hydathodes.

Ans. 1. Odd : Phagocytosis   Category : Plant process

     2. Odd : Guttation   Category : Types of transpiration

     3. Odd : Hydathodes   Category : Structures through which transpiration occurs

Chapter 5. Photosynthesis

1. Grana, Thylakoid, Stroma, Root.
2. Chlorophyll, Chlorophyll b, β-carotene, Photon.
3. Glucose, Water, Oxygen, Carbondioxide.

4. Light intensity, Water content, Temperature, Chlorophyll.

Ans. 1. Odd : Root   Category : Absorb water in photosynthesis

    2. Odd : Photon   Category : Plant pigments

    3. Odd : Carbon dioxide   Category : Products of photosynthesis

    4. Odd : Chlorophyll   Category : absorb light in photosynthesis

Chapter 6. Chemical Coordination in Plants

1. 2,4-D, 2,4,5-T, NAA, Gibberellic acid.

2. Auxin, Cytokinin, Thyroxine, Abscisic acid.

3. Thigmotropism, Albinism, Chemotropism, Geotropism.

Ans. 1. Odd : Gibberellic acid   Category : Synthetic auxins

    2. Odd : Thyroxine   Category : Plant hormones

    3. Odd : Albinism   Category : Tropic movement in plants

Chapter 7. The Circulatory System

1. Human heart, Fish heart, Birds heart, Crocodile heart.

2. Artery, Vein, Portal vein, Lacteal.

3. RBC, ATP, WBC, Platelets.

4. Purkinje fibres, A. V. node, A. V. valve, S. A. node.

5. Mitral valve, Tricuspid valve, Semilunar valve, Venous valve.

6. Systolic pressure, Diastolic pressure, Stethoscope, Sphygmomanometer.

Ans. 1. Odd : Fish heart   Category : Heart with 4 chambers

    2. Odd : Lacteal   Category : Blood capillaries

    3. Odd : ATP   Category : Components of energy

    4. Odd : A. V. Valve   Category : Concerned with conduction of electrical impulses

    5. Odd : Venous Valve   Category : Valves present in heart

    6. Odd : Stethoscope   Category : Terms related to heart Beat

Chapter 8. The Excretory System

1. Liver, Angiotensin, Kidney, ADH

2. Proximal convoluted tubule, Distal convoluted tubule, Henle's loop, Renal corpuscle

3. Afferent arteriole, Efferent arteriole, Vasa recta, Glomerulus

4. Glucose, Amino acids, Urea, Na^+

5. Urea, Carbonic acid, Creatinine, Uric acid.

6. Urea, Uterus, Urinary bladder, Ureter.

7. Selective reabsorption, Glomerular filtration, Tubular secretion, Ureter.

8. Cortex, Bowman's capsule, Proximal convoluted tubule, Loop of Henle.

9. Renal artery, Efferent arteriole, Renal vein, Hepatic vein.

Ans. 1. Odd : Angiotensin   Category : Structures involved in excretion process

    2. Odd : Renal corpuscle   Category : Tubules present in nephron

    3. Odd : Vasa recta   Category : Parts of nephron

    4. Odd : Urea   Category : Substances reabsorbed from nephric filtrate

    5. Odd : Carbonic acid   Category : Substances excreted from the body

    6. Odd : Uterus   Category : Parts of excretory system in women

    7. Odd : Ureter   Category : Processes of excretion

8. Odd : Loop of Henle   Category : Structures lying in cortex region of kidney
9. Odd : Hepatic vein   Category : Blood capillaries related to kidney

Chapter 9. The Nervous System and Sense Organs

1. Cyton, Photon, Axon, Dendron.
2. Cyton, Axon, Dendron, Cerebrum.
3. Coughing, Sneezing, Walking, Blinking.
4. Corpus luteum, Corpus callosum, Pons, Cerebellum.
5. Sneezing, Coughing, Blinking, Typing.
6. Cerebrum, Cranium, Cerebellum, Pons.
7. Sodium pump, Polarized membrane, Threshold stimulus, Action potential.
8. Pons, Cerebellum, Medulla Oblongata, Cerebrum.
9. Rods, Cones, Night blindness.
10. Myopia, Hypermetropia, Xerophthalmia, Astigmatism.
11. Myopia, Cataract, Squint, Cretinism.
12. Ciliary muscle, Choroid, Fovea, Gustatory cells.
13. Incus, Pinna, Malleus, Stapes.
14. Semicircular canals, Cochlea, Tympanum, Utriculus.
15. Eustachian tube, Basilar membrane, Taste buds, Auditory ossicles.

Ans.
1. Odd : Photon   Category : Parts of neuron
2. Odd : Cerebrum   Category : Parts of neuron
3. Odd : Walking   Category : Simple reflexes
4. Odd : Corpus luteum   Category : Structures present in brain
5. Odd : Typing   Category : Simple reflexes
6. Odd : Cranium   Category : Parts of brain
7. Odd : Sodium pump   Category : Action potential and its types
8. Odd : Cerebrum   Category : Parts of hind brain
9. Odd : Night blindness   Category : Light sensitive cells of eye
10. Odd : Xerophthalmia   Category : Defects that can be corrected by using corrective lenses
11. Odd : Cretinism   Category : Defects of eye
12. Odd : Gustatory cells   Category : Parts of eye
13. Odd : Pinna   Category : Ear ossicles
14. Odd : Tympanum   Category : Parts of inner ear
15. Odd : Taste buds   Category : Parts of ear

Chapter 10. The Endocrine System

1. Goitre, Cretinism, Scurvy, Myxoedema.
2. Cretinism, Myxoedema, Simple goitre, Acromegaly.
3. Somatotropin, Gonadotropin releasing hormone, Corticotrophin releasing hormone, Oxytocin.
4. Thyroid gland, Adrenal gland, Pituitary gland, Prostate gland.
5. Adrenal, Liver, Thyroid, Pituitary.
6. Oestrogen, Progesterone, Testosterone, Prolactin.
7. Growth hormone, TSH, Vasopressin, LH.
8. Cushing's syndrome, Eunuchoidism, Addison's disease, Virilism.
9. Aldosterone, Cortisol, Progesterone, Epinephrine.

10. FSH, LH, ADH, HCG.

11. Cortisone, Cortisol, Aldosterone, Epinephrine.

12. Insulin, Glucagon, Diabetes insipidus, Diabetes mellitus.

13. Glucocorticoids, Mineralocorticoids, Corticotropin, Sexcorticoids.

14. Insulin, Blood sugar, Adrenaline, Thyroxine.

15. Adrenal cortex, Adrenal medulla, Cortisone, Pituitary.

16. Larynx, Pancreas, Testis, Ovary.

Ans.

1. Odd : Scurvy — Category : Diseases due to severe and chronic vitamin-C deficiency
2. Odd : Acromegaly — Category : Diseases related to thyroid gland
3. Odd : Oxytocin — Category : Hormones released by anterior pituitary
4. Odd : Prostate gland — Category : Endocrine glands
5. Odd : Liver — Category : Endocrine glands
6. Odd : Testosterone — Category : Female reproductive hormones
7. Odd : Vasopressin — Category : Hormones secreted by anterior pituitary
8. Odd : Eunuchoidism — Category : Disorders related to adrenal gland
9. Odd : Progesterone — Category : Hormones secreted by adrenal gland
10. Odd : ADH — Category : Gonadotropic hormones
11. Odd : Epinephrine — Category : Hormones secreted by adrenal cortex
12. Odd : Diabetes insipidus — Category : Hormones secreted by adrenal cortex
13. Odd : Corticotropin — Category : Terms related to pancreases
14. Odd : Blood sugar — Category : Hormones secreted by adrenal cortex
15. Odd : Cortisone — Category : Endocrine glands
16. Odd : Larynx — Category : Endocrine glands

Chapter 11. The Reproductive System

1. Testes, Prostate gland, Seminal vesicle, Cowper's gland.

2. Vas deferens, Fallopian tube, Epididymis, Cowper's gland.

3. Testis, Penis, Oviduct, Seminiferous tubules.

4. Oxytocin, Insulin, Prolactin, Progesterone.

5. Oestrogen, Progesterone, Testosterone, Oxytocin.

6. Fallopian tube, Uterus, Ovaries, Ureter

7. Vagina, Vulva, Seminal vesicle, Uterus.

8. Ovum, Corpus luteum, Scrotal sacs, Ovary.

Ans.

1. Odd : Testes — Category : Male accessory glands
2. Odd : Fallopian tube — Category : Parts of male reproductive system
3. Odd : Oviduct — Category : Parts of male reproductive system
4. Odd : Insulin — Category : Hormones responsible for pregnancy and lactation
5. Odd : Testosterone — Category : Female reproductive hormones
6. Odd : Ureter — Category : Parts of female reproductive system
7. Odd : Seminal vesicle — Category : Parts of female reproductive system
8. Odd : Scrotal sacs — Category : Terms related to female reproductive system

Chapter 12. Human Population

1. Immigration, Decline in death rate, Emigration, Increase in birth rate.
2. Progestin, Condoms, IUD, Cervical caps.
3. Abortion, Tubectomy, Vasectomy, IUD.
4. Land, Industry, Water, Minerals.

Ans. 1. Odd : Emigration   Category : Terms which result in moving abroad
2. Odd : Progestin   Category : Mechanical methods of contraception
3. Odd : IUD   Category : Surgical methods of contraception
4. Odd : Industry   Category : Natural factors, resources

Chapter 13. Human Evolution

1. Pinna, Diaphragm, Vermiform appendix, Wisdom teeth.
2. *Australopithecus, Homo habilis,* Tuang baby, *Homo erectus.*
3. Java ape man, Peking man, Cro-Magnon man, *Homo erectus erectus.*
4. Neanderthal man, Cro-Magnon man, Modern man, Tuang baby.
5. Natural selection, Survival of fittest, Variations, Overuse of organs.
6. Use and disuse of organs, Overuse of organs, Acquired characters, Natural selection.

Ans. 1. Odd : Diaphragm   Category : Vestigial organs
2. Odd : Homo erectus   Category : Grouped under early pleistocene epoch
3. Odd : Cro-Magnon man   Category : Grouped under mid pleistocene epoch
4. Odd : Tuang baby   Category : Grouped under late pleistcene epoch
5. Odd : Overuse of organs   Category : Postulates of Darwinism
6. Odd : Natural selection   Category : Lamarck's theory

Chapter 14. Pollution

1. Ozone, Carbon dioxide, Sulphur dioxide, Nitrogen oxide.
2. *Rhizobium, Azotobacter, Azospirillum,* Potassium nitrate.
3. Polythene bag, Crop residue, Animal waste, Decaying vegetable.*

Ans. 1. Odd : Ozone   Category : Air pollutants
2. Odd : Potassium nitrate   Category : Bio-fertilizers
3. Odd : Polythene bag   Category : Others are Biodegradable pollutants.

Choose the Odd One Out

* Frequently asked previous years Board Exam Questions.

Multiple Choice Questions | Set 9 |

Select the correct answer out of the four available choices given under each question :

Chapter 1. Cell Division

1. Cytokinesis is the division of :
- (a) Cell
- (b) Cytoplasm
- (c) Cell wall
- (d) Nucleus

2. Karyokinesis is the division of :
- (a) Cytoplasm
- (b) Nucleus
- (c) Cell wall
- (d) Pollen grains

3. Cell division occurring in somatic cells is :
- (a) Mitosis
- (b) Meiosis
- (c) Diplotene
- (d) Diakinesis

4. Duplication of DNA occurs in :
- (a) G_1-phase
- (b) G_2-phase
- (c) S-phase
- (d) M-phase

5. How many chromosomes are found in a cell of human?
- (a) 20 pairs
- (b) 46
- (c) 23
- (d) 46 pairs

6. The nuclear membrane disappears in :
- (a) Prophase
- (b) Anaphase
- (c) Zygotene
- (d) Pachytene

7. Duplicated chromosomes are joined at a point termed :
- (a) Centrosome
- (b) Centromere
- (c) Centriole
- (d) Chromatid

8. The nuclear membrane and nucleolus become indistinguishable during :
- (a) Telophase
- (b) Metaphase
- (c) Prophase
- (d) Interphase

9. The disappearance of spindle and uncoiling of chromosomes takes place in :
- (a) Anaphase
- (b) Telophase
- (c) Pachytene
- (d) Meiosis

10. The centromere divides into two in :
- (a) Prophase
- (b) Metaphase
- (c) Anaphase
- (d) Telophase

11. After mitotic cell division, a female human cell will have :
- (a) 44 + XX chromosome
- (b) 44 + XY chromosome
- (c) 22 + X chromosome
- (d) 22 + Y chromosome

12. The period between two successive mitotic divisions is :
- (a) Diakinesis
- (b) Interphase
- (c) Anaphase
- (d) Mitosis

13. In meiotic cell division, four daughter cells are produced by two successive divisions in which :

(a) First division is equational and second is reductional

(b) First division is reductional and second is equational

(c) Both divisions are reductional

(d) Both divisions are equational

14. Meiosis occurs in :

(a) Vegetative cells

(b) Reproductive cells

(c) Meristematic cells

(d) None of the above

15. The term Meiosis was coined by :

(a) Farmer and Moore

(b) Winiwarter

(c) Flemming

(d) Strasburger

16. Meiosis-I is also known as :

(a) Equational division

(b) Reduction division

(c) Direct cell division

(d) All of the above

17. Leptotene, Zygotene and Diplotene phases are found in :

(a) Mitosis

(b) Prophase of Meiosis-I

(c) Interphase

(d) Prophase of Meiosis-II

18. The process of Meiosis takes place to produce :

(a) Cells of the body

(b) Cells of the brain

(c) Sperms and ova

(d) Testis and ovary

19. The regions where crossing-over takes place are called :

(a) Chiasmata

(b) Cell plate

(c) Spindle fibres

(d) Chromosomes

Ans.

1. (b)	6. (a)	11. (a)	16. (b)
2. (b)	7. (b)	12. (b)	17. (b)
3. (a)	8. (b)	13. (b)	18. (c)
4. (c)	9. (b)	14. (b)	19. (a)
5. (b)	10. (c)	15. (a)	

Chapter 2. Fundamentals of Genetics

1. Genetics is a branch of biology dealing with :

(a) Heredity in living beings

(b) Variation in living beings

(c) Both heredity and variation

(d) None of these

2. Who among the following is called father of genetics?

(a) Mendel

(b) Darwin

(c) Watson and Crick

(d) Lamarck

3. When an individual has both the genes of a contrasting characters, it is said to be :

(a) Homozygous

(b) Heterozygous

(c) Phenotype

(d) Genotype

4. When two individuals differing in at least one character are crossed, the process is known as :

(a) Hybridization

(b) Selection

(c) Pedigree

(d) None of these

5. A cross was made between tall and dwarf plants. In F_1 generation all plants were tall, when the F_1 plants were self pollinated, the tall and dwarf plants appeared in 3 : 1 ratio in F_2 generation. This phenomenon is known as :

(a) Dominance

(b) Segregation

(c) Hybridization

(d) Crossing over

6. What is the effect of sexual reproduction?

(a) Offspring is weak

(b) Offspring is like the parents

(c) Offspring is more vigorous

(d) Offspring is diseased

7. DNA structure was discovered by :

(a) Lamarck

(b) Mendel

(c) Watson and Crick

(d) H. G. Khurana

8. Chromosomal aberrations are caused by :

(a) Change in the structure of gene

(b) Change in the number of chromosomes

(c) Change in the arrangement or position of genes

(d) Both (b) and (c)

9. Which one of the following is a phenotypic monohybrid ratio in F_2 generation?

(a) $3:1$

(b) $1:2:1$

(c) $2:2$

(d) $1:3$

10. The $9:3:3:1$ dihybrid ratio is due to :

(a) Segregation

(b) Crossing over

(c) Independent assortment

(d) Homologous pairing

11. In a human male, a sperm will contain :*

(a) Both X and Y chromosomes

(b) Only Y chromosome

(c) Only X chromosome

(d) Either X or Y chromosome

Ans.

1. (c)	4. (a)	7. (c)	10. (c)
2. (a)	5. (b)	8. (d)	11. (d)
3. (b)	6. (c)	9. (a)	

Chapter 3. Absorption by Roots

1. In the process of osmosis in a cell :

(a) Both protoplasm and cell wall act as a membrane

(b) Only cell wall acts as a membrane

(c) Only outermost layer of protoplast acts as a membrane

(d) The entire protoplast acts as a membrane

2. Osmosis involves :

(a) Cell to cell movement of water

(b) Movement of water through cortical cells

(c) Active absorption of water through roots

(d) All of the above

3. Plasma membrane controls :

(a) Passage of water only

(b) Passage of water and solutes in and out of the cell

(c) Passage of water and solutes into the cell

(d) Movement of cell contents out of the cell

4. The space between the cell wall and plasma membrane in a plasmolysed cell is filled with :

(a) Isotonic solution

(b) Hypotonic solution

(c) Hypertonic solution

(d) Water

---

* Frequently asked previous years Board Exam Questions.

5. Seeds when soaked in water imbibe in it because :

  (a) Osmotic pressure inside the seed is low

  (b) Seed coat contains lot of salts

  (c) The process of absorption works

  (d) There are many vacuoles in the endosperm

6. Process of endosmosis stops :

  (a) When the water concentrations become equal

  (b) When the solutions become isotonic

  (c) When the leaves fall

  (d) When there is no light

7. Marine fish when thrown under tap water bursts because of :

  (a) Endosmosis   (c) Exosmosis

  (b) Diffusion   (d) Plasmolysis

8. Osmosis involves diffusion of :

  (a) Suspended particles from lower to higher concentration

  (b) Suspended particles from higher to lower concentration

  (c) Molecules or ions from the more concentrated solution to the less concentrated solution

  (d) Solvent particles from the less concentrated solution to the more concentrated solution

9. Water will be absorbed by the root hairs when :

  (a) Concentration of solutes in the cell sap is high

  (b) Concentration of solutes in the soil is high

  (c) The plant is rapidly respiring

  (d) None of the above

10. When a plant wilts, the sequence of events will be as follows :

  (a) Exosmosis, plasmolysis, deplasmolysis, temporary wilting

  (b) Exosmosis, deplasmolysis, plasmolysis, temporary and permanent wilting

  (c) Exosmosis, plasmolysis, temporary and permanent wilting

  (d) None of the above

11. When cell is fully turgid, which of the following will be zero?

  (a) Osmotic pressure

  (b) Turgor pressure

  (c) Wall pressure

  (d) Suction pressure (SP) or Diffusion Pressure Deficit (DPD)

Ans. 1. (d)   4. (c)   7. (a)   10. (c)

     2. (d)   5. (c)   8. (d)   11. (d)

     3. (b)   6. (b)   9. (a)

Chapter 4. Transpiration

1. In the mechanism of opening and closing of stomata, the important factor is :

  (a) The presence of chloroplast in the guard cells

  (b) The turgid and flaccid state of the guard cells

  (c) The protein content of the cells

  (d) The starch content of the cells

2. Stomata open during the day and close at night because :
  (a) Photosynthesis occurs during day time only
  (b) Enzymes convert starch into sugar at elevated pH in night
  (c) Loss of sugar increases osmotic concentration of the cell sap
  (d) Loss of starch in day time raises OP of subsidiary cells

3. In hot summer days, plant cooling is due to :
  (a) Loss of water vapours from leaves
  (c) Loss of liquid water
  (b) Transport of water in plant
  (d) Loss of water from entire plant

4. If the rate of transpiration becomes more than the rate of photosynthesis, plants will :
  (a) Continue to live, but will not be able to store food
  (b) be killed instantly
  (c) Grow more vigorously because more energy will be available
  (d) Stop growing and gradually die of starvation

5. Transpiration is very low during the storms due to :
  (a) Presence of moisture in the wind
  (c) High velocity of wind
  (b) Low temperature during storms
  (d) None of the above

6. Transpiration pull will be maximum under which of the following conditions?
  (a) Open stomata, dry atmosphere and moist soil
  (b) Open stomata, high humid atmosphere and well irrigated soil
  (c) Open stomata, high humid atmosphere and dry soil
  (d) Close stomata, dry atmosphere and dry soil

7. Plants lose water by guttation when :
  (a) Rate of transpiration is high
  (b) Soil is wet and the atmosphere is humid
  (c) Soil is dry and atmosphere is dry
  (d) Soil is wet and atmosphere is dry

8. Guttation is the elimination of excess of water from plants through :
  (a) Stomata
  (c) Lenticels
  (b) Hydathodes
  (d) Wounds

9. Which one of the following does not affect the rate of transpiration ?*
  (a) Light
  (c) Wind
  (b) Humidity
  (d) Age of the plant

Ans. 1. (b)   4. (d)   7. (b)
  2. (a)   5. (a)   8. (b)
  3. (a)   6. (a)   9. (d)

Chapter 5. Photosynthesis

1. Chlorophyll is present :
  (a) In the grana of chloroplast
  (c) Dispersed throughout the chloroplast
  (b) On the surface of chloroplast
  (d) In the stroma of chloroplast

2. The specific function of light energy in the process of photosynthesis is to :
  (a) Reduce carbon dioxide
  (c) Activate chlorophyll
  (b) Synthesize glucose
  (d) Split water

3. Which one of the following would not be a limiting factor for photosynthesis?
  (a) Oxygen
  (b) Light
  (c) Carbon dioxide
  (d) Chlorophyll*

* Frequently asked previous years Board Exam Questions.

4. A cell that lacks chloroplast does not :

(a) Evolve carbon dioxide

(b) Liberate oxygen

(c) Require water

(d) Utilize carbohydrates

5. Which would do maximum harm to a tree?

(a) Loss of half of its branches

(b) Loss of half of its flowers

(c) Loss of all of its leaves

(d) Loss of a little bark

6. NADP is expanded as :

(a) Nicotinamide adenosine dinucleotide phosphate

(b) Nicotinamide adenine dinucleotide phosphate

(c) Nicotinamide adenine dinucleous phosphate

(d) Nicotinamide adenosine dinucleous phosphate

7. A plant is kept in a dark cupboard for about 48 hours before conducting any experiment on photosynthesis to :

(a) Remove starch from the plant

(b) Ensure that starch is not translocated from the leaves

(c) Remove chlorophyll from the leaf of the plant

(d) Remove starch from the experimental leaf

8. Compensation point means the condition :

(a) When the entire food manufactured in photosynthesis remains unutilised

(b) When the pot is watered just to meet the full requirement of the plant

(c) When rate of photosynthesis is equal to rate of respiration

(d) Where there is neither photosynthesis nor respiration.

9. The production of starch and not glucose, is often used as a measure of photosynthesis in leaves because :

(a) Starch is an immediate product of photosynthesis

(b) Glucose formed in photosynthesis soon gets converted into starch

(c) Starch is insoluble in water

(d) Sugar cannot be tested

10. The rate of photosynthesis in not affected by :

(a) Light intensity

(b) Humidity

(c) Temperature

(d) Carbon dioxide concentration

11. Which one of these reaction occurs during photosynthesis?

(a) Carbon dioxide is reduced and water is oxidized

(b) Water is reduced and carbon dioxide is oxidized

(c) Carbon dioxide and water both are oxidized

(d) Carbon dioxide and water both are reduced

Ans.

1. (a)	4. (b)	7. (a)	10. (b)
2. (c)	5. (c)	8. (c)	11. (a)
3. (a)	6. (b)	9. (b)	

Chapter 6. Chemical Coordination in Plants

1. A plant hormone used for inducing Morphogenesis in plant tissue culture is :

(a) Ethylene

(b) Gibberellin

(c) Cytokinin

(d) Abscisic acid

2. Cell division in plants is promoted by :

   (a) ABA

   (b) Gibberellin

   (c) Ethylene

   (d) Cytokinin

3. One of the synthetic auxin is :

   (a) IAA

   (b) GA

   (c) IBA

   (d) NAA

4. Which one of the following pairs is not correctly matched?

   (a) IAA - Cell wall elongation

   (b) Abscisic acid - Stomatal closure

   (c) Gibberellic acid - Leaf fall

   (d) Cytokinin - Cell division

5. The phytohormone that helps in the germination of seeds is :

   (a) ABA

   (b) Auxin

   (c) Gibberellin

   (d) Cytokinin

6. Which of the following is not an effect of ethylene?

   (a) Promotes senescence and abscission of plant organs

   (b) Breaks seed and bud dormancy

   (c) Hastens fruit ripening

   (d) Helps to overcome apical dominance

7. Ethylene is used for :

   (a) Retarding ripening of tomatoes

   (b) Hastening of ripening of fruits

   (c) Slowing down ripening of apples

   (d) Both (b) and (c)

8. To increase sugar production in sugarcanes, they are sprayed with :

   (a) IAA

   (b) Cytokinin

   (c) Gibberellin

   (d) Ethylene

9. Internodal elongation is associated with :

   (a) Auxin

   (b) Cytokinin

   (c) Gibberellin

   (d) ABA

10. A plant hormone related with the inhibition of senescence :

   (a) Ethylene

   (b) ABA

   (c) Bromic acid

   (d) Gibberellin

11. Which of the following regulate closure of stomata?

   (a) ABA

   (b) Auxins

   (c) Bromic acid

   (d) Cytokinin

12. Positive geotropism is exhibited by :

   (a) Leaves

   (b) Shoot

   (c) Stem

   (d) Root

13. The phytohormone that prevents germination of seed is :

   (a) Abscisic acid

   (b) Gibberellin

   (c) Cytokinin

   (d) Auxin

14. The hormone responsible for phototropism and geotropism is :

   (a) Auxin

   (b) Gibberellin

   (c) Enzyme

   (d) Starch

15. A phytohormone existing in gaseous state is :

   (a) Auxin

   (b) Ethylene

   (c) Abscisic acid

   (d) Cytokinin

Ans.

1. (c)	5. (c)	9. (c)	13. (a)
2. (d)	6. (d)	10. (a)	14. (a)
3. (d)	7. (b)	11. (a)	15. (b)
4. (c)	8. (c)	12. (d)	

Chapter 7. The Circulatory System

1. The function of WBC is :

   (a) To distribute heat

   (b) To protect enzymes

   (c) To cause blood clotting

   (d) To destroy bacteria

2. The chief function of lymph nodes in mammals is to :

   (a) Produce WBCs

   (b) Produce hormones

   (c) Destroy old RBCs

   (d) Destroy pathogens

3. Agranulocytes are :

   (a) Lymphocytes, monocytes

   (b) Lymphocytes, basophils

   (c) Eosinophils, basophils

   (d) Eosinophils, monocytes

4. What will happen if the spleen of a man is removed?

   (a) WBC production will be lowered

   (b) Removal of dead RBC will not take place

   (c) Antibodies production will be decreased

   (d) RBC production will be stopped

5. Which protein is used in preventing clotting of blood?

   (a) Albumin

   (b) Heparin

   (c) Fibrinogen

   (d) Globulin

6. The beating of the heart is heard on the left side, because :

   (a) The left ventricle is towards the left side

   (b) Both the ventricles are towards the left side

   (c) Contraction of heart is powerful at the open which is on left side

   (d) The dorsal aorta is on the left side

7. Arteries are :

   (a) Thin walled and blood flows under diminished pressure

   (b) Thick walled and blood flows under high pressure

   (c) Thin walled and blood flows under low pressure

   (d) Thick walled and blood flows under diminished pressure

8. Blood pressure is :

   (a) The pressure of blood on the heart muscles

   (b) The pressure of blood exerted on the walls of arteries and veins

   (c) The pressure of blood on the walls of veins only

   (d) The pressure of blood on the walls of arteries only

9. Erythroblastosis foetalis can occur when :

   (a) Man Rh^{+ve} and woman Rh^{+ve}

   (b) Man Rh^{-ve} and woman Rh^{+ve}

   (c) Man Rh^{+ve} and woman Rh^{-ve}

   (d) Man Rh^{-ve} and woman Rh^{-ve}

10. Angina pectoris is due to :

   (a) Defective nutrition

   (b) Chest pain due to inadequate supply of oxygen to the heart muscle

   (c) Defective function of the mitral valve

   (d) Infection by a virus

11. The nearest organ to which the heart supplies oxygenated blood is :
    - (a) Lung
    - (b) Stomach
    - (c) Intestine
    - (d) Heart itself
12. Blood pressure is measured by :
    - (a) Electrocardiogram (ECG)
    - (b) Stethoscope
    - (c) Sphygmomanometer
    - (d) Pulse rate
13. While recording the pulse rate, where exactly does a doctor press on our wrist ?*
    - (a) Nerve
    - (b) Vein
    - (c) Artery
    - (d) Capillary
14. A muscular wall is absent in :*
    - (a) Capillary
    - (b) Venule
    - (c) Arteriole
    - (d) Vein

Ans.

1. (d)	5. (b)	9. (c)	13. (c)
2. (d)	6. (c)	10. (b)	14. (a)
3. (a)	7. (b)	11. (d)	
4. (c)	8. (b)	12. (c)	

Chapter 8. The Excretory System

1. Excretion commonly involves :
   - (a) Removal of all by-products during catabolism
   - (b) Removal of by-products during anabolism
   - (c) Removal of nitrogenous waste
   - (d) All of the above
2. Urea is synthesized from extra amino acids in :
   - (a) Kidney
   - (b) Liver
   - (c) Uriniferous tubules
   - (d) Blood
3. What is the chief nitrogenous waste in mammals?
   - (a) Amino acid
   - (b) Ammonia
   - (c) Uric acid
   - (d) Urea
4. Profuse sweating takes place during heavy muscular exercise. The reason is :
   - (a) To excrete excessive amount of sodium chloride
   - (b) To eliminate excessive lactic acid produced due to anaerobic metabolism
   - (c) To regulate the temperature of the body
   - (d) All of these
5. Which of the following is not an excretory activity in the real sense?
   - (a) Releasing carbon dioxide
   - (b) Passing out faecal matter
   - (c) Sweating
   - (d) Removal of urea
6. Ultrafiltration occurs in :
   - (a) Bowman's capsule
   - (b) Proximal convoluted tubule
   - (c) Henle's loop
   - (d) Distal convoluted tubule
7. In the Bowman's capsule :
   - (a) Afferent arteriole is narrower whereas efferent arteriole is wider
   - (b) Afferent arteriole is wider whereas efferent arteriole is narrower
   - (c) Afferent capillary is wider and efferent capillary is narrower
   - (d) Afferent capillary is narrower and efferent capillary is wider

8. Maximum amount of water from glomerular filtrate is reabsorbed in :

    (a) Proximal convoluted tubule   (c) Ascending limb of loop of Henle

    (b) Descending limb of loop of Henle   (d) Distal convoluted tubule

9. What is located within the glomerular capsule?

    (a) Renal cortex   (c) Several conducting ducts

    (b) Loop of Henle   (d) A knot of capillaries

10. Which of the following organs is the storage area of urine?

    (a) Urinary Bladder   (c) Ureter

    (b) Kidney   (d) Urethra

Ans.

1.	(d)	4.	(d)	7.	(b)	10.	(a)
2.	(b)	5.	(b)	8.	(a)		
3.	(d)	6.	(a)	9.	(d)		

Chapter 9. The Nervous System and Sense Organs

1. The function of nervous system is to :

    (a) Receive stimuli

    (b) Irritability

    (c) Conduction of enzymes

    (d) To prepare the body against reactions during emergency

2. A point of contact between two neurons is termed :

    (a) Synapse   (c) Neuro motor junction

    (b) Synapsis   (d) Sensory

3. Neurilemma is :

    (a) The cell membrane around the nerve cell

    (b) A layer of fatty substance around axon

    (c) A layer of specialized neuroglia around myelin sheath of nerve fibres

    (d) The connective tissue around a nerve tract

4. Cerebellum is the part of the brain which is responsible for :

    (a) Interpreting sensations

    (b) Conducting reflexes in the body

    (c) Maintaining posture and equilibrium

    (d) Controlling thinking, memory and reasoning

5. If the cerebellum is injured :

    (a) Movement becomes shaky and speech become defective

    (b) Movement becomes unbalanced, walk uncontrolled and speech defective

    (c) Movement becomes jerky, walk controlled

    (d) There is no effect as the actions are under the control of will

6. The control of reflex action is through :

    (a) Central nervous system   (c) Autonomic nervous system

    (b) Peripheral nervous system   (d) None of the above

7. The ventral root ganglion of the spinal cord contains cell bodies of the :

    (a) Motor neuron   (c) Intermediate neuron

    (b) Sensory neuron   (d) Association neuron

8. A reflex arc in man is best described as movement of stimuli from :

    (a) Receptor cell, sensory neuron, relay neuron, effector muscles

   (b) Receptor cell, efferent nerve, relay neuron, muscles of the body

   (c) Receptor cell, spinal cord, motor neuron, relay neuron

   (d) Receptor cell, synapse, motor neuron, relay neuron

9. Which of the following is not a natural reflex action?

   (a) Knee-jerk   (c) Salivation at the sight of food

   (b) Blinking of eyes due to strong light   (d) Sneezing when any irritant enters the nose

10. The number of spinal nerves in a human being are :

   (a) 31 pairs   (c) 21 pairs

   (b) 10 pairs   (d) 30 pairs

11. The photoreceptor cells of the retina sensitive to colour are :

   (a) Cones   (c) Rods

   (b) Pupil   (d) Organ of corti

12. The aperture in the eye through which light enters is the :

   (a) Pupil   (c) Ciliary muscles

   (b) Conjunctiva   (d) Choroid

13. The sequence of ear ossicles of vertebrates starting from the tympanum is :

   (a) Incus, Malleus, Stapes   (c) Malleus, Incus, Stapes

   (b) Stapes, Malleus, Incus   (d) Stapes, Incus, Malleus

14. The part of the human eye where rod cells and cone cells are located is the :

   (a) Retina   (c) Choroid

   (b) Cornea   (d) Sclera

15. Aqueous humour is present between the :

   (a) Lens and retina   (c) Cornea and iris

   (b) Iris and lens   (d) Cornea and lens

16. The parts of the human ear concerned with hearing are :

   (a) Cochlea, ear ossicles and tympanum

   (b) Semicircular canals, utriculus and sacculus

   (c) Eustachian tube, tympanum and utriculus

   (d) Perilymph, ear ossicles and semicircular canals

Ans.

1.	(a)	5.	(b)	9.	(c)	13.	(c)
2.	(a)	6.	(a)	10.	(a)	14.	(a)
3.	(c)	7.	(a)	11.	(a)	15.	(d)
4.	(c)	8.	(a)	12.	(a)	16.	(a)

Chapter 10. The Endocrine System

1. Which statement is not for a hormone?

   (a) They act on target organs usually away from the source glands

   (b) They are secreted directly into the blood

   (c) They are used again and again like catalysts

   (d) They are produced in very minute quantities and are biologically very active

2. The basal metabolic rate in body cells is regulated by :

   (a) Parathyroid   (c) Pituitary

   (b) Thyroid   (d) Thymus

3. The mammalian thymus is mainly concerned with :

   (a) Regulation of body temperature   (c) Secretion of thyrotropins

   (b) Regulation of body growth   (d) Immunological functions

4. Which of the following glands has both endocrine and exocrine functions?

   (a) Pituitary gland   (c) Pancreas gland

   (b) Thyroid gland   (d) Adrenal gland

5. Pancreas is a mixed gland in which :

   (a) All cells secrete enzymes and hormones

   (b) Most cells secrete hormones

   (c) Few cells secrete enzymes

   (d) Enzymes and hormones are secreted by separate cells

6. Secretin is secreted by :

   (a) Testes and stimulates male secondary character

   (b) Adrenal glands and stimulates heart beat

   (c) Small intestine and stimulates pancreas

   (d) Pancreas and stimulates conversion of glycogen into glucose

7. Vasopressin is concerned with :

   (a) Quick digestion   (c) Concentration of urine

   (b) Slow heart beat   (d) Dilution of urine

8. Glucagon is secreted by :

   (a) The β cells of Islets of Langerhans   (c) The β cells of pancreas

   (b) The α cells of Islets of Langerhans   (d) The adrenal cortex

9. Leydig cells are meant for :

   (a) Formation of sperms   (c) Production of testosterone

   (b) Production of progesterone   (d) Nutrition of sperm

10. Human Chorionic Gonadotropin :

   (a) Stimulates the growth of placenta

   (b) Stimulates the development of new follicles

   (c) Inhibits the secretion of milk till child birth

   (d) Stimulates the corpus luteum to grow and secrete progesterone

11. The hormone secreted by the posterior pituitary gland is :

   (a) Growth hormone   (c) Antidiuretic hormone

   (b) Adrenocorticotropic hormone   (d) Luteinizing hormone

Ans. 1. (c)   4. (c)   7. (c)   10. (d)

       2. (b)   5. (d)   8. (b)   11. (c)

       3. (d)   6. (c)   9. (c)

Chapter 11. The Reproductive System

1. Which one of the following is the route that a sperm follows when it leaves the testes of a mammal?

   (a) Vas deferens ⟶ epididymis ⟶ urethra

   (b) Urethra ⟶ epididymis ⟶ vas deferens

   (c) Epididymis ⟶ urethra ⟶ vas deferens

   (d) Epididymis ⟶ Vas deferens ⟶ urethra

2. If the vas deferens of a man are surgically disconnected or removed :

   (a) Semen will be without sperms

   (b) Sperms in the semen will be without nuclei

   (c) Spermatogenesis will not take place

   (d) Sperms in semen will be non-motile

3. What will happen if the temperature of the scrotal sacs temporarily goes to about 2°C lower than normal temperature?
    (a) Sperm formation will be stopped
    (b) Testes will start rotation movement
    (c) Scrotal sacs will contract and come close to the body
    (d) Scrotal sacs will relax and go down away from the body
4. The site of maturation of human sperm is the :
    (a) Seminiferous tubule
    (b) Interstitial cells
    (c) Epididymis
    (d) Prostate gland
5. The middle piece of the sperm provides :
    (a) Energy
    (b) Food
    (c) Gene
    (d) Chromosomes
6. The onset of menstruation in the female is termed as :
    (a) Ovulation
    (b) Menarche
    (c) Menopause
    (d) Parthenogenesis
7. In females, after how much time after fertilization does the fertilized egg get implanted in the uterine wall?
    (a) Few months
    (b) One month
    (c) Three weeks
    (d) About seven days
8. Ovulation in mammals is a process in which :
    (a) The egg is released from Graafian follicle
    (b) The egg is fertilized in fallopian tube
    (c) The egg passes through fimbriated funnel of fallopian tube
    (d) The unfertilized egg passes out of female's body
9. Sterilization in the female involves cutting and tying the :
    (a) Ureter
    (b) Uterus
    (c) Urethra
    (d) Oviduct
10. Corpus luteum in mammals is present in :
    (a) Brain and connects the two cerebral hemispheres
    (b) Ovaries and produces progesterone hormone
    (c) Heart and initiates atrial contraction
    (d) Skin and acts as a pain receptor
11. When pregnancy does not occur the life of the Corpus luteum is about :
    (a) 4 days
    (b) 10 days
    (c) 14 days
    (d) 28 days
12. Fertilization means :
    (a) The transfer of male gamete to the female gamete
    (b) The adhesion of male and female reproductive organs
    (c) The fusion of nuclei of male and female gametes
    (d) The shedding of gametes from a reproductive organ
13. On which day of the menstrual cycle does ovulation take place ?*
    (a) 5th day
    (b) 28th day
    (c) 14th day
    (d) 1st day

Ans.
1. (d)   5. (a)   9. (d)   13. (c)
2. (a)   6. (b)   10. (b)
3. (c)   7. (d)   11. (c)
4. (c)   8. (a)   12. (c)

Chapter 12. Human Population

1. The study of human population is referred to as :
    (a) Population dynamics
    (b) Population sociology
    (c) Demography
    (d) Population ecology

---

* Frequently asked previous years Board Exam Questions.

2. The primary reason for increase in human population is :
   (a) The increase in agricultural production
   (b) The increase in birth rate and decrease in death rate
   (c) The improvement in medical technology
   (d) All of the above

3. Population density of a particular area can be computed by :
   (a) Dividing the total number of individuals living in the area by the total land area
   (b) Dividing the total number of individuals living in the area by the total fertile land area
   (c) Dividing the total number of individuals living in the area by total rural area
   (d) Dividing the total number of individuals living in the area by total urban area

4. Which one of the parents is biologically responsible for sex of the child?
   (a) Father
   (b) Mother
   (c) Both the parents
   (d) Supernatural power

5. Which mechanical means is used to cover the penis before coital activity?
   (a) Diaphragm
   (b) Condom
   (c) Loop
   (d) Copper–T

Ans. 1. (c)   3. (a)   5. (b)
      2. (d)   4. (a)

Chapter 13. Human Evolution

1. The brain capacity of *Homo erectus* was about :
   (a) 650 c.c.
   (b) 900 c.c.
   (c) 1200 c.c.
   (d) 1600 c.c.

2. The extinct human who lived 1,00,000 to 40,000 years ago, in Europe, Asia and parts of Africa, with short stature, heavy eye brows, retreating forehead, large jaws with heavy teeth, stocky bodies, a lumbering gait and stooped posture was :
   (a) Cro-Magnon humans
   (b) *Ramapithecus*
   (c) *Homo habilis*
   (d) Neanderthal human

3. The extinct human ancestor who ate only fruits and hunted with stone weapons was :
   (a) *Ramapithecus*
   (b) *Australopithecus*
   (c) *Dryopithecus*
   (d) *Homo erectus*

4. The prehistoric man which lived on earth during late Pleistocene period was :
   (a) Neanderthal man
   (b) *Australopithecus*
   (c) Peking man
   (d) Atlantic man

5. The cranial cavity of the modern man is :
   (a) 450-650 c.c.
   (b) 600-900 c.c.
   (c) 900-1000 c.c.
   (d) 1300-1600 c.c.

6. Which one of the following is not a vestigial part in human beings?
   (a) Coccyx
   (b) Third molar on each side in each jaw
   (c) Finger nails
   (d) Segmental muscles of abdomen

7. Lamarckism cannot explain :
   (a) Webbed toes in aquatic birds
   (b) Weak muscles in the son of a wrestler
   (c) Long, narrow and limbless body of snakes
   (d) Heterophylly

8. During a study session about evolution, one of your fellow students remarks, "The giraffe stretched its neck while reaching for higher leaves; its offspring inherited longer necks as a result" . To correct your friend's misconception, what would you say?

(a)   Spontaneous mutations can result in the appearance of new traits.

(b)   Only favourable adaptations have survival value.

(c)   Overproduction of offspring leads to a struggle for survival.

(d)   Characteristics acquired during an organism's life are not passed on through genes.

Ans. 1.   (b)   3.   (b)   5.   (d)   7.   (b)

2.   (d)   4.   (a)   6.   (c)   8.   (d)

Chapter 14. Pollution

1. Air pollution is caused by :

(a)   Insecticides   (c)   Smoke

(b)   Sewage   (d)   Loud speakers

2. Air is composed of gases, water vapours and :

(a)   Dust particles   (c)   Snowfall

(b)   Rainfall   (d)   Light

3. If waste materials contaminate the source of drinking water, which of the following diseases will spread?

(a)   Scurvy   (c)   Malaria

(b)   Typhoid   (d)   Anaemia

4. Ozone is abundant in this layer. Ozone heats this layer as it absorbs incoming ultraviolet radiation from the sun :

(a)   Thermosphere   (c)   Mesosphere

(b)   Troposphere   (d)   Stratosphere

5. 71% of earth surface is covered with :

(a)   Land   (b)   Air   (c)   Water   (d)   Coal

6. Which poisonous gas is contained in the exhaust of a petrol driven vehicle?

(a)   Ammonia   (c)   Chlorine

(b)   Carbon monoxide   (d)   Carbon dioxide

7. Deforestation is one of the sources of pollution because :

(a)   It increases the oxygen levels produced   (c)   It causes fertilizers to wash away in the water

(b)   It decreases the oxygen levels produced   (d)   None of the above

8. Oil spills are a source of pollution for :

(a)   Water   (c)   Land and Air

(b)   Land and Water   (d)   Air and Noise

9. Which of the following problems is not created by noise pollution?

(a)   Diarrhoea   (b)   Hypertension   (c)   Deafness   (d)   Irritation

10. Maximum permissible smoke density in diesel vehicles is :

(a)   75 HSU   (b)   65 HSU   (c)   50 HSU   (d)   45 HSU

11. Which one of the following is non-biodegradable?

(a)   DDT   (c)   Card board

(b)   Vegetable peel   (d)   Bark of trees

12. Which one of the following is a Greenhouse gas?

(a)   Oxygen   (c)   Sulphur dioxide

(b)   Methane   (d)   Nitrogen

Ans. 1.   (c)   4.   (d)   7.   (b)   10.   (b)

2.   (a)   5.   (c)   8.   (b)   11.   (a)

3.   (b)   6.   (b)   9.   (a)   12.   (b)

Match the Column | Set 10

Column 'II' is a list of items related to terms in Column 'I'. Match the term in Column 'I' with the suitable term given in column 'II'.

Chapter 1. Cell Division

Column I	Column II
(i) Anaphase	(a) Chromosomes become arranged in a horizontal plane at the equator.
(ii) Prophase	(b) Daughter chromosomes move to opposite poles of the spindle.
(iii) Telophase	(c) Chromosomes become visible as fine, long threads.
(iv) Metaphase	(d) Chromosomes lose their distinctiveness and gradually become transformed into chromatin network.

Ans. (i) (b)   (ii) (c)   (iii) (d)   (iv) (a).

Chapter 2. Fundamentals of Genetics

Column I	Column II
(i) Genetics	(a) Chromosomes similar in size and shape.
(ii) Autosomes	(b) The alternative forms of a gene.
(iii) Recessive gene	(c) Study of laws of inheritance of characters.
(iv) Allele	(d) A gene that can express only when in a similar pair.
(v) Homologous chromosomes	(e) Chromosomes other than the pair of sex chromosomes.

Ans. (i) (c)   (iii) (d)   (v) (a).
(ii) (e)   (iv) (b)

Chapter 3. Absorption by Roots

Column I	Column II
(i) Diffusion	(a) The exit or flow of water from the cell to the outer environment.
(ii) Xylem	(b) The shrinkage of protoplasm when the cell is kept in a hypertonic solution.
(iii) Root pressure	(c) The tissue through which water and mineral salts move upward in a plant.
(iv) Isotonic solution	(d) The process by which roots absorb water from the soil.
(v) Exosmosis	(e) The process by which the molecules of perfume spread in the room when the bottle is open.
(vi) Osmosis	(f) The concentration of the solution when lower than that of the cell sap.
(vii) Plasmolysis	(g) The pressure by which water rises upto some feet in a lofty tree.
(viii) Hypotonic solution	(h) Two solutions which have equal osmotic pressure.

Ans. (i) (e)   (iii) (g)   (v) (a)   (vii) (b)
(ii) (c)   (iv) (h)   (vi) (d)   (viii) (f).

Chapter 4. Transpiration

Column I	Column II
(i) Transpiration	(a) Cacti plants
(ii) Movement of water	(b) Stomata
(iii) Guttation	(c) Maize plant
(iv) Low rate of transpiration	(d) Xylem
(v) High rate of transpiration	(e) Hydathodes

Ans. (i) (b) (iii) (e) (v) (c).
(ii) (d) (iv) (a)

Chapter 5. Photosynthesis

Column I	Column II
(i) Grana	(a) Glucose + oxygen
(ii) Autotrophs	(b) Work rooms
(iii) By-products of photosynthesis	(c) Green pigment
(iv) Bacteria and fungi	(d) Raw materials
(v) Chloroplasts	(e) Light reaction
(vi) Oxygen and Hydrogen	(f) Decomposers
(vii) Carbon dioxide and water	(g) Photolysis
(viii) Cells in the leaf	(h) Producers

Ans. (i) (e) (iii) (a) (v) (c) (vii) (d)
(ii) (h) (iv) (f) (vi) (g) (viii) (b).

Chapter 6. Chemical Coordination in plants

Column I	Column II
(i) Cytokinins	(a) Acts as an anti-transpirant
(ii) 2, 4-D and 2,4,5-T	(b) Gibbane ring structure
(iii) Ethylene	(c) Used in tissue culture
(iv) Abscisic acid	(d) Eradication of weeds
(v) Gibberellins	(e) Promotes transverse growth

Ans. (i) (c) (iii) (e) (v) (b).
(ii) (d) (iv) (a)

Chapter 7. The Circulatory System

Column I	Column II
(i) Superior vena cava	(a) Collect deoxygenated blood from the wall of the heart.
(ii) Inferior vena cava	(b) Carry oxygenated blood to heart muscle.
(iii) Pulmonary vein	(c) Collects deoxygenated blood from upper parts of the body.
(iv) Coronary veins	(d) Collects deoxygenated blood from lower parts of the body.

(v) Coronary artery	(e) Brings oxygenated blood from lungs.
(vi) Aorta	(f) Largest artery
(vii) Heart attack	(g) Largest vein
(viii) Blood pressure	(h) Oxygenated blood
(ix) Tricuspid valve	(i) Sphygmomanometer
(x) Bicuspid valve	(j) Allows blood flow from right auricle to right ventricle.
(xi) Contraction and relaxation of heart	(k) Blocking of coronary arteries.
	(l) Cardiac cycle.
	(m) Allows blood flow from left auricle to left ventricle.
	(n) Allows blood flow from right ventricle of pulmonary aorta.

Ans. (i) (c)   (iv) (a)   (vii) (k)   (x) (m)

(ii) (d)   (v) (b)   (viii) (i)   (xi) (l).

(iii) (e)   (vi) (f)   (ix) (j)

Chapter 8. The Excretory System

Column I	Column II
(i) Nephrons	(a) The organ that collects filtrate and urine from renal pelvis and takes it to the bladder for urination.
(ii) Ureter	(b) The triangle-shaped, hollow organ that collects urine.
(iii) Renal artery	(c) The study of normal kidney function and kidney problems.
(iv) Glomerulus	(d) Filtration units in the kidneys.
(v) Nephrology	(e) The outer region of the kidney.
(vi) Bladder	(f) The artery that brings waste-filled blood from the aorta to the kidney.
(vii) Renal cortex	(g) A cluster of blood capillaries surrounded by a bowman's capsule.

Ans. (i) (d)   (iii) (f)   (v) (c)   (vii) (e).

(ii) (a)   (iv) (g)   (vi) (b)

Chapter 9. The Nervous System and Sense Organs

Column I	Column II
(i) Auditory canal	(a) Channels pressure waves of air into the middle ear.
(ii) Eustachian tube	(b) Collects pressure waves of air.
(iii) Sensory neuron	(c) Carry nerve impulses from sense organs to CNS.
(iv) Cerebellum	(d) Controls involuntary responses to regulate physiological functions.
(v) Auditory nerve	(e) Converts pressure waves of air into mechanical vibrations.
(vi) Cranial nerves	(f) Transfers vibrations from a bone to a fluid.
(vii) Incus	(g) Twelve pairs of nerves.
(viii) Malleus	(h) Coordinates muscle movements, maintains posture, and balance.
(ix) Skull	(i) Equalizes air pressure on both sides of the tympanic membrane.
(x) Oval window	(j) Provide information about the spatial orientation of the head.
(xi) Pinna	(k) Gaps between the neurons that allows a signal to pass from one neuron to the next.
(xii) Sacculus	

(xiii) Round window	(l) Basic building blocks of the nervous system.
(xiv) Neuron	(m) Dissipates sound waves.
(xv) Semicircular canals	(n) Transfers vibrations from a bone to a bone in the ear.
(xiv) Synapse	(o) Protects brain from injury.
(xvii) Autonomic nervous system	(p) Transfers vibrations from a bone to a membrane.
(xviii) Stapes	(q) Transfers vibrations from a membrane to a bone.
(xix) Tympanic membrane	(r) Transmits auditory information to the brain.
	(s) Static equalibrium

Ans.

(i) (a)	(vi) (g)	(xi) (b)	(xvi) (k)
(ii) (i)	(vii) (n)	(xii) (s)	(xvii) (d)
(iii) (c)	(viii) (q)	(xiii) (m)	(xviii) (p)
(iv) (h)	(ix) (o)	(xiv) (l)	(xix) (e).
(v) (r)	(x) (f)	(xv) (j)	

Chapter 10. The Endocrine System

Column I	Column II
(i) Pituitary	(a) Produces male sex characteristics.
(ii) Ovaries	(b) Heterocrine gland.
(iii) Thyroid	(c) Increases heart and breathing rate, raises blood pressure.
(iv) Thymus	(d) Produces female sex characteristics.
(v) Adrenal	(e) Emergency hormone.
(vi) Hypothalamus	(f) Regulates the level of calcium and phosphorus.
(vii) Pancreas	(g) Increases rate of metabolism.
(viii) Testes	(h) Maintains the level of calcium.
(ix) Parathyroid	(i) Regulates the amount of water excreted in urine.
(x) Cretinism	(j) Simulates skeletal growth.
(xi) Diabetes mellitus	(k) Master of master gland.
(xii) Insulin shock	(l) Development of a normal, healthy immune system.
(xiii) Gigantism	(m) Shortage of glucose in blood.
(xiv) Cushing's syndrome	(n) Over-secretion of growth hormone in childhood.
(xv) Exophthalmic goitre	(o) Excess of glucose in blood.
(xvi) Acromegaly	(p) Over-secretion of thyroxine.
(xvii) Addison's disease	(q) Dwarfism and mental retardation.
(xviii) Dwarfism	(r) Over-secretion of cortical hormones.
(xix) Adrenaline	(s) Under-secretion of adrenal cortex.
(xx) Vasopressin	(t) Over-secretion of growth hormones in adults.
	(u) Under-secretion of growth hormone.

Ans.

(i) (j)	(vii) (b)	(xiii) (n)	(xix) (e)
(ii) (d)	(viii) (a)	(xiv) (r)	(xx) (i).
(iii) (g)	(ix) (f)	(xv) (p)	
(iv) (l)	(x) (q)	(xvi) (t)	
(v) (c)	(xi) (o)	(xvii) (s)	
(vi) (k)	(xii) (m)	(xviii) (u)	

Chapter 11. The Reproductive System

Column I	Column II
(i) Acrosome	(a) Testosterone
(ii) Ovulation	(b) Fallopian tube
(iii) Sperm	(c) Uterus
(iv) Menopause	(d) Vasectomy
(v) Implantation	(e) Oestrogen
(vi) Fertilization	(f) Stoppage of menstrual cycle
(vii) Contraception in males	(g) Spermatozoa
(viii) Leydig cells	(h) Male gamete

Ans. (i) (g)   (iii) (h)   (v) (c)   (vii) (d)
(ii) (e)   (iv) (f)   (vi) (b)   (viii) (a).

Chapter 12. Human Population

Column I	Column II
(i) Family Planning	(a) Counting of population
(ii) Vasectomy	(b) Sterilization in female
(iii) Tubectomy	(c) Sterilization in male
(iv) Census	(d) Red triangle

Ans. (i) (d)   (ii) (c)   (iii) (b)   (iv) (a)

Chapter 13. Human Evolution

Column I	Column II
(i) Australopithecus	(a) 850-1300 cc
(ii) Homo habilis	(b) Characters acquired during lifetime
(iii) Homo erectus	(c) Vestigial organ
(iv) Peking man	(d) 1400 cc
(v) Neanderthal man	(e) Darwin's theory
(vi) Adaptive characters	(f) 600 cc
(vii) Natural selection	(g) 900 cc
(viii) Pinna	(h) Characters acquired from parents
(ix) Use and disuse of organs	(i) Lamarck's theory
(x) Inherited characters	(j) 735 cc

Ans. (i) (f)   (iv) (a)   (vii) (e)   (x) (h).
(ii) (j)   (v) (d)   (viii) (c)
(iii) (g)   (vi) (b)   (ix) (i)

Chapter 14. Pollution

Column I	Column II
(i) SPM	(a) Release of methane
(ii) Ozone hole	(b) Adds to greenhouse effect
(iii) Melting of polar ice	(c) Affects oxygen transport by blood
(iv) Acid rain	(d) Vehicular standards
(v) Carbon dioxide	(e) Bronchitis and inflammation of the lungs
(vi) Melting of permafrost	(f) Erodes buildings
(vii) Carbon monoxide	(g) Chlorofluorocarbons
(viii) Euro IV norms	(h) Rise in sea level

Ans. (i) (e) (iii) (h) (v) (b) (vii) (c)

(ii) (g) (iv) (f) (vi) (a) (viii) (d).

Explain the Terms | Set 11 |

1. Cell division	**5.** Cell Plate	**9.** Centromeres	**13.** Diplotene
2. Centrioles	**6.** Chromosomes	**10.** Leptotene	**14.** Diakinesis
3. Spindle	**7.** Chromatin.	**11.** Zygotene	
4. Cleavage furrow	**8.** Chromatids	**12.** Pachytene	

Ans.

1. **Cell division :** It is a process by which a cell divides into two or more daughter cells.

2. **Centrioles :** Centriole is a cell structure composed mainly of protein, located in the cytoplasm near the nuclear envelope.

3. **Spindle :** A fan-like microtubule structure formed during mitosis/meiosis that helps separate the chromosomes to the opposite ends is called spindle.

4. **Cleavage furrow :** Structure that forms in animal cells when the cytoplasm divides during cytokinesis.

5. **Cell plate :** It is a disc-like structure that forms in plant cells to form the wall between daughter cells when the cytoplasm divides during cytokinesis.

6. **Chromosomes :** Chromosomes are thread-like structure found in DNA that carry genetic information of an organism in the form of genes.

7. **Chromatin :** Chromatin is a complex combination of DNA and proteins. They condenses to form chromosomes and are present in the nuclei of eukaryotic cells.

8. **Chromatids :** Two identical parts of a chromosome are called sister chromatids.

9. **Centromeres :** It is a part of chromosome through which chromatids are linked.

10. **Leptotene :** It is the first substage of prophase-I in meiosis in which the chromosomes become visible as single threads.

11. **Zygotene :** It is the second substage of prophase-I in which pairing of homologous chromosomes (synapsis) occurs. Each pair of chromosmes are called bivalent.

12. **Pachytene :** It is the third substage of prophase during which the crossing-over begins.

13. **Diplotene :** It is the fourth substage of prophase during which Crossing-over continues and two homologous chromosomes in each pair begin to separate. They are held together at points called chiasmata.

14. **Diakinesis :** It is the last substage of prophase in which nuclear membrane and nucleolus disappear. Spindle begins to be formed at the end of this stage.

1. Heredity	**5.** Heterosomes	**8.** Recessive character
2. Variation	**6.** Alleles.	**9.** Genotype
3. Linkage	**7.** Dominance	**10.** Crossing-over
4. Mutation		

Ans.

1. **Heredity :** The process of transmission of parental characters to the progeny from generations to generations is called heredity.

2. **Variation :** Differences in characters of progeny of same parents and individuals of same species.

3. **Linkage :** The phenomenon of inheritance of a group of genes together during meiosis is called linkage.

4. **Mutation :** Any change brought about into the genetic composition through external or internal factors which may be passed to subsequent generations is termed as mutation.

5. **Heterosomes :** Chromosomes found in reproductive cell and which are responsible for the sex of a child.

6. **Alleles :** Alleles are the alternative forms of the same gene. For example, tallness and dwarfness are the two alternative forms of a gene for height and are called alleles. Similarly, attached ear lobes and free ear lobes are alleles for the type of ear lobes.

7. **Dominant Character :** The character that is expressed in first generation when any two individuals of contrasting characters breed is called dominant character and the phenomenon is called dominance.

8. **Recessive character :** The character which remains hidden in F_1 generation and expressed in the second generation.

9. **Genotype :** The genetic composition of any organism is called genotype.

10. **Crossing-over :** The phenomenon of the exchange of genetic material between two non-sister chromatids of homologous chromosomes during meiosis is called crossing over.

Chapter 3. Absorption By Roots

1. Diffusion	**3.** Endosmosis	**5.** Plasmolysis	**7.** Root pressure
2. Osmosis	**4.** Exosmosis	**6.** Ascent of sap	**8.** Transpiration pull.

Ans.
1. **Diffusion :** It is the free movement of molecules of solid, liquid or gas from their higher concentration area to their lower concentration area when the two are in a direct contact.

2. **Osmosis :** Osmosis is a special type of diffusion which involves the movement of solvent molecules from a region of their higher concentration to the region of their lower concentration across a semi permeable membrane.

3. **Endosmosis :** It is the movement of water molecules from the surroundings into the cell through a semi-permeable membrane.

4. **Exosmosis :** It is the outward diffusion of water molecules from the cell into the outer surroundings through a semi-permeable membrane.

5. **Plasmolysis :** It is the shrinkage of protoplasm from cell wall when a cell is placed in a hypertonic solution.

6. **Ascent of sap :** The upward movement of water along with the minerals from the root to aerial parts of the plant body is called ascept of sap or translocation of water.

7. **Root pressure :** It is the transverse osmotic pressure within the cells of a root system that causes sap to rise through a plant stem to the leaves.

8. **Transpiration pull :** Suction force that helps in drawing the water upward from roots to the leaves of a plant is known as transpiration pull.

Chapter 4. Transpiration

1. Transpiration	**4.** Stomatal transpiration	**7.** Lenticel
2. Cuticular transpiration	**5.** Guttation	**8.** Hydathode
3. Lenticular Transpiration	**6.** Bleeding	**9.** Wilting.

Ans.
1. **Transpiration :** It is defined as the loss of water in the form of vapour from the aerial parts of a plant.

2. **Cuticular transpiration :** Transpiration that takes place through the cuticle (waxy layer) covering the leaves is called cuticular transpiration.

3. **Lenticular transpiration :** Transpiration that takes place through the small openings in the corky tissue covering the stem is called lenticular transpiration.

4. **Stomatal transpiration :** Transpiration that takes place through the stomata of the leaves is called stomatal transpiration.

5. **Guttation :** The exudation of water in the form of water droplets along with sugar and mineral salts through specialized openings *i.e.,* hydothodes, present along the margins of a leaf is called Guttation.

6. **Bleeding :** Exudation of cell sap or watery solution from the injured parts of a plant.

7. **Lenticel :** It is a pore in the periderm of a woody stem. It acts as an organ of gaseous exchange.

8. **Hydathode :** A water secreting gland found on the edges and tips of leaves of many plants.

9. **Wilting :** The collapsing of plant cells due to unfavourable water relations is called wilting. It may be due to excessive transpiration as compared to absorption of water by roots. It may also be due to blocking of the xylem elements, pathogens or parasites.

Chapter 5. Photosynthesis

1. ATP
2. Free energy
3. NADPH
4. Plastoquinone
5. Photosynthesis
6. Photosynthetic membrane
7. Phosphorylation
8. NADP
9. Photophosphorylation
10. Carbon cycle.

Ans. 1. **ATP :** Adenosine triphosphate is a complex organic molecule that acts as an energy currency in cells.

2. **Free energy :** The amount of energy available to do work in a biochemical reactions.

3. **NADPH :** It is a reduced form of nicotinamide adenine dinucleotide phosphate ($NADP^+$), and a small water soluble molecule that acts as a hydrogen carrier in biochemical reactions.

4. **Plastoquinone :** It is a small molecule involved in electron and proton transfer in photosynthesis.

5. **Photosynthesis :** The physical-chemical process for plants by which certain chlorophyll containing organisms use light energy for the biosynthesis of organic molecules.

6. **Photosynthetic membrane :** Photosynthetic membrane which is also known as the thylakoid membrane, is a bilayer of lipid molecules in which proteins are embedded. It is a site of light reaction of photosynthesis during which light energy is converted into chemical energy.

7. **Phosphorylation :** The phosphorylation is a bio-chemical process which involves covalent attachment of a phosphate group to an organic molecule.

8. **NADP (Nicotinamide Adenine dinucleotide phosphate) :** It is a coenzyme which acts as a reducing agent in certain anabolic reactions. During electron transfer, NADP gains electron from hydrogen and get reduced to $NADPH_2$.

9. **Photophosphorylation :** The phosphorylation of ADP to form ATP in the chloroplast during the light dependent reaction of photosynthesis is called photophosphorylation.

10. **Carbon cycle :** The various processes resulting in the circulation of carbon in different forms to the earth and then back into the atmosphere constitute the carbon cycle.

Chapter 6. Chemical Coordination in Plants

1. Parthenocarpy	3. Bolting	5. Antitranspirants	7. Phototropism
2. Apical Dominance	4. Epinasty	6. Tropism	8. Hydrotropism.

Ans. 1. **Parthenocarpy :** Parthenocarpy is the production of fruits without the fertilization of egg in the ovary.

2. **Apical dominance :** It is a phenomenon through which the apical bud suppresses the growth of the lateral buds.

3. **Bolting :** It is defined as the unusual lengthening of plant stem by inducing plant hormones such as gibberellins to produce stem with long internodes.

4. **Epinasty :** A nastic movement in which leaf is bent downwards as the upper surface of the leaf part shows more growth in comparison to the lower surface is known as Epinasty. This phenomenon is controlled by ethylene in many plants.

5. **Antitranspirants :** Hormones that are applied to plants to control transpiration are called anti-transpirants.

6. **Tropism :** The phenomenon of directional movement of plant in response to a environmental stimulus is known as tropism.

7. **Phototropism :** The tropic movement of plant in response to stimulus of light is called phototropism.

8. **Hydrotropism :** The tropic movement of plant in response to stimulus of water is called Hydrotropism.

Chapter 7. The Circulatory System

1. Diapedesis

2. Hematopoiesis

3. Phagocytosis

4. Double circulation

5. Blood pressure

6. Pulse rate

7. Pacemaker.

8. Electrocardiogram (ECG)

9. Hepatic portal system

Ans. 1. **Diapedesis :** The passage of White Blood Corpuscles through the unruptured walls of blood vessels is known as diapedesis. It helps in engulfing the germs and also protects the body from getting infected.

2. **Hematopoiesis :** Formation of blood corpuscles like WBC and RBC by the bone marrow and lymph nodes is called Hematopoiesis. Bone marrow and lymph nodes are called Haemopoietic tissues.

3. **Phagocytosis :** Phagocytosis is a process by which certain cells like WBCs engulf the damaged tissues, bacteria and germs and digests them.

4. **Double circulations :** In mammals, the heart produces two separate circulations, the pulmonary to the lungs and systemic to the rest of the body. These two separate circulations are jointly called double circulation. From the right ventricle, deoxygenated blood goes to the lungs for purification and comes back to left auricle through pulmonary vein which is known as pulmonary circulation. Distribution of oxygenated blood from left ventricle to different parts of the body and back to the hearts as deoxygenated blood is known as systemic circulation.

5. **Blood pressure :** The pressure exerted on the elastic walls of the arteries by the blood while flowing in the arteries is called blood pressure. It is greater during systole (contraction) than during diastole (relaxation) of the heart. In a normal adult, the blood pressure is 120/80 where systolic is 120 and diastolic pressure is 80 mm of Hg (mercury).

6. **Pulse rate** indicates the rate at which the heart beats. Each heart beat results from the contraction (systole) and relaxation (diastole) of the heart. On an average, the systole and diastole take 0.8 seconds., which makes 75 beats per minute.

7. **Pacemaker :** The specialized tissue present on the wall of the right auricle which controls the movement of heart muscles is known as a pacemaker.

8. **Electrocardiogram :** It is the recorded report of an electrocardiograph which is produced by the heart muscles during the cardiac cycle of contraction and relaxation.

9. **Hepatic portal system :** System of veins carrying blood capillaries of intestine to the liver in mammals is called hepatic portal system. The blood from the intestine carries digested carbohydrates and proteins, *i.e.,* glucose and amino acids to the liver where they are converted into glycogen and urea respectively.

Chapter 8. The Excretory System

1. Ureotelism
2. Malpighian body
3. The Bowman's capsule
4. Glomerulus
5. Loop of Henle
6. Ureter
7. Urinary bladder
8. Tubular reabsorption.

Ans. 1. **Ureotelism :** Certain animals predominantly excrete urea as their nitrogenous waste. Such animals are called ureotelic animals and the phenomenon is termed as ureotelism.

2. **Malpighian body :** It is a part of the nephron consisting of the Glomerulus and the Bowman's capsule.

3. **Bowman's capsule :** It is a thin walled cup like hollow ball pressed deep on one side. Its hollow internal space continues into the tubule.

4. **Glomerulus :** A single afferent arteriole of the renal artery breaks up into a number of capillary branches to form the glomerulus. The blood in the glomerulus is subjected to higher pressure since the diameter of the afferent arteriole is wider than that of the efferent arteriole that leaves the glomerulus, so ultrafiltration takes place.

5. **Loop of Henle :** It is a hair-pin shaped structure and it is not convoluted. It runs in medulla to turn back and to re-enter the cortex to continue into the next convoluted region of the tubule.

6. **Ureter :** From the hilum of a kidney, arises a narrow tube called ureter which carries the urine collected from the pelvis of the kidney to the urinary bladder which is situated at the base of the abdomen.

7. **Urinary bladder :** It is a large, thin walled, highly distensible muscular bag-like organ situated at the base of the abdomen. The urinary bladder receives the urine from the ureter. The wall of the bladder relaxes and the bladder expands to hold and store the urine.

8. **Tubular Reabsorption :** The process by which proximal and distal tubules reabsorb all the useful products present in the glomerular filtrate.

Chapter 9. The Nervous System and Sense Organs

1. Nerve
2. A Mixed nerve
3. Cyton
4. Ganglion
5. Voluntary action
6. Synapse
7. Reflex action
8. Natural reflex
9. Accommodation of the eye
10. Hypermetropia
11. Presbyopia
12. Astigmatism
13. Cataract.

Ans. 1. **Nerve :** It is a thread-like white structure which emerges from the brain and the spinal cord. It consists of a large number of axons or nerve fibres surrounded by a connective tissue sheath. The nerves arising from the brain are called cranial nerves while those arising from the spinal cord, are called spinal nerves.

2. **Mixed nerve :** It is one which carries both sensory and motor fibres. For example, a spinal nerve. These are mixed nerves and they have two separate connections with the spinal cord—(i) A dorsal root which is a sensory root and (ii) A ventral root which is a motor root.

3. **Cyton :** Cyton is the cell body of a nerve cell (neuron), containing cytoplasm and the cell nucleus.

4. **Ganglion :** A Ganglion is a small, solid mass of nervous tissue containing numerous cell bodies of a neuron.

5. **Voluntary actions :** Voluntary actions are responses to the stimuli that are consciously coordinated and controlled by the brain.

6. **Synapse :** It is a gap between two neurons where dendrites of one neuron meet the axon of the next neuron but they never unite, as there is no continuity between the nerve cells.

7. **Reflex action :** It is an instantaneous and involuntary response to a stimulus. The impulse passes from the sensory cells of the receptor organ along the dorsal root into the spinal cord. From here two messages pass simultaneously—one to the brain and the other travels out along the ventral root to reach the muscle which immediately responds.

8. **Natural reflex :** It is the one in which no previous experience or learning is required and are inborn and protective, *e.g.,* the sucking of milk by an infant from the breast of the mother or reflex of the eyelid.

9. **Accommodation of the eye :** It is the process of adjusting the focal length of the lens according to the near or distant objects so that the image can be focused on the retina clearly. This is done by altering the curvature of the lens by the contraction or relaxation of the ciliary muscles.

10. **Hypermetropia :** Hypermetropia is a condition of eye in which the near objects are not seen clearly as the image of the objects is formed behind the retina. It is corrected by using convex lens.

11. **Presbyopia :** It is a natural condition affecting older people in which near objects cannot be seen clearly. Their lens loses flexibility resulting in a kind of far-sightedness. This is corrected by bifocal lens.

12. **Astigmatism :** It is a defect in which some parts of the object are seen clearly while others are seen blurred. It arises due to the uneven curvature of the cornea. This is corrected by using cylindrical lenses.

13. **Cataract :** It is a condition in which the lens turns opaque and the vision is cut down even to total blindness. It can be corrected by surgically removing the lens and replacing with artificial one and also by using spectacles with highly convex lenses.

Chapter 10. The Endocrine System

1. Exocrine glands
2. Cretinism
3. Myxoedema
4. Castration
5. Feedback mechanism
6. Cushing's syndrome
7. Acromegaly.

Ans. 1. **Exocrine glands :** The glands which have ducts to discharge their secretions in the body are called exocrine glands.

2. **Cretinism** is a condition of mental retardation and dwarfism due to insufficient secretion of thyroxine by the thyroid gland during fetal life or early infancy.

3. **Myxoedema** is a condition that occurs because of the under-secretion of thyroxine in adults. It is characterized by low metabolic rate and symptoms include slow speech, enlarged tongue, puffiness of the face etc.

4. **Castration :** It is the removal of the testes or ovaries from an animal.

5. **Feedback mechanism :** An in-built mechanism that regulates the production and release of hormones in the body is termed as feedback mechanism.

6. **Cushing's syndrome** is a condition which arises due to excessive production of ACTH (adrenocorticotropic hormone). Its symptoms includee obesity, hyperglycemia, weakness, high blood pressure etc.

7. **Acromegaly :** A condition that develops when pituitary gland produces too much growth hormone during adulthood is termed as acromegaly.

Chapter 11. The Reproductive System

1. Vas deferens
2. Penis
3. Cowper's glands
4. Scrotum
5. Androgens
6. Secondary sexual characters
7. Graafian follicle
8. Gametogenesis
9. Foetus
10. Parturition

Ans. 1. **Vas deferens :** The vas deferens also known as the sperm duct, is a duct which receives the sperms from the epididymis and passes it to the urethra after receiving the secretions from the seminal vesicles, prostate gland and Cowper's gland.

2. **Penis :** The penis is a muscular and highly vascular copulatory organ composed of erectile tissue which serves to deposit the semen of the male into the vagina of the female during copulation or mating.

3. **Cowper's gland :** Cowper's gland is either of the two pea shaped gland located beneath the prostate gland. It secretes a fluid which mixes with the sperms, offers chemical protection and supports the swimming motion of the sperms. The mucous secretion of Cowper's gland serves as lubricant and helps to decrease the acidity of the semen.

4. **Scrotum :** Scrotum is a special sac in which two testes are present. It is located outside the abdominal cavity so that the testes are maintained at a temperature lower than the body temperature.

5. **Androgens :** These are the male sex hormones that have been produced by the interstitial cells of the testes. The androgens are essential for the maturation of sex organs, development of the sperm and for promoting secondary sexual characters such as beard, moustache, the deepening of the voice etc.

6. **Secondary Sexual characters :** These are the characters that develop at the time of puberty due to hormonal activity. In a female, there is development of breasts and change in body shape and size of hips. In a male, there is development of a beard and moustache and deepening of the voice.

7. **Graafian follicle :** Graafian follicle is a fluid filled follicle in the ovary which ruptures after every 28 days to release an ovum.

8. **Gametogenesis :** Gametogenesis is a process by which gametes are produced in an organism. Formation of sperms in testes is called spermatogenesis and formation of ova in ovary is called oognesis.

9. **Foetus :** Foetus is a fertilized zygote that gets implanted in the endometrial lining of the uterus after undergoing cell division.

10. **Parturition or birth :** It is the expelling of the foetus from the body of the mother. It begins by the contraction of the uterine walls resulting in labour pains.

Chapter 12. Human Population

1.	Age ratio	5.	Death rate	9.	Tubectomy
2.	Natality	6.	Emigration	10.	Vasectomy.
3.	Physical enumeration	7.	Carrying capacity		
4.	Population density	8.	IUD.		

Ans. 1. **Age ratio :** The number of individuals belonging to different age groups is called Age ratio.

2. **Natality :** The number of children born per 1000 of living population per year is termed as natality.

3. **Physical enumeration :** It is the estimation of human population by physically counting of individuals per unit area. The Census Bureau physically verifies the number of persons living in each house.

4. **Population density :** Population density is the number of individuals living per square kilometere (km^2) at any given time.

5. **Death rate** is defined as the number of individuals eliminated from a population by death in a year per 1000 living population. It is also called Mortality rate.

6. **Emigration :** Emigration is the act of leaving one region in order to settle elsewhere permanently. This results in decrease in the population of that region.

7. **Carrying capacity :** The maximum number of individuals that an environment can support without undergoing any deterioration is called the carrying capacity. Available space, water, resources etc., determine it.

8. **IUD :** Intra Uterine device (IUD) is a contraceptive device placed in the uterine passage to prevent the sperms from reaching the ovum. This checks pregnancy.

9. **Tubectomy :** It is an operative procedure in females in which a small segment of oviduct is removed to prevent the entry of ovum in the uterus. This is a permanent method to avoid pregnancy.

10. **Vasectomy :** It is an operative procedure in males in which a small segment of the vas deferens is removed.

Chapter 13. Human Evolution

1. Biological evolution
2. Mutation
3. Natural selection or survival of the fittest
4. Vestigial organs
5. Adaptive characters
6. Industrial melanism

Ans. 1. **Biological evolution :** It is a long process of change in the characteristics of population of the organisms over successive generations.

2. **Mutation :** Any change brought about into the genetic composition through external or internal factors which may be passed to subsequent generations is termed as mutation.

3. **Natural selection or Survival of fittest :** The process of selective choosing of individuals with useful variations from a population with mixed characters was termed as Natural selection by Darwin and survival of the fittest by Wallace.

4. **Vestigial organs :** The organs that were completely developed and functional in the ancestors but are in a reduced, non-functional form in the current species are known as Vestigial organs.

5. **Adaptive characters :** The characters developed during the life time of an individual are called acquired or adaptive characters.

6. **Industrial melanism :** The phenomenon of evolution of dark body colours (melanic forms) in animal species during the time of industrial revolution is known as industrial melanism.

Chapter 14. Pollution

1. Noise pollution
2. Pollution
3. Pollutant
4. Particulate matter
5. Smog
6. Bio-fertilizer
7. Manure
8. Decibel
9. Ammonification
10. Nitrification.

Ans. 1. **Noise pollution :** The unfavourable alteration in the environment brought about by an unreasonably loud noise affecting our physical and mental health is called noise pollution.

2. **Pollution :** Addition of any unwanted substance in the environment that may cause harm to the environment is called pollution.

3. **Pollutant :** Any substance which on adding to the environments pollutes the environment is called pollutant.

4. **Particulate matter :** The fine solid and liquid particles present in the atmosphere that causes serious health disease are called particulate matter.

5. **Smog :** Smog is a combination of smoke and fog.

6. **Bio-fertilizer :** The micro-organisms which, when added to the soil, increase the fertility of the soil, are termed as bio-fertilizer.

7. **Manure :** Any organic matter of plant or animal source which when added to soil improves its quality to raise better crops is called manure.

8. **Decibel :** The unit to measure the intensity of sound is called decibel.

9. **Ammonification :** The process of breaking down of nitrogenous organic matter into ammonia by the action of micro-organisms is called ammonification.

10. **Nitrification :** The process of converting ammonia into nitrite and nitrates by the action of micro-organisms in the soil, is called nitrification.

Differentiate Between | Set **12** |

Chapter 1. Cell Division

1. Mitosis and Meiosis.
2. Cytokinesis and Karyokinesis.
3. Centrifugal cytokinesis and Centripetal cytokinesis.
4. Anaphase of Mitosis and Anaphase of Meiosis-I.
5. Gametic meiosis and Zygotic meiosis.
6. Centrosome and Centromere.
7. Chromatin and Chromosome.
8. Cytokinesis in plant and animal cell.
9. Chiasmata and Crossing over.

Ans.

1.

Mitosis	Meiosis
(i) It occurs in somatic cells.	It occurs in generative cells.
(ii) It involves a single division resulting into two daughter cells.	It involves two successive divisions resulting in the formation of four daughter nuclei.
(iii) Prophase is short and simple.	Prophase is of longer duration and complex.
(iv) Number of chromosomes in daughter cells is equal to that of parent cell.	Number of chromosomes in daughter cells is half to that of the parent cells.
(v) It is also known as equational division.	It is also known as reductional division.
(vi) Mitosis brings about growth, repair and healing.	Meiosis forms gametes and spores and maintains the chromosome number in each cell division constant from generation to generation.

2.

Cytokinesis	Karyokinesis
(i) It is the division of cytoplasm.	It is the division of nucleus.
(ii) It is followed by Karyokinesis.	It is the first division which takes place in a cell.

3.

Centrifugal cytokinesis	Centripetal cytokinesis
(i) During the partition of the cytoplasm following karyokinesis, when the cell plate formation begins in the centre and proceeds towards outwards, the division is said to be centrifugal.	When the cell membrane starts constricting from the sides and proceeds inwards, till the mother cell is divided into two daughter cells, the division is known as centripetal cytokinesis.
(ii) All plant cells follow centrifugal cytokinesis by cell plate formation.	All animal cells follow centripetal cytokinesis through cell furrow formation.

4.

Anaphase of mitosis	Anaphase of meiosis-I
During this phase of mitosis, the centromeres divide, the spindle fibres contract and move towards opposite poles, pulling the daughter chromosomes apart.	With the contraction of microtubules of the spindle apparatus, each homologous chromosome with its two chromatids and unbroken centromeres (unlike anaphase of mitosis) start moving towards the opposite poles of the cell.

Differentiate Between

5.

Gametic meiosis	Zygotic meiosis
(i) When the reproductive cells of a diploid organism undergo meiosis to produce haploid gametes, it is called Gametic meiosis.	When a diploid zygote undergoes meiosis to form haploid cells, it is called Zygotic meiosis.
(ii) These haploid gametes unite during fertilization to form diploid organisms.	Diploid zygote divides to form haploid organisms.

6.

Centrosome	Centromere
(i) It is an organelle of the animal cell.	It is a non-stainable part of chromosome at which two chromatids join.
(ii) It contains two centrioles which move towards the opposite poles and forms spindle fibres during cell division.	It provides attachment of spindle fibres during cell division.

7.

Chromatin	Chromosome
(i) Uncondensed form of nucleoprotein.	Condensed form of nucleoprotein.
(ii) Seen in interphase stage of cell division.	Seen in M-phase.
(iii) Control of metabolic activities.	Vehicles of heredity.

8.

Cytokinesis in Plant cell	Cytokinesis in Animal cell
(i) It starts with a plate formation.	Plate formation is absent. A constriction forms in the middle of cell membrane.
(ii) It is centrifugal.	It is centripetal.

9.

Chiasmata	Crossing Over
It is the part of attachment of non-sister chromatids of homologous chromosomes where crossing over takes place.	It is exchange of genetic material between non-sister chromatids of homologous chromosomes.

Chapter 2. Fundamentals of Genetics

1. Homozygous and Heterozygous.
2. Genotype and Phenotype.
3. Monohybrid and Dihybrid cross.

4. Y-linked inheritance and X-linked inheritance.
5. Haemophilia and Colour blindness.

Ans.

1.

Homozygous	Heterozygous
An individual having two identical alleles (alternative form of the same gene) is known as homozygous.	An individual having two different alleles is known as heterozygous.

2.

Genotype	Phenotype
It designates the genetic constitution of an individual which determines the characters. The individuals of the same genotype interbreed and have the same phenotype if they are present in the same environment.	It designates the external appearance of an individual. The individual of the same phenotype may appear alike but may not interbreed if genetically different.

3.

Monohybrid	Dihybrid
Crosses involving a single pair of alleles. It yields a phenotypic ratio of $3:1$ in F_2 generation.	Crosses involving two pairs of alleles. It yields a phenotypic ratio of $9:3:3:1$ in F_2 generation.

4.

Y-linked inheritance	X-linked inheritance
There are certain traits like baldness or hypertrichosis that occur in male but not in female because the dominant genes controlling these traits are found on the Y chromosome, which is present only in males.	Certain inherited defects such as colour blindness and haemophilia are far more common in males than in females because these defects are due to recessive genes present on the X-chromosome.

5.

Haemophilia	Colour blindness
Haemophilia is a X-linked inheritance disorder. It is a recessive character genetic disease in which individuals suffering from disease lack a factor responsible for clotting of blood.	It is an inherited disorder. The gene of red, green colour blindness is located on X-chromosome. When this gene is affected, the person is unable to differentiate between the red and green colour.

Chapter 3. Absorption by Roots

1. Osmosis and Diffusion.
2. Turgid and Flaccid.
3. Permeable and Semi-permeable membrane.
4. Active transport and Passive transport.
5. Turgor pressure and Wall pressure.
6. Turgor pressure and Root pressure.
7. Plasmolysis and Deplasmolysis.
8. Endosmosis and Exosmosis.

Ans.

1.

Osmosis	Diffusion
Osmosis is a special type of diffusion which involves the movement of solvent molecules from a region of their higher concentration to a region of their lower concentration through a semi-permeable membrane.	Diffusion is the movement of solute molecules or ions from a region of their higher concentration to a region of their lower concentration without the influence of any semi-permeable membrane.

2.

Turgid	Flaccid
(i) In turgid condition, the cell is filled with water so that its cell wall is in a state of tension. (ii) It occurs due to endosmosis.	In flaccid condition, the cell loses water from the vacuole and cytoplasm under plasmolytic condition. It occurs due to exosmosis plasmolysis.

3.

Permeable Membrane	Semi-permeable Membrane
A permeable membrane has pores which allow free movement of solute as well as solvent molecules.	A semi-permeable membrane has pores which allow only solvent molecules to pass through them.

4.

Active Transport	Passive Transport
In active transport, minerals present in solution are transferred from a region of their lower concentration to the one of their higher concentration by using metabolic energy.	In passive transport, minerals are transferred from a region of their higher concentration to a region of their lower concentration without using metabolic energy.

5.

Turgor Pressure	Wall Pressure
It is the pressure applied by the contents of a turgid cell on its cell wall.	It is the pressure exerted by the cell wall on its content.

6.

Turgor Pressure	Root Pressure
(i) It is the pressure applied by the contents of a turgid cell on its cell wall.	It is the pressure within the cells of a root system that causes sap to rise through a plant stem to the leaves.
(ii) It is caused when a cell becomes turgid.	It is caused due to alternate turgidity and flaccidity of root cells.

7.

Plasmolysis	Deplasmolysis
(i) In this, the protoplasm of the cell shrinks away from the cell wall.	In this, the protoplasm of the cell swells up and touches the cell wall.
(ii) It results in the flaccid condition of the cells and the plant.	It results in the turgid condition of the cells and the plant.
(iii) It is caused due to exosmosis.	It is caused due to endosmosis.

8.

Endosmosis	Exosmosis
(i) It occurs when a cell is placed in a hypotonic solution.	It occurs when a cell is placed in a hypertonic solution.
(ii) Water moves into the cell.	Water moves out of the cell.

Chapter 4. Transpiration

1. Transpiration and Guttation.
2. Transpiration and Evaporation.
3. Stomata and Lenticels.
4. Cuticular and Lenticular transpiration.
5. Transpiration and Translocation.
6. Transpiration and Perspiration.
7. Stomata and Hydathodes.
8. Guttation and Bleeding.
9. Cobalt chloride paper and Goat's bladder.

Ans.

1.

Transpiration	Guttation
(i) It is regulated by guard cells.	It is due to root pressure.
(ii) It occurs at day time.	It occurs at night.
(iii) Water escapes through stomata and lenticels.	Water escapes through hydathodes only.
(iv) Water escapes in the form of water vapour.	Water escapes from the hydathodes present on the margin of the leaves in the form of water droplets.

2.

Transpiration	Evaporation
(i) Loss of water in the form of vapour from aerial parts of the plant.	Loss of water from the surface of the water bodies in the form of vapour.
(ii) It is a vital and partly a physical process controlled by both internal and external factors.	It is a physical process controlled by the temperature and humidity of the atmosphere.
(iii) It is a slow process.	It is a fast process.

3.

Stomata	Lenticels
(i) These are located on the lower surface of dicot leaves and both upper and lower surfaces of monocot leaves.	These are located on the stems of woody plants.
(ii) Loss of water through stomata is termed stomatal transpiration.	Loss of water from the lenticels is called lenticular transpiration.

4.

Cuticular Transpiration	Lenticular Transpiration
It takes place through the cuticle, covering the leaves of the plant.	It takes place through the opening on the stems of woody plants, called lenticels.

5.

Transpiration	Translocation
(i) It is the loss of water in the form of water vapour from the aerial parts of the plant.	It is the transfer of prepared food to the different parts of the plant, including the storage organs.
(ii) It occurs through stomata, cuticles and lenticels.	It occurs through vascular tissues.

6.

Transpiration	Perspiration
(i) It takes place in plants.	It takes place in animals.
(ii) Only water vapour is removed.	Sweat containing urea, uric acid and salts are removed with water.
(iii) It takes place through the leaves and stem and through the stomata and lenticels.	It takes place through the skin; sweat pores of the sweat glands.

7.

Stomata	Hydathodes
Stomata pass out water in the form of vapours.	Hydathodes send out water in the form of droplets.

8.

Guttation	Bleeding
It is the process in which water droplets oozes out from the hydathodes present at the tip and margins of leaves.	It is the process in which plant sap oozes out through injured or cut ends of the plant.

9.

Cobalt Chloride Paper	Goat's Bladder
It is used for the process of transpiration to check the presence of water.	It is used for the process of osmosis as semi-permeable membrane.

Chapter 5. Photosynthesis

1. Light reaction and Dark reaction.
2. Stroma of chloroplast and Grana of chloroplast.
3. Chloroplast and Chlorophyll.
4. Autotrophs and Heterotrophs.
5. Photosynthesis and Respiration.

Ans.

1.

Light Reaction	Dark Reaction
(i) It takes place in the presence of light.	It does not require light.
(ii) It occurs in the grana of chloroplast.	It occurs in the stroma of chloroplast.
(iii) Its products are ATP and $NADPH_2$.	Its products are organic compounds.

2.

Stroma of Chloroplast	Grana of Chloroplast
(i) It is the site of dark reaction.	It is the site of light reaction.
(ii) It is a non-green granular matrix.	It is a green flattened sac-like structure.

3.

Chloroplast	Chlorophyll
(i) It is an organelle of the cell.	It is the green pigment in chloroplast.
(ii) It is living.	It is non-living.

4.

Autotrophs	Heterotrophs
(i) They can produce their own food.	They cannot prepare their own food.
(ii) They contain chlorophyll.	They do not contain chlorophyll.

5.

Photosynthesis	Respiration
(i) It is an anabolic process.	It is a catabolic process.
(ii) It takes place only in chlorophyll bearing cells.	It takes place in all cells.
(iii) Oxygen and glucose released as end-products.	Carbon dioxide and water released as end-products.
(iv) It takes place only in presence of light.	Light is not required.

Chapter 7. The Circulatory System

1. Blood and Lymph.

2. Arteries and Veins.

3. Red blood cells and White blood cells.

4. Open circulatory system and Closed circulatory system.

5. Diastole and Systole.

6. Blood plasma and Serum.

Ans.

1.

Blood	Lymph
(i) Blood contains plasma, RBCs, WBCs and platelets.	Lymph contains only the soluble parts of plasma.
(ii) It contains albumin, globulin and fibrinogen.	It does not contain these substances.
(iii) It is an opaque, red coloured fluid of alkaline nature.	It is a colourless fluid resembling blood in other respects.

2.

Arteries	Veins
(i) These carry blood from the heart to different organs of the body.	These collect blood from different organs of the body.
(ii) These carry oxygenated blood except pulmonary artery.	These carry deoxygenated blood except pulmonary vein.
(iii) Blood flows rapidly with jerks under pressure.	Blood flows slowly at a constant slow speed.
(iv) The wall of arteries are thick and elastic.	The wall of veins are thin and non-elastic.
(v) Valves are absent.	Valves are present.

3.

RBCs	WBCs
(i) These are minute biconcave disc-like structures, flat in centre, thick and round at the periphery.	These are amoeboid and can produce pseudopodia.
(ii) Nuclei are absent in mature RBCs.	WBCs have nucleus.
(iii) These contain respiratory pigment haemoglobin.	Haemoglobin is not present.
(iv) RBCs help in transport of oxygen and carbon dioxide.	WBCs help in protection of the body against infections from the germs.
(v) The number of RBCs in adult male is 5 million per mm^3.	Their number is usually about 4000-8000 per mm^3.
(vi) Their average life span is about 120 days.	Their average life span is about two weeks.

4.

Open circulatory system	Closed circulatory system
(i) Blood may flow in vessels but also remains in direct contact with tissues.	Blood flows in definite vessels known as arteries and veins.
(ii) Blood spaces or sinuses are present.	Blood spaces or sinuses are absent.
(iii) Haemocoel is present.	Haemocoel is absent.

(iv) Found in insects, e.g., cockroach, housefly, etc.	Found in annelids and higher vertebrates.

5.

Diastole	Systole
(i) It is the condition of the heart when the chambers relax.	It is the condition of the heart when the chambers of the heart contract.
(ii) It is the condition when the blood enters the chamber, e.g., when left atrium relaxes, blood enters from the pulmonary vein under low pressure.	It is the condition when the blood is pumped out of the heart, e.g., when the left ventricle contracts, the blood is pumped to the body under high pressure.

6.

Blood Plasma	Serum
It is transparent fluid part of blood that contains Blood corpuscles, Fibrinogen and Prothrombin.	It is a transparent fluid secreted from blood clot that does not contain Blood corpuscles, Fibrinogen and Prothrombin.

Chapter 8. The Excretory System

1. Renal artery and Renal vein.

2. Renal cortex and Renal medulla.

3. Afferent arteriole and Efferent arteriole.

4. Ureter and Urethra.

5. Excretion and Egestion.

6. Urea and Urine.

7. Excretion and Secretion.

Ans.

1.

Renal Artery	Renal Vein
(i) Blood is rich in urea.	Blood is nearly free from urea.
(ii) Blood has more salts of Na^+, K^+, NH_4^+.	The blood has less salts of Na^+, K^+, and NH_4^+.
(iii) Blood is rich in oxygen.	Blood is rich in carbon dioxide.

2.

Renal cortex	Renal medulla
(i) It is dark red in colour.	It is light red.
(ii) It forms the outer layer of kidney.	It forms the inner layer of the kidney.
(iii) It contains the malphigian corpuscles, the proximal and distal parts of renal tubule.	It contains elements of Henle's loop and the collecting tubules.

3.

Afferent arteriole	Efferent arteriole
(i) It brings blood into the kidney.	It carries blood away from the kidney.
(ii) It is formed by the branching of the renal artery.	It is formed by the fusing of glomerular capillaries.
(iii) Its diameter is two times wider than that of the efferent arteriole.	Its diameter is two times narrower than that of the afferent arteriole.

4.

Ureter	Urethra
(i) It transports urine from kidneys to urinary bladder.	It transports urine from urinary bladder to the exterior.
(ii) Sphincter muscle is absent.	It is guarded by sphincter muscle.

5.

Excretion	Egestion
(i) It is the removal of metabolic wastes from the body.	It is the removal of undigested food material from the body.

| (ii) It is related with kidney. | It is related with alimentary canal. |

6.

Urea	Urine
(i) It is a chemical compound.	It is a mixture of metabolic wastes and other substances.
(ii) It is produced in the liver.	It is formed in the kidney.

7.

Excretion	Secretion
It is the removal of metabolic wastes from the body. The excretory materials include tears, sweat, urine, CO_2, etc.	Secretion is an active process of elimination of unwanted materials from the body. It is mainly meant for the movement of materials from one point to another point in the body. Secretory materials include hormones, saliva, enzymes etc.

Chapter 9. The Nervous System and Sense Organs

1. Sensory neuron and Motor neuron (function).
2. Cerebrum and Spinal cord (arrangement of neurons).
3. Cerebrum and Cerebellum.
4. Afferent and Efferent nerve.
5. Vitreous humour and Aqueous humour.
6. Yellow spot and Blind spot.
7. Short-sightedness and Long-sightedness.
8. Rods and Cones.
9. Retina and Choroid.
10. Myopia and Hypermetropia.
11. Middle ear and Inner ear.
12. Cochlea and Concha.

Ans.

1.

Sensory Neuron	Motor Neuron
A sensory neuron sends nerve impulses to the central nervous system from the receptor organs.	A motor neuron sends nerve impulses from the central nervous system to the effector organs.

2.

Cerebrum	Spinal cord
The inner portion of the cerebrum consists of white matter, mainly containing the axons (nerve fibres) of the neurons whereas the outer portion consists of gray matter, containing cell bodies of neuron.	The inner portion of the spinal cord consists of gray matter containing the cell bodies, motor and associated neurons whereas the white matter forms outer layer.

3.

Cerebrum	Cerebellum
It is the seat of intelligence, memory and controls of voluntary activities.	It co-ordinates muscular activities and maintains body balance.

4.

Afferent (sensory) Nerve	Efferent (motor) Nerve
(i) It conducts nerve impulse from periphery to the central nervous system.	It conducts nerve impulse from central nervous system (C.N.S.) to the periphery of the body.
(ii) It is generally made up of pseudo-unipolar neurons.	It is generally made up of multipolar neurons.
(iii) Its dendrites are comparatively longer than the axon.	Its axon is comparatively longer than dendrites.
(iv) Its axon enters into the C.N.S.	Its axon emerges out from C.N.S.

5.

Vitreous Humour	Aqueous Humour
(i) It is found between the retina and the lens, posterior in the eye.	It is found between the cornea and the lens, anterior in the eye.
(ii) It has high specific gravity.	It has low specific gravity.

6.

Yellow Spot	Blind Spot
(i) It has only cone cells.	It has neither cone cells nor rod cells.
(ii) Clear images are formed here.	No images are formed here.

7.

Short-Sightedness	Long-Sightedness
(i) The inability of the eye lens to focus images of distant objects on the retina.	The inability of the eye lens to focus near object images on the retina.
(ii) The images fall in front of the retina.	The images fall beyond the retina.
(iii) It is corrected by using glasses of concave lens.	It is corrected by using glasses of convex lens.

8.

Rods	Cones
(i) These are photoreceptor cells concerned with vision in poor light.	These are photoreceptor cells concerned with detailed clear vision and colour perception.
(ii) They contain rhodopsin.	They have iodopsin.

9.

Retina	Choroid
(i) It is the innermost layer of the eyeball.	It is the middle layer of eyeball tunics.
(ii) It contains neurons.	It contains blood capillaries.

10.

Myopia	Hypermetropia
(i) The lengthening of the eyeball or the lens is too curved causes this defect.	The shortening of the eyeball or flattening of the eye lens causes this defect.
(ii) It is corrected by using glasses of concave lens.	It is corrected by using glasses of convex lens.

11.

Middle Ear	Inner Ear
(i) It has three ear ossicles and eustachian tube.	It has Cochlea, Urticulus, Sacculus and semi-circular canals.
(ii) It transmits sound vibrations.	It is concerned with hearing, balance and equilibrium.

12.

Cochlea	Concha
(i) It is a part of the inner ear.	It is the ear pinna of cartilage.
(ii) It is associated with hearing.	It collects the sound waves.

Chapter 10. The Endocrine System

1. Endocrine gland and Exocrine gland
2. Hormones and Enzymes
3. Insulin and Glucagon
4. Nervous control and Hormonal control
5. Cretinism and Myxoedema
6. Gigantism and Acromegaly
7. Acromegaly and Myxoedema.
8. Diabetes mellitus and Diabetes insipidus
9. Simple Goitre and Exophthalmic Goitre

Ans.

1.

Endocrine gland	Exocrine gland
(i) These are ductless glands.	They may or may not have ducts.
(ii) They pour their secretion directly into the blood.	The secretion is poured directly at the sight of action or reaches the target.

Differentiate Between

(iii) They secrete hormones.	They secrete enzymes.
(iv) They control long term activities of target organs, *e.g.,* thyroid glands.	They control short term activity, *e.g.,* gastric gland.

2.

Hormones	Enzymes
(i) Act at sites usually far away from source.	Act usually within the same cell or at the most close to the cell.
(ii) Always transported by blood.	Not transported by blood. In some cases, transported by ducts.
(iii) Chemically may be proteins, steroids or amino acids.	Chemically always protein.

3.

Insulin	Glucagon
(i) It is secreted by β-cells of Islets of Langerhans.	It is secreted by α-cells of Islets of Langerhans.
(ii) It converts the excess glucose into glycogen.	It converts the glycogen into glucose.

4.

Nervous Control	Hormonal Control
(i) The information is sent in the form of electric signals.	The information is sent in the form of chemical signals.
(ii) The signals travel through nerve fibres to specific target cells like muscle fibres and glands.	The signals travel through blood stream to the cells in different organs.
(iii) Nervous system causes muscles to contract or relax, glands to secrete more or less. But it cannot bring about growth.	Endocrine system brings about changes in metabolic activities of all body tissues. It affects growth.
(iv) Action is immediate (within few milliseconds.)	Action is slow (can take hours or days to produce response).
(v) Effect lasts for a short time.	Effect is more lasting and permanent.

5.

Cretinism	Myxoedema
(i) Caused due to hyposecretion of thyroxine in children.	Caused due to hyposecretion of thyroxine in adults.
(ii) It is characterized by stunted growth, pot belly, protruding tongue and pigeon chest.	It is characterized by puffy appearance due to accumulation of fat in the subcutaneous tissue and oedema (accumulation of water in tissue space).
(iii) Mental and sexual retardation takes place.	Mental and sexual development is not affected but patients lack alertness.

6.

Gigantism	Acromegaly
(i) Caused by over-secretion of somatotropin in childhood.	Caused by over-secretion of somatotropin after adolescence.
(ii) Due to abnormal elongation of bones and muscles, person is of abnormally large height.	Abnormal increase of bones of hands, legs and the lower jaw, person has gorilla like appearance but is not a giant.

7.

Acromegaly	Myxoedema
(i) It occurs due to malfunctioning of pituitary gland.	It occurs due to malfunctioning of thyroid gland.

	(ii) Occurs due to over-secretion of growth hormone.	Occurs due to low secretion of thyroxine.
	(iii) It is hyperactivity disorder.	It is hypoactivity disorder.

8.

Diabetes mellitus	Diabetes insipidus
(i) It is caused by the deficiency of insulin.	It is caused by the deficiency of ADH.
(ii) Patient's urine contains glucose.	No glucose is lost in the urine.

9.

Simple Goitre	Exophthalmic Goitre
(i) It is caused by the deficiency of iodine.	It is caused by the over activity of thyroid gland.
(ii) It can be cured by adding iodine in the diet.	It can be cured by killing the thyroid cells or removing a portion of the thyroid gland.

Chapter 11. The Reproductive System

1. External fertilization and Internal fertilization.

2. Sexual reproduction and Asexual reproduction.

3. Isogametes and Heterogametes.

4. Structure of the sperm and the Structure of the ovum.

5. Urogenital system and Urinary system.

6. Uterus and Urethra.

7. Urogenital duct and Ureter.

8. Amnion and Chorion.

9. Graafian follicle and Corpus luteum.

10. Foetus and Embryo.

Ans.

1.

External fertilization	Internal fertilization
It occurs outside the body of the animal through a medium such as water.	It occurs inside the body of the female.

2.

Sexual Reproduction	Asexual Reproduction
(i) It involves the gametes.	No gamete formation.
(ii) Two individuals are needed.	One individual involves in this reproduction.

3.

Isogametes	Heterogametes
These are similar in shape and size and unite to form a zygote.	These are dissimilar male and female gametes which produce zygote in fertilization.

4.

Structure of Sperm	Structure of Ovum
Sperm is motile, consisting of head, neck, middle piece and tail. It is haploid.	Ovum is rounded, immotile and haploid structure.

5.

Urogenital System	Urinary System
It is a combined system of excretory and reproductive functions.	It is an excretory system.

6.

Uterus	Urethra
It is a sac that holds, nourishes and protects the foetus.	It is a tubular passage for the exit of sperms and urine in mammals.

7.

Urogenital Duct	Ureter
It carries both gametes and urine.	It carries only urine.

8.	Amnion	Chorion
	It is the innermost foetal membrane which secretes amniotic fluid.	It is the outer membrane which forms placenta with endometrium and allantois. It does not secrete amniotic fluid.

9.	Graafian Follicle	Corpus Luteum
	It is a fully developed ovarian follicle containing ovum.	It is a yellow mass formed after the release of an egg from the Graafian follicle. It acts as an endocrine gland.

10.	Foetus	Embryo
	It is an unborn infant after two months of intra-uterine life till birth.	It is an unborn infant during the first two months of intra-uterine life.

Chapter 12. Human Population

1. Natality and Mortality.

2. Immigration and Emigration.

3. Tubectomy and Vasectomy.

Ans.

1.	Natality	Mortality
	(i) It is the number of offsprings produced per year per 1000 of living population.	It is the number of deaths per year per 1000 of living population.
	(ii) It increases population.	It decreases population.

2.	Immigration	Emigration
	(i) The movement of individuals into the population is known as immigration.	The movement of individuals out of the population is known as emigration.
	(ii) It results in an increase in the population.	It results in a decrease in the population.

3.	Tubectomy	Vasectomy
	It is the tying up of oviducts with nylon thread to close the passage of egg towards uterus.	It is the surgical removal of a small bit from each Vas deferens (sperm duct) between two ligatures. Thus, the sperms cannot travel down.

Chapter 13. Human Evolution

1. Man and Apes

Ans.

Man	Apes
(i) Limited proportion of skin is covered with hair,. *e.g.,* top, back and sides of head, armpits and genitals (adults), sometimes chest and limbs (adult males).	Dense hairs cover most of the skin except face, plantar surfaces of feet and palm surfaces of hands.
(ii) Skull supported on top of vertebral column.	Skull hangs forward from vertebral column.
(iii) Cranium is larger than face.	Face is larger than the cranium.
(iv) Walking upright with a "bipedal gait".	Walking with a "quadrupedal gait".
(v) Shows advanced communication and have the capacity to make tools.	Communication is limited to certain signals and gestures.

Chapter 1. Cell Division

1. What is direct cell division ? Explain with an example.

Ans. Amitosis is the direct cell division, it is the simplest type of cell division in which there is no spindle formation or condensation of fibres. Nucleus is directly divided into two, *e.g.*, bacteria.

2. Why is cell division important ?

Ans. The cell division is important as it serves four important functions which are : growth, replacement, repair and reproduction.

3. Name the two kinds of cell division found in living organisms.

Ans. Meiosis and Mitosis.

4. What type of cell division does occur in somatic cells of the body ?

Ans. The mitotic cell division occurs in somatic cells of the body.

5. Where does Meiosis occur in our body ?

Ans. In our body meiosis occurs in germ cells *i.e.,* in gonads.

6. What do you mean by cell cycle ?

Ans. Every cell capable of cell division passes through different stages or phases in a cyclic manner. It is called the cell cycle.

7. Write the name of various steps of cell cycle.

Ans.

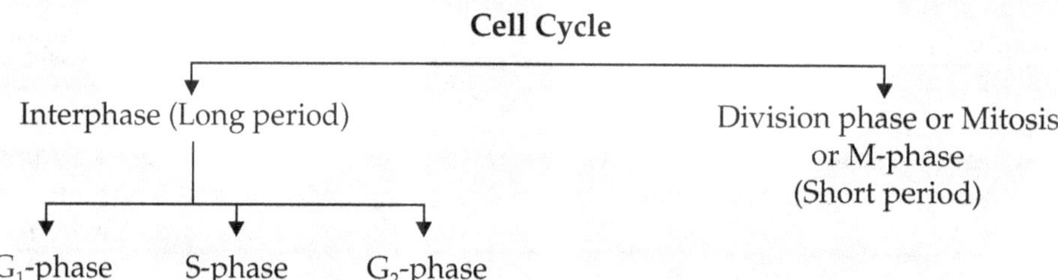

8. Name the structure which initiates cell division.

Ans. Centrosome.

9. Why gametes have a haploid number of chromosomes ?

Ans. The gametes are produced as a result of Meiosis hence they have haploid number of chromosomes.

10. Mention three significant changes that occur in a cell during interphase.

Ans. The three significant changes that occur in a cell during interphase are :

    (i)   The cell grows in size.

    (ii)   New DNA is synthesized as per the old DNA template.

    (iii) Synthesis of RNA and protein takes place.

11. What is cytokinesis ?

Ans. During cell division, karyokinesis (division of nucleus) is followed by the division of cytoplasm. This is called cytokinesis. In other words, cytokinesis is the division of cytoplasm of a cell.

12. How does colchicine act as mitotic poison ? Is there any advantage of it ?

Ans. Colchicine is an alkaloid obtained from *Autumn crocus (Colchicum autumnale)*. It inhibits the formation of mitotic spindle. As a result, chromosomes duplicate but they remain within the same cell (endoreplication). Such cells are called polyploid cells.

Its advantage is that, plant breeders have used colchicine-induced polyploidy as a means of producing variants of agricultural and horticultural crops.

13. Explain the significance of mitosis.

Ans. (i) It helps to maintain linear heredity of an organism by keeping the chromosome number constant in daughter cells.

(ii) It helps in development of organism from zygotic stage to adult stage.

(iii) It is the means of repair and regeneration of cells.

(iv) Asexual reproduction is accomplished only through mitosis.

(v) Details of mitosis are similar in all organisms which emphasizes the unity of life.

14. Why is meiosis referred to as reduction division ?

Ans. Meiosis is referred to as reduction division because the number of chromosomes in the daughter cells is halved during this process. This means the daughter cell has half the number of chromosomes as that of the mother cell.

15. What is the importance of meiosis in creating variations ?

Ans. During meiosis, the exchange of chromosomal material takes place between the non-sister chromatids, forming new combinations. These new combinations give rise to variations which result in the evolution of species and even in the origin of new species.

16. State how does meiosis maintain chromosome number in a species.

Ans. The gametes are formed by meiosis. During meiosis, the number of chromosomes is reduced to half *i.e.,* the gametes contain haploid number of chromosomes. The male and female gametes fuse to form a diploid zygote. In this way, meiosis maintains chromosome number in a species.

17. How prophase-I of meiosis differs from prophase of mitosis in an essential way ? Describe how it affects the daughter cells.

Ans. Prophase-I of meiosis has five sub-stages namely Leptotene, Zygotene, Pachytene, Diplotene and Diakinesis. In pachytene, exchange of genetic material between non-sister chromatids takes place through crossing-over and chiasma formation which does not occur in prophase of mitosis. As a result, the daughter cells have a variation in their genetic composition contrary to identical daughter cells of mitosis.

18. What is the importance of Chiasma formation ?

Ans. Chiasma is the region where crossing-over takes place. By the formation of chiasma, exchange of genetic material between non-sister chromatids of the homologous chromosomes is accomplished. So, Chiasma is the means of bringing about recombination of characters and thus variations in multicellular organisms.

19. What is the importance of meiosis ?

Ans. The meiosis is important to maintain the constant number of chromosomes in a species. It also brings about variations which result in the evolution or origin of new species.

Chapter 2. Fundamentals of Genetics

1. What is a gene ? How is it related to heredity ?

Ans. Genes are hereditary units located on a chromosomal thread. A gene can be defined as "ultimate unit of recombination, mutation and self-reproduction". They are responsible for various characteristics externally shown by the plants and animals. A single gene may affect one or more characteristics of offsprings.

2. Why did Mendel selected pea plants for his experiment ?

Ans. Mendel selected pea plants for his experiment because of the following reasons :

(i) A pea plant has many contrasting characters.

(ii) Self-fertilization takes place in pea plants and so it is possible to get a pure line with contrasting traits.

(iii) Flowers are bisexual and hermaphrodite. Therefore, cross pollination can be achieved easily.

3. A pea plant which is homozygous for Green pods which are inflated [GGII] is crossed with a homozygous plant for yellow pods which are constricted [ggii]. Answer the following questions :*

(i) Give the phenotype and genotype of the F_1 generation.

Which type of pollination has occurred to produce F_1 generation ?

(ii) Write the phenotypic ratio of the F_2 generation.

(iii) Write the possible combinations of the gametes that can be obtained if two F_1 hybrid plants are crossed.

(iv) State Mendel's law of 'Segregation of Gametes'.

(v) What is the scientific name of the plant which Mendel used for his experiments on inheritance ?

Ans. (i)

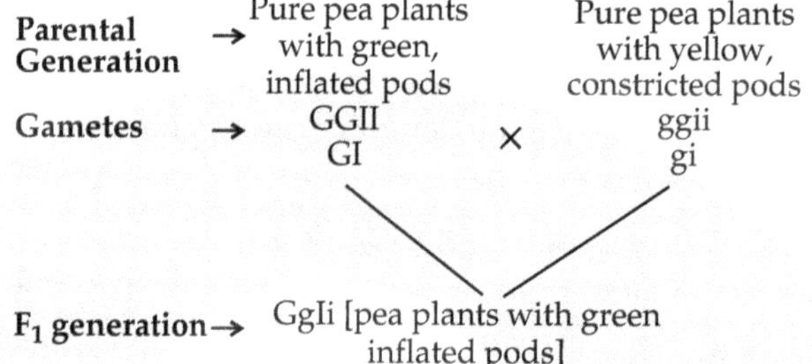

Phenotype : Inflated, green pods

Genotype : GgIi.

Cross pollination has occurred to produce F_1 generation.

(ii) $9 : 3 : 3 : 1$

(iii)

Gametes ⇒ ⇓	GI	Gi	gI	gi
GI	GGII	GGIi	GgII	GgIi
Gi	GGIi	GGii	GgIi	Ggii
gI	GgII	GgIi	ggII	ggIi
gi	GgIi	Ggii	ggIi	ggii

So, the possible combination of gametes in F_2 generation are GI, Gi, gI, gi.

(iv) Law of segregation states that the two members of a pair of factors separate during the formation of gametes. They do not blend but segregate into different gametes.

(v) Pisum sativum.

4. Define Mendel's law of segregation.*

Ans. Law of Segregation or the law of purity of gametes : The two members of a pair of factors separate during the formation of gametes. They do not blend but segregate or separate into different gametes. The gametes combine together by random fusion at the time of zygote formation.

5. In a homozygous pea plant, axial flowers (A) are dominant over terminal flowers (a).*

(i) What is the phenotype and genotype of the F_1 generation if a plant bearing pure axial flowers is crossed with a plant bearing pure terminal flowers ?

(ii) Draw a Punnett square board to show the gametes and offsprings when both the parent plants are heterozygous for axial flowers.

(iii) What is the phenotypic ratio and genotypic ratio of the above cross shown in **(ii)** ?

(iv) State Mendel's Law of Dominance.

(v) Name two genetic disorders commonly seen in human males.

Ans. (i) The phenotype of the F_1 generation is plants with axial flowers will be produced. The genotype of F_1 generation plants is Aa, i.e., all plants are heterozygous dominant for axial flowers.

(ii)

$$Aa \quad \times \quad Aa$$

	A	a
A	AA	Aa
a	Aa	aa

(iii) From the above cross, 3 plants with axial flowers (AA, Aa, Aa) and 1 plant with terminal flower (aa) is produced. So, phenotypic ratio is :

3 : 1. Genotypic ratio is 1 : 2 : 1 *i.e.*, 1AA : 2Aa : 1aa

(iv) Mendel's Law of Dominance states that – " Out of a pair of contrasting characters present together, only one is able to express itself while the other remains suppressed. The one that expresses itself is the dominant character and the one unexpressed is the recessive. The recessive character can express only when the pair is homozygous recessive."

(v) Haemophilia and colour blindness are two common genetic disorders commonly seen in human males.

6. What is monohybrid cross ? How did Mendel perform this cross ?

Ans. Monohybrid cross : It is a cross between two individuals where two forms of a single trait are crossed or hybridized.

Mendel performed this experiment on pea plant. He crossed the true breeding forms of tall and dwarf plants and obtained the hybrid progeny. This is called as first generation (F_1) offspring plant. Later, he self pollinated these plants to produce the second generation (F_2).

7. What is crossing-over ? What are the factors affecting it ?

Ans. Crossing-over is the interchange of the chromosomal parts between non-sister chromatids of a homologous pair of chromosomes. High temperature, X-rays and radiation treatment are the factors affecting crossing-over.

8. Define mutation and give its significance.

Ans. Any change in genetic composition of an individual brought about by internal or external factors is called mutation. Mutations plays a significant role in the evolution and speciation because they cause variation. However, some harmful mutations cause diseases.

9. A certain couple got four daughters in a sequence and no son. Does it mean that the husband does not produce Y-chromosome bearing sperms ? Explain. What is the chance of this couple having a daughter ?

Ans. Daughter or son is a matter of chance for Y- or X-chromosome carrying sperm to fertilize the egg. It is always 50%. The couple got four daughters as the sperms carrying the X-chromosome fertilized the egg and this was a matter of chance.

The chance of the couple getting another daughter is again 50% (so is for the son).

10. Mutation alters the hereditary material. Explain.

Ans. Mutation alters the hereditary material of an organism's cell and results into change in certain characters of traits. For example :

(i) Sickle-cell anaemia is a blood disease caused by gene mutation. The mutation causes change in the DNA which controls productivity of RBCs.

(ii) Radioactive radiations also alter the gene structure and their effects can be seen generation after generation.

11. Why do men suffer from haemophilia and colour blindness ? Under what conditions do women suffer from these disorders ?

Ans. Haemophilia and colour blindness are sex-linked disorders caused by recessive genes located on X-chromosome. These disorders occur more frequently in men because males are heterozygous for the defect. They have one X-chromosome and one Y-chromosome. Y-chromosome does not carry alleles for these traits, therefore the recessive genes are able to express even in single dose.

Females have two X-chromosomes, therefore, both the alleles have to be present in recessive form to be able to be expressed. Thus, females suffer only if they are homozygous for the trait which is possible only when a carrier or sufferer female marries a sufferer male.

12. What is genetic engineering and what is its application ?

Ans. Genetic engineering is a technique through which the genetic constitution of an organism is altered by the introduction of new genes. This method is now being used to generate insulin and several other vital substances.

13. What is the role of genetic counselling ?

Ans. Genetic counselling is given to increase the family's understanding about genetic diseases and to control the transmission of several genetic disorders like haemophilia, sickle cell anaemia and thalassaemia.

14. A homozygous dominant tall pea plant bearing red flowers (TTRR) is crossed with a hormozygous recessive dwarf pea plant bearing white flowers (ttrr).*

  (i)   What is the phenotype and genotype of F_1 individuals?

  (ii) Write the possible combination of gametes that are obtained when two F_1 hybrid plants are crossed.

  (iii) Mention the phenotypic ratio of the F_2 generation.

  (iv) State Mendel's Law of Independent Assortment.

  (v)   Name two X-linked disorders found in humans.

Ans. (i)   Phenotype is tall pea plants bearing red flowers.

        Genotype is TtRr

  (ii) Possible combination of gametes is TR, tR, Tr, tr.

  (iii) Phenotypic ratio is 9:3:3:1

  (iv) Law of Independent Assortment states that the two pairs of factors in a dihybrid cross are segregated independently during gamete formation and are randomly combined in F_2 generation. Inheritance of factors controlling a particular trait in an organism is independent of the other.

  (v)   Colour blindness, Haemophilia

Chapter 3. Absorption By Roots

1. Give at least three uses of water to green plants.

Ans. (i)   Water is major component of protoplasm.

  (ii) It is an important raw material for photosynthesis.

  (iii) Most metabolic and enzymatic reactions take place in the presence of water.

2. What is the significance of diffusion ?

Ans. Significance of Diffusion :

  (i)   It helps in the exchange of respiratory gases.

  (ii) It helps in the transport of food molecules throughout the plant body.

3. What is the water potential ?

Ans. Water potential is a measure of potential energy of water per unit volume or the difference in potential energy between a given water sample and pure water.

4. What is tonicity ?

Ans. Tonicity is the relative concentration of two solutions that determines the extent of diffusion and its direction.

5. Explain why the grass in your lawn becomes greener if you add a little fertilizer to it, but it dies if you add a lot of it.

Ans. If a little fertilizer is added, it provides minerals and other nutrients, so the leaves synthesize more chlorophyll and appear greener. If a lot of fertilizer is added, it forms a hypertonic solution resulting in plasmolysis and consequently wilting of parts of the plant. Ultimately, the plant dies.

---

* Frequently asked previous years Board Exam Questions.

6. A few RBCs were kept in three test tubes containing isotonic, hypotonic and hypertonic solutions. What will be the expected observations after a few hours ? Explain.

Ans. The shape and size of the RBCs will remain unchanged in isotonic solution, because the cells will neither lose nor gain water in it.

RBCs will swell up in hypotonic solution as water will enter in it due to endosmosis.

RBCs will shrink in hypertonic solution as water will move out of the cell due to exosmosis.

7. Root hairs become flaccid when fertilizers are added to the moist soil around it. Explain.

Ans. When fertilizers are added to the moist soil around it, it forms hypertonic solution, resulting the protoplasm to shrink and plasma membrane withdraws itself from the cell wall. Hence, the root hairs also become limp or flaccid.

8. Define the cohesive and Adhesive forces.

Ans. Cohesive Force : The force produced by the molecular attraction between water particles is called cohesive force.

Adhesive Force : The force of attraction between the molecules of unlike bodies that tends to hold them together is called adhesive force.

9. How is root hair structurally adapted for absorption of water from the soil ?

Ans. (i) The root hair has a large surface area in contact with the soil particle.

(ii) The minute root hair can penetrate between the soil particles and when it comes in contact with soil water, the cell membrane allows efficient entry of water into the root.

(iii) The cytoplasm and the vacuoles also help in the water absorption by osmosis.

10. What do you mean by transpiration pull ?

Ans. Transpiration pull : As the water is lost from the surface of leaf by transpiration, more water molecules are pulled up due to the tendency of water molecules to remain joined (cohesion), and produces a continuous column of water through the stem. This phenomenon is known as transpiration pull.

11. "Grapes shrink when immersed in a very strong sugar solution". Explain.

Ans. Very strong sugar solution is hypertonic to the grapes juice. Therefore, water from inside the grapes moves to outside hypertonic solution. It results in shrinkage of the grapes.

Chapter 4. Transpiration

1. Define transpiration.

Ans. Transpiration is a process in which excess of water is lost in the form of vapours from the aerial parts of a plant.

2. Name the three types of transpiration.

Ans. (i) Stomatal transpiration.

(ii) Lenticular transpiration.

(iii) Cuticular transpiration.

3. What is meant by the term 'transpiration stream' ?

Ans. The continuous flow of water from the roots to the leaves of a plant through xylem vessels due to suction force is known as transpiration stream.

4. Where are stomata generally found ?

Ans. Stomata are generally found on the epidermis of a leaf.

5. State the functions of guard cells.

Ans. Guard cells regulate opening and closing of stomata, thus control exchange of gases and transpiration.

6. How does stomata differ from lenticels ?

Ans. Stomata are present on the leaves and open only during the day, while lenticels are present on the stem of woody plants and are open all the times.

7. What are lenticels ? Where are they found ?

Ans. Lenticels are minute, permanent openings which develop in the barks of older stems of woody plants. Some water is lost continuously through the lenticular openings in the form of water vapour.

8. (i) Name the organ in which guard cells are located and mention the main functions of these.

(ii) Give the function of thick cuticle layer present in desert plants.

Ans. (i) The guard cells are located in the leaves. These regulate the opening of stomata for transpiration and diffusion of gases and close in order to reduce transpiration.

(ii) It lowers the rate of transpiration thus conserving water.

9. What is the advantage of wilting to a plant ?

Ans. Wilting causes guard cells to lose their turgidity due to which the stomata closes, thus reducing the loss of water by the leaves due to transpiration.

10. Briefly explain how the rate of transpiration is affected by :

(i) Intensity of light.

(ii) Humidity of the atmosphere.

Ans. (i) Light intensity : It increases or decreases the rate of transpiration. In strong light, the rate of transpiration is more because stomata are wide open. In dim light or on a cloudy day, the stomata are partially closed, reducing the rate of transpiration.

(ii) Humidity of the atmosphere : If the air outside is humid, the rate of transpiration is reduced, since the outward diffusion of internal water vapour is affected.

11. Describe any three conditions which affect transpiration.

Ans. The three conditions which affect transpiration are the following :

(i) Sunlight : In bright sunlight, the stomata remains fully open and transpiration takes place through the stomatal pores. At night, stomata remains closed, so transpiration is reduced.

(ii) Wind : If the wind velocity is high, transpiration becomes rapid because the water vapour is carried away before the air around the leaf becomes saturated.

(iii) Availability of water : If availability of water in the soil is less, the transpiration is low and the leaves may even begin to wilt.

12. What are the advantages of transpiration to the plant ?

Ans. (i) It results in ascent of sap by creating a suction force.

(ii) It helps in cooling of the plant in summer.

(iii) It helps in distribution of water to all parts of the plants.

(iv) It helps in elimination of excess of water absorbed by the roots.

13. What are the disadvantages of transpiration ?

Ans. (i) Some plants die due to excessive water loss by transpiration.

(ii) Due to high rate of transpiration plant suffers from loss of turgidity.

14. "A higher rate of transpiration is recorded on a windy day rather than on a calm day." Explain.

Ans. Wind causes faster movement of air and removes the moist air around the leaf. This reduces the humidity of air, so more water from the plant comes near the surface, causing more evaporation of water and therefore higher rate of transpiration.

15. Explain the relationship between transpiration through the aerial parts and absorption by the root hairs.

Ans. The loss of water due to transpiration tends to lower the concentration of water in the cell sap. Thus, the root hair with its semi-permeable membrane and hypertonic cell sap establish an osmotic system with the water available in the soil surrounding the root hair. This is how the two processes are inter-related.

16. Describe an experiment to prove that transpiration occurs more from the under surface of dorsiventral leaves.

Ans. Two equal pieces of cobalt chloride paper are dried and placed one on the upper surface and the other on the lower surface of dorsiventral leaves. They are firmly held in place by pieces of cello tape or glass slides.

After a few minutes the cobalt chloride paper shows change in colour from blue to pink. The time taken for the cobalt chloride paper on the upper surface of the leaf to turn pink is much longer than for the under surface.

Thus, it proves that the rate of transpiration is greater from the under surface of dorsiventral leaves.

17. Transpiration is a necessary evil. Comment.

Ans. A major portion of the water absorbed by the plants is lost to the atmosphere by transpiration. Even then it is advantageous to the plant due to the following reasons :

(i)   It allows the ascent of sap.

(ii) It brings cooling effect.

(iii) It helps in absorption and conduction of minerals.

However, transpiration is also a threat to the plant life as excessive transpiration leads to wilting and finally to the death of the plant. Thus we can say transpiration is a necessary evil.

Chapter 5. Photosynthesis

1. What are the basic requirements of photosynthesis ?

Ans. The basic requirements of photosynthesis are :

(i)   Solar energy from the sun

(ii)   Green chlorophyll

(iii) Carbon dioxide from the air

(iv)   Water

2. (i)   Where is chlorophyll present in a cell ?

(ii) Name the membrane that connects thylakoid of one granum with the other granum.

Ans. (i)   In the cell organelle called plastids (or chloroplasts).

(ii) Stroma lamellae.

3. Give some adaptations in a green leaf for photosynthesis.

Ans. (i)   Presence of broad leaves for maximum exposure to light.

(ii)   Leaves are positioned at a right angle to the light to get maximum light.

(iii) There are numerous stomata to allow rapid exchange of gases.

(iv)   Leaves are thin to allow rapid transport or diffusion of materials.

4. What is the importance of photosynthesis in the life of the following :

(i)   Green plants   (ii)   Non-green plants   (iii)   Animals.

Ans. (i)   Green plants are able to build up complex energy-rich molecules of carbohydrates which are further used for different metabolic activities of cells.

(ii)   Non-green plants such as saprophytes and parasites use the food prepared by green plants during photosynthesis as a source of their own nutrition.

(iii) Animals eat green plants or animals that feed on green plants. Thus, they obtain their energy from the food prepared by green plants during photosynthesis.

5. A leaf is a food factory. Explain.

Ans. The leaves of green plants are specially developed for the purpose of synthesizing food. The leaf anatomy is best suited for collecting the raw materials. The leaf absorbs CO_2 from the atmosphere through its stomatal openings. It gets water from the stem. The chloroplasts are the actual sites of photosynthetic reactions which result in the formation of glucose. Hence, due to the ability to collect raw materials and to carry on chemical reactions to synthesize food, it is called as the food factory of the plant.

6. Why are green leaves thin and broad ?

Ans. Green leaves are thin and broad so that they can receive more light and can photosynthesize more efficiently.

7. State one important function of Chloroplast.

Ans. Chloroplast contains chlorophyll which is used to trap the solar energy from the sunlight falling on the leaf. This energy is used during photolysis to split the water molecule into hydrogen and oxygen.

8. Which tissues and cells are mainly concerned with photosynthesis ?

Ans. The tissues and cells which contain chloroplasts are mainly the palisade parenchyma and spongy mesophyll cells of a green leaf and they are mainly concerned with photosynthesis.

9. Why is photosynthesis important in nature ?

Ans. Photosynthesis is necessary in nature because of the following reasons :

(i) The body of all living organisms, both plants and animals, is dependent on the food that has been synthesized in a green cell by photosynthesis.

(ii) The purification of the atmosphere whereby the volume of CO_2 remains fairly constant due to the photosynthetic activity of green plants.

(iii) Oxygen is given out during photosynthesis which is necessary to sustain life on earth.

10. How do non-green plants such as fungi and bacteria obtain their nourishment ?

Ans. Non-green plants such as fungi and bacteria obtain their nourishment from decaying organic matter which comes from dead animals and plants.

11. "Oxygen is a waste product of Photosynthesis." Comment.

Ans. Oxygen liberated during photosynthesis is a waste for the plant, so it is released into air and is used by living organisms in respiration.

12. What is meant by Photolysis of water ?

Ans. *Photo* means 'light' and *lysis* means 'breaking', thus photolysis of water is the splitting of water molecule into its two component ions by light.

$$H_2O \longrightarrow H^+ + OH^-$$

13. Oxygen given out during photosynthesis comes from water. Explain this statement.

Ans. During the process of photolysis under light reaction, the water molecule splits up to release H^+ and OH^- ions. These OH^- ions react to liberate oxygen. Thus, we can say that oxygen liberated during photosynthesis comes from water.

14. How is the rate of Photosynthesis affected when a green plant gets green light ?

Ans. The rate of photosynthesis decreases and finally stops when the green plant gets green light because green light is not absorbed but reflected back by the plants.

15. Why is it not possible to demonstrate respiration in a green plant kept in the sunlight ?

Ans. In the sunlight *i.e.*, during the day time, plants consume CO_2 and release O_2 in the atmosphere. During respiration, plants release CO_2 which occurs only at night. Hence, it is not possible to demonstrate respiration in the sunlight.

16. Explain why transpiration and photosynthesis are interlinked during the day.

Ans. During the day, the chloroplast in the guard cells are able to carry out photosynthesis, so the osmotic pressure in the cell sap of the guard cells is high and water enters the guard cells which lead to opening of the stomatal aperture. Thus, stomatal transpiration can take place and CO_2 can also enter the green leaf to enable it to perform photosynthesis. So, during day time photosynthesis and stomatal transpiration occur simultaneously.

17. Explain why respiration is said to be a reverse process of photosynthesis ?

Ans. In respiration, energy is released as a result of oxidation of food, whereas in photosynthesis, it is stored up as a carbohydrate molecule. Oxygen is used in respiration whereas it is given out as a by-product in photosynthesis. Thus, respiration is a reverse process of photosynthesis.

18. Name the molecules which are called assimilatory power. Why are they called so ?

Ans. ATP and $NADPH_2$ molecules are called assimilatory power. They are called so, because they provide the energy requirement for CO_2 assimilation during dark reaction of photosynthesis.

19. What is the law of limiting factor ?

Ans. Blackman (1905) established the law of limiting factor in connection with photosynthesis. According to this law, when a process is conditioned to its rapidity by a number of separate factors, the rate of process is limited by the pace of the lowest factor, *i.e.*, the factor which is present in minimum amount.

20. Complete the following food chains by writing the names of appropriate organisms in the blanks :

    (i)   Grass → ....→ Snake →..................... .

    (ii)   .... →................. → Hen → Man.

    (iii)   Grass → .... → Lion.

    (iv)   .... → Mouse → .... → Peacock.

Ans. (i)   Grasshopper, Hawk; (ii) Grass, Insects; (iii) Rabbit; (iv) Corn, Snake.

21. On a bright sunny day water weeds growing in an aquarium were actively giving off bubbles of gas. Use this information to answer questions that follow :

    (i)   Name the process occurring in the water weed that has resulted in evolution of these bubbles.

    (ii)   Of what gas do these bubbles consist ?

    (iii) Briefly describe the reactions occurring in the leaves of the water weeds leading to the evolution of these bubbles.

    (iv) Give an overall balanced chemical equation to represent the process named in (i) above.

Ans. (i)   Photosynthesis.

    (ii)   Oxygen.

    (iii) The process that takes place first is the photolysis of water to form H^+ and OH^- ions with the help of energy from sunlight. The hydroxyl ions combine to form hydrogen peroxide ($2OH^- \rightarrow H_2O_2$) which decompose to give molecular oxygen *i.e.*,

$$2H_2O_2 \longrightarrow 2H_2O + O_2$$

    (iv) $6CO_2 + 12H_2O \xrightarrow[\text{Chlorophyll}]{\text{Light}} C_6H_{12}O_6 + 6O_2 + 6H_2O$

22. List the events taking place in the photochemical phase of photosynthesis.

Ans. Photochemical phase of photosynthesis is light dependent. A series of chemical reactions occur in quick succession initiated by light, therefore, the phase is called photochemical phase. It takes place in chlorophyll containing thylakoids of chloroplast.

It occurs in following steps :

    (i)   The chlorophyll on exposure to light energy becomes activated by absorbing photons.

    (ii)   This energy is used in splitting the water molecules (photolysis) as below :

$$H_2O \longrightarrow H^+ + OH^-$$

    (iii) OH^- ions, through a series of steps, produce water (H_2O) and oxygen (O_2). Water may be used inside the plant but O_2 get released into the atmosphere.

    (iv) H^+ combines with CO_2 in dark reaction to produce glucose.

23. Using a destarched plant, describe step by step how would you proceed to prove that in the absence of light the leaf cannot manufacture starch ?

Ans. (i)   In a dark room, a leaf on the destarched plant is covered on either side with strips of black paper which is kept in place by paper clips or cellophane tape.

    (ii)   Now the potted plant is kept in light.

    (iii) After a few hours, the leaf is detached from the plant and the black strips are removed.

    (iv) Then the leaf is boiled in water for 2-3 minutes and then boiled in alcohol to remove the green chlorophyll.

    (v)   The leaf is then washed in water and tested with iodine.

    (vi) The region of the leaf that was under the black strip turns yellowish-brown showing that no starch was made, while the rest of the leaf turns bluish-black showing that starch was made in the presence of light.

24. A healthy croton plant bearing variegated leaves was kept in a dark cupboard to destarch it after which it was placed in sunlight for a few hours. One of the leaves was then plucked and an outline of the leaf marking the green and the non-green regions was drawn. The leaf was then tested for starch. Using the above information, answer the following questions :

    (i)   State the aim of the above experiment.

    (ii)   Name the chemical used for testing the presence of starch.

    (iii) Why is the leaf boiled in water and alcohol before testing for the presence of starch ?

    (iv) What change is seen on the leaf after the starch test ?

    (v)   Give the chemical equation to represent the process of starch formation in plants.

Ans. (i)   To show that chlorophyll is necessary for photosynthesis.

    (ii)   Iodine solution.

    (iii) Leaf is boiled in water to kill the cells and boiled in alcohol to remove chlorophyll.

    (iv) The green parts of the leaf turned blue-black while non green parts turned brown.

    (v) $6CO_2 + 12H_2O \xrightarrow[\text{Chlorophyll}]{\text{Light energy}} C_6H_{12}O_6 + 6H_2O + 6O_2\uparrow$

25. A candidate, in order to study the importance of certain factors in photosynthesis, took a potted plant and kept it in the dark for over 24 hours. Then in the early hours of the morning she covered one of the leaves with black paper in the centre only. She placed the potted plant in the sunlight for a few hours, and then tested the leaf which was covered with black paper for starch.

    (i)   What aspect of photosynthesis was being investigated ?

    (ii)   Is there any control in this experiment ? If so, state the same.

    (iii) Why was the plant kept in the dark before the experiment ?

    (iv) Describe step by step how the candidate proceeded to test the leaf for the presence of starch.

Ans. (i)   The student is investigating the necessity of sunlight for photosynthesis.

    (ii)   The leaf portion which is not covered with black paper is the control as it receives sunlight.

    (iii) The plant is kept in the dark before the experiment to destarch the leaves.

    (iv) The leaf is tested for presence of starch as follows :

    (1)   The leaf is boiled with alcohol over a water bath till it becomes colourless.

    (2)   It is rinsed with hot water to remove alcohol and then placed it on a white tile.

    (3)   Iodine solution was poured on it. The portion covered with black paper turns brown while rest of the leaf turns blue-black.

26. A potted plant was taken in order to prove a factor necessary for photosynthesis. The potted plant was kept in the dark for 24 hours. One of the leaves was covered with black paper in the centre. The potted plant was then placed in sunlight for a few hours.

    (i)   What aspect of photosynthesis was being tested ?

    (ii)   Why was the plant placed in the dark before beginning the experiment ?

    (iii) During the starch test why was the leaf :

    (1)   boiled in water

    (2)   boiled in methylated spirit.

    (iv) Write a balanced chemical equation to represent the process of photosynthesis.

Ans. (i)   That light is necessary for photosynthesis.

    (ii)   To remove all starch from the leaves of the plant.

    (iii) (1) To kill the cells.

        (2) To destroy the chlorophyll.

    (iv) $6CO_2 + 12H_2O \xrightarrow[\text{Chlorophyll}]{\text{Light}} C_6H_{12}O_6 + 6H_2O + 6O_2$

27. Write an experiment to demonstrate that CO_2 is necessary for photosynthesis.

Ans. Take a destarched plant. Insert one of its leaves in a conical flask which contains potassium hydroxide. Leave it in the sunlight. After a few hours, test this leaf and any other leaf of this plant for starch. The leaf which was exposed to the atmospheric air turns blue black and the one in the flask containing KOH does not turn blue black after iodine test. This experiment shows that CO_2 is necessary for photosynthesis as KOH absorbs CO_2.

28. What is meant by destarched plant ? How can it be destarched ?

Ans. A destarched plant has no starch present in the leaves and a leaf remains yellowish-brown when tested with iodine during a starch test.

A plant can be destarched by keeping it in the dark for two or three days, so that the leaves are free from stored starch.

29. If you are planning an experiment to show the effect of light on photosynthesis :

    (i)   Will you select white light or green light ? Justify your answer.

    (ii)   Why would you select a destarched plant ?

Ans. (i)   We will select white light because photosynthesis is maximum in white light while it is minimum in green light as green light is reflected by green plants.

    (ii)   We will select destarched plant to demonstrate the synthesis of starch through iodine test.

Chapter 6. Chemical Coordination in Plants

1. Give one main difference between the plant and animal growth.

Ans. Animals stop growing in size after they reach maturity whereas plants continue to grow in size indefinitely.

2. How does light affect the growth in plants ?

Ans. Light is required for tissue differentiation, synthesis of photosynthetic pigments and photosynthesis. It adds contents to the protoplasm and thus promotes growth.

3. What is the contribution of gravity to growth ?

Ans. Gravity decides the direction of the root or shoot growth.

4. What are the two types of plant growth regulators ?

Ans. The two types of plant growth regulators are :

    (i)   Growth promoters

    (ii)   Growth inhibitors

5. Name the three growth promoting hormones.

Ans. The three growth promoters in plants are auxins, gibberellins and cytokinins.

6. What is apical dominance?

Ans. It is a phenomenon in which the apical bud suppresses the growth of lateral buds. The lateral buds can develop into new branches only when the apical bud is removed.

7. How does auxin contribute to apical dominance ?

Ans. Auxins induce the formation of ethylene, which acts as an inhibitor of the formation of the lateral buds and in turn promotes and maintains apical dominance.

8. Why are the hedge plants pruned ?

Ans. The hedge plants are pruned at regular intervals to remove the apical buds and to promote the growth of the lateral buds. This leads to the dense growth of the hedges.

9. What is parthenocarpy ? Name any two auxins which induce parthenocarpy.

Ans. Parthenocarpy is the formation of seedless fruits without the act of fertilization. Auxins such as IAA and IBA are applied at low concentrations to the unpollinated pistils to develop them into parthenocarpic or seedless fruits.

10. What are Gibberellins ?

Ans. Gibberellins are weakly acidic growth hormones having gibbane ring structure that regulate growth and other developmental processes in the plants.

11. What causes Geotropism ?

Ans. The unequal distribution of auxins in plants leads to Geotropism. The auxin accumulates on the lower side of the stem and this promotes the growth of the roots.

12. Give an example to describe Chemotropism.

Ans. Chemotropism is the tropic movement of plant part in response to some chemical. For example, the movement of pollen tube towards ovary takes place due to the absorption of calcium and borate from the style of carpel.

Chapter 7. The Circulatory System

1. Why is circulatory system also known as transport system ?

Ans. Circulatory system is also called transport system because it transports food, water, hormones, enzymes, electrolytes, antibodies and respiratory gases to or away from the body tissues.

2. Write about origin and functions of Red Blood Corpuscles.

Ans. Origin : In the early childhood stage, RBCs are formed in the liver, spleen and thymus. In the later stages, red bone marrow starts producing RBCs.

Function : They help in the transportation of oxygen and carbon dioxide to the different parts of body.

3. Complete the following table :

Components	Origin	Function	Approx. No. (per mm^3)	Life span
RBCs				
WBCs				
Platelets				

Ans.

Components	Origin	Function	Approx. No. (per mm^3)	Life span
RBCs	Bone marrow	Carry O_2 to th different parts of body.	4·8 million-6·5 million	120 days
WBCs	Bone marrow	Develop immunity.	4,500-11,000	Two weeks
Platelets	Large bone marrow cells	Initiate blood clotting.	150,000-400,000	8–9 days

4. Define the term diapedesis.

Ans. Diapedesis is the process by which the leucocytes or white blood cells squeeze out through the walls of blood capillaries at the site of injury to fight against pathogens.

5. What is the meaning of double circulation ? In which animals is this type of circulation observed ?

Ans. During one complete cycle of flow of blood through the whole body, if the blood flows through the heart twice then the circulation is called double circulation. The heart produces two separate circulations, the pulmonary to the lungs and systemic to the rest of the body. These two separate circulations are jointly called double circulation. Double circulation is observed in crocodiles, birds and mammals.

6. State any five functions of blood.

Ans. (i) It transports oxygen from lungs to body tissues.

(ii) It transports carbon dioxide from the tissues to the lungs partly in combination with haemoglobin and partly as solution in blood plasma.

(iii) It transports digested food to different organs of the body.

(iv) It helps in keeping the temperature of the body uniform by distributing heat.

(v) It forms a clot wherever there is a cut in a blood vessel. The clot not only prevents further loss of blood but also prevents the entry of disease causing germs.

7. The table below is designed to indicate the transport of certain substances in our body. Fill in the blanks with suitable answers :

S. No.	Substance	From	To
(i)	....	Lungs	Whole body
(ii)	Carbon dioxide	....	....
(iii)	Urea	....	....
(iv)	Diggested carbohydrates	Intestine	....
(v)	....	....	Target organs
(vi)	Heat	....	Whole body

Ans. (i) Oxygen

    (ii) Whole body, Lungs

    (iii) Liver, Kidney

    (iv) Liver

    (v) Hormones, Endocrine glands

    (vi) Tissues.

8. Why are capillaries thin walled ?

Ans. The capillaries are thin walled because they help in the exchange of gases and diffusion of materials into the cells. This diffusion is possible due to the thinness of its walls.

9. Describe the role of lymph.

Ans. (i) Transport of nutrients and oxygen to the cells and tissues.

    (ii) Removal of CO_2 and nitrogenous wastes from the tissues and carry them to the blood.

    (iii) It absorbs fatty acids and glycerol through lacteals.

    (iv) It destroys harmful pathogens by its lymphocytes.

    (v) It maintains body temperature.

    (vi) It regulates protein level in the tissue fluid.

10. Name the blood vessels entering the heart and leaving the heart.

Ans. Blood vessels entering the heart : The auricles receive blood from three large vessels :

    (i) Anterior vena cava   (ii) Posterior vena cava   (iii) Pulmonary vein.

Blood vessels leaving the heart : Arising from the ventricle are two large blood vessels :

    (i) The pulmonary artery   (ii) The aorta

11. Name the blood vessels entering liver and kidney and blood vessels leaving liver and kidney.

Ans. (i) Blood vessels entering liver :

    (1) Hepatic artery (from aorta into liver).

(2) Hepatic portal vein (from stomach and intestine into liver).

    (ii) Blood vessel entering kidney :

        Renal artery (from aorta into kidney).

    (iii) Blood vessel leaving liver :

        Hepatic vein (from liver into posterior vena cava).

    (iv) Blood vessel leaving kidney :

        Renal vein (from kidney into posterior vena cava).

12. In what ways does the blood entering the kidney differ from that leaving the kidney ?

Ans. The blood entering the kidneys contains excretory substances such as urea, uric acid, etc. These substances are removed from the blood in the kidneys and the blood is free from the waste products of metabolism when it leaves the kidneys.

13. What is blood pressure ? How is it measured ?

Ans. The blood flowing through the arteries exert some pressure on its walls. This pressure is known as blood pressure. It is measured by an instrument named as Sphygmomanometer.

14. What is the value of systolic B. P. and diastolic B. P. of a normal human adult ?

Ans. Systolic B. P. is 120 mm of Hg.

Diastolic B. P. is 80 mm of Hg.

15. Write short note on tissue fluid.

Ans. Tissue fluid or intercellular fluid : As the blood flows in the capillaries of the tissues, the plasma and the leucocytes leak out through their walls. This fluid bathes the cells and is called the tissue fluid or the intercellular fluid. It is from this fluid that the cells absorb oxygen and other required substances, and in turn, give out CO_2 and other wastes back into it.

16. The table below is designed to indicate the major arteries emerging from the aorta and supplying blood to different organs.

Fill in the blanks with suitable answers.

	Name of artery	Supplying to
(i)	....	Kidney
(ii)	Genital	....
(iii)	....	Right forelimb
(iv)	Phrenic	....
(v)	....	Liver
(vi)	....	Chest.

Ans. (i) Renal (iii) Right subclavian (v) Hepatic

(ii) Gonads (testis, ovary) (iv) Diaphragm (vi) Intercostal.

17. Describe in brief the cardiac cycle.

Ans. Cardiac cycle : It is the sequential phenomenon of contraction and relaxation of heart. The action potential causes atria and then ventricles to undergo contraction (systole) followed by their relaxation (diastole). Systole forces the blood to move from the atria to the ventricles and then to the pulmonary artery and the aorta. The heart beats 72 times in a minute. So, several cardiac cycles are done per minute. The duration of cardiac cycle is 0·8 seconds. Two heart sounds are heard by stethoscope during each cardiac cycle.

18. When are the sounds 'LUBB' and 'DUB' produced during heartbeat ?

Ans. The first sound 'LUBB' is produced when the atrio-ventricular valves get closed sharply at the start of ventricular systole. The second sound 'DUB' is produced at the beginning of ventricular diastole when the semilunar valves, at the roots of aorta and pulmonary artery get closed.

19. What is the Rh-factor ?

Ans. Rh-factor is a protein found on the surface of red blood cells. The Rh-factor was first discovered in the Rhesus monkey. It was found that Rh (rhesus) antigens were causing many of the transfusion failures that were unexplained by A–B–O system. There are at least eight different Rh antigens so far. The person bearing Rh-factor is Rh^{+ve} and person who does not possess this factor is Rh^{-ve}.

20. Describe the significance of the hepatic portal system.

Ans. The hepatic portal system is significant in the following ways :

(i) This system is responsible for proper action of various drugs on the body as many drugs are activated in the liver before they reach to other organs.

(ii) It also helps in neutralizing many toxic materials absorbed from the digestive tract.

(iii) It helps in venous drainage from the pancreas and spleen.

Chapter 8. The Excretory System

1. Give a simple definition of excretion.

Ans. Excretion is the removal of all harmful and unwanted products (specially the nitrogenous products) from the body of living beings.

2. Describe in short about different body parts that perform excretion in mammals.

Ans. (i) Kidneys : Kidneys play a vital role in the process of excretion and are responsible for removal of nitrogenous metabolic waste from the body in the form of urine.

(ii)	Sweat glands : Primary function of sweat glands is thermoregulation (cooling). Sweat secreted by these glands consists of nitrogenous wastes in small quantities and is passed out only when cooling is required.

(iii)	Lungs : They help in the excretion of carbon dioxide during exhalation.

3. "Kidneys are the master chemists of the body." Comment.

Ans. The kidneys purify the blood by removing toxic and waste products from the blood. They maintain the proper concentration of salts in the body and also regulate the proper amount of water in the body. Hence, we can say that kidneys are the master chemist of the body.

4. Think of the following :

Tears, sweat, saliva, milk, insulin, urine.

Which of these are secretions ? Give reason for your answer.

Ans. Except urine, all others listed are secretions, because in the secretion, substances that have some utility for the body is given out by a cell or gland. While excretion is the passing out of substances that have no further use in the body or are harmful.

5. Write about the excretory role of the lungs.

Ans. Lungs possess blood capillaries which absorb O_2 and pass on CO_2 to the alveoli by the simple process of diffusion to remove it from the body. If retained inside the body, it may prove fatal. So, lungs are excretory organ which removes CO_2 from the body.

6. What is Osmoregulation ?

Ans. It is the mechanism by which the osmotic pressure is maintained and regulated between the body cells and the intercellular fluid by providing fluid or by taking out excess of fluid in the cell.

7. Explain the functioning of kidney.

Ans. Kidney plays a major role in the formation of urine. The formation of urine takes place in three steps :

(i)	Ultrafiltration : The blood flows through the glomerulus under great pressure. This high pressure causes the liquid part of the blood to filter out from the glomerulus into the renal tubule. During ultrafiltration, almost all the liquid part of the blood comes out of the glomerulus and passes into the renal tubule. The fluid entering the renal tubule is called the glomerular filtrate consisting of water, urea, salts, glucose and other plasma solutes. The thicker part of the blood left behind in the glomerulus after ultrafiltration, contains the two kinds of corpuscles RBCs, WBCs, proteins and other large molecules that are carried forward through the efferent arteriole. Thus, the blood proceeding away from the glomerulus is relatively thick.

(ii)	Reabsorption : The glomerular filtrate entering the renal tubule is an extremely dilute solution containing a lot of usable materials including glucose and some salts such as those of sodium. As the filtrate passes down the tubule, much of the water is reabsorbed together with the usable substances. But their reabsorption is only to the extent that the normal concentration of the blood is not disturbed. This is called selective reabsorption. The fluid which flows through the last part of the tubule is urine.

(iii)	Tubular secretion : Certain substances like potassium (K) in the normal course and a large number of foreign chemicals including drugs like penicillin are passed into the forming urine by the cells of tubular wall to remove toxic substances from the body. The liquid that passes into the collecting tubule is termed as final urine.

8. How is urea produced ?

Ans. Amino acids from the intestine are carried to the liver where, by the process of deamination, they are converted into ammonia, which is then combined with CO_2 to form urea and water. This process of conversion of ammonia into urea is known as ornithine cycle.

9. (i)	Give the working of nephron.

(ii)	What kind of urine (concentration) is produced in human body ?

Ans. (i)	In a nephron, the blood enters by afferent arteriole and is filtered through the glomerulus. The filtrate is passed into the Bowman's capsule by the process called ultrafiltration. The filtrate contains useful products like glucose, amino acids, salts etc. The plasma proteins, blood corpuscles and platelets are retained in the glomerular mass. The filtrate now passes through Henle's loop where selective reabsorption of useful products takes place but urea and uric acid are not absorbed. Now, filtrate with the excretory substances is passed to proximal and distal convoluted tubule where fluid is filtered again. The essential minerals are reabsorbed and urine is formed which is removed from the body through urethra.

   (ii)   Hypertonic.

10. What are the functions of ureter and urethra ?

Ans. The ureter carries urine from the kidneys to the urinary bladder.

The urethra carries urine from the urinary bladder to the outside of the body.

11. Why is urine yellow in colour ?

Ans. Urine is yellow in colour due to the presence of a pigment Urochrome, formed due to breakdown of haemoglobin of old RBCs.

12. Describe about physical properties of urine.

Ans. Physical properties of urine :

   (i)   Colour : Straw-yellow colour (due to presence of Urochrome).

   (ii)   Volume : 1 - 1.5 litre per day but varies.

   (iii) pH : 5 to 8, *i.e.,* slightly acidic

   (iv)   Odour : On standing, the smell of urine becomes strong, ammonia-like due to bacterial activity otherwise faint smell.

   (v)   Specific gravity : 1.000 to 1.030.

13. Write constituents of urine.

Ans. Constituents of urine : The normal human urine consists of about 95% of water and 5% of solid wastes dissolved in it. The percentage of the solid wastes may slightly vary according to the food taken and according to the time after taking food but usually these are approximately as follows :

Organic Constituents in (g/L)		**Inorganic Constituents in (g/L)**	
Urea	— 2.3	Sodium chloride	— 9.0
Creatinine	— 1.5	Potassium chloride	— 2.5
Uric acid	— 0.7	Sulphuric acid	— 1.8
Others	— 2.6	Ammonia	— 0.6
		Others	— 2.5

Besides the normal constituents, the urine may pass out certain hormones and medicines like the antibiotics and the excess vitamins.

14. "Urine is formed from alkaline blood, but it is acidic in nature." Comment.

Ans. Blood is alkaline in nature but urine formed from blood is acidic. It is due to the reason that during urine formation, certain acidic substances like H^+ ions are added to the blood in the renal tubule which gives acidic nature to urine.

15. How does hydrostatic pressure develop in the glomerulus ?

Ans. The efferent arteriole is narrower than the afferent arteriole. This creates some resistance to blood flow, producing the back-up of blood in the glomerulus. This causes a build-up of pressure in the glomerulus which is known as hydrostatic pressure.

16. What is dialysis ? Under what conditions is it carried out ?

Ans. The process of removing nitrogenous waste from the body by artificial means is known as dialysis.

When both the kidneys fail to work, the dialysis machine is used. The patient's blood is led from the radial artery in his arm through the machine where the urea and excess salts are removed and the purified blood is returned to a vein in same arm. In case of permanent damage to the kidneys, dialysis has to be repeated for about 12 hours twice a week.

Chapter 9. The Nervous System and Sense Organs

1. What are the functions of the nervous system ?

Ans. The nervous system regulates, co-ordinates and links the activities of different organs and the entire organism, making it an integrated whole. It also brings about an adjustment between the organism and its environment.

2. Name the three layers that cover the axon.

Ans. The three layers that cover the axon are :

(i)   Axolemma (the innermost layer).

(ii)   Myelin sheath or medullary sheath (the middle layer).

(iii)   Neurilemma, the outermost white isolating sheath surrounding the axon.

3. How does an impulse travel across a synapse ?

Ans. When the impulse reaches the end of one neuron, it triggers the neuron to release some chemicals in the synapse. These chemicals diffuse across the synapse and bind with receptor molecules of the next neuron. In this way, a path is created between two neurons for the continuous transmission of impulse.

4. What are the different parts of a neuron ? Give a brief explanation of each part.

Ans. The different parts of a neuron are :

(i)   Cell body (cyton or perikaryon) : The cell body has a large, central nucleus surrounded by granular cytoplasm.

(ii)   Dendrites : Several short, thread-like branches called dendrites arise from the cell body. The dendrites conduct nerve impulses to the cyton.

(iii)   Axon : One of the branches grows very long in comparison to others. This branch is called the axon. It conducts nerve impulses away from cyton.

5. Explain the divisions of nervous system.

Ans. The nervous system is divisible into three regions :

(i)   Central nervous system : Includes brain and spinal cord.

(ii)   Peripheral nervous system : Includes spinal and cranial nerves.

(iii)   Autonomic nervous system : Includes the sympathetic and parasympathetic nervous system.

6. How does the arrangement of nerve cells in the spinal cord differ from that in the brain ?

Ans. In spinal cord, the cytons of the nerve cells forming gray matter is located in the interior of the spinal cord while in the brain, gray matter is located in the exterior.

7. Name the part of the human brain which is concerned with the following :

(i)   Seat of memory   (ii)   Coordinates muscular activity.

Ans. (i)   Cerebrum

(ii)   Cerebellum.

8. Give the functions of spinal cord.

Ans. (i)   It controls all the reflex actions.

(ii)   It conducts sensory impulses from skin to the brain and motor impulses from brain to the muscles of trunk and limbs.

9. Explain the terms : (i) Sensory nerve, (ii) motor nerve, and (iii) mixed nerve.

Ans. (i)   A sensory nerve is one which sends nerve impulses from a receptor (sense organs) to the central nervous system.

(ii)   A motor nerve is one which carries the impulses from the central nervous system to an effector.

(iii)   A mixed nerve is one which carries both sensory and motor fibres. For example, a spinal nerve.

10. (i)   What is meant by 'reflex action' ?

(ii)   State whether the following are simple reflexes, conditioned reflexes, or neither of the   two :

1. Sneezing.
2. Blushing.
3. Constriction of pupil.
4. Lifting up a book.
5. Knitting without looking.
6. Sudden application of brakes without thinking.
7. Blinking
8. Cleaning
9. Playing on the keyboard
10. Salivation when food is put in the mouth.

Ans. (i) The reflex action is an immediate short-lived response to a stimulus, brought about by the nervous system without the involvement of brain.

(ii)
1. Simple reflex
2. Simple reflex
3. Simple reflex
4. None
5. Conditioned reflex
6. Conditioned reflex
7. Simple reflex
8. None
9. Conditioned reflex
10. Simple reflex.

11. What type of reflexes are the following ?

(i) Sweating in summer.

(ii) Knitting and swimming.

(iii) Solving mathematical sums.

(iv) Formation of goose-pimples in cold weather.

(v) Blinking of the eye.

Ans. (i) Simple reflex.

(ii) Conditioned and modified reflex.

(iii) Conditioned reflex.

(iv) Simple reflex.

(v) Simple reflex.

12. What are the functions of tears ?

Ans. The functions of tears are :

(i) To lubricate the surface of eye.

(ii) To wash away dust particles.

(iii) To kill the germs.

(iv) To communicate emotions.

13. What is a lacrimal gland ?

Ans. Lacrimal gland is a secretory gland present above the lateral end of each eye. Its secretion is tears which lubricates the eye and is antiseptic in nature.

14. In what way is yellow spot different from blind spot ?

Ans. Yellow spot has more cones and less rod cells. Blind spot has no photosensitive cells.

15. Mention the characteristics of the image that falls on the retina of the eye.

Ans. It is real, inverted and diminished.

16. What is meant by power of accommodation of the eye ? Name the muscles of the eye responsible for the same.

Ans. The power of accommodation of the eye is the process of adjusting the focal length of the lens according to the near or distant objects so that the image can be focused on the retina clearly. The ciliary muscles attached to the lens controls its curvature and alters its focal length.

17. What is stereoscopic vision ?

Ans. The capacity to perceive three-dimensional image due to simultaneous focusing of both eyes on an object is called stereoscopic (binocular) vision.

18. During a street flight between two individuals, mention the effects on the following organs by the autonomous nervous system in the table given below : (one has been done for you as an example)

Organ	Sympathetic system	Parasympathetic system
e.g. Lungs	Dilates bronchi and bronchioles	Constricts bronchi and bronchioles
(1) Heart		

| (2) Pupil of the eye | |
| (3) Salivary gland | |

Ans.

Sympathetic system	Parasympathetic system
(1) Increases heart beat.	Return heart beat to normal.
(2) Dilates	Constricts.
(3) Secretion of the salivary gland decreases.	Increases.

19. Name the common defects of the eye.

Ans. Common defects of the eye are :

(i)	Near or short sightedness (Myopia)	(v)	Night blindness
(ii)	Far or long sightedness (Hypermetropia)	(vi)	Colour blindness
(iii)	Astigmatism	(vii)	Squint
(iv)	Presbyopia	(viii)	Cataract

20. With reference to the functioning of the eye, answer the questions that follow :

    (i)   What is meant by power of accommodation of the eye ?

    (ii)   What is the shape of the lens during (1) near vision, (2) distant vision ?

    (iii)   Name the two structures in the eye responsible for bringing about the change in the shape of the lens.

    (iv)   Name the cells of the retina and their respective pigments which get activated (1) in the dark, (2) in light.

Ans. (i)   It is the ability of the eye to focus objects clearly, both close and distant from the eye.

    (ii)   (1) Almost round

           (2) Less convex, almost flat

    (iii)   Ciliary muscles and suspensory ligaments.

    (iv)   (1) Rods, rhodopsin

           (2) Cones, iodopsin

21. Name an old age eye defect. Why is it caused ?

Ans. Presbyopia. It is caused due to hardening of eye lens.

22. What are thermoreceptors ?

Ans. Thermoreceptors are specialized cells, present in the skin, that are sensitive to change in temperature. They are in the form of free nerve endings.

23. What are the functions of proprioceptors ?

Ans. Proprioceptors are the sensors present in the muscles. They detect position and movement of muscles, muscle tension, internal movement of organs etc.

24. Describe the structure and location of various taste buds.

Ans. Structure of taste buds : There are four primary tastes–sweet, salty, sour and bitter. The taste receptors are called taste buds. Each taste bud opens on the tongue surface through a taste pore. Each taste bud contains 60–65 spindle-shaped cells, out of which 5-15 are taste receptor cells and others are supporting cells. The taste receptor cells produce protoplasmic outgrowths called taste hair. The taste hair projects through taste pores and receive the stimulus of taste.

Taste buds	Location
Sweet	Front of the tongue
Salt	Tip and sides of the tongue
Bitter	Rear side of the tongue
Sour	Back and sides of the tongue

25. Name three involuntary actions controlled by medulla in the hind brain.

Ans. Salivation, vomiting and blood pressure.

26. Which part of the human ear gives 'Dynamic balance' and 'Static balance' to the body ?*

Ans. Sensory cells in semi-circular canals are concerned with dynamic balance of the body. Sensory patches in Utriculus and Sacculus are concerned with static balance of the body.

Chapter 10. The Endocrine System

1. What do you mean by endocrine system ?

Ans. In human body there are two types of glands—exocrine and endocrine. The exocrine glands have ducts and discharge their secretions through them, *e.g.*, salivary glands, liver, etc. The endocrine glands are those which do not possess any duct and discharge their secretion (hormones) directly into the blood stream to send them to the various parts of the body. The endocrine glands and their secretion (hormones) constitute the endocrine system which along with nervous system coordinates the activity of various parts of the body.

2. What is a hormone ?

Ans. A hormone is defined as a chemical substance produced by the endocrine glands situated in one part of the body and carried by the blood to some other parts of the body in order to exert its regulation and co-ordination effect on the cells of a specific organ or tissue.

3. What are Endocrine glands ?

Ans. The endocrine glands are ductless glands which secrete hormones. Hormones are poured directly into the blood stream and carried to different parts of the body. Endocrine glands include pituitary gland, thyroid gland, adrenal gland, thymus gland etc.

4. What is the chemical nature of hormone ?

Ans. Chemically, hormones may be proteins, amino acids or steroids *i.e.*, they are of different chemical nature. They may be protein as insulin, polypeptide like parathyroid hormone and epinephrine or steroid as oestrogen, testosterone etc.

5. Why are hormones called 'chemical messengers' ?

Ans. Hormones are chemical substances that are carried to all parts of the body through blood circulation to bring about the harmonious working of the body. So, they are called chemical messengers.

6. What are the general properties of hormones ?

Ans. General properties of hormones :

    (i)   Hormones are secreted by the endocrine glands.

    (ii) Hormones are specific in function.

    (iii) Hormonal effects are long lasting.

    (iv) Hormones are required in very minute quantities.

    (v)   They are secreted independent of one another.

    (vi) They act as chemical co-ordinators or chemical messengers.

    (vii) They are protein or steroid in nature.

    (viii) They are secreted in response to specific stimuli.

7. Which parts of the alimentary canal produce hormones ?

Ans. The parts of the alimentary canal which produce hormones are the stomach and intestine. The stomach produces a hormone gastrin, while intestinal glands produce secretin.

8. Name the different Endocrine glands found in the body of man.

Ans. (i)   Pituitary gland   (iv) Adrenal gland

    (ii) Thyroid gland   (v)   Gonads (Testes, ovary)

    (iii) Parathyroid gland   (vi) Thymus gland

9. What are tropic hormones ?

Ans. The hormones that stimulate certain other endocrine glands to release hormones, are called tropic hormones *e.g.*, hormones secreted by anterior pituitary.

10. Name the hormone produced by the following glands giving one function of each.

   (i)   Thyroid
   (ii) Pancreas
   (iii) Adrenal medulla

Ans. (i)   The thyroid secretes thyroxine. It controls basal metabolic rate (BMR), growth and differentiation of the body.

   (ii) Pancreas secretes insulin and glucagon. These hormones control blood glucose level. Insulin decreases while glucagon increases blood glucose level.

   (iii) Adrenal medulla secretes adrenaline. It controls heartbeat and blood pressure and helps in providing glucose to the body in order to overcome emergency situations. It is also called the emergency hormone.

11. Write about some functions of adrenal glands.

Ans. Functions of adrenal glands :

   (i)   Prepare the body for emergencies.
   (ii)   Regulate the kidney in maintaining salt and water balance.
   (iii) Control blood pressure and pulse rate.
   (iv)   Control concentration of sodium, potassium and sugar in the body.
   (v)   Control some sexual characteristics.
   (vi)   Influence the breakdown of tissue proteins into amino acids.

12. What is the effect of the hyposecretion of cortical hormones ?

Ans. Hyposecretion of cortical hormones is responsible for Addison's disease.

   The symptoms of this disease are loss of energy, skin pigmentation, loss of weight, nausea, hypoglycemia (low blood sugar), sensitivity to cold and low threshold for pain, increased susceptibility to infections, increased Na^+ in urine, vomiting and diarrhoea.

13. Classify the following as endocrine or exocrine gland.

   (i)   Salivary gland   (iii) Thyroid gland   (v)   Adrenal.
   (ii) Liver   (iv) Pancreas

Ans. (i)   Salivary glands : Exocrine gland.
   (ii) Liver : Exocrine gland.
   (iii) Thyroid gland : Endocrine gland.
   (iv) Pancreas : Has acinar cells which act as exocrine glands and the Islets of Langerhans act as endocrine glands.
   (v)   Adrenal : Endocrine gland.

14. Which hormones are secreted by anterior pituitary gland ?

Ans. (i)   Growth hormone.   (iv) Luteinizing hormone.
   (ii) Thyroid stimulating hormone.   (v)   Adrenocorticotropic hormone.
   (iii) Follicle stimulating hormone.

15. How is iodine important to our body ?

Ans. Iodine is the active ingredient in the production of thyroxine hormone. If there is insufficient quantity of iodine in food, the thyroxine hormone is not produced. As a result, thyroid gland increases in size which is visible as a swelling in the neck. This condition is known as goitre.

16. Where is the thymus gland located and what is its function ?

Ans. The thymus gland is located in the mediastinum in front of the heart. It secretes a hormone thymosin which stimulates the lymphocytes to destroy invading micro-organisms and antigens. It gradually becomes smaller with advancing years and in the adult, it is degenerated.

17. People living in hilly regions usually suffer from simple goitre. Explain.

Ans. Iodine is essential for the production of thyroxine by the thyroid gland. The people living in hilly regions receive insufficient iodine in their diet due to the fact that they drink iodine deficient water from rivers and streams fed by melting snow. Even their diet has little or no iodine. When there is a deficiency of iodine in the diet, the thyroid gland enlarges in size resulting in goitre.

18. What is osteoporosis and what is its cause ?

Ans. Osteoporosis is a disease caused due to excessive secretion of parathormone. In this, the bones become weak, elastic and bent.

19. Write in brief about the causes and symptoms of exophthalmic goitre.

Ans. Exophthalmic goitre or Grave's disease is caused by overactivity of the thyroid gland. The thyroid increases in size and leads to an increased metabolic rate, a high rate of heart beat and wasting away of the tissues of the body.

The apparent symptoms are :

(i)   Swelling in the neck.

(ii)   Protuberance of the eyeballs.

(iii)   The patient feels tired, nervous and restless.

20. List some of the functions of pituitary gland.

Ans. Functions of pituitary gland :

(i)   Regulates growth.

(ii)   Influences the thyroid gland, the adrenals and gonads.

(iii)   Can produce changes in the skin colour of many amphibians.

(iv)   Controls and stimulates the secretion of other endocrine glands.

21. What are the two kinds of diabetes ? Mention their symptoms and the causes.

Ans. The two kinds of diabetes with their symptoms and effects are :

(i)   Diabetes insipidus

Cause : It is caused due to deficiency of antidiuretic hormone (ADH).

Symptom: In this, urination is frequent and copious, resulting in loss of water from the body and the person feels thirsty.

(ii)   Diabetes mellitus

Cause : It is caused due to insufficient secretion of insulin hormone.

Symptom : Fatigue, weight loss, slow healing and blurred vision.

22. What is feedback mechanism ?

Ans. Feedback mechanism is a regulatory mechanism, in-built in our body, in which one gland regulates the secretions of other gland to ensure that the hormones are produced in right quantities.

23. Explain how thyroxine levels are controlled through negative feedback mechanism.

Ans. Thyroid stimulating hormone (TSH) is a tropic hormone that stimulates normal development and secretion of the thyroid gland. Thyroid releasing hormone (TRH) from the hypothalamus stimulates TSH release. Thermal changes like low body temperature and increased food intake act as a stimuli which stimulate the neuro-secretory cells of the hypothalamus to secrete thyroid releasing hormone (TRH).

This releasing factor stimulates the adenohypophysis to secrete thyrotropic hormone (TSH). The TSH in turn stimulates the acinar cells of the thyroid follicles to secrete thyroxine in the blood. When the thyroxine level of blood plasma reaches the permissible limits, the thyroxine begins to send a negative feedback (or feedback inhibition) on the hypothalamus and anterior pituitary lobe to inhibit or decrease the secretion of TRH and TSH respectively.

24. Complete the following :

	Gland/Organ	Hormone	Function
(i)	Stomach	....	....
(ii)	Parathyroid	....	....
(iii)	....	....	Lowers blood sugar level
(iv)	Adrenal medulla	....	....
(v)	Pancreas (Alpha cells)	....	....
(vi)	Testes	....	....

Ans.

Gland/Organ	Hormone	Function
(i) Stomach	Gastrin	Stimulates secretion of gastric juices.
(ii) Parathyroid	Parathormone	Regulates calcium metabolism.
(iii) Pancreas (Beta cells)	Insulin	Lowers blood sugar level.
(iv) Adrenal medulla	Adrenaline	Helps body to adapt stress and other extreme conditions.
(v) Pancreas (Alpha cells)	Glucagon	Raise blood sugar level.
(vi) Testes	Testosterone	Development of primary and secondary sexual characters in males.

25. Complete the table given below by filling in the blanks numbered (i) to (viii).

Gland	Hormone Secreted	Effect on Body
(i)	(ii)	Regulates basal metabolism
Pancreas (β-cells)	(iii)	(iv)
(v)	(vi)	Increases heart beat
(vii)	Thyroid stimulating hormone	(viii)

Ans.

(i)	Thyroid	(vi)	Adrenal
(ii)	Thyroxine	(vi)	Adrenaline
(iii)	Insulin	(viii)	Pituitary
(iv)	Controls blood sugar level		
(viii)	Stimulates the production of thyroid hormone		

26. Complete the table :*

Name of the Hormone	Endocrine Gland	Function
(i)	(ii)	Deposits extra glucose of blood as glycogen
Growth Hormone	(iii)	(iv)
(v)	Thyroid	(vi)
(vii)	(viii)	Prepare body for any emergency
Oxytocin	(ix)	(x)

Ans.

(i)	Insulin	(vii)	Adrenaline
(ii)	Pancreas	(viii)	Adrenal gland
(iii)	Anterior Pituitary gland	(ix)	Posterior Pituitary gland
(iv)	It promotes the normal growth of the whole body.	(x)	It stimulates contraction of uterus during child birth and stimulates milk ejection.
(v)	Thyroxine		
(vi)	It regulates the basal metabolism of the body.		

Chapter 11. The Reproductive System

1. What is sexual reproduction ?

Ans. It is a type of reproduction usually found in higher animals and plants where male and female sexes produce male and female heterogametes separately, which on fertilization produce a zygote.

2. Give two important unique features of the human reproductive system.

Ans. (i)   It has the longest reproductive phase.

(ii)   There is no specific breeding season. It can take place any time during the year.

3. Name the various organs of reproductive system of man.

Ans. Reproductive organs of man are :

(i)   A pair of testes

(ii)   A pair of epididymis

(iii)   A pair of vas deferens

(iv)   Urethra

(v)   Penis

(vi)   Accessory glands

4. What are the functions of testes ?

Ans. The main function of testes is the production or formation of sperms. They also secrete male sex hormone testosterone which is responsible for the development of secondary sexual characters in male.

5. Write in sequence the regions which a mature sperm travels from the seminiferous tubules upto the urethral opening.

Ans. Course of sperms in a male :

Seminiferous tubules

(Produce sperms)

↓

Network of tubules

↓

Efferent ducts

↓

Upper part (head) of epididymis

↓

Middle part (body) of epididymis

↓

Hind part (tail) of epididymis

↓

Sperm duct (vas deferens)

↓

Urethra (in penis).

6. What is semen ?

Ans. Semen is an organic fluid which contains sperm cells, secretion of accessory glands, fibrinogen, i.e. prostate gland, seminal vesicles etc.

7. What do you understand by Inguinal hernia ?

Ans. Inguinal hernia is a condition in which the intestine bulges into the scrotum through inguinal canal due to pressure in the abdomen.

8. What are the signs of puberty in human male and female ?

Ans. In a boy : Change of voice and discharge of semen.

In a girl : Appearance of the menses, appearance of mammary glands and widening of the hips.

9. What differences are there in number, structure and activity of the male and female gametes in human ?

Ans.

Male Gametes	Female Gametes
Number : Very large.	Normally one at a time.
Structure : A sperm is about 50-55 microns long with head, acrosome neck and lashing tail.	It is spherical and non-motile.
Activity : With the help of lashing tail, it moves actively towards the oviducts.	Passively carried from ovary to oviduct.

10. (i) Name the female sex hormones and structures which secrete them.

(ii) How is the foetus protected ?

Ans. (i) (1) Oestrogen, produced by ovarian follicle and placenta.

(2) Progesterone, produced by corpus luteum.

(3) Relaxin, produced by ovary and placenta.

(ii) The human foetus is protected by the amnion layer having amniotic fluid and the yolk sac.

11. Define the four stages in the uterine cycle.

Ans. The uterine cycle consists of four distinct stages as follows :

(i) Menstruation : It lasts for about five days.

(ii) Follicle stage : From the end of menstruation to the release of ovum, it lasts for 10-14 days.

(iii) Ovulation : It is the release of ovum from the ovary.

(iv) Corpus luteum stage : It lasts from ovulation to menstruation for about 10-14 days.

12. (i) Where does fertilization occur ?

(ii) Name two essential structures which take part in fertilization.

(iii) What happens to the zygote after fertilization ?

Ans. (i) In the fallopian tube at the ampullary isthmus junction.

(ii) The egg and sperm fuse to form zygote during fertilization.

(iii) After fertilization, the zygote divides to form several celled embryo which is implanted in the uterus for further development.

13. (i) Rewrite the following terms in a correct and logical sequence :

Luteal phase, follicular phase, menstrual phase, ovulatory phase.

(ii) Differentiate on the basis of what is indicated in brackets :

Prostate gland and Cowper's gland (the nature of secretion)

Ans. (i) Menstrual phase, follicular phase, ovulatory phase, luteal phase.

(ii) Prostate gland secretes an alkaline secretion for the maintenance of the sperms while Cowper's gland secretion is meant for lubrication.

14. What is fertilization ? Name the site of fertilization in human female.

Ans. The fusion of male and female gametes to form a zygote is called fertilization. In human female, the site of fertilization is oviduct or fallopian tube.

15. Mention three functions of placenta.

Ans. (i) It connects the foetus with the uterus of mother.

(ii) It helps in the exchange of nutrients, gases and waste products between mother and the foetus.

(iii) It acts as an endocrine gland and secretes chorionic gonadotrophin hormone which maintains the pregnancy.

16. The circulatory system of the foetus and that of the mother are never connected directly. What are the advantages ?

Ans. (i) The separate circulatory system facilitates quick diffusion of nutrients, metabolic waste and respiratory gases between the foetus and the mother.

Short Questions

(ii)   Bacteria and other pathogens cannot pass from the mother to the foetus because they are filtered out by the placenta.

(iii)   Blood pressure changes in the maternal circulation cannot affect the foetus which has delicate blood vessels.

17. What is placenta ? How is it formed ? What are its functions ?

Ans. The placenta is an organ composed of blood capillaries, villi, connecting tissue and latent endocrinal cells. It is formed by the union of uterine endometrial tissue, chorion and allantois (embryonic tissue). It is attached to the wall of the uterus and through it, exchange of nutrients, hormones, respiratory gases and waste products occurs between the foetal and maternal circulation.

18. Describe briefly the ways how a mammalian embryo is—(i) protected (ii) nourished, and (iii) respires.

Ans. (i)   The mammalian embryo is protected by two sacs :

(1) The chorion

(2) The amnion, which contains the amniotic fluid to protect the embryo from shocks.

The embryo is also protected by the thick, muscular wall of the uterus.

(ii)   The mammalian embryo is nourished by the nutrients which diffuse through the placenta of the mother to pass through the umbilical cord to the embryo.

(iii)   The mammalian embryo respires by the diffusion of oxygen through the placenta to enter the blood stream of the embryo. The waste carbon dioxide passes through the umbilical cord and leaves through the placenta.

19. What changes occur at the time of birth ?

Ans. A cycle of uterine contractions followed by labour pains, dilation of cervix occurs and the vagina slowly pushes the foetus out of the uterus. The uterine contractions are initiated by decreased progesterone secretion and the secretion of oxytocin hormone by the pituitary gland. After the child delivery, the placenta is expelled out.

20. What do you mean by identical and fraternal twins ?

Ans. Identical Twins : Sometimes, a single fertilized egg may get split and separated into two parts during its early stages of cell division. Each of these two split parts then behaves like an independent egg and produces one complete individual each. Such twins are called identical twins.

Fraternal Twins : Sometimes, two eggs are released from ovaries at a time and both may get fertilized to produce two individuals. Such twins are called fraternal twins.

Chapter 12. Human Population

1. Define growth rate of population. In what situation can this rate be negative ?

Ans. The growth rate of population is defined as the rate at which the number of individuals in a population increases at a given period of time. It is calculated as the difference between birth rate and death rate. The growth rate of population can be negative when the death rate is higher than the birth rate of the population.

2. What factors govern the growth of population ?

Ans. (i)   Birth rate

(ii)   Death rate

(iii)   Emigration and immigration.

3. What is meant by population density ? How are women operated to prevent the entry of eggs into oviduct ?

Ans. Population density is defined as the number of individuals living per square kilometre (km^2) at any given time. Women are operated to prevent the entry of eggs into the oviduct by tubectomy in which a small portion of fallopian tubes are cut and the ends are tied with nylon thread.

4. What is a census ? Why is it important ?

Ans. Census is an official procedure of counting the existing number of population at a given time and acquiring information of name, age, sex, occupation, date of birth, matrimonial status, number of dependents in a family, race, religion, language spoken, residence etc.

A census is taken in India every ten years by the government to count the number of people in the country. The census is important to estimate the death rate and growth rate of the population of a country.

5. Write difference between immigration and emigration.

Ans. Immigration refers to the addition of individuals to an existing population while emigration refers to the act of leaving the existing population leading to decrease in a population.

6. How will you find out the following ?

    (i)   Birth rate   (ii)   Infant mortality rate   (iii) Fertility rate

Ans. (i)

$$\text{Birth rate} = \frac{\text{Number of births in a year}}{\text{Total population of that year}} \times 1000$$

    (ii)

$$\text{Infant mortality rate} = \frac{\text{Number of Infant death}}{\text{Number of live births}} \times 1000$$

    (iii)

$$\text{Fertility rate} = \frac{\text{No. of births in a year}}{\text{No. of women between 16 and 40 years of age}} \times 1000$$

7. Our resources cannot keep pace with the ever increasing population. Give three examples in support of this statement.

Ans. (i)   With the growing number of people, there is insufficient food as growth in population is in geometric progression whereas increase in food production is in arithmetic progression.

   (ii) There is a corresponding lack of housing, recreational facilities, clinics and hospitals to cope with the ever-increasing population.

  (iii) There is limited land for factories and industries so there is unemployment due to ever-increasing population.

8. Mention any two reasons for the rapid increase in population in recent times.

Ans. The two reasons for the rapid increase in population in recent times are :

    (i)   The death rate in India has fallen down due to increased scientific medical knowledge.

   (ii) Improved standard of living due to increased food production and industrial development and education has brought about an increase in population.

9. Write some benefits of a small family.

Ans. The benefits of having a small family are :

    (i)   Basic needs like food, clothing, shelter, education, etc., will be satisfied more easily.

   (ii) Children can get better education. Parents can often be able to provide higher education to their children.

  (iii) Children will be healthy; physically and mentally.

  (iv) Parents can take better care of the children in a small, well-planned family.

10. Write some major disadvantages of large family.

Ans. The main disadvantages are :

    (i)   The children are not able to get good variety and proper quantity of food resulting in malnutrition and deficiency diseases.

   (ii) The mother will have poor health due to which she can't look after the children properly.

  (iii) There will be a high economic pressure on father's income.

  (iv) The children won't get proper education and medical facilities due to lack of money.

11. Why is there need to control population ?

Ans. There is need to control population because :

    (i)   The number of people is increasing in geometric progression.

    (ii)   It is leading to great economic pressure on the parents which is affecting their quality of life.

    (iii)   There is struggle for existence.

    (iv)   Natural resources are overexploiting to meet human demands.

12. Explain briefly the idea contained in the following statement : "There will be increasing dependence on sources of energy other than coal and petroleum in the future."

Ans. There will be increasing dependence on sources of energy other than coal and petroleum in the future because these two fossil fuels are non-renewable sources of energy and they are being consumed very quickly by the increasing human population. Further, man is trying to obtain energy from non-polluting sources of energy such as wind, hydroelectric power, etc., to prevent excessive pollution that is caused by the use of coal and petroleum.

13. Give five reasons why has family planning often failed in the rural villages and countryside.

Ans. Family planning has often failed in the rural villages and countryside because :

    (i)   Less awareness about family planning methods.

    (ii)   There is a low educational level.

    (iii)   The people still follow traditional, cultural and religious beliefs and superstitions.

    (iv)   The villagers also feel that with more children, family income will increase which will help in the survival of family.

    (v)   The people of the rural areas often fail to precisely follow the methods of birth control.

14. Explain briefly the relation between poverty and population.

Ans. The poorer and lower classes of people feel that children will be able to supplement the income of the parents by working. The more the children, the more will be the income of the family.

Infant mortality is very high among the poor people because the mother does not receive pre-natal and post-natal care. Further, many children die at an early age. This high infant mortality causes many of the poor to have more children so that some of them may survive.

15. How is the electronic media educating people about the importance of small families ?

Ans. The electronic media such as Radio and Television convey the message of family planning to the citizens every day. The newspapers also provide the daily increase in the population of India to tell us about the danger and seriousness of population explosion.

16. Mention three steps to control the increasing human population in India.

Ans. Three steps by which the increasing human population can be controlled are :

    (i)   Family Planning : There can be a decrease in birth rate by voluntary family planning aided by incentives. The methods include sterilization, use of contraceptives and pills.

    (ii)   Education of the people about small family norms and its benefits.

    (iii)   Providing a health, educational or even financial incentive can be highly effective in controlling population growth.

17. How is human population checked at present ?

Ans. At present, human population is checked by death due to old age, disease, wars, epidemics, natural calamities such as earthquakes and floods and also by family planning methods.

18. What are the problems faced by India owing to the 'population explosion' ?

Ans. Consequences of 'population explosion' in India are :

    (i)   Scarcity of food, space and water : Although the population is growing rapidly, but the living and food, space available per person has remained constant.

    (ii)   Increase in epidemics and diseases as a result of unhygienic and crowded living conditions in cities, towns and villages.

(iii) Unemployment and poverty will be uncontrollable and may lead to social unrest and lack of educational facilities.

(iv) Destruction of forests and their fauna and flora so that more land can be brought under cultivation or for human dwellings.

(v) Problems of sanitation, cleanliness and clean drinking water for the increasing population.

(vi) Lack of facilities such as schools, colleges, hospitals, transportation, etc.

(vii) Non-renewable resources such as coal, oil, water, minerals, etc., will be consumed very quickly.

(viii) Disturbances in ecological balance due to deforestation and pollution.

19. (i) Describe the four methods of birth control practiced in India.

(ii) Name two surgical techniques (for man and woman) to prevent pregnancy.

Ans. (i) The four methods of birth control are :

(1) Surgical methods : This includes vasectomy in males and tubectomy in females.

(a) Vasectomy : This involves the breaking of the contact between the sperms and ovum, by cutting the vas deferens or sperm duct which carries sperms from the testes to the outside in man. It prevents pregnancy.

(b) Tubectomy : Severing and sealing off the fallopian tubes so that the mature ovum may not come in contact with the incoming sperms.

(2) Barrier methods : Loops, condoms, IUDs, diaphragms, etc., are used to prevent the sperms from meeting the ovum.

(3) Contraceptive pills : Many birth control pills are available nowadays that prevent the release of the egg from the ovary.

(4) Voluntary methods : It include :

(a) Avoiding sexual intercourse during the unsafe period of ovulation.

(b) Frequent use of contraceptive.

(ii) For man—Vasectomy, For woman—Tubectomy.

20. What is the popular sign for the Family Planning and Welfare Centres in India ?

Ans. The popular sign for the Family Planning and Welfare Centres in India is the inverted Red Triangle.

21. State two methods of contraception, one a barrier method and one which is not a barrier method. For each method named, give two advantages and one disadvantage of the method.

Ans. A barrier method—condom.

Non-barrier—contraceptive pill.

Advantages of the condom include the fact that it is readily available, needs no medical supervision and can help reduce the transmission of venereal diseases. A disadvantage is that it is not the most reliable method. Advantages of the contraceptive pill are that it is highly reliable if taken according to instructions and also a woman can take responsibility for her own fertility. A disadvantage is that it should be taken under medical supervision as there is a small risk of side effects.

Chapter 13. Human Evolution

1. Give any five similarities to show that man and apes have evolved from a common ancestor.

Ans. The similarities that suggest the phylogenetic relationship between man and apes are :

(i) Absence of tail in both

(ii) Large sized head with well developed brain

(iii) Long neck and limbs

(iv) Capability to communicate through vocal means

(v) Menstruation in females

2. *Australopithecus* belonged to which period and what were its characteristic features ?

Ans. The fossils of *Australopithecus africans* (the first African ape-man) were discovered from late Pliocene and early Pleistocene rocks of about 13 million years ago. Some of their ape-like characters are :

(i)   Small cranial cavity (600 cm^3)

(ii)   Long canines and incisors

(iii) Small stature (4 feet)

Some of the man-like characters are :

(i)   Erect or semi-erect posture

(ii)   Bipedal locomotion that helped them in hunting

(iii) Distinct lumbar curve in the vertebral column

3. List out any three characteristicss of *Homo habilis.*

Ans. The characteristics are :

(i)   Cranial cavity was about 735 cm^3

(ii)   Smaller moderately-prognathic face and smaller teeth

(iii) Showed bipedal gait

4. What were the two forms of erect man noticed in the past ?

Ans. The two forms of erect man were :

(i)   *Homo erectus erectus* (Java ape man)

(ii)   *Homo erectus pekinensis* (Peking man)

5. Which two adaptations helped the Java man to walk erect ?

Ans. The two adaptations were :

(i)   Modern human-like body proportions

(ii)   Relatively elongated legs and shorter arms

6. Give an example to show that the overuse of an organ can help in its evolution.

Ans. The ancestors of giraffe were short necked and had horse-like forelimbs. These giraffes were forced to extend their necks and stretch their forelimbs to reach higher vegetation as the surface vegetation had disappeared suddenly. This attempt of catching leaves from small trees and bushes led to a slight elongation of these parts. This elongation in the neck and forelimbs was transmitted to the next generation. As a result, the modern giraffes have a long neck and long forelimbs. Thus, it is an example of overuse of certain organs.

7. What are vestigial organs ? Why is Vermiform appendix considered to be vestigial in human ?

Ans. The organs that were completely developed and functional in the ancestors but are in a reduced, non-functional form in the current species are known as vestigial organs. Vermiform appendix and caecum are long in herbivorous animals like rabbit, horse, etc. The symbiotic bacteria present in these organs secrete cellulase enzyme that helps in the digestion of plant food. As man evolved, he started to cook the plant food before consumption. The process of cooking simplifies the cellulose present in plant food so that it can get digested even in the absence of cellulase. Thus, Vermiform appendix and caecum become vestigial in man.

8. Describe how wisdom teeth have gradually become vestigial ?

Ans. The skull of human ancestors had larger jaws with more teeth, which were possibly used to help chew coarse, rough food like leaves, roots, nuts and meat. The modern human diet consists of softer and cooked foods. With a reduction in human jaw size, molars, particularly the third molars or wisdom teeth became highly prone to impaction and they gradually turned out to be vestigial.

9. What was the explanation provided by August Weismann while criticizing the principle of inherited characters ?

Ans. August Weismann proved that environmental factors can affect the somatic cells that do not get transmitted to the next generation. As the germs cells that get transmitted to the next generation remain unaffected, the effects produced by the environmental factors are lost with the death of the organism and have no role in evolution.

10. What were the examples proposed to criticize the postulates of Lamarckism ?

Ans. The postulates of Lamarckism were criticized based on certain examples that prove them to be untrue.

   (i)   Environment cannot always instigate new needs. For example, we cannot develop wings even if we have a desire to fly. Hence, new needs and environment cannot always trigger evolution.

   (ii)   Even though the evolution of horse, elephant, etc., supports the first proposition of Lamarck, it does not stand true in all circumstances. In many species, there has been a gradual reduction in size with evolution. For example, in angiosperms, the trees are considered to be more primitive and shrubs, herbs and grasses with reduced sizes have evolved from the trees.

11. Why are variations considered to be very essential for evolution ?

Ans. Variations make the population heterogeneous. Variations are observed at the phenotypic and genotypic level. Natural selection chooses only those genetic variations that get expressed in the phenotype. Thus, genetic variations are the pre-requisites for evolution and serve as agents for evolution. They help the organisms to adapt to the environment and make them more fit. Thus, variations are very essential for evolution.

12. Natural selection is the key concept of Darwinian theory of evolution. Explain with the help of an example.

Ans. The process of selective choosing of individuals with useful variations from a population with mixed characters is termed as natural selection.

Example : Industrial Melanism

Prior to industrial revolution, white moth were present in greater numbers as they could hide themselves in the light coloured lichens present on the trunks of trees. Gradually, with industrial revolution, the black coloured moths increased in numbers and white coloured moth got killed. With industrial revolution, the deposition of soot and smoke particles on the tree trunks increased. This killed the lichens and the white peppered moths were killed as they lost the hiding places and were exposed to the predators. The number of black coloured moths increased as they got naturally selected due to the better chances of survival.

13. How does the availability of food and space limit the growth of population ?

Ans. Every organism tries to produces offsprings similar to parents in large numbers, so that the continuity of race is maintained. However, as the availability of natural resources such as food and space is limited, an indefinite growth of the population is not possible. These limiting factors do not allow the population to cross the carrying capacity of the environment.

14. What are the three different types of struggle for existence seen in nature ?

Ans. The three different types of struggles are :

   (i)   Struggle between organisms of the same species.

   (ii)   Struggle between organisms belonging to two different species.

   (iii)   Struggle between living beings and the changes in the environmental conditions.

15. Give any two evidences that do not support Darwinism.

Ans. (i)   Darwin did not explain anything about the sources of variations and how they got transmitted to the next generation. Moreover, the mechanism of natural selection was also not clear to him.

   (ii)   The survival of the fittest was explained by explaining how only the fittest members of the species surviving in a particular environment continue to proliferate in a particular area. However, there is no explanation provided on how the first fit individual of that species came into existence.

Chapter 14. Pollution

1. What is pollution ?

Ans. Pollution is the addition of any such constituent to air, water or land which deteriorates the natural quality of the environment.

2. Name the major pollutants of air.

Ans. Major pollutants of air are : Sulphur dioxide, nitrogen oxides, carbon dioxide, fly ash and suspended particulate matter (SPM).

3. How can we control air pollution ?

Ans. (i)   From domestic combustion : Reducing pollution from domestic cooking, using clean cooking-kerosene as a desirable cooking fuel in rural areas.

     (ii)   From industries : Measures for controlling industrial air pollution—technological measures (energy efficient devices, cleaning technologies), meteorological controls, zoning strategy, penalties and subsidies, Case Study : The Taj Trapezium.

     (iii)   From vehicles : Vehicle emission control—modify engine design (catalytic converters, four stroke engines), clean fuels, public transport options, traffic management, economic policy measures.

4. Describe the impact of air pollution.

Ans. Global warming and climate change are the result of air pollution. Global warming causes depletion of ozone layer due to which entry of harmful ultraviolet rays from the sun is now possible. These radiations cause various skin diseases including skin cancer. In plants, such enhanced level of these radiations cause stunted growth, thick stems, smaller leaves, etc. Similarly, climate change has a bad effect on the environment in which rain cycle is adversely affected and as a result, certain regions are facing floods, whereas other regions are facing drought.

5. What is water pollution ?

Ans. Water pollution is the introduction of chemical, physical or biological material into fresh or ocean waters such that it degrades the quality of the water and affects the organisms living in it.

6. List the cause of water pollution.

Ans. Industrial effluents, mining wastes, sewage disposal, domestic wastes and agricultural wastes.

7. What are some types of pollutants found in water ?

Ans. Disease-causing organism, pesticides and fertilizers, industrial chemicals, metals, radioactive waste, petroleum products etc.

8. How could warm water act as a pollutant ?

Ans. Warm water released by a factory into a nearby river or pond raises the temperature of the water, sometimes enough to harm the living things there.

9. Describe some ways how industries and agriculture can help lessen pollution.

Ans. Farmers can modify the farming practices to control pollution. For example, they can practice crop rotation to minimize the use of fertilizers. Industries can also contribute in controlling pollution by the following ways :

     (i)   By installing electrostatic precipitator in the chimneys.

     (ii)   By treating hot water before releasing it into water bodies.

10. How is soil pollution caused ?

Ans. Soil pollution usually results from the disposal of non-biodegradable solid and semi-solid wastes, excessive use of pesticides and insecticides in agricultural practices, toxic chemicals from industrial processes and insanitary habits.

11. What is the effect of pollution on soil ?

Ans. Soil is the foundation of a healthy biosphere. Precipitation from air as acid rain and dry deposition of pollutants on land surface contribute to soil pollution. Pollutants combine with plant nutrients and are consumed by animals. Polluted soil unfavourably affects the microbial environment resulting in reduction in mineralization and decomposition processes. Soil fertility and aeration are also reduced and earthworms, nematodes etc., are destroyed by toxic chemicals.

12. What are the adverse effects of oil spill ?

Ans. Replacement of coal by the oil fuel has increased the problem of pollution. The presence of oil in a water course is undesirable since it creates aesthetic problems. It has a tendency to spread over the surface of water due to which diffusion of oxygen into water is inhibited and re-aeration of water is affected.

13. What is radioactivity ?

Ans. Some substances are highly unstable and thus to attain stability, they dissociate themselves continuously and emit certain type of harmful radiations as energy. Such substances are called radioactive substances and the phenomenon is called radioactivity.

14. What is the effect of radiation on health ?

Ans. Radiation can lead to severe health hazards. Effects of non-ionizing radiation at low level are uncertain but ionizing radiation at high level can cause cancer and increase in chromosome damage.

15. Discuss the health hazards associated with the pollution.

Ans. The impact of pollution on health may be primary or secondary. The primary impact occurs immediately but the secondary impact is delayed and may persist in future.

(i) When contaminated water is supplied to the residents of a locality, it may spread water borne diseases like diarrhoea, hepatitis etc.

(ii) Release of smoke as vehicular exhaust pollutes the air. When this air is inhaled by the humans, it causes asthma and bronchitis.

(iii) Large amount of soluble nitrates are released and dissolve in the water. It may contaminate the groundwater including wells of the area. Heavy intake of nitrates by humans may cause serious health hazards.

(iv) People who work in the deep coal mines, inhale the fine coal dust. It leads to a disease called black lungs. Many gases are also released in the process of mining like methane and carbonmonoxide.

16. What are the health effects of carbon monoxide ?

Ans. When we breathe air containing carbon monoxide, it gets absorbed in the bloodstream where it displaces oxygen and binds with the haemoglobin. Carbon monoxide has a greater affinity to haemoglobin and thus; binds to haemoglobin about 250 times better than oxygen. Without oxygen, vital organs, heart and brain become deprived and will begin to deteriorate. To compensate, heart rate increases, breathing may become difficult and in the most serious circumstances cardiac trauma, brain damage, coma and even death will result.

17. Why is pollution prevention important ?

Ans. Preventing pollution offers important benefits, as pollution created never avoids the need for expensive investments in waste managements and cleanup. By anticipating the future, pollution prevention reduces both financial costs (waste management and cleanup) and real environmental costs (health problems and environmental damage). As a result, pollution prevention holds the exciting potential of protecting the environment and strengthening economic growth through more efficient production and natural resource use.

18. What is acid rain ?

Ans. Acid rain is the term used for rain which is unusually acidic in nature. Acid rain is caused when oxides of sulphur and nitrogen combine with atmospheric moisture to form acids.

19. What are the effects of acid rain ?

Ans. Effects of acid rain :

(i) Acid rain increases acidity in the soil and destroys forests and crops.

(ii) It corrodes fences, buildings, monuments, bridges and statues.

(iii) It affects the human nervous system by causing neurological diseases.

(iv) It poses a serious threat to human health, since it contaminates air and water.

20. What causes acid deposition ?

Ans. Acid deposition, commonly called acid rain, is caused by emissions of sulphur dioxide and nitrogen oxides. Although natural sources of sulphur oxides and nitrogen oxides do exist, more than 90% of the sulphur and 95% of the nitrogen emissions occurring in eastern North America are of human origin.

These primary air pollutants arise from the use of coal in the production of electricity, from base-metal smelting and from fuel combustion in vehicles. Once released into the atmosphere, they can be converted chemically into such secondary pollutants as nitric acid and sulphuric acid, both of which dissolve easily in water. The resulting acidic water droplets can be carried along long distances by prevailing winds, returning to Earth as acid rain snow or fog.

21. What is Ozone ?

Ans. Ozone is a gas that is made up of three oxygen atoms (O_3). Ozone is classified as either stratospheric (good ozone) or ground level (bad ozone).

22. What are CFCs ?

Ans. Chlorofluorocarbons (CFCs) are non-toxic, non-flammable chemicals containing atoms of carbon, chlorine, and fluorine. They are used in the manufacture of aerosol sprays, blowing agents for foams and packing materials, as solvents and as refrigerants. CFCs react with sunlight in the earth's stratosphere to break down the protective ozone layer, a layer of gas that shields the earth's surface from damaging UV-B rays.

23. Discuss in detail the process of ozone depletion.

Ans. The upper part of stratosphere contains large amount of Ozone gas. The ozone gas blocks the harmful ultraviolet rays from reaching the earth. It has been proved that chlorofluorocarbons or CFCs are released from the refrigeration system, air conditioning systems, spray cans etc. These CFCs are lighter than air and are able to reach at height of stratosphere. Here they react with the sunlight. In this process, the chlorine gas is released which reacts with the ozone gas. It breaks apart the ozone molecules thus reducing them in the stratosphere. As a result, the ultraviolet radiation is able to reach the surface of earth. These rays can cause skin cancer, cataract and affect the immune system of the body.

24. Is ozone depletion related to global warming ?

Ans. Ozone depletion and global warming are separate problems, though some agents contribute to both. Chlorofluorocarbons (CFCs) are the principle cause of ozone depletion, but they also happen to be potent heat-trapping gases. Still, CFCs are responsible for less than 10 per cent of total atmospheric warming, far less than the 63 per cent contribution of carbon dioxide. Thus, attention paid to CFCs has been on their ozone depletion role. This will change as CFCs are phased out and replaced by hydro chlorofluorocarbons (HCFCs) and hydro fluorocarbons (HFCs such as R-134a). These chemicals have little or no effect on the ozone layer but are strong heat-trapping gases. As their concentration in the atmosphere is already rising, the likely net effect in the future is that reductions in the CFC-related contribution to global warming will be offset by the presence of HCFCs and HFCs.

25. What is the difference between stratospheric and ground level ozone ?

Ans. Stratospheric ozone or good ozone is a layer surrounding the earth's atmosphere. It protects all life on earth from the damaging effects of the sun's rays. Ground level ozone is formed by a photochemical reaction between atmospheric oxygen (O_2) and smog forming chemicals at the earth's surface. Ground level ozone is odourless and colourless, but can have profound effects on the human respiratory system.

26. What is greenhouse effect and how is it caused ?

Ans. Carbon dioxide gas is released into the atmosphere in a large quantity. Excessive release of carbon dioxide leads to greenhouse effect that increases the average temperature of earth. It is also referred to as the global warming. Amount of carbon dioxide has increased by 28% in the last one hundred years which is attributed to burning of fossil fuels like coal, gas and oil.

27. What are the effects of global warming ?

Ans. Effects of global warming are :

    (i)   The increase in temperature will be uniform all over the surface of the world. There will be serious climatic changes. This will bring various changes in wind and rain pattern.

    (ii)   Higher temperature will cause rise in transpiration. This in turn, will affect the groundwater table.

    (iii)   As the climatic belts shift from equator towards pole, the vegetation would also shift away from the equator.

(iv) Insects and pests will increase in the warmer climatic conditions. Thus, pathogenic diseases will multiply.

28. Give a short description about Swachh Bharat Abhiyan.

Ans. Swachh Bharat Abhiyan is a national level campaign that aims to clean the streets, roads and infrastructure throughout the length and breadth of the country. This campaign was officially launched on 2 October, 2014 at Raj Ghat, New Delhi, by Prime Minister Narendra Modi. The campaign aims to achieve the vision of a 'Clean India' by 2 October, 2019.

29. What is social forestry ? How does it help to prevent pollution ?

Ans. Social forestry means management and protection of forests and afforesting trees in barren and deforested areas. The aim of social forestry is to plant several trees in private wastelands. It is a multifaceted solution for several pollution problems. Social forestry started with NCA (National Commission on Agriculture) in 1976 with an aim of making use of all unused land.

30. What do you understand by Euro Bharat Vehicular Standard ?

Ans. Emission standards specify the maximum output of pollutants from petrol, diesel or gas driven engines used in motor vehicles and other equipments. Emission norms were first introduced in India in 1991 to regulate the level of pollution. These were made more stringent in the later years.

Give Reason | Set 14 |

Chapter 1. Cell Division

1. Mitosis is called the equational division.

Ans. Mitosis is called equational division because during mitosis the cell divides equally into two identical daughter cells.

2. Meiosis is called the reduction division.

Ans. The meiosis is called reduction cell division because the chromosome number in the four daughter cells formed is reduced from diploid to haploid.

3. Gametes must be produced by meiosis for sexual reproduction.

Ans. The number of chromosomes in sex cell is halved so when the male and female sex cells unite, the embryo will get diploid number of chromosomes. Also, meiosis causes variation in offspring.

4. Chromosomes are the carriers of heredity.

Ans. The chromosomes contain gene which carry genetic information to the offsprings.

Chapter 2. Fundamentals of Genetics

1. Law of independent assortment holds good for the gene pairs that occur in different pairs of chromosomes.

Ans. It is chromosome and not the individual gene which segregates during gamete formation.

2. Heritable variations are called genetic variations.

Ans. Because these variations arise due to change in the genetic material of gametes.

3. Discontinuous variations are inheritable.

Ans. Because they are produced by the effects of environment.

4. X-linked recessive diseases are more common among males than in females.

Ans. Because females have two copies of the X-chromosome so if one X-chromosome is recessive, its effect can be suppressed by other X-chromosome but males have only one X-chromosome and if this chromosome is recessive, its effect cannot be suppressed by Y-chromosome.

5. In honey bees, female is diploid and male is haploid.

Ans. Because in honey bees, females develop from fertilized eggs which are diploid and males develop from unfertilized eggs which are haploid.

6. Haemophilia shows criss-cross inheritance.

Ans. The gene that causes haemophilia is recessive and lies in the X-chromosomes.

Chapter 3. Absorption by Roots

1. Potato cubes when placed in water become firm and increase in size.

Ans. Cell sap inside potato cubes is a hypertonic medium, so when these cubes are placed in water, water enters inside potato cubes by endosmosis making them firm and their size also increases.

2. Salt and sugar are used in preserving food.

Ans. Salt and sugar increase concentration of food, thus destroying bacteria by plasmolysis.

3. On sprinkling common salt on grass growing in a lawn, the grass is killed.

Ans. Sprinkling salt makes soil solution hypertonic hence grass loses water due to exosmosis.

4. The raisins swell up in water.

Ans. The raisins are dry grapes. When these are kept in water, water enters into the raisins by osmosis (endosmosis) and raisins swell up.

5. We gargle with saline water in case of throat infection.

Ans. The salt solution (saline water) is hypertonic and when we gargle with it, it comes in contact of infection causing bacteria in the throat. The water present in the bacterial cell comes out causing plasmolysis and they get killed, thus giving us relief from infection.

6. The leaves of wilted lettuce, if kept in cold water, become crisp.

Ans. The leaves of wilted lettuce are plasmolysed which when kept in the water get deplasmolysed and become turgid. Hence the leaves become crisp.

7. Bacteria and fungi do not grow in pickles, jams, jellies and squashes, etc.

Ans. Pickles, jams, jellies and squashes are kept in hypertonic solution of sugar or salt which causes the plasmolysis of bacteria and fungi. So, they cannot grow in such an unfavourable environment.

8. Fresh water fish cannot survive in sea water.

Ans. The sea water is saline (having more concentration of salts) and acts as hypertonic solution for the fresh water. So fresh water fish cannot survive in sea water as it causes the plasmolysis of the cells of the fish and ultimately the fish will die.

9. A closed can of dried seeds bursts open if some water enters it by accident.

Ans. If some water enters in a closed can of dried seeds, the seeds absorb water by imbibition and osmosis and will swell up. The swelling up of seeds exerts a force on the walls of the can, and hence the can bursts open.

10. Drops of water on a leaf of plant like peepal does not enter the leaf by osmosis.

Ans. Due to the presence of cuticle, which does not allow water molecules to pass through it.

11. Plants growing in fertilized soil are often found to wilt, if the soil is not adequately watered.

Ans. If the soil is fertilized and not watered properly, then the concentration of soil becomes high. As a result, soil becomes hypertonic as compared to the root cells of the plant, so exosmosis takes place which may result in wilting of plants.

12. Plants begin to die when excess of soluble fertilizers are added to the soil.

Ans. Excess application of soluble fertilizers in the soil makes the soil solution hypertonic as compared to the cell sap of the roots of the plant. Hence, exosmosis takes place and plants begin to die.

13. Root hairs become flaccid and droop when excess fertilizers are added to the moist soil around them.*

Ans. When excess fertilizers are added to moist soil, solute concentration increases, making the soil a hypertonic solution, in turn outward flow of water occurs from root hair cells causing plasmolysis of cell. Hence root hairs become flaccid and droop down.

Chapter 4. Transpiration

1. Transplanting of seedlings to flower bed in the evening is better than doing so in the morning.

Ans. During day time transpiration rate is very high. As a result, the seedling will wilt and ultimately die. However in the evening, transpiration rate is very slow so the seedling will be able to retain the water absorbed from the soil and as a result of this, they will remain healthy.

2. Land plants die if their roots remain water logged.

Ans. Older portions of the root do not have root hairs. They are covered with a protective layer of dead calls having tiny openings called lenticels. Through these lenticels, gaseous exchange occurs between the soil and inner living cells. If the roots of land plants remain water logged, then lenticels will not be able to do gaseous exchange and as a result of this, plants will die.

3. Young plants wilt on a hot sunny day.

Ans. On a hot sunny day, the rate of transpiration exceeds the rate of water absorption by roots. As a result of this, leaves collapse and plant wilts.

---

* Frequently asked previous years Board Exam Questions.

4. Plants absorb more water than their requirement.

Ans. The plants absorb much more water than their requirement because :

    (i)   They require more mineral salts for their growth and minerals are present in very small quantity in water.

    (ii)   Most of the water is lost through transpiration. Therefore, to prevent wilting they require excess of water.

5. Balsam plants wilt during mid-day even if the soil is well watered.

Ans. Transpiration rate in such plants is very high during mid-day and exceeds the water absorption rate of the roots. So, more water is lost than absorbed. This water deficiency in cells causes them to lose turgidity and the plants wilt.

6. Forests bring in the rain and transpiration is the cause behind this.

Ans. When water is lost by evaporation (transpiration), heat energy is taken up from the plant body to vapourize the water. The water is then rapidly taken up by the roots and again released into the air through leaves by transpiration. In the air above, the moisture forms clouds and soon falls as rain.

7. Why do some herbaceous plants show wilting of leaves during mid-day which again recover in the evening ?

Ans. During mid-day, the rate of transpiration is maximum. During this time, in some herbaceous plants, the rate of transpiration exceeds the amount of water absorbed. Thus, the leaves lose its turgid state and show wilting but in evening there is no minimum transpiration hence they recover.

8. Guard cells are small in size and are kidney shaped in outline.

Ans. Because of their small size, guard cells are rapidly influenced by turgor changes. Because of their kidney shaped outline, they remain joined at their ends. This concave-convex curvature of the two guard cells can be varied easily and this further facilitates the stomatal pore to open and close easily.

Chapter 5. Photosynthesis

1. All life on earth would come to an end if there were no green plants.

Ans. Green plants manufacture food during the process of photosynthesis and give out oxygen; a life supporting gas for all organisms.

2. Photosynthesis is considered as a process supporting all life on earth.

Ans. This process produces food and releases oxygen, both of which are necessary to maintain life on earth.

3. Chlorophyll is necessary for photosynthesis.

Ans. The chlorophyll traps solar energy and converts it into chemical energy.

4. Chloroplasts are called energy converters.

Ans. Chloroplast contains chlorophyll which traps Solar energy and converts it into Chemical energy.

5. ATP is needed for dark reaction.

Ans. ATP provides energy for dark reaction.

6. Respiration is said to be the reversal of photosynthesis.

Ans. Respiration is a catabolic process while photosynthesis is an anabolic process. During respiration, O_2 is consumed and CO_2 is given out while during photosynthesis, CO_2 is consumed and O_2 is given out.

Chapter 6. Chemical Coordination in Plants

1. Gibberellins can increase the sugar yield.

Ans. Carbohydrate is stored in the form of sugar in the stems of sugarcane. If gibberellins are sprayed over the sugarcane crop, the length of the stems increases and this helps to increase the sugar yield by as much as 20 tons per acre.

2. Gibberellins increase the photosynthetic area.

Ans. The treatment with gibberellins makes the leaves broader and elongated. This increases the photosynthetic area.

3. You can keep green leafy vegetables fresher and greener for a longer duration of time using cytokinins.

Ans. Cytokinins delay the senescence (ageing) of leaves and other organs by controlling protein synthesis and mobilization of resources and thus food substances tend to remain fresher for a longer duration when dipped in cytokinins.

Chapter 7. The Circulatory System

1. Circulatory system is also known as transport system.

Ans. The circulatory system is also known as transport system because it carries various substances from one part of body to another.

2. People have a common belief that the heart is located on the left side of the chest.

Ans. The narrow end of the roughly triangular heart known as the apex is pointed to the left side and during working, the contraction of the heart is most powerful at this end, giving a feeling of the heart being on the left side. Actually it is right in the centre between the two lungs and above the diaphragm.

3. Veins have valves at intervals in their inner lining whereas the arteries do not have valves.

Ans. In arteries, blood flows with pressure but in veins the pressure falls considerably, so the back flow of blood is possible which is prevented by the valves.

4. SA node is called pacemaker of the heart.

Ans. The SA node is called the pacemaker of the heart because the wave of contraction which conducts heartbeat originates in it.

5. It is necessary to know the blood groups before giving transfusion of blood.

Ans. In blood transfusion, it is necessary that the type of blood to be transfused should be matched with the type of blood of the receiving person. Otherwise, the RBCs of the donor blood will stick to each other and block the passage of blood vessels of the receiver, leading to death. Hence, it is necessary to know the blood groups before giving transfusion of blood.

6. Can the blood clot inside the blood vessels ? Give reason in support of your answer.

Ans. The blood inside the blood vessels does not clot because of a chemical "heparin" which is a naturally occurring anticoagulant secreted by basophil cells. Heparin released in blood vessels prevents blood from clotting.

7. The number of leucocytes increases during infection.

Ans. The number of leucocytes increases during infection to fulfil the defence demand of the body.

8. A matured mammalian erythrocyte lacks nucleus and mitochondria.

Ans. Loss of nucleus gives RBCs a biconcave shape thus increasing their surface area volume ratio for absorbing more oxygen. RBCs do not have mitochondria so that they cannot use oxygen for themselves. All oxygen can be efficiently transported without any consumption by RBCs and delivered to the tissues. Thus for their efficient function matured mammalian RBCs lack nucleus and mitochondria.

Chapter 8. The Excretory System

1. All living things must excrete.

Ans. Metabolic activities of all living things produce waste materials. These substances, if accumulate in the body, become poisonous and destroy the vital organs. So excretion is must.

2. Excretion is necessary.

Ans. Excretion is necessary to remove the harmful and toxic substances from the body.

3. It is necessary to maintain a normal osmotic concentration of blood.

Ans. It is necessary to maintain a normal osmotic concentrtion of blood to prevent osmosis in body cells and tissues which would otherwise lead to gain or loss of water by cells and tissues thus resulting in cells and tissues damage.

4. Urine is acidic while blood is alkaline in nature.

Ans. The urine is acidic in nature due to the secretion of acidic chemicals into the glomerular filtrate while blood is alkaline due to reabsorption of alkaline substances from it.

5. As a result of ultrafiltration, along with excretory products certain useful products like glucose, salt etc. are also filtered but are not excreted.

Ans. Glucose, salt etc. in the glomerular filtrate are reabsorbed in the proximal part of renal tubule.

6. Glucose is absent in the urine of a healthy person.

Ans. The glucose is absent in the urine of a healthy person because it is completely reabsorbed from the glomerular filtrate.

7. The urine is slightly thicker in summer than in winter.

Ans. During summer, the water is also lost in the form of sweat from the body hence more water is reabsorbed from the glomerular filtrate to keep the fluid balance in the body. That is why, the urine is slightly thicker in summer than in winter.

8. There is frequent urination in winter than in summer.

Ans. In winter, sweating is less so more water is given out in the form of urine to maintain water balance in the body. Reverse process happens in summer.

Chapter 9. The Nervous System and Sense Organs

1. The spinal cord and brain are called as the central nervous system.

Ans. Because they give rise to all the nerves and control all the actions of the body.

2. Injury to medulla oblongata results in death.

Ans. Medulla oblongata controls involuntary functions like heart beat, rate of respiration, secretion of saliva, gut peristalsis, etc. Injury to the medulla oblongata may result in cessation of heart beat and breathing, thus leading to death.

3. The hand automatically shows the direction to turn a cycle without thinking.

Ans. It is because of conditioned reflex which we learn by experience and gradually respond to it unconsciously.

4. A person after consuming alcohol walks clumsily.

Ans. Alcohol affects the cerebellum which is the center of body balance and co-ordination. Due to the alcohol effect, the cerebellum is unable to co-ordinate muscular movements properly.

5. Deficiency of vitamin A causes night blindness.

Ans. Because the visual purple (Rhodopsin) of the rods, which are responsible for vision in the dark, is not formed in the absence of vitamin A.

6. When you enter into a dark room from bright sunlight, you cannot see things for a few seconds.

Ans. In bright light, the visual purple or rhodopsin pigment is destroyed and the diameter of pupil is reduced to allow the entry of less light which is called dark adaptation.

7. We see objects clearly when their image is formed at the central region of retina.

Ans. The central region of the retina has Fovea Centralis which has high density of cone cells around it. These cone cells are responsible for clear vision and details of the objects.

8. Older people require glasses to read and write.

Ans. In old age, the flexibility of the lens declines and it become less convex or opaque leading to weakness of eye sight.

Chapter 10. The Endocrine System

1. Hormones are called 'chemical messengers'.

Ans. The hormones are chemical substances that are carried to all the parts of the body through blood circulation to bring about the harmonious working of the body. So, they are called chemical messengers.

2. Organs like the stomach and intestine are also endocrine glands.

Ans. The mucous lining of the stomach and intestine produce certain hormones which regulate the secretion and flow of certain digestive juices. So these are endocrine glands.

3. Goitre is usually observed in people living in hilly regions.

Ans. The soil and water in hilly regions is deficient in iodine. Hence goitre is usually observed in people living in hilly regions.

4. The thymus is larger and more prominent in children than in adults.

Ans. The thymus gland is supposed to stimulate growth and provide immunity in children. Hence it is larger and more prominent in children than in adults.

5. Pancreas is both an exocrine gland and an endocrine gland.

Ans. Pancreas is a heterocrine or myxocrine gland, as it contains two types of secretary structures, *i.e.,* (i) Islet of Langerhans which secrete hormones insulin and glucagon, and these are transported by way of blood, and (ii) Acini that secretes pancreatic juice which is transported by way of ducts.

6. Insulin is injected into the body of a highly diabetic patient and not given orally.

Ans. Insulin is a protein hormone and if it is given orally, it would be acted upon by the protein digesting enzymes in the alimentary tract. So it is injected into the body of highly diabetic patient and is able to travel in the blood stream to bring about the required, specific effect.

7. The pituitary is called the master gland.

Ans. The hormones of pituitary gland regulate the activities of the body and other endocrine glands. Hence, it is called master gland.

8. Adrenaline is also known as emergency hormone.

Ans. Adrenaline is secreted at the time of emergency (stress or strain) and prepares the body to fight or flight. So, it is also known as emergency hormone.

9. Our hair stand on their ends during fear.

Ans. During fear, adrenal medulla secretes adrenaline which prepares the body to face fear by increasing heartbeat, blood pressure and energy production. It is also responsible for goosebumps which makes our hair stand on their ends.

10. Some adult women may develop facial hairs.

Ans. If there is an overgrowth of the adrenal cortex in an adult woman, she develops facial hairs. This condition is known as adrenal virilism.

11. The release of progesterone in the urine is an indication of pregnancy.

Ans. Because progesterone brings about changes in the uterus for the retention and growth of pregnancy.

Chapter 11. The Reproductive System

1. Gametes have a haploid (n) number of chromosomes.

Ans. The gametes take part in fertilization and after fertilization form the zygote in which the number of chromosomes is doubled. Hence, to maintain a constant number of chromosomes in a species, the gametes have haploid number of chromosomes.

2. Urethra is also called urogenital duct.

Ans. Since the urethra carries both urine and semen in males, it is called urogenital duct.

3. At the time of birth, the testes descend into the scrotal sacs.

Ans. In human beings (mammals), the temperature required for the production and survival of sperms is lower than that of the normal body temperature. Hence, to provide a suitable temperature that is about 2–3°C lower than that of normal body temperature, the testes descend into the scrotal sac at the time of birth.

4. Missing of menses is the first indication of pregnancy.

Ans. Because the endometrium of uterus along with the unfertilized egg is given out in the form of menstrual flow.

5. The chances of pregnancy to occur are most favourable on or about the 14th day of the menstrual cycle.

Ans. The chances of pregnancy to occur are most favourable on or about the 14th day of the menstrual cycle because ovulation occurs on the 14th day and the egg so released remains viable for one to two days.

6. The oviduct funnel is lined with cilia.

Ans. The ovum is non-motile and inactive female gamete and is released into the abdominal cavity. So, to pick up and push the ovum into the uterus, the oviduct funnel is lined with cilia.

7. Most often only one embryo is formed at a time although there are two ovaries in women.

Ans. One ovum under the influence of hormones is released alternatively every month.

8. The acrosome of sperm secretes an enzyme called hyaluronidase at the time of fertilization.

Ans. This enzyme dissolves the membranous covering of the ovum to facilitate the entry of sperm into the ovum.

9. A large number of sperms are required for fertilizing one egg.

Ans. The ovum does not exert any distant chemical attraction over the sperms. Hence, to ensure that sperms reach every part of the female reproductive tract so that at least one sperm becomes available to ovum for its fertilization, large number of sperms are required.

10. Millions of sperms are produced at ejaculation yet one sperm actually fertilizes the ovum.

Ans. Only one ovum is released at a time in the human female during ovulation. Although millions of sperms are ejaculated, only one sperm is enough to fertilize the single ovum. This arrangement is to control and maintain the growth rate of human population. The ovum secretes a protective wall that prevents the entry of other sperms.

11. The fully grown human embryo respires but does not breathe.

Ans. The fully grown human embryo respires because the dissolved oxygen in the mother's blood diffuses into the embryo and is used in the oxidation of glucose in the cells with the liberation of energy. However, there are no breathing movements as the lungs lie collapsed in the embryo and only function after the foetus is expelled out from the mother's body.

Chapter 12. Human Population

1. Birth rate is high in India.

Ans. (i) Most of rural population which forms the bulk of our society are illiterate, ignorant and superstitious.

(ii) Children are considered to be the helping hand to increase the family income.

2. There is a stability or a decline in the population of developed countries.

Ans. In developed countries, both death-rate and birth-rate are low due to better medical facilities and family planning methods.

3. Medical discoveries such as antibiotics and vaccinations have indirectly contributed to the sharp rise in human population in the present century.

Ans. Medical discoveries such as antibiotics and vaccinations have resulted in the decrease of death rate resulting in a corresponding rise in growth rate which leads to an increase in population.

Chapter 13. Human Evolution

1. *Australopithecus* was a human ancestor.

Ans. *Australopithecus* is considered to be the human ancestor as it showed the following man like features.

(i) Erect or semi-erect posture.

(ii) Bipedal locomotion that helped them in hunting.

(iii) Distinct lumbar curve in the vertebral column.

(iv) They used weapons and stones.

(v) Canines did not project beyond other teeth.

2. Cro-Magnon man is considered to be very near to modern humans.

Ans. Cro-Magnon man is considered to be very near to modern humans because they showed the following features :

(i)   They had a long stature (1.8 meteres long), well built body and an erect posture.

(ii) The cranial cavity was increased to 1660 cc.

(iii) The chin became prominent and the nose got elevated.

(iv) The distribution of hair resembles that of the modern man.

3. Natural selection explains the evolution of giraffes.

Ans. Giraffes with long neck and forelimbs were better adapted to the environment as the climatic change had removed the grass lands and replaced them with trees and shrubs. Natural selection had acted in favour of these long necked individuals for many generations. This led to the evolution of the modern-day giraffes.

4. Peppered Moths explain the phenomenon of survival of the fittest.

Ans. The body colour of the peppered moth, *Biston betularia* is a genetic trait and various alleles of this gene exhibit different shades of body colour. Prior to the industrial revolution in England, the population of white peppered moth was higher, as they were well adapted to protect themselves from predatory birds. During this period, light coloured lichens covered the trunks of the oak trees and moths rested on the lichens during the day time. Gradually, with industrial revolution, the black coloured moth increased in number and white coloured moth got killed. Industrial revolution had brought a great environmental change. It increased the deposition of soot and smoke particles on the tree trunks. The lichens died as they could not survive the soot and smoke. The white peppered moth lost their hiding places and were exposed to predators like birds as they were now clearly visible in the day time. A dominant gene mutation appeared in some members of white-winged *Biston betularia*. This mutation resulted in the origin of dark-winged melanic moth or black coloured moths (a completely new species).

5. There is a co-relation between the position of nectaries in flowers and length of Proboscis of pollinating insects.

Ans. Flowers and insects which pollinate flowers have evolved simultaneously. The co-evolution of these organisms makes them mutually interdependent. This co-evolution can be explained by natural selection.

Chapter 14. Pollution

1. Use of CFCs is banned in some countries.

Ans. The CFCs causes damage to the ozone layer which protects us from the harmful effects of ultraviolet rays present in sunlight. Hence, its use is banned in some countries.

2. It is advised to use electrostatic precipitators in the chimneys.

Ans. Some solid particles (pollutants) are also present in the smoke. Hence, to remove these solid pollutants from smoke, it is advised to use electrostatic precipitators in the chimneys.

3. It is mandatory to take a pollution certificate for the vehicles from the Traffic Police.

Ans. In cities, about 80% of the total air pollution is caused by automobiles (vehicles). Hence, to control air pollution, it is mandatory to take a pollution certificate for the vehicles from the traffic police.

4. Use of pressure horn is prohibited in certain places.

Ans. The pressure horn causes noise pollution which increases blood pressure, disturbs concentration, lowers working capacity and may lead to nervous disorders. Hence, use of pressure horn is prohibited in certain places like near hospitals, schools and residential complexes etc.

5. Carbon monoxide is dangerous when inhaled.*

Ans. Haemoglobin has a very strong affinity for Carbon monoxide and a stable compound called Carboxy-haemoglobin (HbCO) is formed when carbon monoxide is inhaled. It cuts down the capacity of blood to transport oxygen which may lead to death. Hence it is very dangerous to inhale carbon monoxide.

6. Acid rain is harmful to the environment.*

Ans. Acid rain has oxides of nitrogen and sulphur dissolved in it which decreases its pH value thus making it acidic. This damages vegetation, corrodes monuments, statues, buildings etc., and also causes harm to human health, aquatic life and crops and pollutes soil.

---

* Frequently asked previous years Board Exam Questions.

Sketch and Label the Diagram Set 15

Chapter 1. Cell Division

1. Give a labelled diagram to illustrate amitosis.

Ans.

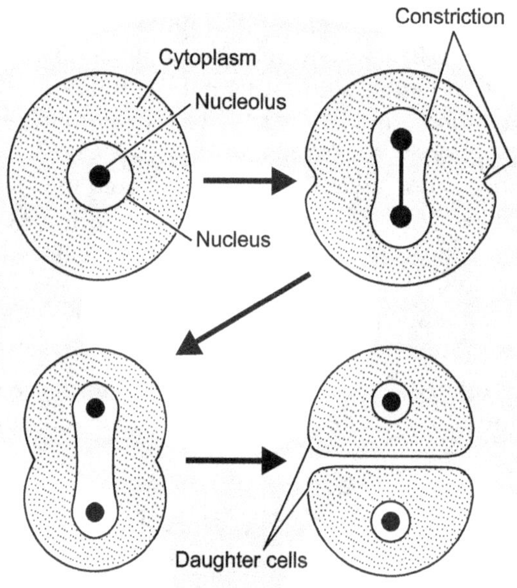

Process of amitosis

2. Draw a labelled schematic representation of mitotic cell division.

Ans.

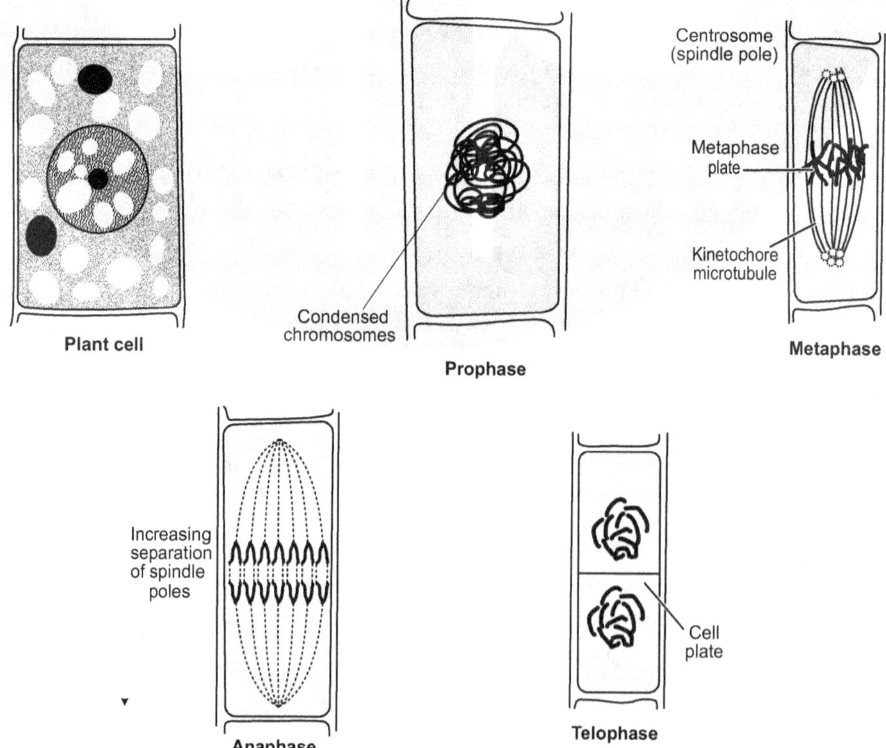

3. Draw a duplicate chromosome and label its part.

Ans.

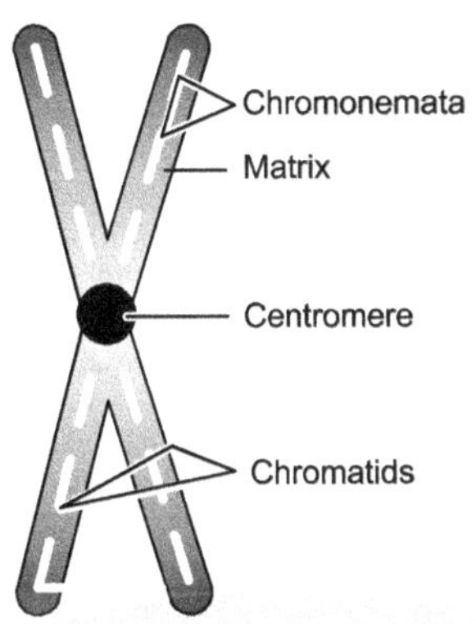

Structure of Chromosome

4. Draw a well labelled diagram to show the anaphase stage of mitosis in a plant cell having four chromosomes.

Ans.

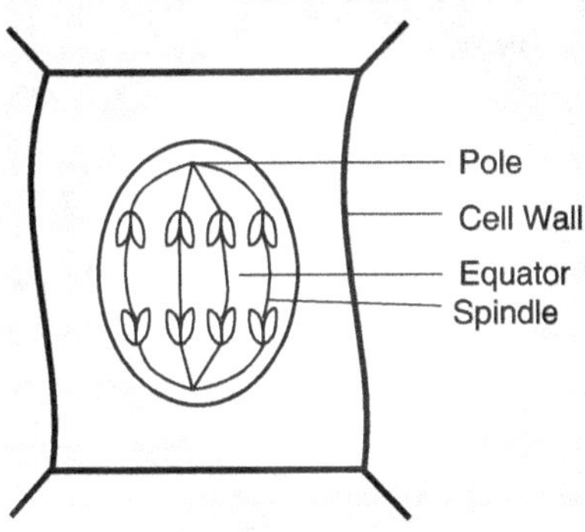

Anaphase of mitosis in plant cell

Chapter 3. Absorption by Roots

1. Give a diagrammatic representation of plasmolysis in a cell.

Ans.

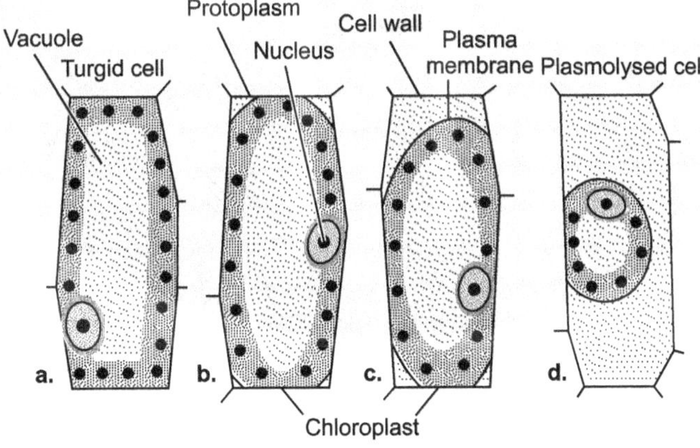

(a) A cell in normal turgid condition; (b) – (d) Successive stages in shrinkage of protoplasm from the cell wall after being placed in a hypertonic solution.
Diagrammatic representation of plasmolysis in a cell

2. Draw a cross-section of root showing association of soil particles with root hairs.

Ans.

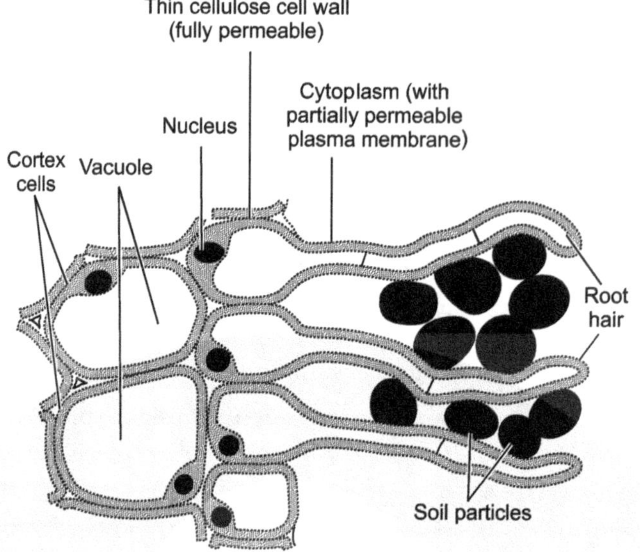

Cross-section of root showing association of soil particles with root hairs

3. Draw a diagram of the root hair cell as it would appear when a concentrated solution of fertilizers is added near it.

Ans.

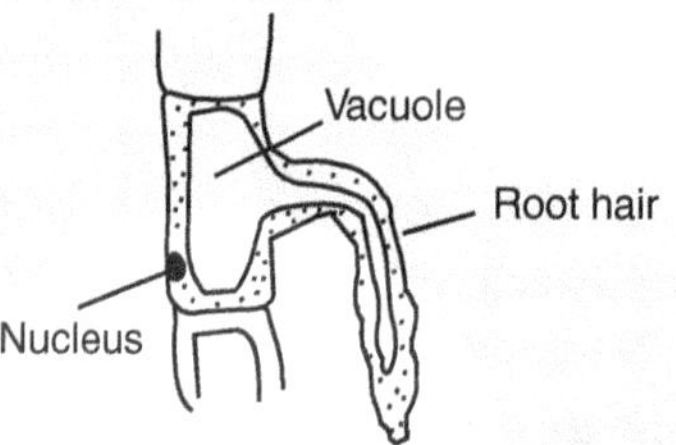

4. A thin strip of epidermal cells of a leaf was observed in a drop of water. They all looked turgid and normal.

(i) Draw a diagram of such a cell.

(ii) Draw a diagram of a cell if this strip is transferred to a strong concentrated solution of sugar. What is term used for the effect on the cells?

Ans. (i)

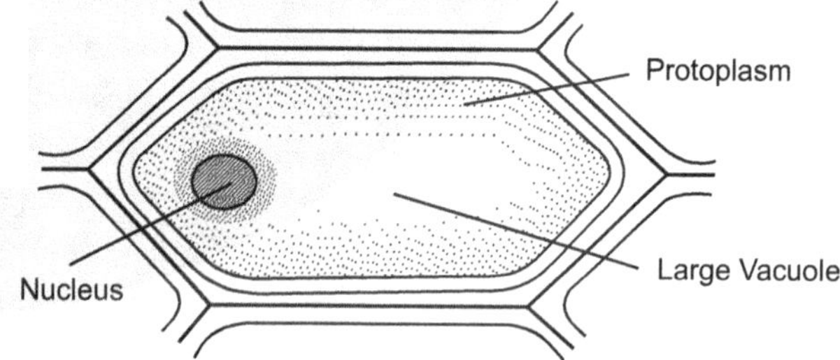

(ii) Plasmolysis.

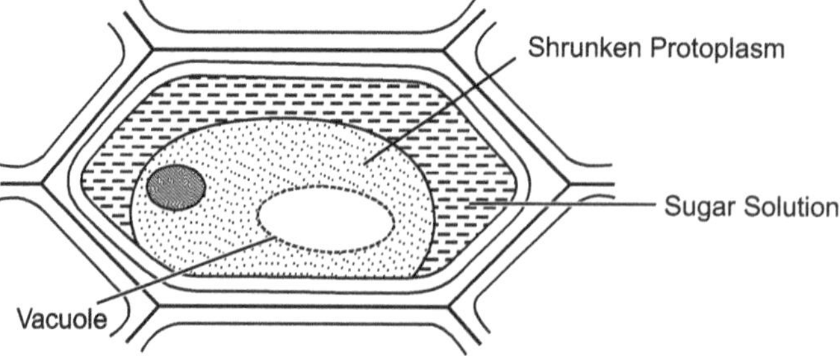

Chapter 4. Transpiration

1. Draw a neat diagram of the stomatal apparatus found in the epidermis of leaves and label the Stoma, Guard cells, Chloroplast, Epidermal Cells, Cell wall and Nucleus.

Ans.

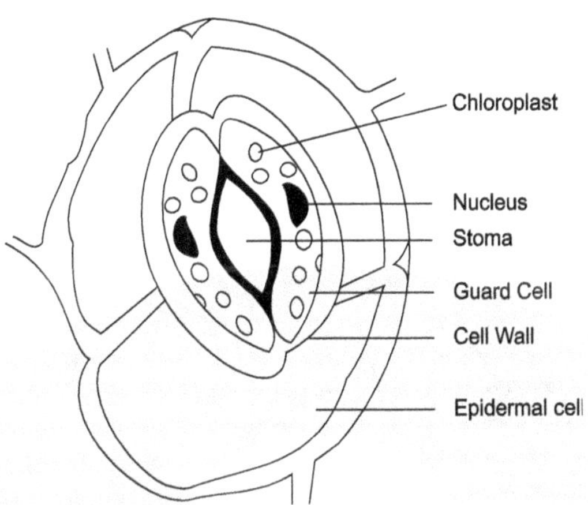

2. The diagram below represents a process in plants.*

The setup was placed in bright sunlight. Answer the following questions :

(i) Name the physiological process depicted in the diagram.

Why was oil added to the water ?

(ii) When placed in bright sunlight for four hours, what do you observe with regard to the initial and final weight of the plant ?

Give a suitable reason for your answer.

(iii) What happens to the level of water when this setup is placed in :

1. Humid conditions ?

2. Windy conditions ?

(iv) Mention any three adaptations found in plants to overcome the process mentioned in (i).

(v) Explain the term 'Guttation'.

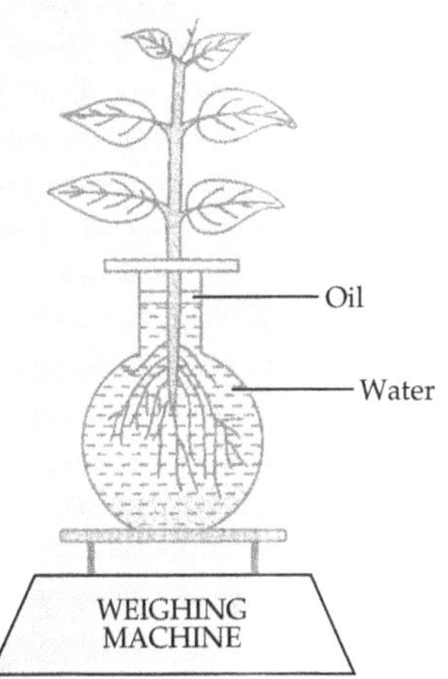

Ans. (i) Absorption of water by roots, Transpiration through leaves.

Oil was added to water to prevent loss of water through evaporation.

(ii) The final weight of the plant will be lesser than its initial weight since the rate of transpiration is more than the rate of absorption of water hence leaves transpire, causing the reduction in the weight of the plant.

(iii) 1. In humid conditions, transpiration rate is very low so level of water in jar will not show much change.

2. On a windy day, transpiration rate increases so level of water in the jar will fall rapidly.

(iv) 1. Sunken stomata

2. Modification of leaves into spines.

3. Presence of thick layer of cuticle on the leaf surface.

(v) Guttation is the process of loss of water in the form of droplets from special openings called hydathodes present on the margins of leaves.

Chapter 5. Photosynthesis

1. Draw a neat and well-labelled diagram of the chloroplast.

Ans.

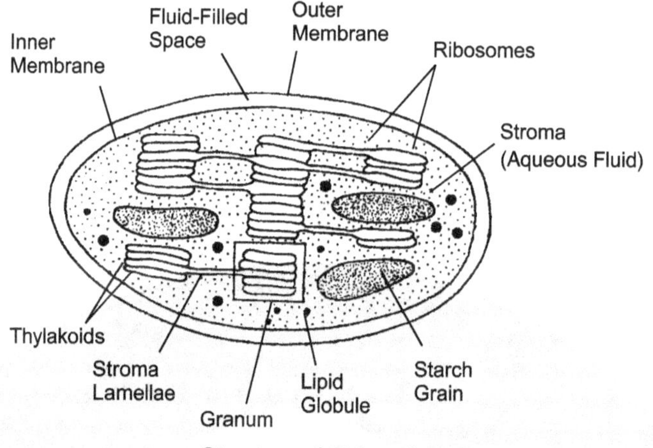

Structure of Chloroplast

2. Draw a neat and well-labelled diagram of the apparatus you would set up to show that oxygen is given out during photosynthesis.

Ans.

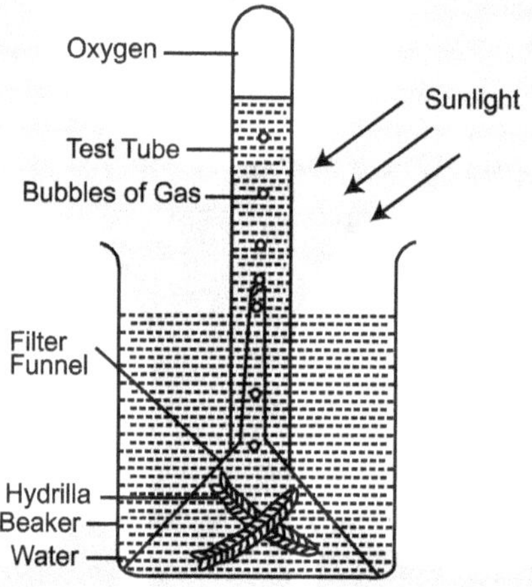

Apparatus to show that Oxygen is evolved out during Photosynthesis

Chapter 7. The Circulatory System

1. Draw a diagram showing external features of heart.

Ans.

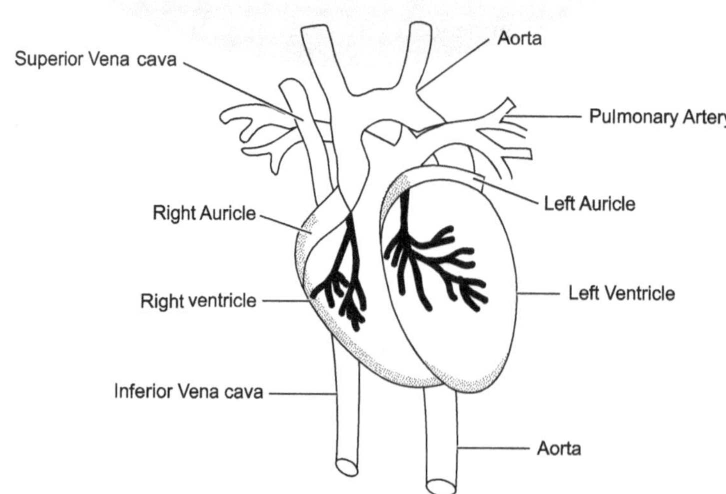

2. Draw a digram showing position of valves in human heart.

Ans.

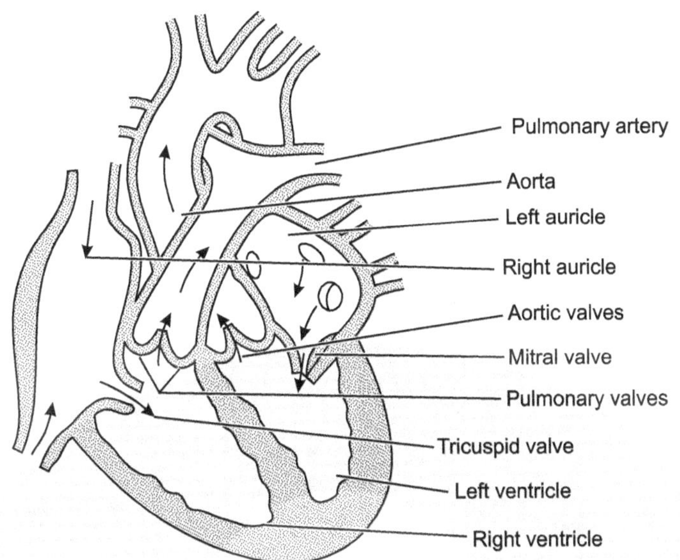

3. Draw well-labelled diagrams of Artery and Superior vena cava to show the structural difference betwween them.

Ans. (i) Artery   (ii) Superior vena cava

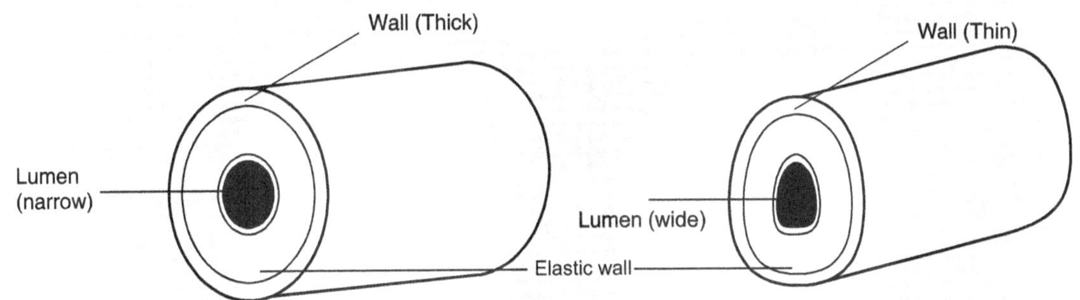

Chapter 8. The Excretory System

1. Draw a labelled diagram of the human kidney as seen in a longitudinal section.

Ans.

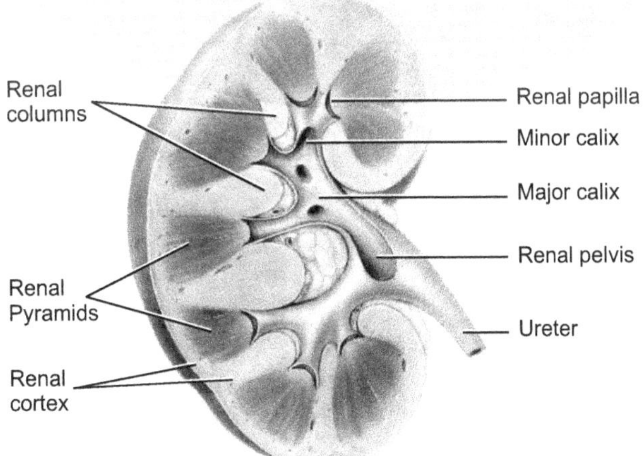

L. S. of Human Kidney

2. Draw a well-labelled diagram of the human excretory system.

Ans.

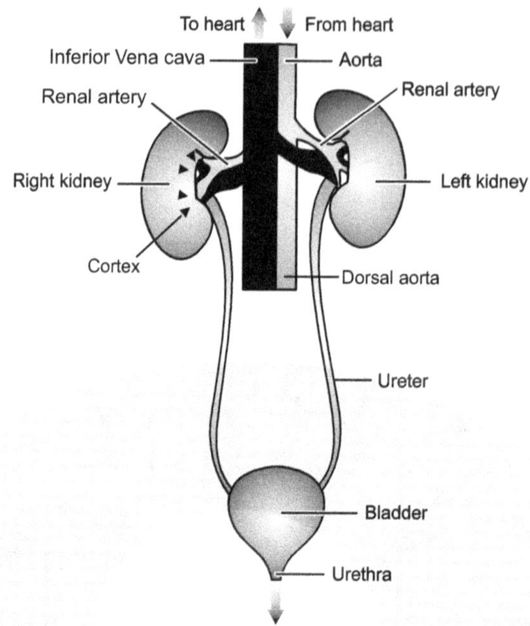

3. Sketch and label the structure of malpighian body.

Ans.

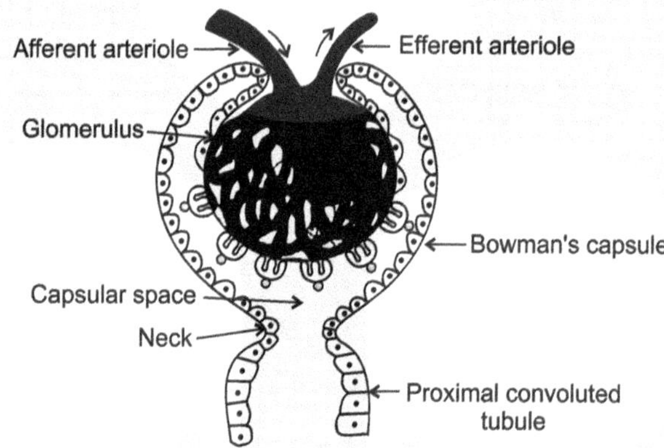

4. Sketch and label the ultrastructure of nephron.

Ans.

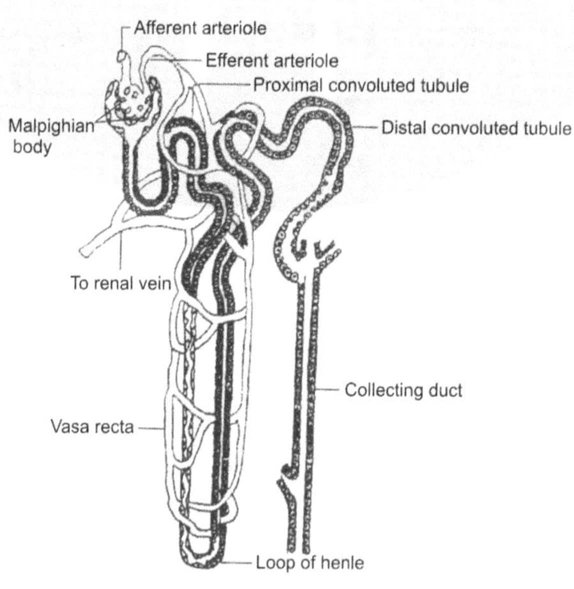

Ultrastructure of Nephron

Chapter 9. The Nervous System and Sense Organs

1. Draw a neat labelled diagram to show how hypermetropia can be rectified.

Ans.

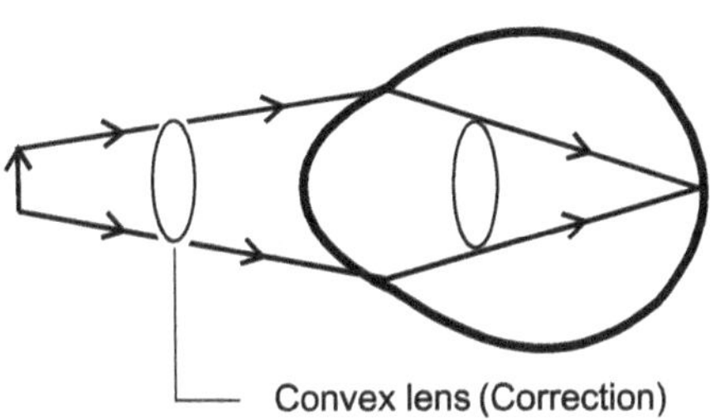

2. Draw well labelled diagram of a 'Neuron' and label the following parts :

  (i) Node of Ranvier   (ii) Nissl's granules   (iii) Cyton

Ans.

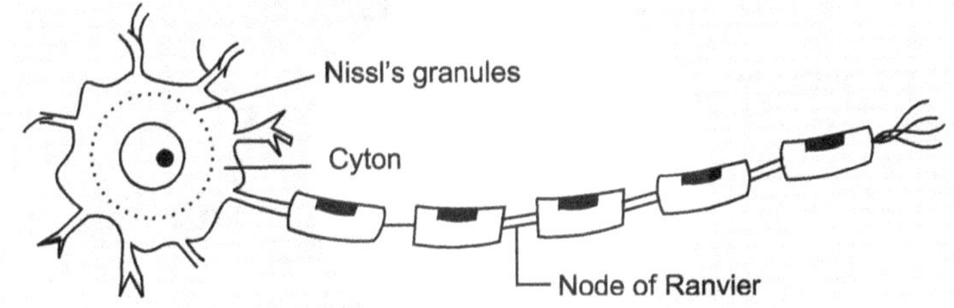

3. Draw a labelled diagram of a the path of conduction of the impulse in the neuron.

Ans.

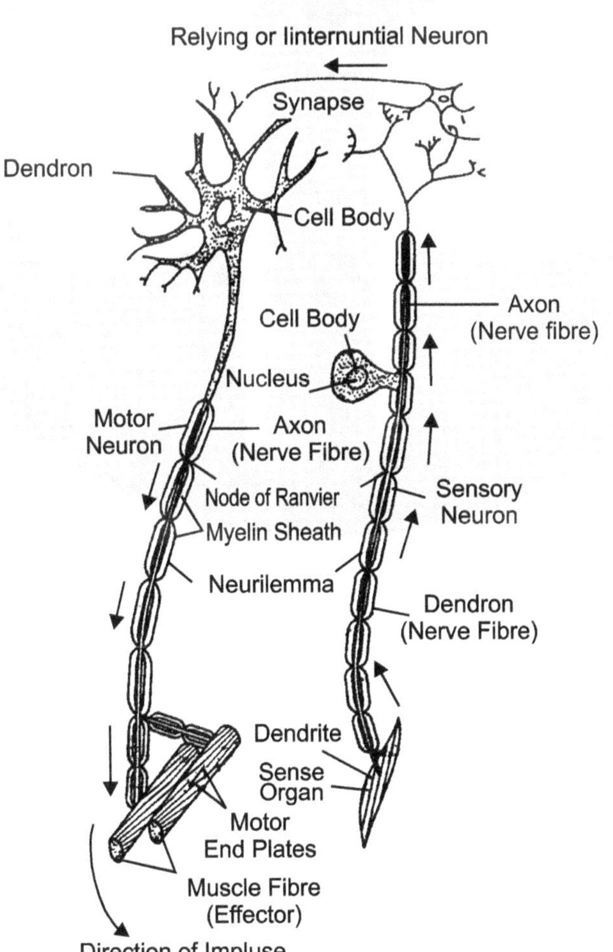

4. Draw a diagram of the human eye as seen in a vertical section and label the parts which suits the following descriptions relating to the :

(i)   photosensitive layer of the eye.

(ii) structure which is responsible for holding the eye lens in its position.

(iii) structure which maintains the shape of the eye ball and the area of no vision.

(iv) anterior chamber seen in front of the eye lens.

(v)   outermost transparent layer seen in front of the eye ball.

Ans.

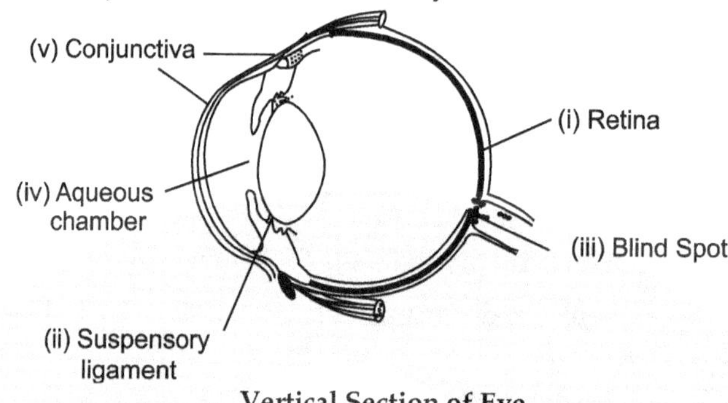

Vertical Section of Eye

5. Draw a labelled diagram of the front view of human eye.

Ans.

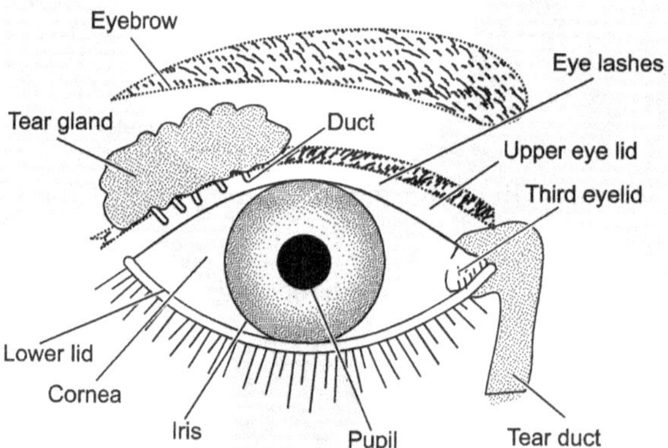

6. Draw a labelled diagram of the ear. Name the part of the ear that is responsible for static balance in human beings.

Ans.

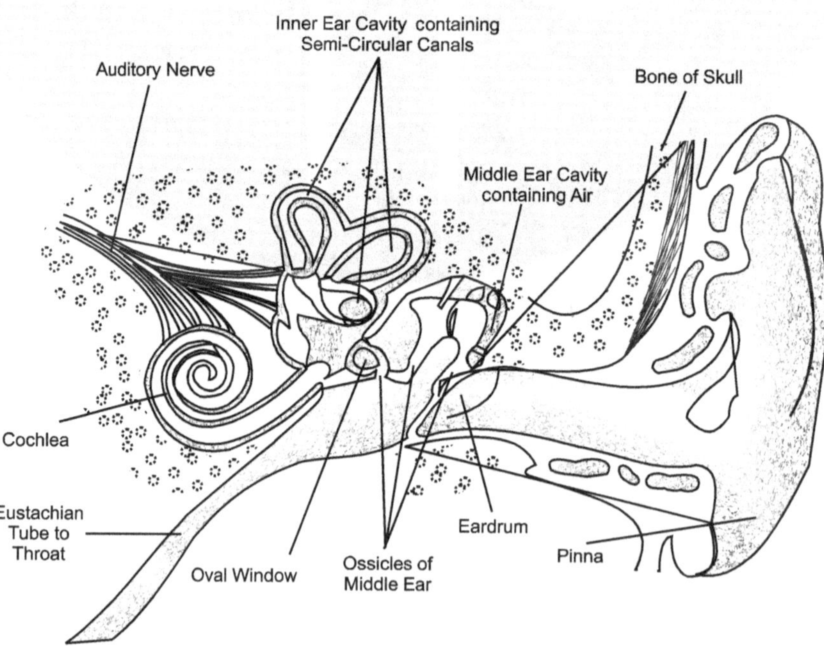

The static balance in the ear of human beings is achieved by the gravity receptors located in the utriculus and sacculus in the inner ear.

Chapter 10. The Endocrine System

1. Sketch and label the V. S. of pituitary gland.

Ans.

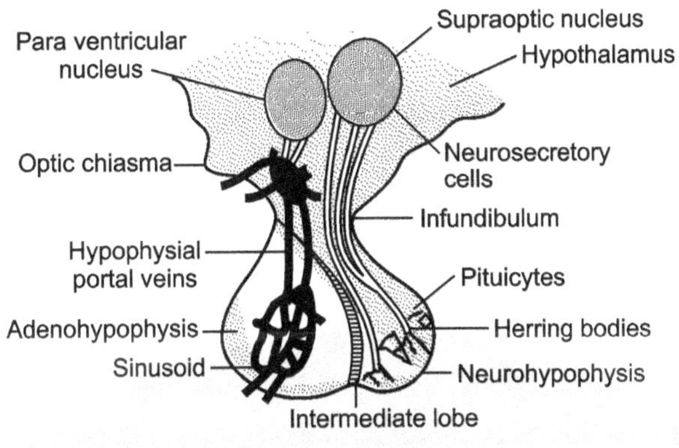

V. S. Pituitary gland

2. Draw and label the structure of thyroid gland.

Ans.

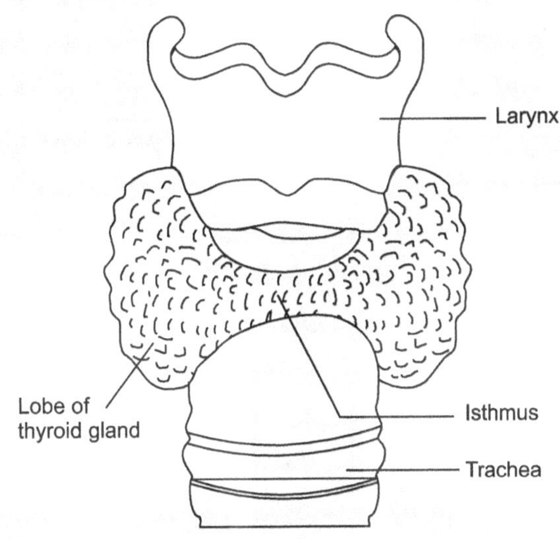

Thyroid gland

3. Give a labelled diagram of parathyroid gland.

Ans.

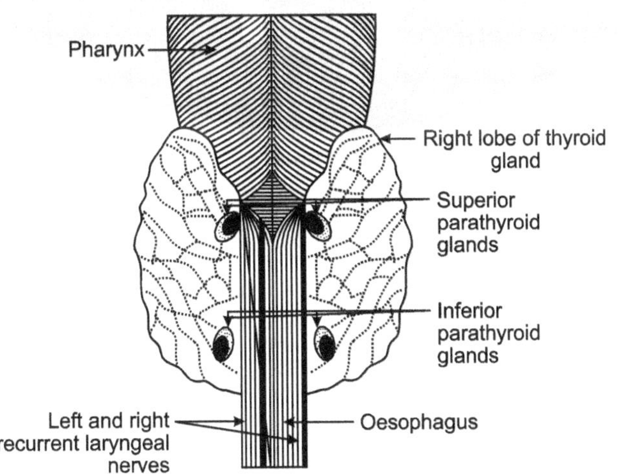

Parathyroid gland

4. Sketch and label the structure of adrenal gland.

Ans.

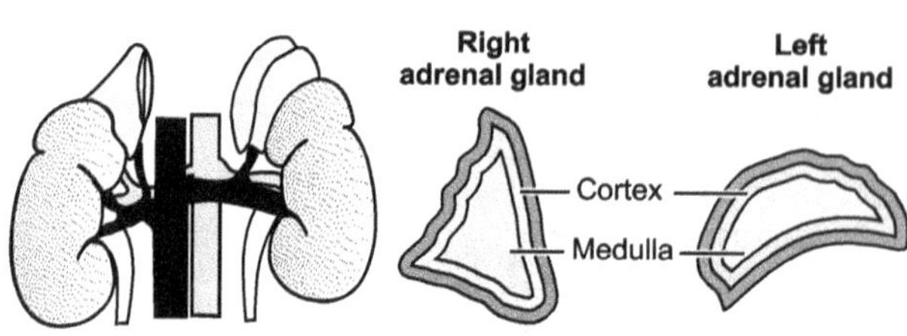

5. Give a labelled diagram of thymus gland.

Ans.

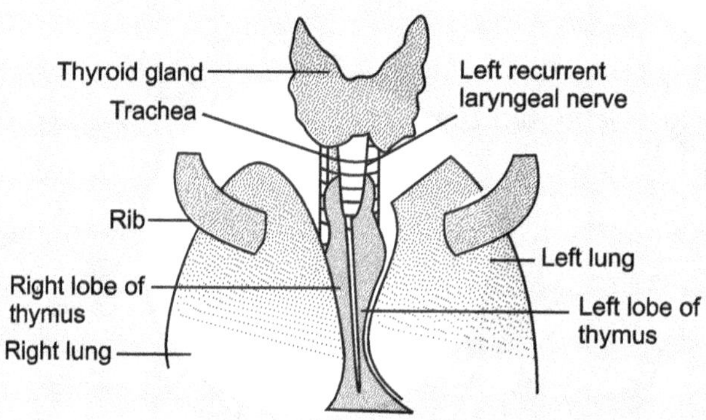

Chapter 11. The Reproductive System

1. Draw a labelled diagram of sperm.

Ans.

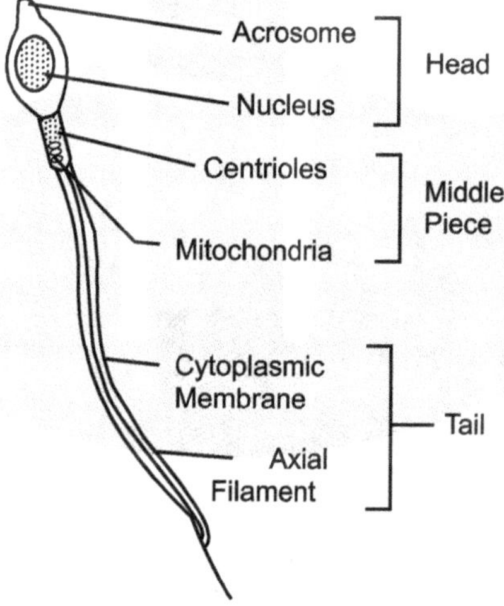

2. Sketch and label the human male reproductive system.

Ans.

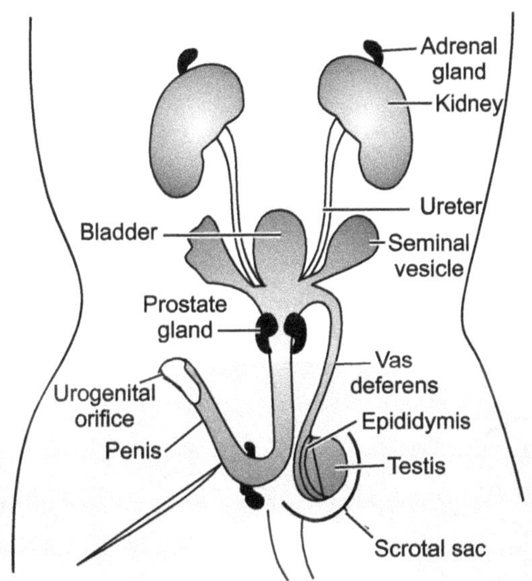

3. Draw a labelled diagram of human female reproductive system.

Ans.

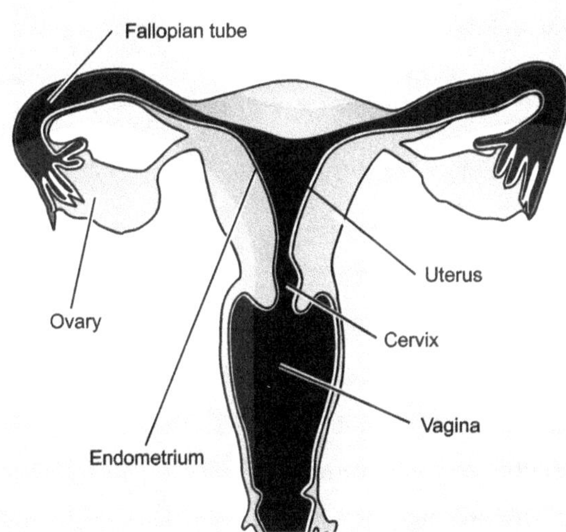

4. Give a labelled structure of ovum.

Ans.

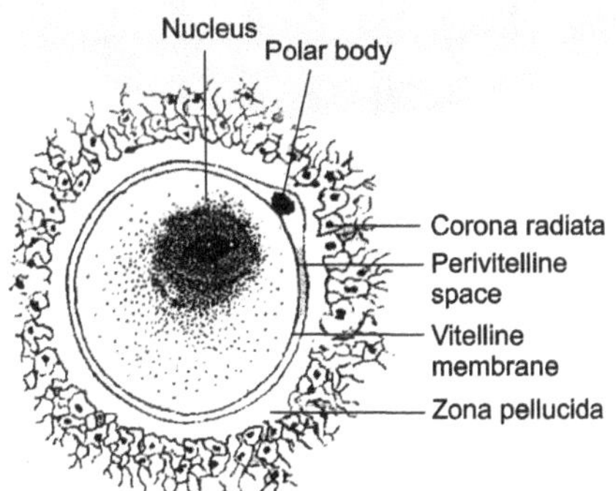

Structure of ovum (unfertilized)

Chapter 1. Cell Division

1. Identify the stages of mitosis given below and label the figures.

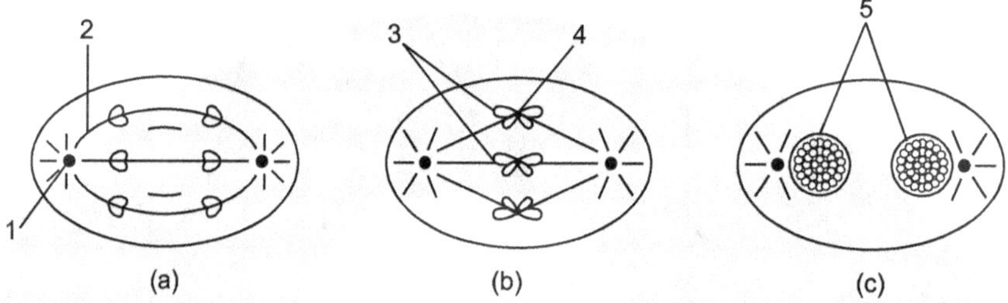

Ans. (a) Anaphase, (b) Metaphase, (c) Telophase.

1. Centrosome, 2. Spindle fibres, 3. Chromosomes, 4. Centromere, 5. Daughter nuclei.

2. Identify the stages of meiosis given below.

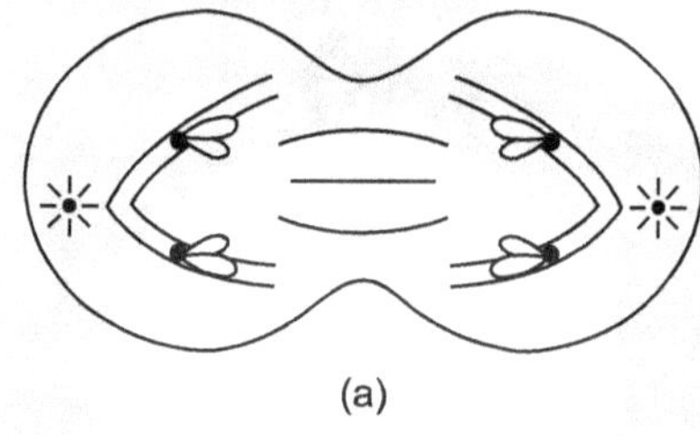
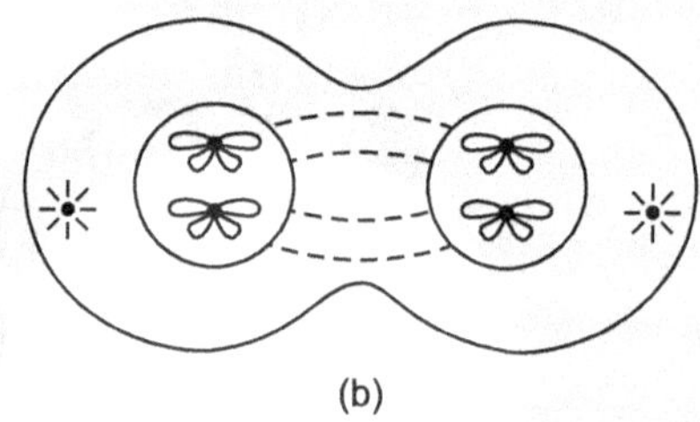

Ans. (a) Anaphase I, (b) Telophase I.

3. The diagram given below represents a stage during cell division.*

Study the same and answer the questions that follow :

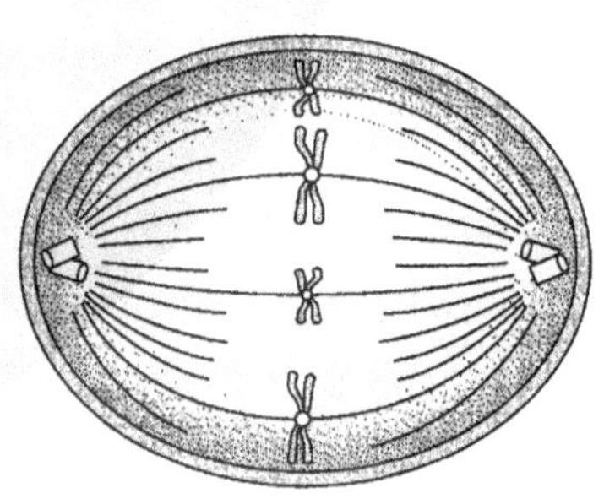

(i)   Identify whether it is a plant cell or an animal cell.

Give a reason in support of your answer.

(ii)   Name the stage depicted in the diagram.

What is the unique feature observed in this stage ?

(iii) Name the type of cell division that occurs during :

1. Replacement of old leaves by new ones.

2. Formation of gametes.

(iv) What is the stage that comes before the stage shown in the diagram ?

(v)   Draw a neat, labelled diagram of the stage mentioned in.

(iv) above keeping the chromosome number constant.

Ans. (i)   It is an animal cell as centrioles are present.

(ii)   Metaphase of mitosis

All the duplicated chromosomes are aligned on the equatorial plane and the chromosomes are attached to the spindle fibres through centromere.

(iii) 1. Mitosis   2. Meiosis

(iv) Prophase

(v)

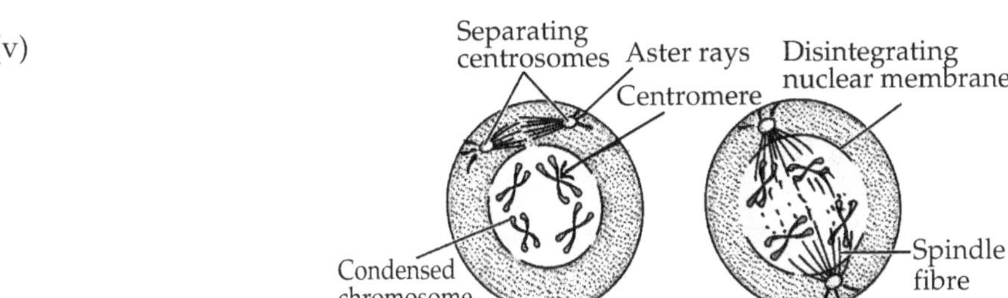

4. The diagram given alongside represents a certain stage of a cell.

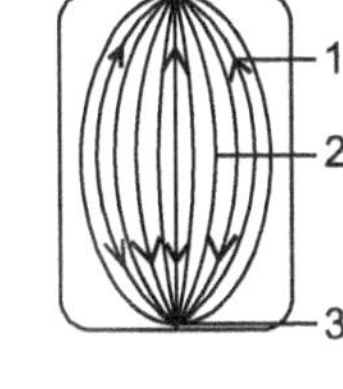

   (i) Is it an animal cell or a plant cell? Give one reason in support of your answer.

   (ii) Label the parts numbered 1–3.

   (iii) Which stage (phase) of mitosis is represented in this diagram?

Ans. (i) It is a plant cell because it has cell wall.

   (ii) 1. Chromatids　　　　　2. Spindle fibres　　　　　3. Pole.

   (iii) Anaphase.

5. (i) Draw a neat labelled diagram to show the metaphase stage of mitosis in an animal cell having '6' chromosome.

   (ii) How many daughter cells are formed at the end of mitosis and at the end of meiosis?

   (iii) With reference to cell division explain the following terms :

   Chromatid , Centromere, Haploid.

   (iv) Name the type of cell division that occurs during :

   1. Growth of shoot　　　　　　3. Repair of worn out tissues.

   2. Formation of pollen grains

Ans. (i) See diagram.

   (ii) **Mitosis :** Two daughter cells.

   Meiosis : Four daughter cells.

   (iii) **Chromatid :** Duplicated chromosomes consist of two identical strands, each of these is called a chromatid.

   Centromere : It is the point at which the two chromatids remain attached. It is also the point of attachment for spindles.

   Haploid : A cell having only one set of chromosomes is called haploid.

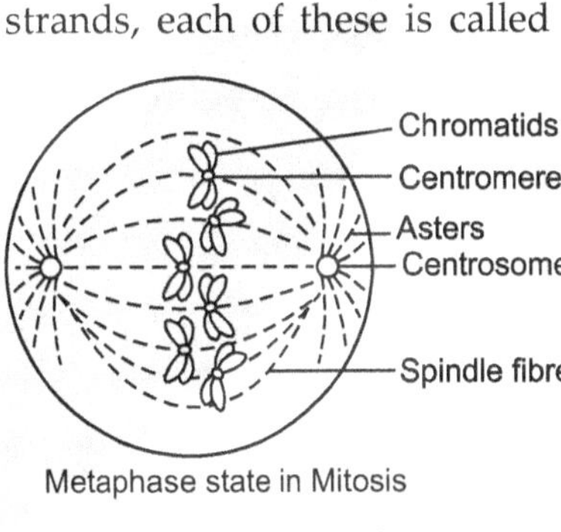

   (iv) 1. Mitosis

   2. Meiosis

   3. Mitosis

6. The diagram below represents a stage during cell division. Study the same and then answer the questions that follow :

   (i) Name the parts labelled 1, 2 and 3.

   (ii) Identify the above stage and give a reason to support your answer.

   (iii) Mention where in the body this type of cell division occurs.

   (iv) Name the stage prior to this stage and draw a diagram to represent the same.

Ans. (i) 1. Centrosome

   2. Spindle fibres

   3. Chromatid

   (ii) **Anaphase**—Sister chromatids get separated and the daughter chromosomes are reaching to the opposite poles of the cell.

   (iii) In the somatic cells of the body.

   (iv) Metaphase

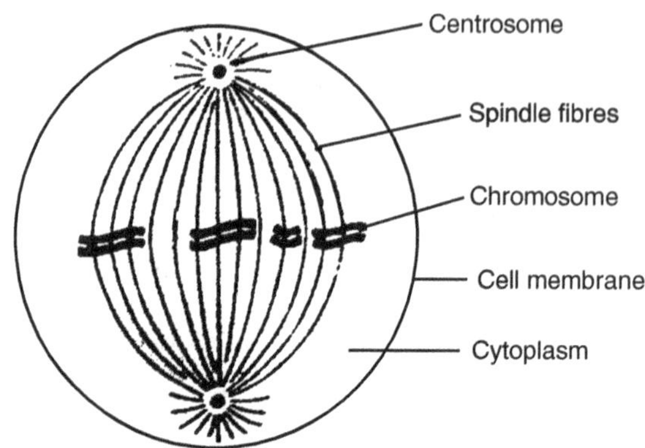

7. Given alongside is a diagram representing a stage during mitotic cell division. Study it carefully and answer the questions that follow :

(i)   Is it a plant cell or an animal cell? Give a reason to support your answer.

(ii) Identify the stage shown.

(iii) Name the stage that follows the one shown here. How is that stage identified?

(iv) How will you differentiate between mitosis and meiosis on the basis of the chromosome number in the daughter cells?

Ans. (i)   It is plant cell, because centrosome is absent and spindle apparatus is not connected to it.

(ii) Prophase.

(iii) Metaphase. In this stage, the chromosome lies in one plane at equator and gets attached to a spindle fibre by its centromere.

(iv) **Mitosis** : Same diploid number of chromosomes are present in the daughter cells.

  Meiosis : Haploid number of chromosomes are present in the daughter cells.

8. The figure alongside shows a certain stage of mitosis :

(i)   Name the stage.

(ii) Label the part 1-4.

(iii) How many chromosomes are shown here?

Ans. (i)   Metaphase

(ii) 1. Chromatid

  2. Centromere

  3. Centriole

  4. Spindle fibre

(iii) 43 chromosomes

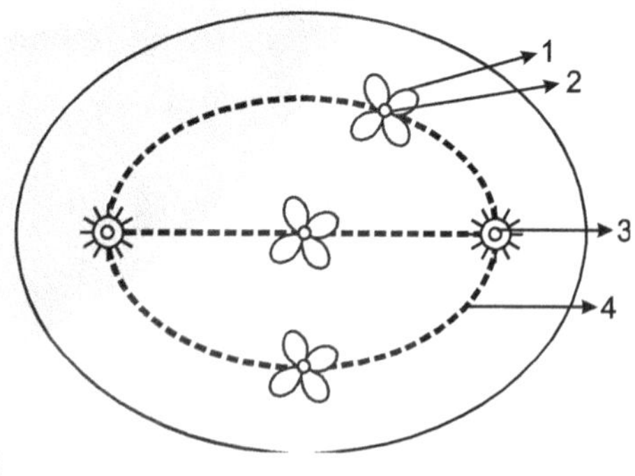

9. Study the diagram given below which represents a stage during the mitotic cell division and answer the questions that follow :*

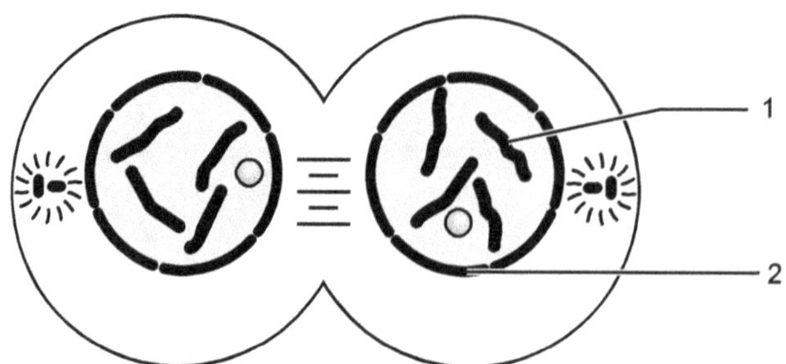

Diagram Based Questions

(i) Identify the stage giving suitable reasons.

(ii) Name the parts numbered 1 and 2.

(iii) What is the technical term for the division of nucleus?

(iv) Mention the stage that comes before the stage shown in the diagram. Draw a neat labelled diagram of the stage mentioned.

(v) Which is the cell division that results in half the number of chromosomes in daughter cells?

Ans. (i) The stage shown in the figure is telophase due to the following reasons :

(1) Nuclear membrane and nucleolus have reappeared.

(2) Spindle fibres are disappearing.

(3) Furrows have been formed for the division of cytoplasm.

(4) Sister chromatids reach opposite poles,

(5) The two sets of daughter chromosomes have reached the opposite poles.

(ii) 1- Chromatin fibres

2- Nuclear membrane

(iii) The division of nucleus is called Karyokinesis.

(iv) The stage comes before this stage that is shown in the diagram is Anaphase.

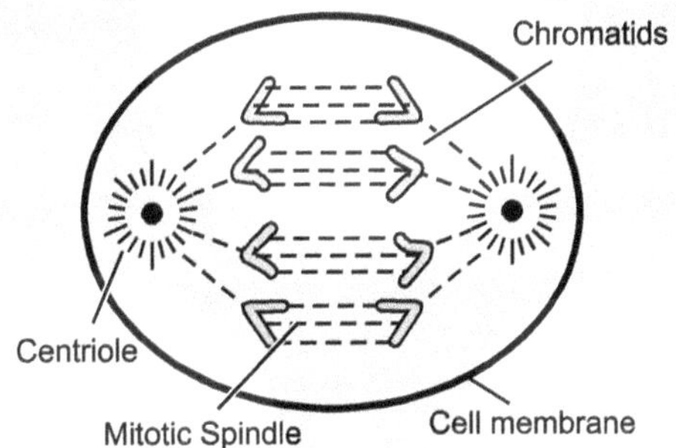

(v) Meiosis is the cell division that results in half the number of chromosomes in daughter cells.

10. In the given diagram, name the parts labelled 1, 2, 3, 4 and 5 and describe about them in short.

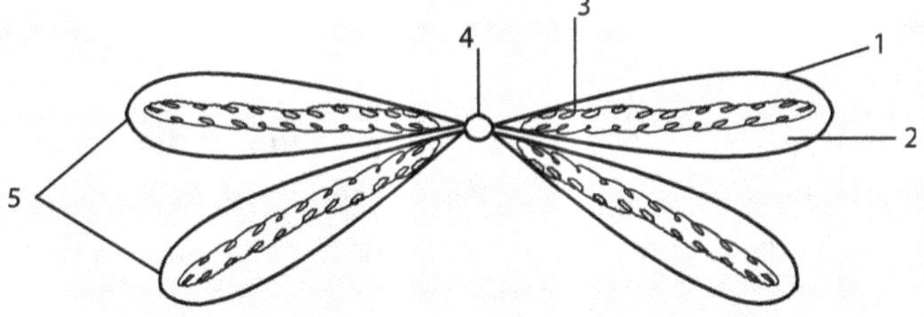

Ans. 1. **Pellicle :** The matrix of chromosome is enclosed in a sheath called as pellicle.

2. **Matrix :** The chromatin of chromosome is embedded in the achromatic substance known as matrix.

3. **Chromatin :** Chromatin is the heredity material made-up of long fibres of DNA combined with proteins.

4. **Centromere :** Centromere is a point at which the two chromatids remain attached. It is also the point of attachment for spindles.

5. **Chromatids :** Chromatid is either of the two strands of chromosome joined together by a centromere.

Chapter 2. Fundamentals of Genetics

1. (i) State Mendel's Law of Dominance.

(ii) A pure tall plant (TT) is crossed with a pure dwarf plant (tt).

Draw Punnet squares to show (1) F_1 generation, (2) F_2 generation.

(iii) Give the Phenotype of the F_2 generation.

(iv) Give the Phenotypic and Genotypic ratio of the F_1 and F_2 generation.

(v) Name any one X-linked disease found in humans.

Ans. (i) **Law of Dominance** : Out of a pair of contrasting characters present together, one is able to express itself while the other remains suppressed.

(ii) Parents   Tall plant   Dwarf plant

                          TT   ×   tt

(1) F_1 generation

	t	t
T	Tt	Tt
T	Tt	Tt

(2)   Tt   ×   Tt

           F_2 generation

	T	t
T	TT	Tt
t	Tt	tt

(iii) In F_2 generation 75% plants will be tall and 25% dwarf.

(iv) F_1 Phenotypic ratio—1 : 1 : 1 : 1 (All tall plants)

        Genotypic ratio—1 : 1 : 1 : 1 (All hybrids)

  F_2 Phenotypic ratio—3 : 1

        Genotypic ratio—1 : 2 : 1

(v) Haemophilia.

2. (i) State Mendel's law of Independent Assortment.

(ii) A homozygous Tall plant (T) bearing red coloured flowers (R) is crossed with a homozygous Dwarf plant (t) bearing white flowers (r) :

(1) Give the Genotype and Phenotype of the F_1 generation.

(2) Give the possible combinations of the gametes that can be obtained from the F_1 hybrid.

(3) Give the dihybrid ratio and the phenotype of the offsprings of the F_2 generation when two plants of the F_1 generation above are crossed.

Ans. (i) Mendel's law of independent assortment states that in a dihybrid cross, the alleles of one pair segregate independently of the alleles of other pair and the gametes assort independently at the time of zygote formation. Thus, inheritance of one character does not interfere the inheritance of other character.

(ii)

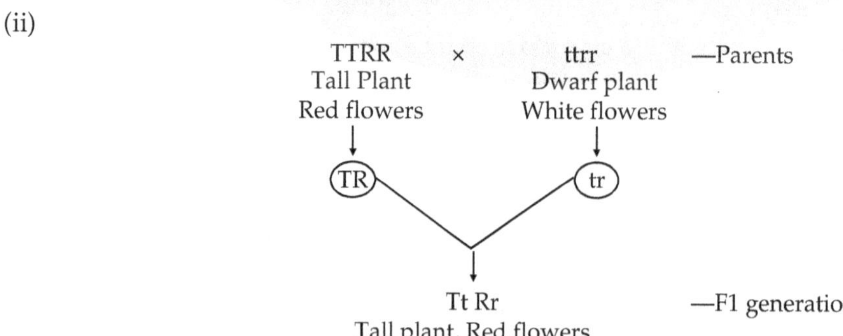

(1) Genotype — TtRr. Phenotype — All tall with red flowers.

(2) Gametes — TR, Tr, tR, tr.

(3) 9 : 3 : 3 : 1, 9 — Tall with red flowers, 3 — Tall with white flowers, 3 — Dwarf with red flowers, 1 — Dwarf with white flowers.

Diagram Based Questions

3. Given below is a schematic diagram showing Mendel's experiment on sweet pea plants having axial flowers with round seeds (AARR) and terminal flowers with wrinkled seeds (aarr). Study the same and answer the questions that follow :

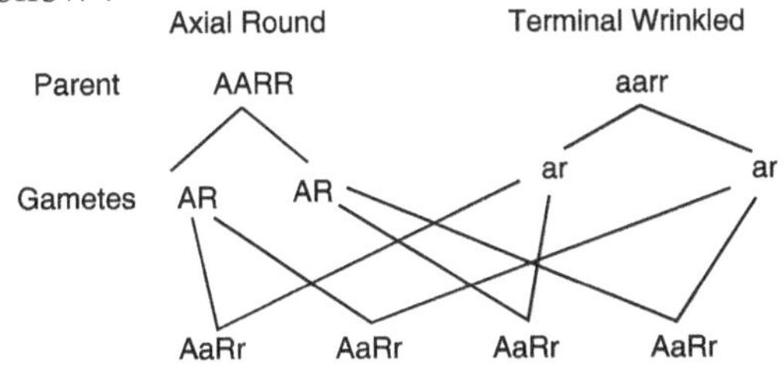

  (i) Give the phenotype of F_1 progeny.

 (ii) Give the phenotypes of F_2 progeny produced upon by the self-pollination of F_1 progeny.

(iii) Give the phenotypic ratio of F_2 progeny.

(iv) Name and explain the law induced by Mendel on the basis of the above observation.

Ans. (i)   Axial round

    (ii)   Axial round, axial wrinkled, terminal round, terminal wrinkled.

   (iii) $9 : 3 : 3 : 1$

   (iv) **Law of independent assortment :** When there are two pairs of contrasting characters, the distribution of factors of each pair in the gametes is independent of the distribution of other pair of characters.

4. What is dihybrid cross? How did Mendel perform this cross?

Ans. Dihybrid Cross : A cross between two parents taking into consideration alternative traits of two different characters. For example, a cross between round and yellow seed bearing plant with wrinkled and green seed bearing plant.

Mendel crossed the rounds & yellow seeds with wrinkled & green seeds :

<table>
<tr><td align="center">RRYY
Round and Yellow
seeded plant</td><td align="center">×</td><td align="center">rryy
Wrinkled and green
seeded plant</td></tr>
<tr><td align="center" colspan="3">↓</td></tr>
<tr><td align="center">Rr Yy
All Round and Yellow
seeded plant</td><td></td><td align="center">F_1 generation</td></tr>
</table>

Then, Mendel selfed the F_1 plants. Interestingly, some of the resulting plants were round and green seeded, some were wrinkled and yellow seeded, and wrinkled and green seeded plants had reappeared.

F_1 Gametes	RY	Ry	rY	ry
RY	RRYY	RRYy	RrYY	RrYy
Ry	RRYy	RRyy	RrYy	Rryy
rY	RrYY	RrYy	rrYY	rrYy
ry	RrYy	Rryy	rrYy	rryy

F_2 generation :

Round yellow : Round green : Wrinkled yellow : Wrinkled green—$9 : 3 : 3 : 1$

5. The karyotype (set of chromosomes) shown below is taken from a dividing cell in a certain individual.

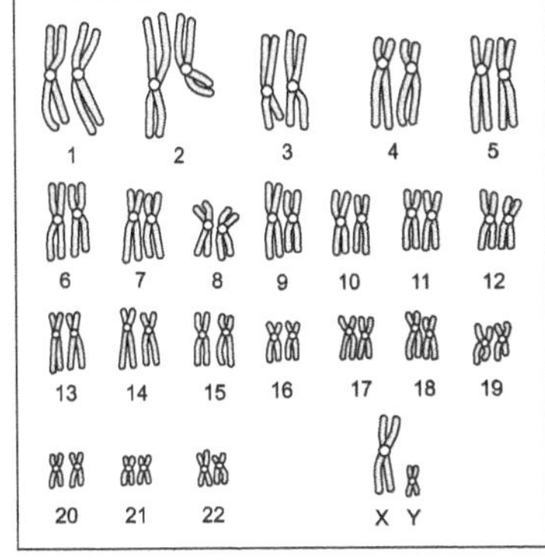

    (i)   Is the individual male or female? Explain your answer.

    (ii) How would you expect (1) a female cell and (2) sperm cell to differ in chromosome composition?

Ans. (i)   Male, because there is a Y-chromosome and an X-chromosome.

    (ii) (1) A female cell would have two X-chromosomes and no Y-chromosome.

          (2) A sperm cell would have one X-chromosome and one Y-chromosome.

6. Write a short note on sex determination in man.

Ans. The difference between two individuals of same species with respect to heredity is known as sex. So, an individual can either be a male or female in normal circumstances. Scientists have discovered that sex is transmitted by definite sex-chromosomes, also called heterosomes. The human body cells have two sex-chromosomes. A woman has two X-chromosomes while a man has one X-chromosome and one Y-chromosome. Therefore, an egg cell has one X-chromosome and

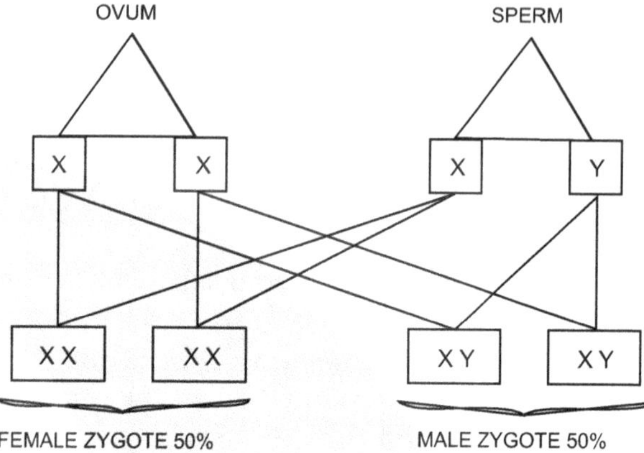

a sperm cell has either an X- or a Y-chromosome. This means that the sex of a baby is determined by the type of sperm cell fertilizing the egg. If the egg is fused with a sperm having Y-chromosome, then the male zygote will develop and when fused with a sperm having X-chromosome then a female zygote will develop.

7. A woman with normal vision marries a man with normal vision. They have a colourblind son. Her husband dies and she marries a colourblind man. Show the type of children that might be expected from this marriage and the proportion of each.

Ans. In the first marriage of woman, the son was colourblind therefore the woman is a carrier. Genotype of that woman : $X\overset{\bullet}{X}$

The man in the second marriage is colourblind.

Genotype of that man : $\overset{\bullet}{X}Y$

Possible combination of this marriage :

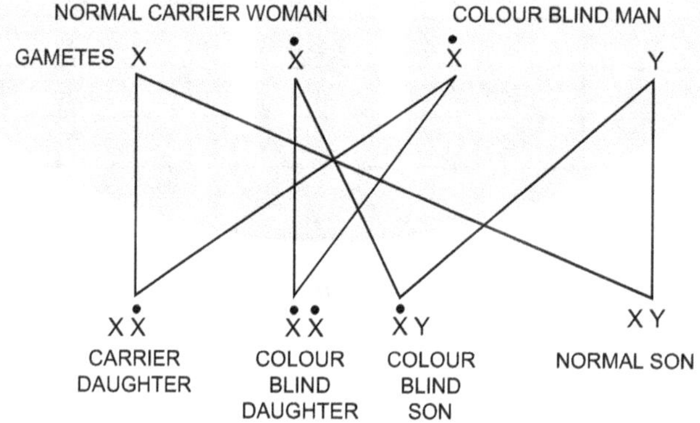

Expected result :

Son	:	50%	Normal	:	25%
			Colourblind	:	25%
Daughter	:	50%	(Carrier) Normal	:	25%
			Colourblind	:	25%

Diagram Based Questions

8. A woman had normal vision, but her father was colour-blind. She marries a man, who is colour-blind. Find out the probability of the first child being colourblind, whether it is a boy or girl.

Ans. That woman is heterozygous and carrier of that trait because her father was colourblind. She marries a colourblind man, then it might be possible that her first child will be colour-blind whether a son or a daughter, because mother and father both possess an inherited chromosome.

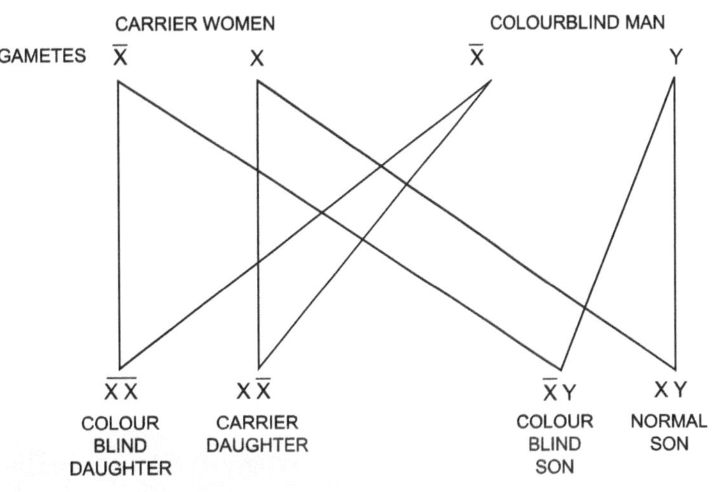

9. A haemophilic man marries a carrier women. Find out the probability of their offsprings being haemophilic.

Ans. The gene of haemophilia is present on X-chromosome. This disease is only found in males and females can only act as carriers.

X^hY
Male
Haemophilic

$\times$
$\downarrow$

X^hX
Female
Carrier

♂	X^h	Y
X^h	X^hX^h	X^hY
X	X^hX	XY

(♀)

Expected results : 25% Haemophilic girls

25% Haemophilic boys

25% Carrier girls

25% Normal boys

Chapter 3. Absorption by Roots

1. In the figure alongside, 'A' shows a cell in the normal state and 'B' shows the same cell after leaving it in a certain solution for a few minutes.

(i) Describe the change which has occurred in the cell as seen in B.

(ii) Give the technical term for the condition of the cell as reached in B and as it was in A.

(iii) Define the process which led to this condition.

(iv) What was the solution–isotonic, hypotonic or hypertonic, in which the cell was kept?

(v) How can the cell in B be brought back to its original condition?

(vi) Name the parts numbered 1 to 3.

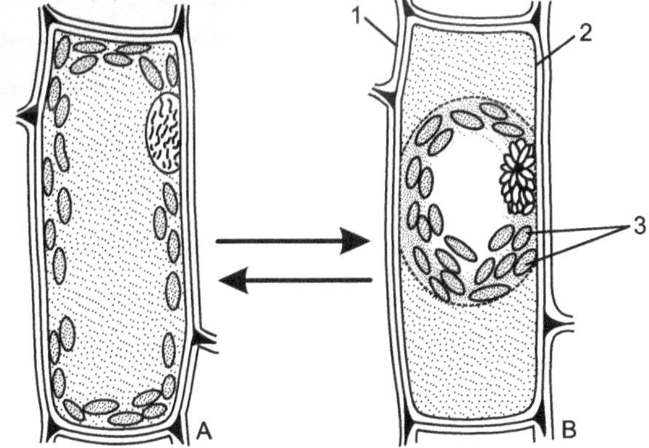

Ans. (i) Exosmosis (exit of water) has resulted in the shrinkage of the protoplasm of cell B.

(ii) Plasmolysis and deplasmolysis.

(iii) Plasmolysis is the process of shrinkage of the protoplasm of a plant cell as a result of loss of water from the cell.

(iv) Hypertonic solution.

(v) The cell in B can be brought back to its original condition by placing it in a drop of distilled water.

(vi) 1. Cell wall,   2. Plasma membrane,   3. Chloroplast.

2. Given alongside is the diagram of a cell as seen under the microscope after having been placed in a certain solution :

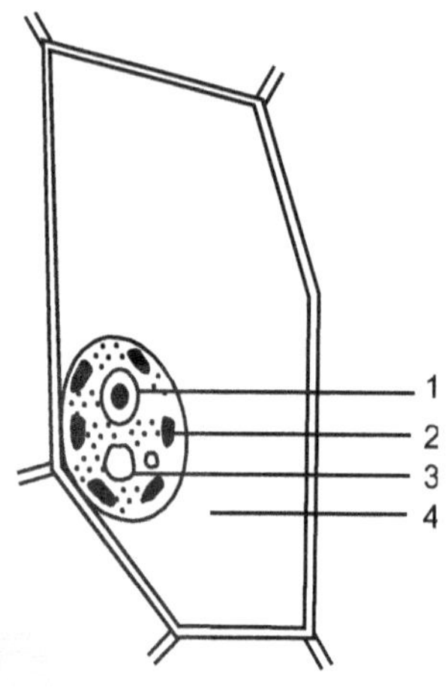

(i)   What is the technical term used for the state/condition of the cell given above?

(ii)   Give the technical term for the solution in which the cell was placed.

(iii) Name the parts numbered 1 to 4.

(iv) Is the cell given above a plant cell or an animal cell? Give two reasons in support of your answer as evident from the diagram.

(v)   What would you do to bring this cell back to its original condition.

Ans. (i)   Flaccidity

(ii)   Hypertonic solution

(iii) 1. Nucleus, 2. Plastids, 3. Small vacuole, 4. Hypertonic solution.

(iv) Plant cell

Reason : (1) Presence of cell wall, (2) Presence of plastids.

(v)   It has to be placed in a hypotonic solution.

3. The alongside diagram represents a plant cell after being placed in a strong sugar solution. Guidelines 1 to 5 indicate the following:

1.   Cell wall   3.   Protoplasm

2.   Plasma membrane   4.   Large vacuole

5.   Nucleus

Study the diagram and answer the questions that follow :

(i)   What is the state of the cell shown in the diagram?

(ii)   Name the structure which acts as a selectively permeable membrane.

(iii) If the cell had been placed in distilled water instead of strong sugar solution which feature would not have been present?

(iv) If the cell in the diagram possessed chloroplasts, where would these be present?

(v)   Name any one feature of this plant cell which is not present in animal cells.

Ans. (i)   Flaccid.

(ii)   Plasma membrane.

(iii) If the cell has been placed in distilled water it remains in a fully distended condition. Its plasma membrane remains in close contact with the cell wall and presses against it.

(iv) Chloroplast will be present in the protoplasm outside the vacuole.

(v)   Cell wall.

4. A plant cell kept in a drop of water was examined under the low power magnification of a microscope, as shown.

(i)   What would you do to bring this cell back to its original condition?

(ii)   What scientific term is used for such condition?

(iii) Draw the same cell if it is kept in a strong sugar solution.

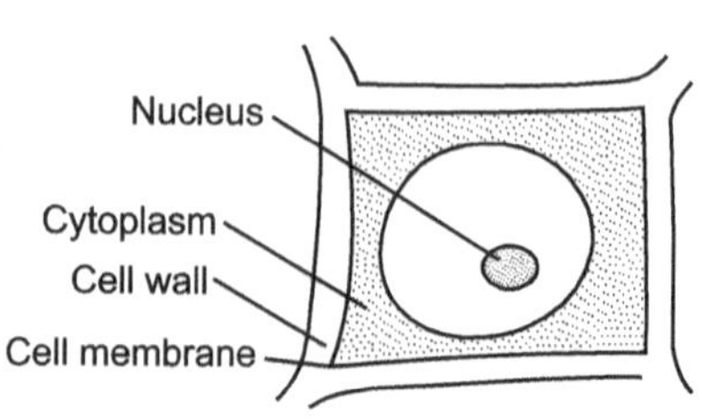

Ans. (i) Put the cell back into a drop of water for some time. Deplasmolysis occurs.

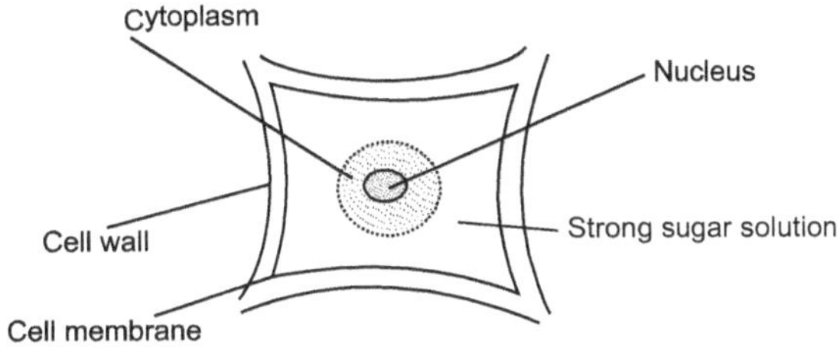

(ii) Flaccid.

(iii) Plasmolysed cell.

5. A thin strip of epidermal cells from the fleshy scales of an onion bulb was examined in a drop of water, under a microscope. All the epidermal cells looked alike and the figure alongside represents one of them. The thin strip was then transferred to a drop of strong sugar solution and re-examined under the microscope after about five minutes.

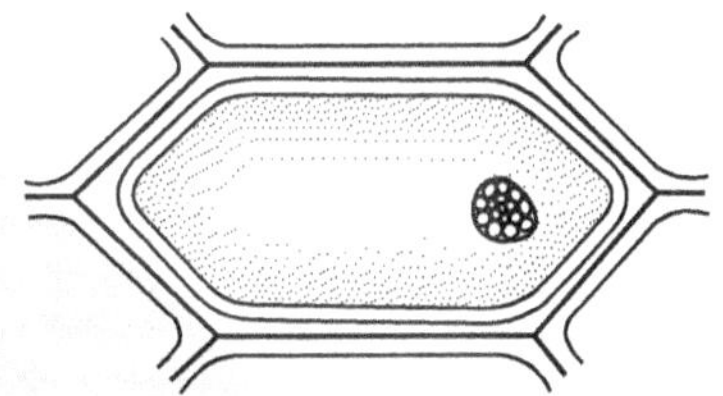

(i) Make a sketch of one of the epidermal cells, as it might appear after immersion in strong sugar solution. Label any two parts which has undergone a change.

(ii) Give the scientific term for the change shown in Q. (i) above.

(iii) What would you do to bring this cell back to its original condition?

(iv) Give the scientific term used for the recovery of the cell as a result of the step taken in Q. (iii) above.

Ans. (i) See figure.

(ii) Plasmolysis.

(iii) We would immerse this cell into fresh water, *i.e.*, hypotonic solution.

(iv) Deplasmolysis.

6. The diagram given represents a plant cell after being placed in a strong sugar solution. Study the diagram and answer the questions that follow :*

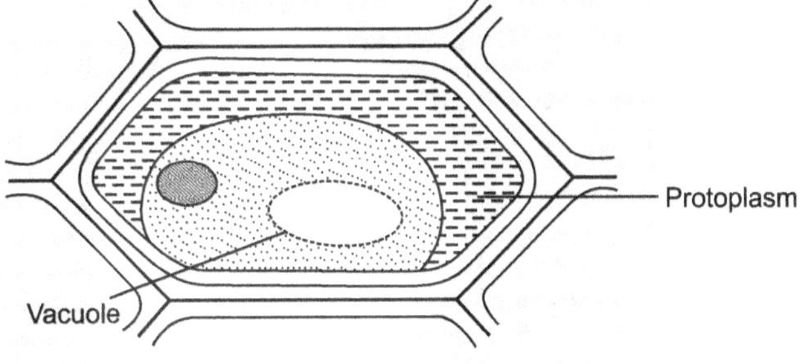

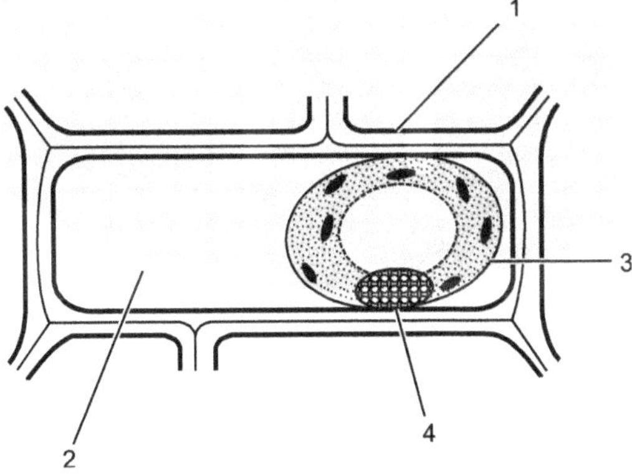

(i) What is the state of the cell shown in the diagram?

(ii) Name the structure that acts as a selectively permeable membrane.

(iii) Label the parts numbered 1 to 4 in the diagram.

(iv) How can the above cell be brought back to its original condition? Mention the scientific term for the recovery of the cell.

(v) State any two features of the above plant cell which is not present in animal cells.

Ans. (i) The cell shown in the diagram is in flaccid [plasmolysed] state.

    (ii) Plasma membrane acts as a selectively permeable membrane.

    (iii) 1- Cell wall   3- Plasma membrane

          2- Strong sugar solution   4- Nucleus

    (iv) If this flaccid or plasmolysed cell is placed in water, its protoplasm again swells up and cell can retain back its original condition. This recovery of the cell is called deplasmolysis.

    (v) In plant cell, cell wall, a large vacuole in the centre and chloroplasts are present which is not seen in an animal cell.

7. Given below is an experimental demonstration.

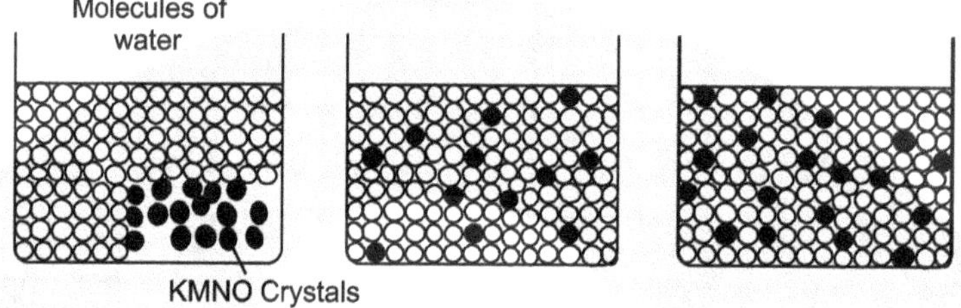

    (i) Which phenomenon has been demonstrated in the given figure?

    (ii) What is solute and what is solvent in the above experiment?

    (iii) Define the phenomenon in Q. (i) above.

    (iv) Give one example from your daily life experiences based on this principle.

Ans. (i) Diffusion.

    (ii) $KMnO_4$ crystals represent the solute and water is solvent.

    (iii) The movement of the molecules of a substance from the region of their higher concentration to the region of their lower concentration until a state of equilibrium is achieved in both the regions.

    (iv) If a bottle of scent or spirit is opened in one corner of a closed room, its smell can be felt in every part of the room.

8. In an experiment, two sets of apparatus were set up as shown below :

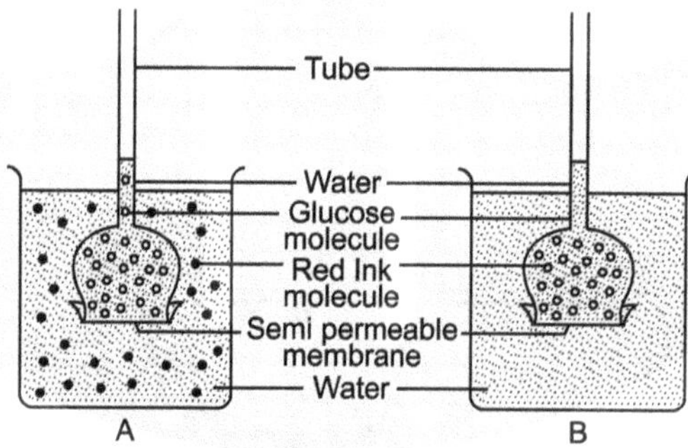

In A there is concentrated sugar solution inside the thistle funnel and red ink in the water outside the funnel. In B there is concentrated glucose solution with red ink inside the thistle funnel and water outside the thistle funnel.

In both A and B the level of liquid inside the funnels rises up the tubes. In A, the sugar solution turns red and in B, the water turns red.

Study the given observations and answer these questions :

    (i) Name the process by which red ink moves in A and B.

    (ii) Which type of pressure forces the water molecules to move towards thistle funnels and causes rise in the water level?

    (iii) Where does this process occur in plants and animals?

    (iv) What material could be used as semi-permeable membrane?

Ans. (i) Osmosis.

   (ii) Osmotic pressure.

   (iii) In plants, in the root cells and in animals, in the RBCs.

   (iv) Cellophane paper, goat bladder, etc.

9. The beaker is divided into two chambers A and B. The big circle represents solute and the small circles solvent.

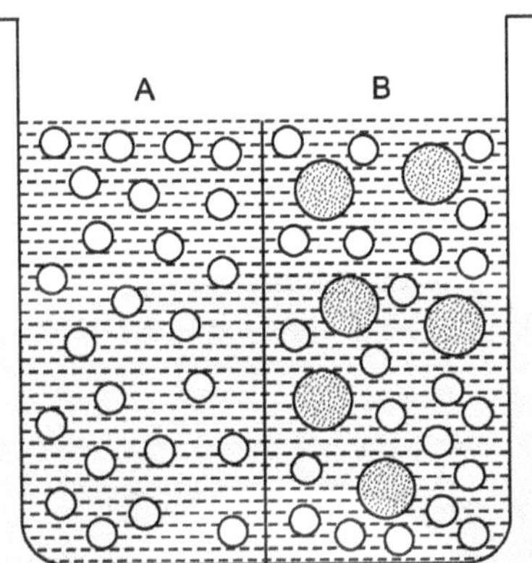

   (i) What can you say about the size of the holes in the membrane, if it is to behave semi-permeably between these two?

   (ii) Will the solvent molecules pass through the membrane from left to right, from right to left, in either direction or in both directions?

   (iii) In which direction will there be a net movement of solvent molecules?

Ans. (i) The size of the holes in the membrane is large enough to allow only the solvent particles to pass through it. But solute particle cannot pass through it. Thus, the membrane acts as the semi-permeable.

   (ii) Solvent molecules will pass through the membrane in both directions. Since solvent molecules are present on both the sides they will strike the semi-permeable membrane and pass through the same.

   (iii) There is a net movement of solvent molecules from the place of its higher chemical potential to the place of its lower chemical potential, *i.e.*, from left to right.

10. The diagram alongside represents an experimental set up to demonstrate a vital process. Study the same and then answer the questions that follow :

   (i) Name the process.

   (ii) Define the above named process.

   (iii) What would you observe in the experimental set up after an hour or so?

   (iv) What control experiment can be set up for the above experiment?

   (v) Keeping in mind the root hair cell and its surrounding, name the part that corresponds to (1) Concentrated sugar solution, (2) Cellophane, (3) Water in the beaker.

   (vi) Name any other substance that can be used instead of Cellophane paper in the above experiment.

   (vii) Mention two advantages of this process to the plant.

Ans. (i) Osmosis.

   (ii) Transfer of water or solvent molecules from a region of their higher concentration to a region of their lower concentration through a semi-permeable membrane is called osmosis.

   (iii) Level of sugar solution rises in the stem of thistle funnel, whereas water level in the beaker falls.

   (iv) A non-permeable membrane can be used in place of Cellophane for a control experiment.

   (v) (1) Root hair cell sap corresponds to concentrated sugar solution.

(2) Cell membrane of root hair cell corresponds to Cellophane.

(3) Soil solution corresponds to water in the beaker.

(vi) Goat's bladder or pig's bladder.

(vii) (1) Helps in water absorption.

(2) Helps in opening and closing of stomata, thus facilitating gaseous exchange.

11. A complete ring of bark was removed from a tree in spring. The tree continued to live in summer but a swelling appeared on the bark above the ring while the bark below shriveled up. Answer the questions given below :

   (i)   Account for the swelling in the bark above the ring.
   (ii) Account for the shrinking of the bark below the ring.
   (iii) Name the tissue that distributes food in plants.
   (iv) Name the tissue that distributes water in plants.
   (v)   What is the role of a bark in a plant?

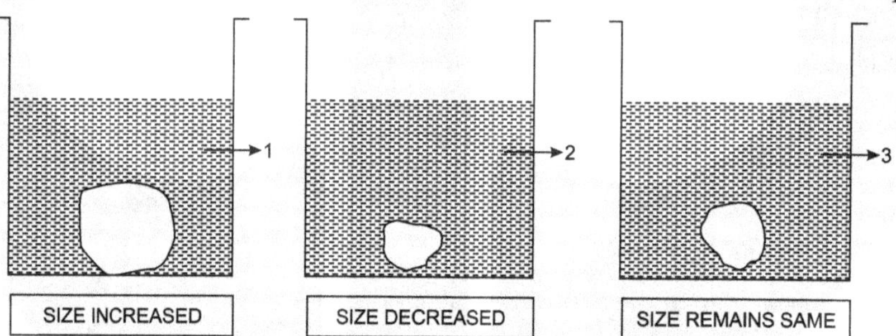

Ans. (i)   The phloem has been removed from a part of the ring. The food prepared by leaves comes down through phloem, but since the phloem is cut off, the food gets collected in the upper part of the ring and hence the swelling appears.

   (ii) The food prepared by leaves is not able to pass on downward as the phloem has been removed, resulted in the shrinking of the bark.

   (iii) Phloem.

   (iv) Xylem.

   (v)   Bark protects from the attack of fungi and insects, against loss of water by evaporation and against variation of external temperature.

12. A candidate in order to study the process of osmosis has taken 3 potato cubes and put them in 3 different beakers containing 3 different solutions. After 24 hours, in the first beaker the potato cube increased in size, in the second beaker the potato cube decreased in size and in the third beaker there was no change in the size of the potato cube. The following diagram shows the result of the same experiment :

   (i)   Give the technical terms of the solutions used in beakers, 1, 2 and 3.
   (ii) In beaker 3 the size of the potato cube remains the same. Explain the reason in brief.
   (iii) Write the specific feature of the cell sap of root hairs which helps in absorption of water.
   (iv) What is osmosis?
   (v)   How does a cell wall and a cell membrane differ in their permeability?

Ans. (i)   **Beaker 1:** Hypotonic solution

   Beaker 2 : Hypertonic solution

   Beaker 3 : Isotonic solution

   (ii) In beaker 3 the size of potato cube remains the same because of isotonic solution which has same concentration of solutes as that of potato cells. So water is neither lost nor gained by the potato cells.

   (iii) Cell sap of root hairs is much more concentrated than the soil solution and this causes entry of water into the root cells.

   (iv) Osmosis is the movement of water molecules from a region of their higher concentration to a region of their lower concentration through a semi-permeable membrane.

   (v)   Cell wall is freely permeable while cell membrane is selectively permeable.

13. The diagram given below is of an experiment just at the start. Study the diagram carefully and answer the following questions :

   (i)   What does the experiment demonstrate?

   (ii)   Define the process demonstrated in the experiment.

   (iii)   What changes are observed after a few hours?

   (iv)   Give two examples of a semi-permeable membrane.

   (v)   Which limb of the U-tube contains more concentrated sucrose solution, A or B?

   (vi)   Why is the membrane separating the two solu-tions labelled as semi-permeable membrane?

Ans. (i)   The process of osmosis.

   (ii)   Osmosis is a special type of diffusion of solvent molecules through a semi-permeable membrane from region of their higher concentration to the region of their lower concentration.

   (iii)   The level of water in column A will rise along with passage of time and will ultimately stop when concentration of water molecules is equal on both sides of the membrane.

   (iv)   (1) Parchment paper,   (2) Egg membrane.

   (v)   Limb A.

   (vi)   It permits only certain molecules to pass through it.

14. The apparatus arranged here signifies an important process.

   (i)   Name the process.

   (ii)   Where does this process occur in plants?

   (iii)   What solution is placed inside the dialysis tubing?

   (iv)   What happens to the level of the solution in the capillary tube?

   (v)   Define the process mentioned in Q. (i) above.

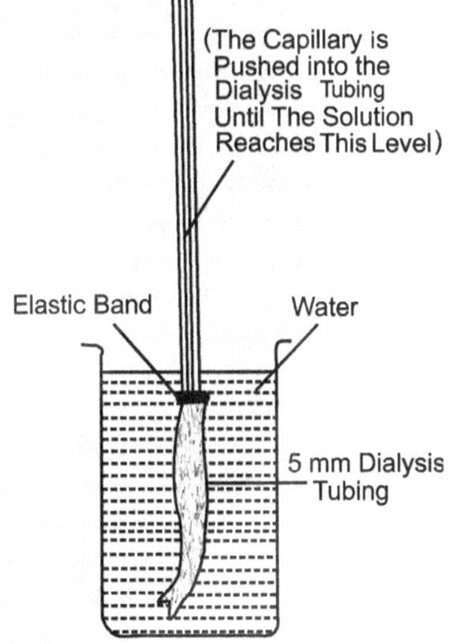

Ans. (i)   The process is called osmosis.

   (ii)   This process occurs in the root hair cells of plants.

   (iii)   The solution placed inside the dialysis tubing is generally strong sugar solution or salt solution.

   (iv)   The level of the solution in the capillary tube rises above the original level.

   (v)   Osmosis is a physiological process where the water molecules or solvent molecules move through a semi-permeable membrane from a solution having a higher concentration of solvent molecules to the solution having a lower concentration of water or solvent molecules.

15. Given alongside is the figure of an experimental set up to demonstrate root pressure.

   (i)   Define root pressure.

   (ii)   What change would you observe in the water level after some time?

   (iii)   What role is being played by the root pressure in the given experiment?

   (iv)   Why the oil has been sprinkled on water?

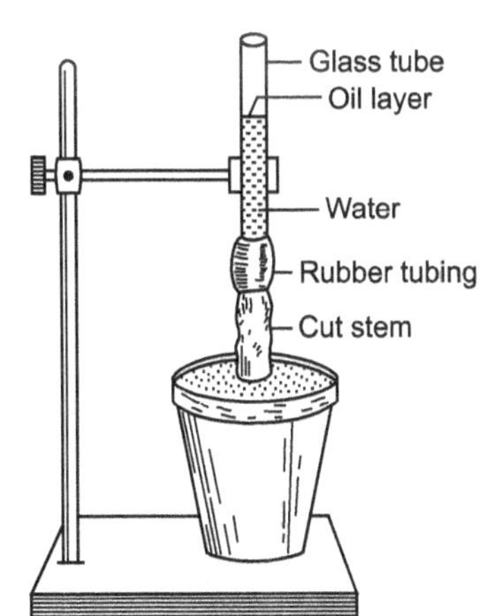

Ans. (i)   The collective force exerted by the cortical cells of the root in forcing water upward into the xylem is known as root pressure.

   (ii)   The water level will rise in the glass tube.

   (iii)   Root pressure is forcing the water up in the stem.

   (iv)   To prevent evaporation of water from the tube.

16. The diagram given below represents the result of an experiment conducted on two freshly taken shoots of a green herbaceous plant. The lower ends are dipped in water.

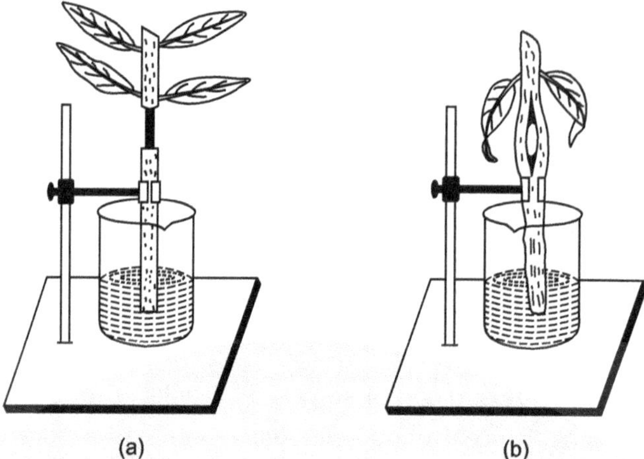

(a)   (b)

 (i) What is the aim of the experiment?

 (ii) Some parts of the stem in both the shoots have been removed. Name the conducting tissue in shoot A and in shoot B, that have been removed.

 (iii) What are the results of this experiment?

Ans. (i) To demonstrate the role of xylem and phloem in flowering plants.

 (ii) In shoot A, phloem tissue has been removed. In shoot B, central xylem tissue has been removed.

 (iii) Plant A gets water and minerals and synthesizes its food and remains healthy.

  Plant B due to lack of xylem does not get its supply of water and minerals. The leaves are seen drooping and will dry.

17. The figure given below is a diagrammatic representation of a part of the cross-section of the root in the root hair zone. Study the same and then answer the questions that follow :

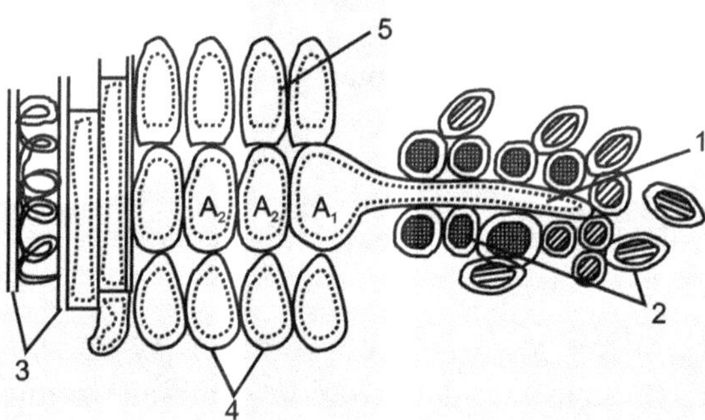

 (i) Name the parts indicated by guidelines '1' to '5'.

 (ii) Is the root hair cell unicellular or multicellular?

 (iii) Draw a labelled diagram of the root hair cell as it would appear if some fertilizer is added to the soil close to it.

 (iv) Name the process responsible for the entry of water molecules from the soil into A_1 and then A_2.

 (v) What pressure is responsible for the movement of water in the direction indicated by arrows?

 (vi) How is this pressure set up?

Ans. (i) 1. Vacuole (containing cell sap)   4. Cortex cells

   2. Soil particles   5. Vacuole in cortical cells.

   3. Xylem vessel

 (ii) Root hair cell is unicellular.

 (iii) See diagram below.

Diagram Based Questions

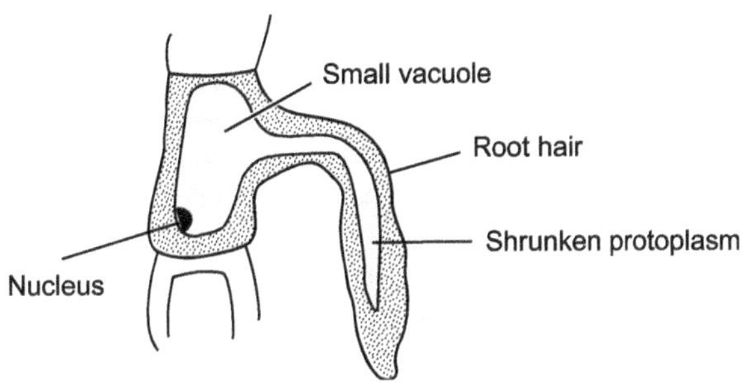

(iv) Osmosis

(v) Root pressure

(vi) This pressure is set up due to difference in osmotic gradient.

18. The alongside figure shows a root hair.

(i) Label the parts 1 to 4.

(ii) What is the role of part 4?

(iii) Why is the root hair one-celled?

(iv) What will happen to the root hair if some fertilizer is added to the soil near the root hair?

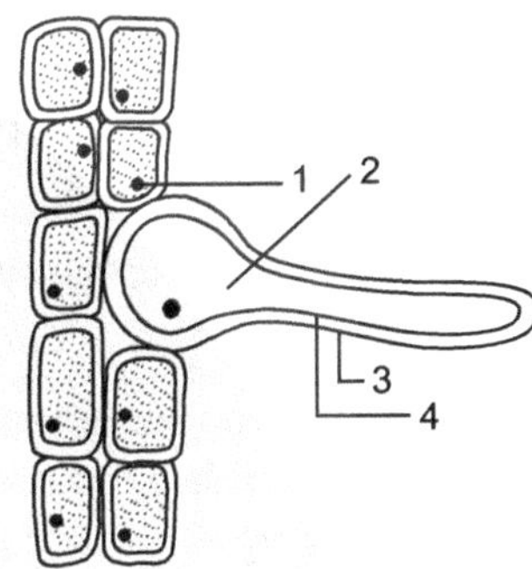

Ans. (i) 1. Nucleus   3. Cell wall

2. Vacuole   4. Cell membrane

(ii) Part 4 is the cell membrane. It is semi-permeable. It allows only water molecules to pass through it.

(iii) Because it is an extension of epidermal cell.

(iv) By the addition of fertilizer, root hair becomes flaccid because water will move out of it as soil water becomes hypertonic.

19. The below diagram A shows a root hair growing through the soil particles. The diagram B is the root hair of an aquatic plant.

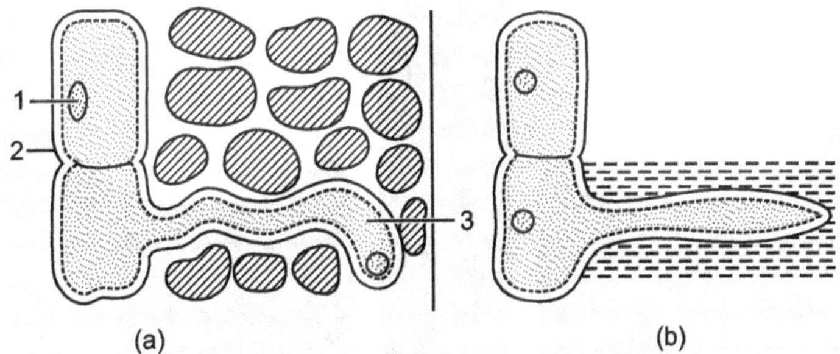

(i) Name the parts 1, 2, 3.

(ii) Name two substances which enter the root hair. What are their uses?

(iii) By what process do these substances enter the root hair?

(iv) Account for the different shapes of root hairs in the two diagrams.

Ans. (i) 1–Nucleus 2–Cell wall 3–Cytoplasm of the root hair cell.

(ii) 1. Water : Carries minerals to the plant required for photosynthesis .

2. Minerals : They are needed for healthy plant growth.

(iii) Osmosis and minerals by active transport.

(iv) In the Fig. A, the root hair has to pass through the soil particles and so they are not straight. In the Fig. B, the root hair has no obstruction in water, so it grows straight.

Chapter 4. Transpiration

1. The diagram alongside represents a structure found in a leaf.

   Study the same and answer the questions that follow :

   (i)   Name the parts labelled A and B.

   (ii) What is the biological term for the above structure?

   (iii) What is the function of the part labelled A?

   (iv) Mention two structural features of A, which help in the function mentioned in (iii) above.

   (v)   Where is this structure likely to be found in a leaf?

   (vi) The above structure helps in the process of transpiration. Explain the term transpiration.

   (vii) How many other cells are found surrounding this structure as seen in the diagram?

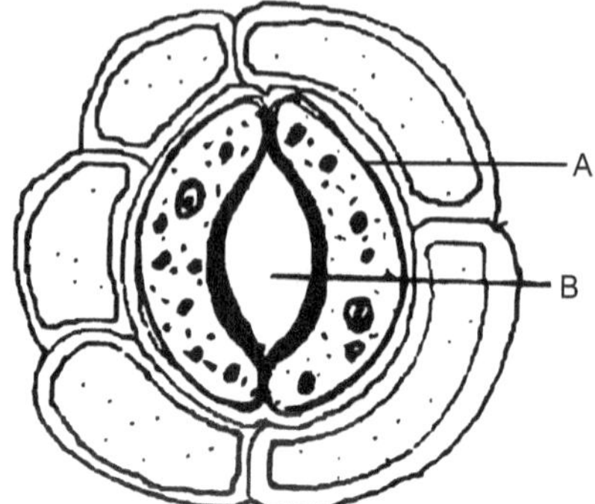

Ans. (i)   A—Guard cell   B—Stoma.

   (ii) Stomatal apparatus.

   (iii) Regulates the opening and closing of stomata.

   (iv) Guard cells have a thick inner wall facing the opening of stomata and a thin outer wall on the opposite side which makes it bulge outwards when rigid. Thus it helps in closing and opening the stomata.

   (v)   On the epidermis of leaf.

   (vi) Transpiration is the loss of water as water vapours from the aerial parts of the plant.

   (vii) Five.

2. The figure below represents the vertical section of a leaf :

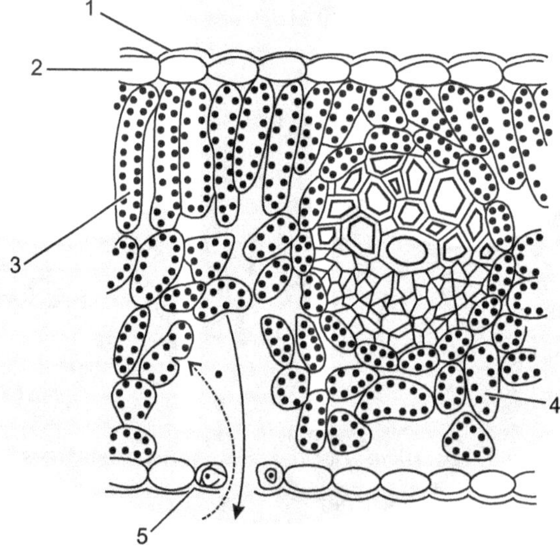

   (i)   Name the parts labelled 1 to 5.

   (ii) What do the two arrows (dotted and solid) indicate in the day time and at night?

   (iii) Could you add one more arrow in the figure? If yes, what for?

   (iv) How many leaf veins have been shown in this section?

Ans. (i)   1. Cuticle, 2. Upper epidermis, 3. Palisade tissue, 4. Spongy parenchyma, 5. Guard cell of stoma.

   (ii) In the day time, dotted arrow shows the path of CO_2 while solid arrow shows the path of oxygen. At night, dotted arrow shows the path of oxygen while solid arrow shows the path of CO_2.

   (iii) Yes, we can add one more arrow in the figure to show the loss of water during transpiration.

   (iv) Only one leaf vein has been shown in this section.

3. Given alongside are the diagrams of a certain structure in plants in two conditions.

  (i) Name the structure shown.

  (ii) Name the parts numbered 1-5.

  (iii) What is the most apparent difference between A and B in the structure shown?

  (iv) Describe the mechanism which brings about the change in the structure depicted in A and B.

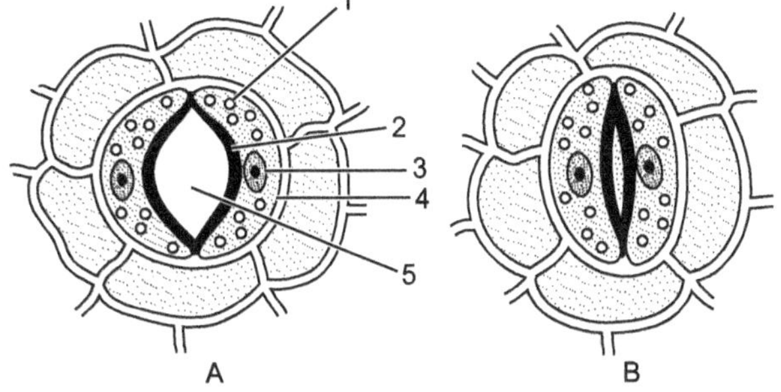

Ans. (i) Stomata surrounded by epidermal cells.

  (ii) 1. Chloroplast, 2. Inner wall of guard cells, 3. Nucleus, 4. Guard cells, 5. Stoma.

  (iii) The stoma is open in A and is almost closed in B.

  (iv) The opening and closing mechanism of stomata is regulated by the amount of water and solutes present in the guard cells. The guard cells have a thick inner wall facing the opening and a thin outer wall on the opposite side; their cytoplasm contains chloroplasts. During the day, guard cells begin photosynthesis and the sugar produced during the process increases the osmotic pressure which draws in water from the adjoining cells. Hence, the guard cells become turgid and bulge outward due to their thin outer wall, thus widening the stomatal opening lying in between (Fig. A). As the stomata open, the diffusion of gases in and out begins for fulfilling the need for photosynthesis and for allowing transpiration. If for any reason, the water content of the leaf is falling short, the guard cells fail to remain turgid, they turn flaccid or lose turgidity, thereby closing the stomatal opening (Fig. B) and the transpiration stops.

4. Given below is an experimental set up to study a particular process :

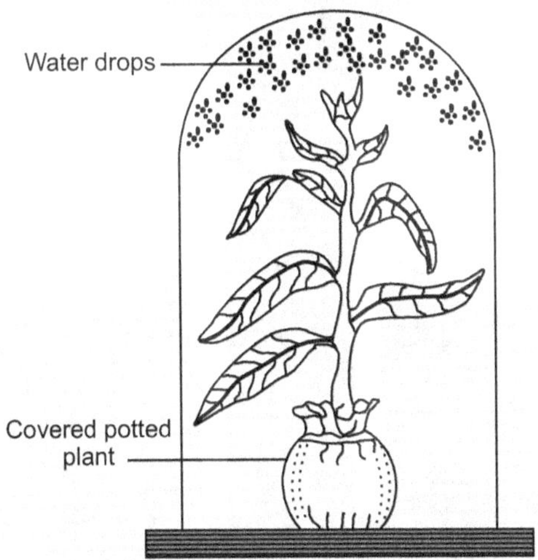

  (i) Name the process being studied.

  (ii) Explain the process named in (i) above.

  (iii) Why is the pot covered with a plastic sheet?

  (iv) Mention one way in which this process is beneficial to the plant.

  (v) Suggest a suitable control for this experiment.

Ans. (i) Transpiration.

  (ii) It is process in which water in the form of vapours are released from the aerial parts like leaves and soft stems of the plant.

  (iii) The plastic sheet will not allow the moisture of the mud of the pot to come out by evaporation process and affect the result.

  (iv) It helps in ascent of sap in the plant.

(v) A similar apparatus is set up without the potted plant. In its place, a same plastic bag with its mouth tied, is kept in the bell jar. No water drops will appear in the bell jar.

5. The figure given below represents an experimental set up with a weighing machine to demonstrate a particular process in plants. The experimental set up was placed in bright sunlight. Study the diagram and answer the following questions :

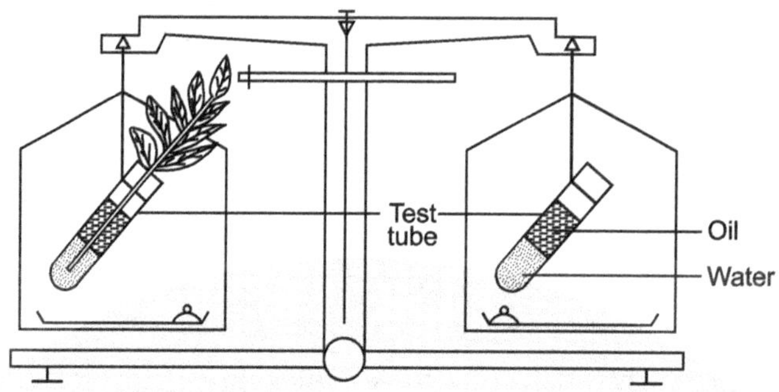

(i) Name the process intended for study.

(ii) Define the above mentioned process.

(iii) When the weight of the test tube (A and B) is taken before and after the experiment, what is observed? Give reasons to justify your observation in A and B.

(iv) What is the purpose of keeping the test tube B in the experimental set up?

Ans. (i) Transpiration.

(ii) It is the release of water vapours from the aerial parts of the plant.

(iii) Weight of test tube A will decrease after the experiment because water will be lost from it through the leaves by transpiration. Weight of test tube B will remain same after the experiment because water will not be lost by transpiration as there is no plant in and nor by evaporation as oil is spread over it, which will not allow evaporation.

(iv) It is a control experiment where the purpose of using test tube B is to compare the level of water in both test tubes.

6. Study the diagram given below and answer the questions that follow :

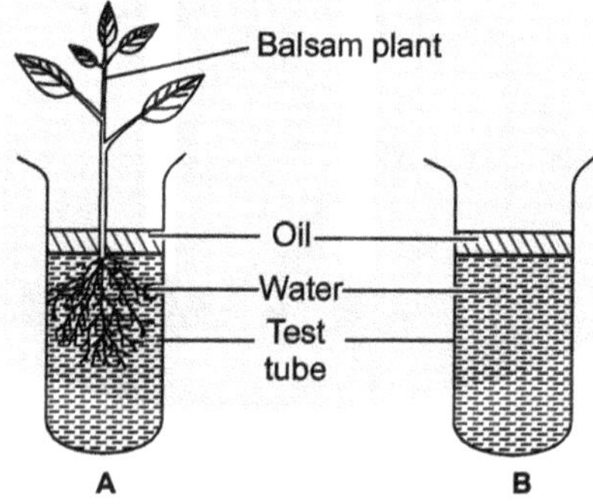

(i) Explain the physiological process being studied.

(ii) What will be the observations in the two test-tubes after about 2-3 days?

(iii) Give a reason for your answer in (ii) above.

(iv) Why is the surface of water covered with oil?

(v) State the purpose of setting up test tube B.

Ans. (i) **Transpiration :** Loss of water as water vapour from aerial parts of the plant.

(ii) After 2-3 days the level of water falls in test-tube A while it remains constant in test tube B.

(iii) The fall in the level of water in test-tube A is due to the absorption of water by the roots.

(iv) The oil has been put in each test-tube to prevent the loss of water by evaporation.

(v) The purpose of setting up test-tube B is to show that in the absence of plant, there is no change in the level of water.

7. Study the diagram given below and answer the questions that follows :

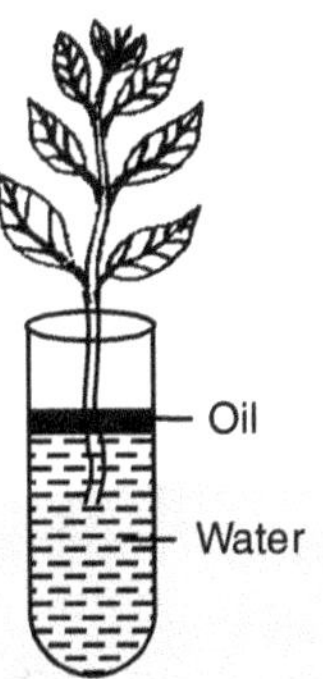

(i) Name the process being studied in the above experiment.

(ii) Explain the process mentioned in (i) above.

(iii) Why is oil placed over water?

(iv) What do we observe with regard to the level of water when this set up is placed in :

1. Bright sunlight

2. Humid conditions

3. On a windy day

(v) Mention any three adaptations in plants to overcome the process mentioned in (i).

Ans. (i) Transpiration

(ii) It is the process by which plants lose water as vapours through the aerial parts.

(iii) To prevent evaporation of water from the test tube.

(iv) 1. In bright sunlight the level of water decreases quickly.

2. In humid conditions level of water does not decrease for a long time.

3. On windy day level of water decreases very quickly.

(v) 1. The stomata may be sunken or covered by hairs.

2. The leaves may become narrower.

3. A thick layer of cuticle on the leaf surface help to decrease transpiration.

8. Given below is the diagram of an experimental set up to study the process of transpiration in plants. Study the same and then answer the questions that follow :

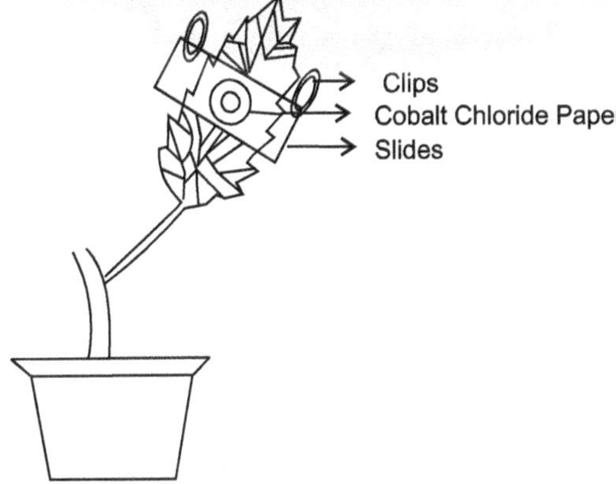

(i) What is the colour of dry cobalt chloride paper?

(ii) Is the experimental leaf a monocot or a dicot ? Give a reason to support your answer.

(iii) Why are glass slides placed over the dry cobalt chloride paper?

(iv) After about half an hour what change, if any, would you expect to find in the cobalt chloride paper placed on the dorsal and ventral sides of the leaf? Give a reason to support your answer.

(v) Define the term 'transpiration'.

Ans. (i) The colour of dry cobalt chloride paper is blue.

(ii) Dicot leaf. It has reticulate venation.

(iii) To prevent water vapour of the air from interfering the experiment.

(iv) The cobalt chloride paper placed on the lower surface of the leaf will show more pink dots as there are more stomata. The upper surface has less stomata than the lower surface so cobalt show chloride paper placed on upper surface will can pink dots.

(v) Transpiration is defined as the loss of water as water vapour from the aerial parts of the plant.

9. The apparatus shown here is Garreau's potometer designed to demonstrate unequal transpi ration from the two surfaces of a dorsiventral leaf. Before keeping the leaf in between the cups, anhydrous calcium chloride ($CaCl_2$) contained in two small vials were weighed and placed in both the cups. The ends of the cups were closed with corks through which two mercury manometers were connected. After a few hours, $CaCl_2$ vials were taken out and weighed again.

(i) What is the purpose of keeping $CaCl_2$ vials inside the cup?

(ii) After a few hours, the $CaCl_2$ vials were taken out and weighed again. Will you expect any difference in weight? If so, give reasons.

(iii) What was the purpose of using a manometer?

(iv) What do you mean by transpiration?

Ans. (i) The $CaCl_2$ vials are kept inside the cup to absorb water.

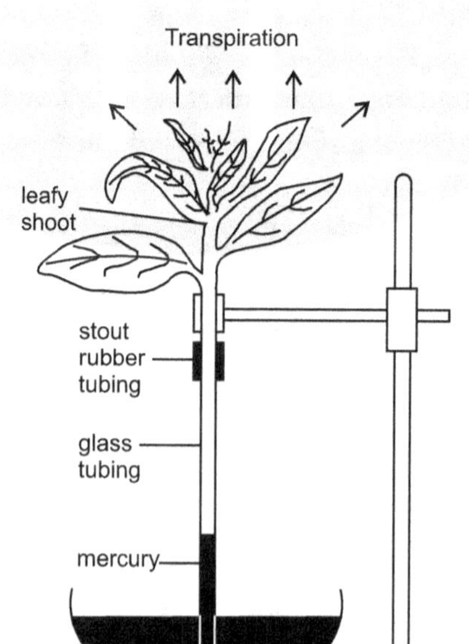

(ii) After few hours, the weight of the $CaCl_2$ vials will increase because they will absorb the water which is transpired by the leaf of the plant.

(iii) Manometers are used to indicate the unequal transpiration from the two surfaces of a dorsiventral leaf by showing difference in rise in their mercury levels.

(iv) Transpiration is the loss of water in the form of water vapour from the aerial parts of the living plants.

10. The diagram below represents an experiment to demonstrate a certain phenomenon in a green plant :*

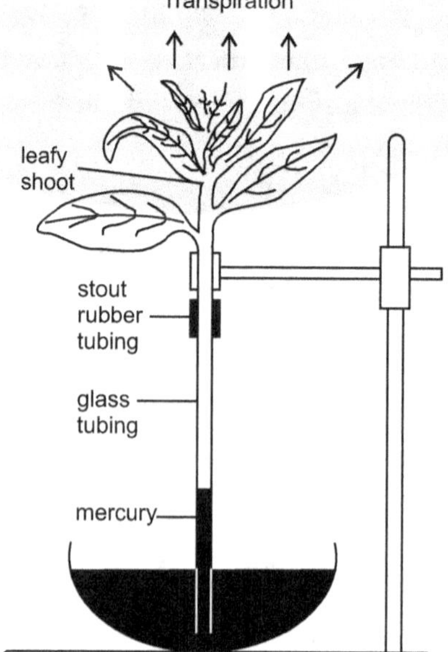

Diagram Based Questions

(i) Will the level of mercury in the glass tubing rise or fall?

Which conducting tissue of the plant does the glass-tubing represent?

(ii) Define Transpiration.

(iii) How will the rate of the above process differ if the environment of the plant has:

1. Less humidity   2. High temperature?

(iv) State any two advantages of transpiration to the plant.

(v) Draw a neat labelled diagram of a Plasmolysed cell.

Ans. (i) Mercury in the glass tube will rise.

Xylem

(ii) Transpiration is the loss of water in the form of water vapours from the leaves and other aerial parts of the plant.

(iii) 1. Less humidity increases the rate of transpiration.

2. High temperature increases the rate of transpiration.

(iv) Two advantages of transpiration are:

1. It provides cooling effect to the plant.

2. It provides a suction force which helps in ascent of sap.

(v)

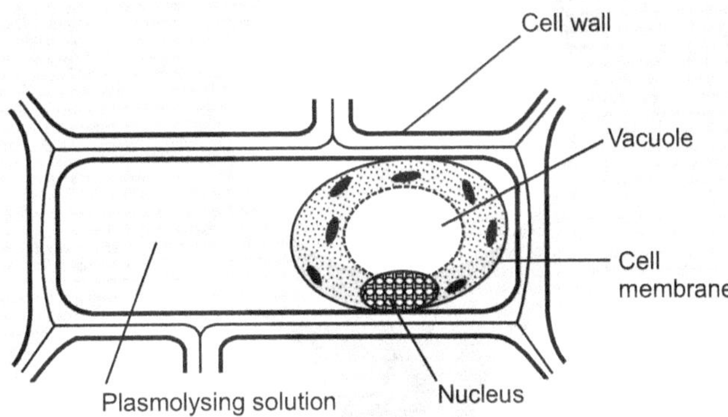

11. The following diagram is set up to demonstrate an experiment.

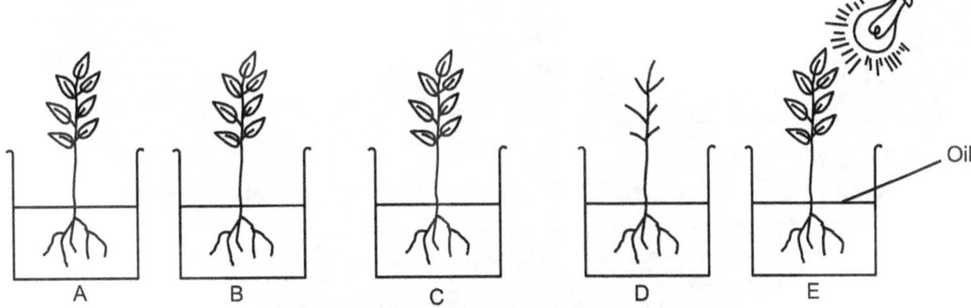

Five plants A, B, C, D and E were placed in a beaker containing water. The water in each beaker was covered with a layer of oil. The leaves were removed from plant D, in plant B upper surfaces of all the leaves were covered with Vaseline, in plant C the lower surfaces of all the leaves were covered with Vaseline and plant E was exposed to strong light. The beakers were then left for few hours and at the end of the experimental period, weights of each beaker were taken.

Write the correct answer out of the five available choices given under each question :

(i) In which beaker would you expect the greatest decrease in weight?

(I)   A   (III) C   (V) E

(II) B   (IV) D

(ii) In which beaker the change of weight would be minimum?

(I) A   (III) C   (V) E

(II) B   (IV) D

(iii) Which plant would remain healthy for a longer period of time?

    (I) A   (III) C   (V) E

    (II) B   (IV) D

(iv) In this experiment which plant can be considered as the uncontrolled one?

    (I) A   (III) C   (V) E

    (II) B   (IV) D

(v) The difference of weight would be maximum between :

    (I) A and B   (III) A and D   (V) D and E

    (II) A and C   (IV) A and E

Ans. (i) (V) E,   (ii) (IV) D,   (iii) (I) A,   (iv) (I) A, (v) (V) D and E.

12. Given below is an apparatus used to study a particular process in plants. Study the same and answer the questions that follow :—

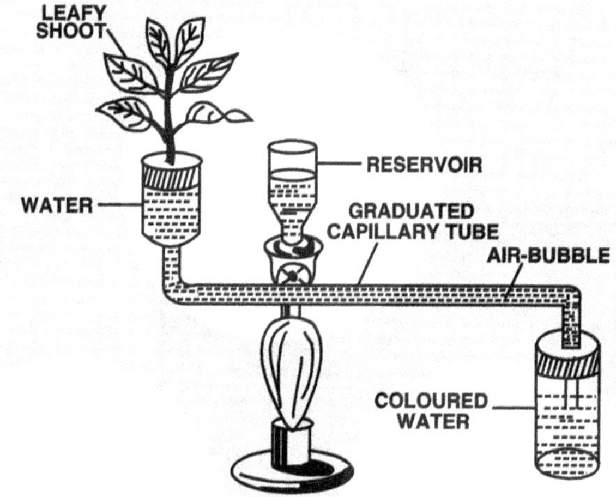

  (i)   Name the apparatus.

  (ii) Mention one limitation of this apparatus.

  (iii) Which phenomenon is studied with the help of this apparatus?

  (iv) What is the function of the part marked 'reservoir'?

  (v) What is the role of the air bubble in the experiment?

Ans. (i)   Ganong's Potometer.

  (ii) Potometer cannot measure rate of transpiration precisely as not all of the water taken up by plant is used for transpiration.

  (iii) Transpiration.

  (iv) It is used to adjust the position of air bubble in graduated capillary tube.

  (v) The movement of air bubble in graduated tube in a minute gives the rate of transpiration.

13. Give below is an experimental set up to demonstrate a particular process. Study the same and answer the questions that follow—

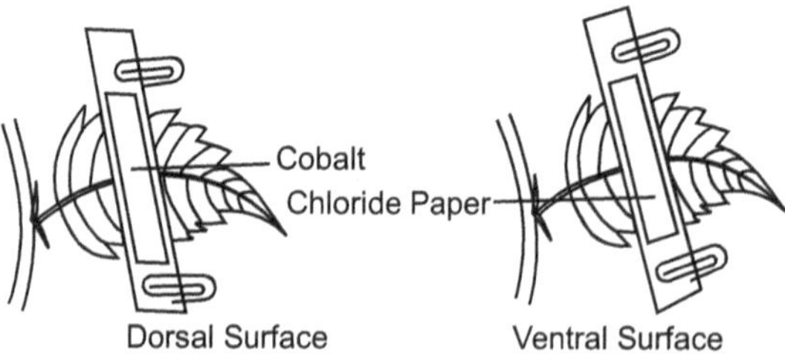

  (i)   Name the physiological process being studied.

  (ii) Explain the process mentioned above.

  (iii) What is the aim of the above experiment?

(iv) What would you observe in the experimental set-up after an hour? Give a reason to support your answer.

(v) Mention any three adaptations found in plants to overcome the physiological process mentioned in i. above.

Ans. (i) Transpiration

(ii) Transpiration is the process by which water is lost in form of vapours from the aerial parts of the plant.

(iii) The aim of the experiment is to show that transpiration occurs more form the lower surface of the leaves as compared to upper surface.

(iv) After an hour we will observe that the cobalt chloride paper placed under the lower surface of the leaf will turn pink faster as compared to the cobalt chloride paper placed on upper surface of the leaf. This is because of presence of numerous stomata on the under surface of the leaf as compared to the upper surface.

(v) Three adaptations in plants to overcome transpiration are—

Presence of thick cuticle on leaves surface.

- Sunken stomata
- Fewer stomata

Chapter 5. Photosynthesis

1. The figure below represents the vertical section of a leaf :

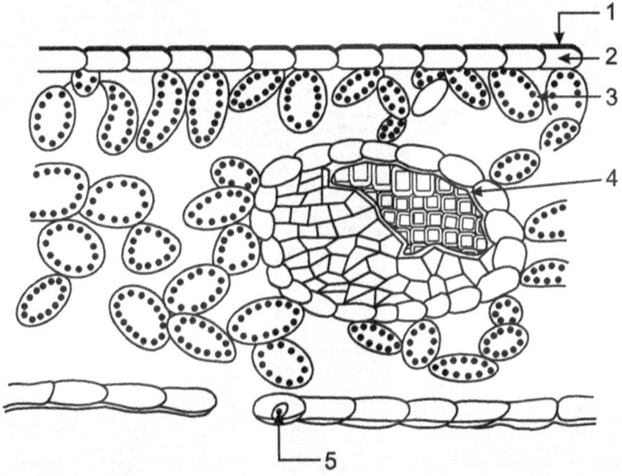

(i) Name the parts 1 to 5.

(ii) How many veins have been shown in the figure?

(iii) State the functions of part 4 and 5.

Ans. (i) 1. Cuticle
   2. Upper Epidermis
   3. Palisade tissue/chloroplast
   4. Xylem
   5. Stomata

(ii) One vein has been shown.

(iii) Xylem—helps in the conduction of water.

Stomata —exchange of gases takes place through it.

2.

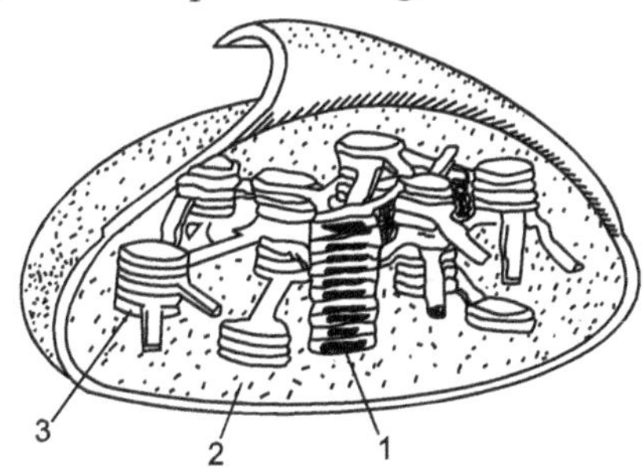

    (i)   Identify the above diagram.

    (ii) Label the guidelines 1-3.

    (iii) Name the phenomenon which takes place in the above diagram.

    (iv) Define the phenomenon.

    (v) What is the importance of the above phenomenon?

Ans. (i)   Chloroplast.

    (ii) 1. Granum   2. Stroma   3. Thylakoid

    (iii) Photosynthesis.

    (iv) Photosynthesis is the process by which living plant cells, containing chlorophyll, produce food substances (glucose and starch) from carbon dioxide and water, by using light energy. Plants release oxygen as a waste product during photosynthesis.

    (v) Photosynthesis is the source of energy, food and oxygen.

3. (i)   Draw a neat and well-labelled diagram of the chloroplast.

    (ii) List the events taking place in the photochemical phase of photosynthesis.

    (iii) If you are planning an experiment to show the effect of light on photosynthesis :

        (1) Will you select white light or green light? Justify your answer.

        (2) Why would you select a destarched plant?

Ans. (i)

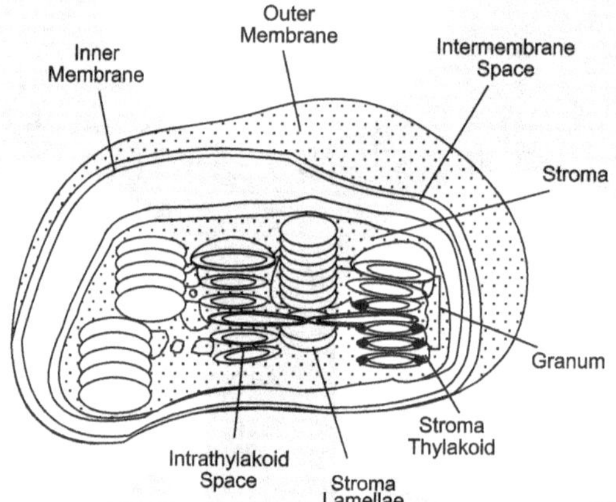

    (ii) Photochemical phase of photosynthesis is light dependent. A series of chemical reactions occur in quick succession initiated by light, therefore the phase is called photochemical phase. It takes place in chlorophyll containing thylakoids of chloroplast.

        It occurs in following steps :

        (1) The chlorophyll on exposure to light energy becomes activated by absorbing photons.

        (2) This energy is used in splitting the water molecules (photolysis) as below :

$$H_2O \longrightarrow H^+ + OH^-$$

        (3) OH^- ions through a series of steps produce water (H_2O) and oxygen (O_2). Water may be used inside the plant but O_2 is released into the atmosphere.

        (4) H^+ combines with CO_2 in dark reaction to produce glucose.

    (iii) (1) We will select white light because photosynthesis is maximum in white light while it is minimum in green light as green light is reflected by green plants.

        (2) We will select destarched plant so that we can demonstrate the synthesis of starch through iodine test.

4. A potted plant with variegated leaves was taken in order to prove a factor necessary for photosyn-thesis. The potted plant was kept in dark for 24 hours and then placed in bright sunlight for a hours. Observe the diagrams and answer the questions —*

Diagram Based Questions

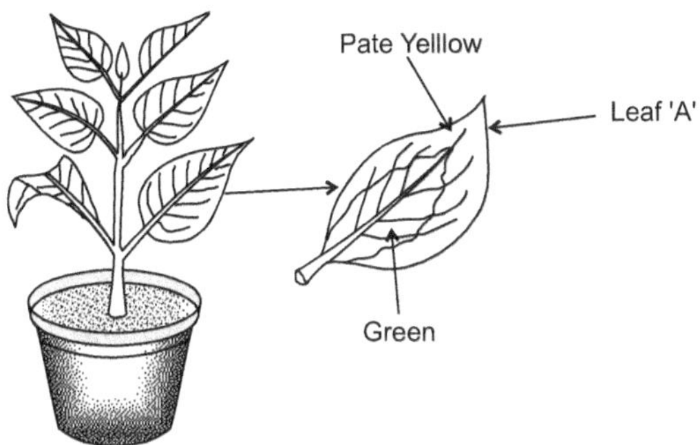

(i) What aspect of photosynthesis is being tested in the above diagram?

(ii) Represent the process of photosynthesis in the form of a balanced equation.

(iii) Why was the plant kept in the dark before beginning the experiment?

(iv) What will be the result of starch test performed on leaf A shown in the diagram. Give an example of a plant with variegated leaves.

(v) Draw a neat, labelled diagram of a chloroplast.

Ans. (i) Chlorophyll is necessary for photosynthesis.

(ii) $6CO_2 + 12H_2O$ [in presence of light energy and chlorophyll] $\rightarrow C_6H_{12}O_6 + 6O_2 + 6H_2O$

(iii) Plant was kept in dark to destarch the leaves so that the already present starch in the plants will not interfere with the results of the experiment.

(iv) The green portion of leaf after starch test will turn blue-black colour showing presence of starch but non-green portions will turn brown.

Example-Croton.

(v)

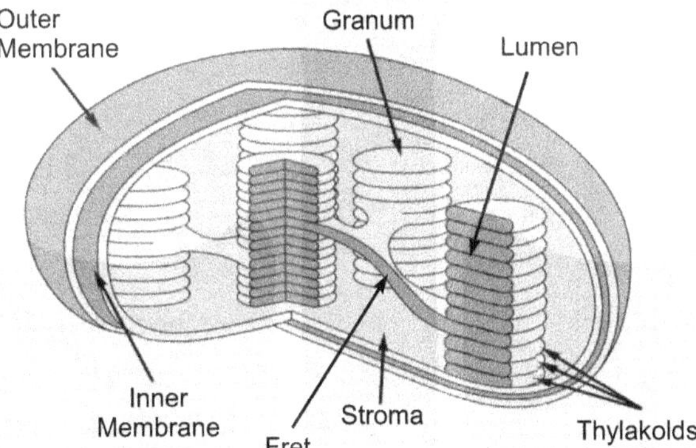

5. The figure alongside represents an experiment set up to study a physiological process in plants.*

(i) Name the physiological process being studied.

(ii) Explain the process.

(iii) What is the aim of the experiment?

(iv) Give a well balanced equation to represent the process.

Ans. (i) Photosynthesis.

(ii) It is the process in which green plants manufacture food from carbon dioxide and water, in the presence of sunlight.

(iii) To show that oxygen is given out during photosynthesis.

(iv) $6CO_2 + 12H_2O \xrightarrow[\text{Chlorophyll}]{\text{Light}} C_6H_{12}O_6 + 6H_2O + 6O_2$

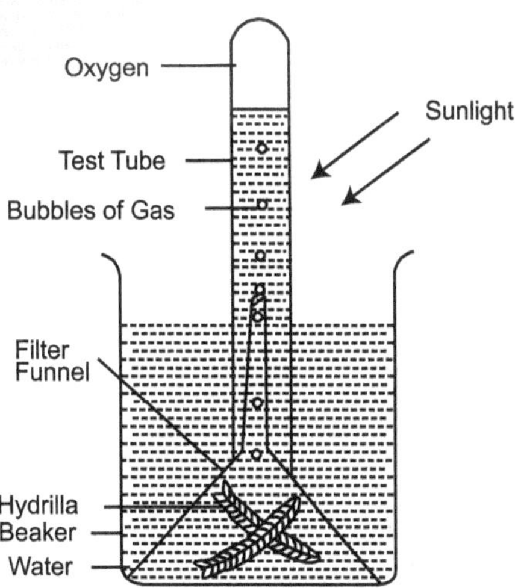

6. The figure given below is for performing an experiment on photosynthesis. Answer the following :

(i) What is the aim of this experiment?

(ii) Describe an experiment to show that light is necessary for photosynthesis.

(iii) What do you conclude from this experiment?

(iv) What is the role of light in photosynthesis?

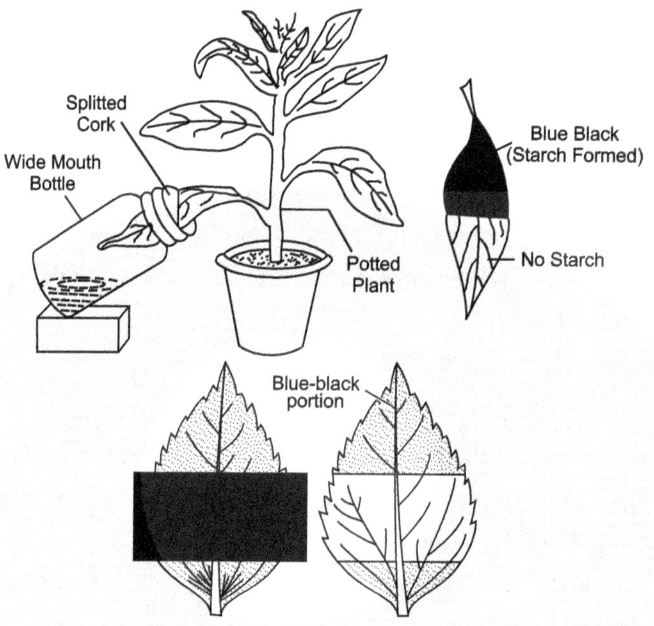

Ans. (i) To demonstrate that sunlight is necessary for photosynthesis.

(ii) Take a potted plant and keep it for 2-3 days in dark to destarch its leaves. Take one leaf and cover it on both sides with two black paper strips, as shown in the diagram, with the help of cellophane tape. Now keep the potted plant in light. After a few hours, pluck the leaf and remove the black strips. Boil the leaf in alcohol and wash in water. Test the leaf for starch with iodine solution. The leaf will turn blue-black all over except the region covered with black strips. This shows that the region which did not receive light could not synthesise starch. Thus, light is necessary for photosynthesis.

(iii) Light is necessary for photosynthesis.

(iv) Light supplies energy in the form of photons to split water during light reaction of photosynthesis.

7. A well watered healthy potted plant with variegated leaves was kept in darkness for about 24 hours. It was then set up as shown in the diagram and exposed to light for about 12 hours. At the end of this time leaf X and leaf Y were tested for starch. Study the diagram and answer the questions that follow:

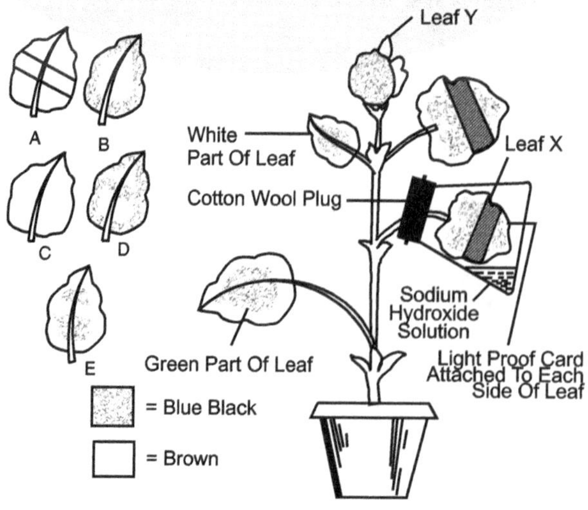

(i) Why was the plant initially kept in darkness for 24 hours?

(ii) What is the function of sodium hydroxide solution in the flask?

(iii) Select the correct leaf from the five available choices shown in the diagram as A, B, C, D and E. Rewrite the correct answer for the filling in the appropriate letter from the questions that follow:

1. After the starch test, leaf X would look like……

2. After the starch test, leaf Y would look like……

(iv) The experiment with leaf Y shows that photosynthesis requires the presence of certain factors. Mention any one factor.

Ans. (i) To remove starch from the leaves.

(ii) Sodium hydroxide absorbs CO_2 present in the air inside the flask.

(iii) 1. C   2. E

(iv) Carbon dioxide/light/chlorophyll.

8. The diagram given below represents an experiment to prove the importance of a factor in photosynthesis. Answer the questions that follow :*

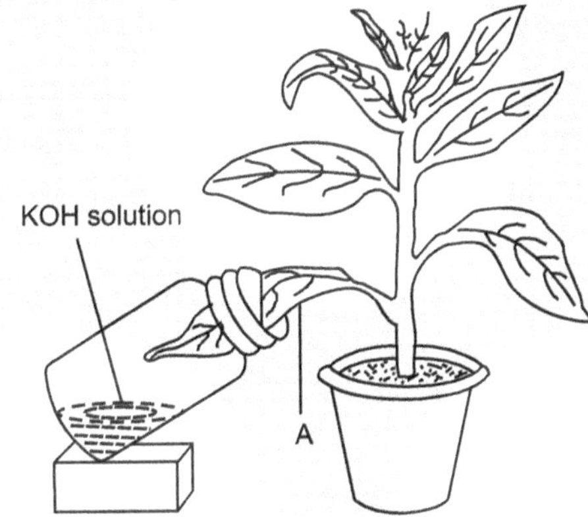

(i) Which factor is being studied here?

(ii) What is the purpose of keeping KOH in the flask?

(iii) Explain the term Photosynthesis.

(iv) What will you observe when the leaf A is tested for starch?

(v) Write a well balanced chemical equation for the process of photosynthesis.

Ans. (i) Carbon dioxide is necessary for photosynthesis.

(ii) KOH absorbs carbon dioxide.

(iii) Photosynthesis is the process by which cells containing chlorophyll using carbon dioxide and water in presence of light energy produce glucose and release oxygen as by-product.

(iv) When leaf A is tested for starch for the portion inside the flask, it does not show blue-black colour indicating absence of starch whereas the portion that is outside will show blue-black colour.

(v) $6CO_2 + 12H_2O \xrightarrow[\text{Sunlight}]{\text{Chlorophy II}} C_6H_{12}O_6 + 6H_2O + 6O_2$

9. The diagrams given below represent the relationship between a mouse and a physiological process that occurs in green plants. Study the diagram and answer the questions that follow :*

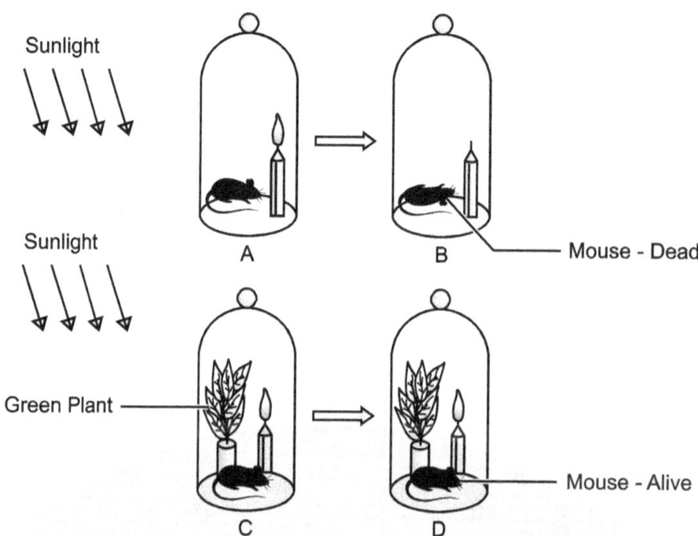

(i) Name the physiological process occurring in the green plant that has kept the mouse alive.

(ii) Explain the physiological process mentioned above.

(iii) Why did the mouse die in bell jar B?

(iv) What is the significance of the process as stated in (i) for life on earth?

(v) Represent the above mentioned physiological process in the form of a chemical equation.

Ans. (i) Photosynthesis is the physiological process that is occurring in the green plant which kept the mouse alive.

(ii) Photosynthesis is the process by which living plant cells containing chlorophyll produce food substances like glucose and starch from carbon dioxide and water by using light energy. Plants release oxygen gas during this process which is a life supporter for the living organisms on the earth's surface.

(iii) In bell jar B, there is no green plant so no oxygen is produced by photosynthesis process. The oxygen gas that is present in the bell jar has already been consumed by the mouse and the burning candle. So due to lack of oxygen, the mouse died and also the candle got extinguished.

(iv) The significance of photosynthesis process is that it is the only biological process which releases oxygen into the atmosphere that supports all life forms on the earth's surface.

(v) $6CO_2 + 12H_2O \xrightarrow{\text{In presence of light energy and chlorophyll}} C_6H_{12}O_6 + 6H_2O + 6O_2$

10. Study the graph and select the correct answer out of the available choices given under each question.

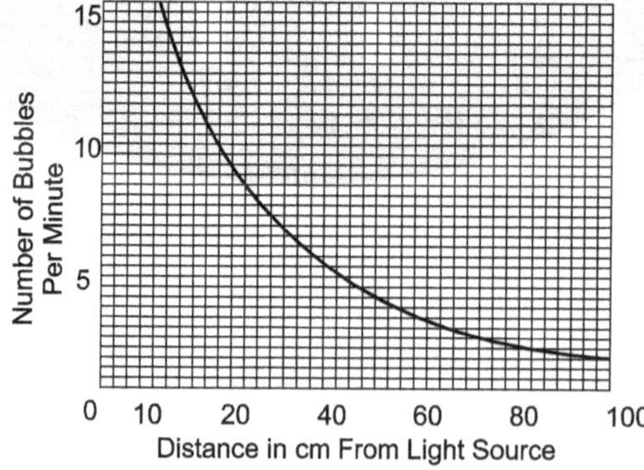

(i) From the graph it seems likely that the rate of bubbling per minute at 50 cm would have been :

(a) 2·0   (c) 3·0   (e) 4·0

(b) 2·5   (d) 3·5

(ii) The gas produced by the plant during the photosynthesis is :

(a) Air   (b) Oxygen   (c) Carbon dioxide

    (d) Nitrogen   (e) Hydrogen

(iii) The gas collected comes due to the breakdown of :

    (a) Glucose   (c) Water   (e) ATP

    (b) Starch   (d) Air

(iv) If ice cubes were added to the water, the rate of bubble formation would :

    (a) Remain the same.

    (b) Increase because more water is added.

    (c) Decreases because the temperature drops.

    (d) Decreases because water freezes.

    (e) Cannot tell from the information given.

(v) If some sodium bicarbonate is added to the water, the rate of bubble formation :

    (a) Increases because more respiration occurs.

    (b) Increases because more photosynthesis occurs.

    (c) Increases because the gas become less soluble.

    (d) Decreases because carbon dioxide acts as a limiting factor.

    (e) Decreases because respiration decreases.

Ans. (i)   3·5, (ii) Oxygen, (iii) Water, (iv) Decreases because the temperature drops, (v) Increases because photosynthesis increases.

11. The figure given below represents an experiment to demonstrate a particular aspect of photosynthesis. The alphabet 'A' represents a certain condition inside the flask.

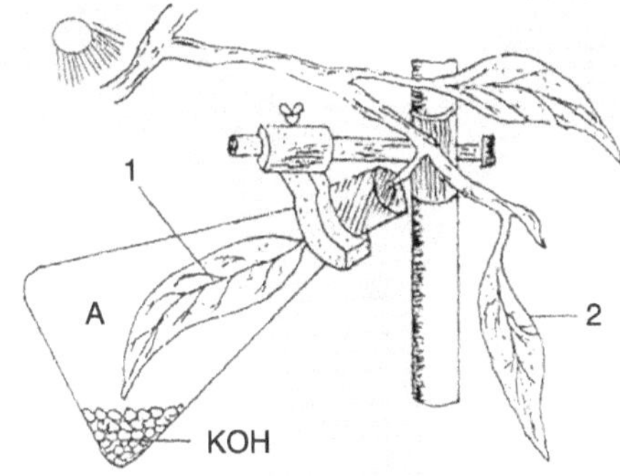

    (i)   What is the aim of the experiment?

    (ii)   Identify the special condition inside the flask.

    (iii) Name an alternative chemical that can be used instead of KOH.

    (iv) In what manner do the leaves 1 and 2 differ at the end of the starch test?

Ans. (i)   To prove that CO_2 is necessary for photosynthesis.

    (ii)   No CO_2 in the flask.

    (iii) CaO (limestone), potassium pyrogallate.

    (iv) Leaf 1, no change in colour with starch test.

         Leaf 2, will turn blue black at the end of starch test.

12. The diagram given below is an experiment conducted to study a factor necessary for photosynthesis. Observe the diagrams and then answer the questions—

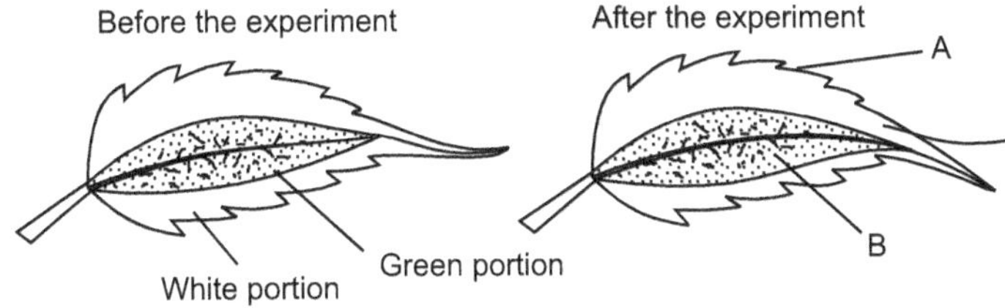

    (a)   What is the aim of the experiment?

Diagram Based Questions

(b) Name the test performed on the leaf and the solution used for the test.

(c) What type of leaf was used for t he experiment? Give an example.

(d) What is the expected result of the above test on the parts labelled A and B?

(e) Give a balanced chemical equation to represent the process of photosynthesis.

Ans. (a) Chlorophyll is necessary for photosynthesis .

(b) Starch test is performed on leaf and iodine solution is used for this test.

(c) Variegated leaf is used, examples is croton.

(d) Green part [B] will turn blue black/whereas non-green portion [A] will turn brown on performing starch test.

(e) $6CO_2 + 12H_2O \rightarrow C_6H_{12}O_6 + 6O_2 + 6H_2O$

13. The figure below represents an experiment performed to demonstrate a particular aspect of photosynthesis. The apparatus was kept in sunlight for almost the whole day. The numeral '1' represents a certain condition inside the flask and the numeral '2' represents a chemical responsible for this condition.

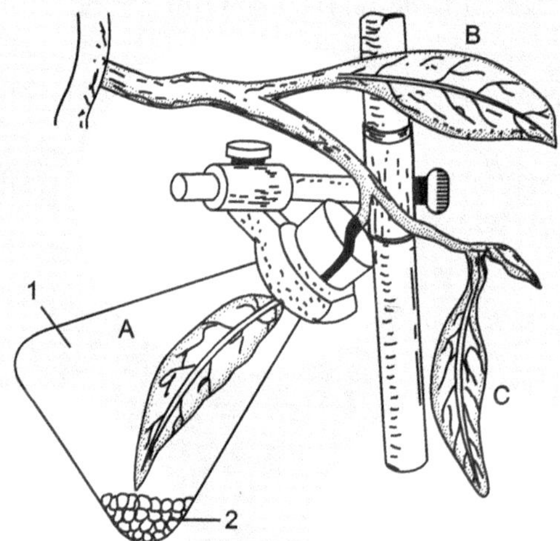

(i) What is the objective of the experiment?

(ii) What is the special condition inside the flask?

(iii) What is the chemical substance numbered '2'?

(iv) In what way will the three leaves (A, B and C) differ at the end of the experiment, when tested with iodine solution?

Ans. (i) The objective of this experiment is to show that CO_2 is necessary for photosynthesis.

(ii) The special condition inside the flask is that there is no CO_2 in the air as it has been absorbed by the KOH.

(iii) KOH or NaOH pellets.

(iv) Leaf A will be yellowish-white. Leaf B and Leaf C will turn blue-black.

Chapter 6. Chemical Coordination in Plants

1. Given below is an experimental set up to demonstrate a particular tropic movement in germinating seeds. Study the diagram and answer the questions that follow :*

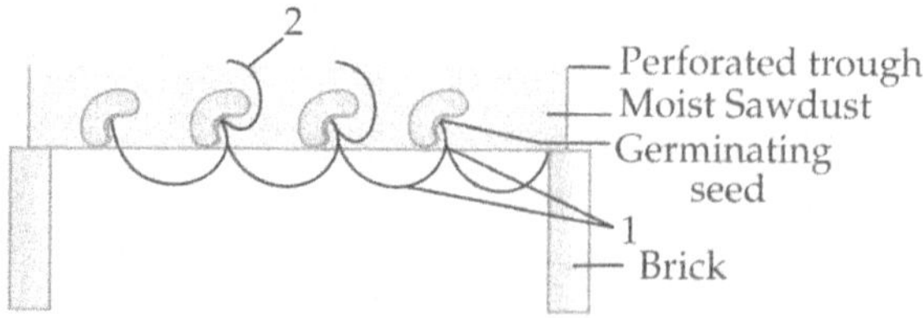

---

* Frequently asked previous years Board Exam Questions.

(i) Label the parts 1 and 2.

(ii) Name the tropic movement shown by part 1.

(iii) Part 1 is affected by two stimuli. Name them.

Which one of the two is stronger ?

(iv) What is Thigmotropism ? Give one example.

(v) What is meant by 'Positive' and 'Negative' tropic movements in plants ?

Ans. (a) (i) 1- Radicle; Plulule

(ii) Geotropism *i.e.* the movement of the parts of the plant towards earth's gravity.

(iii) The two stimuli are water/moisture and gravity of earth.

Water is a stronger stimulus as compared to earth's gravity.

(iv) Thigmotropism is the growth movement of plants in response to touch stimulus. Example- The tendrils of *Cuscuta* coil around a support in response to touch.

(v) If the growth movement of plant parts is towards the stimuli then the plant shows positive tropic movement but if the growth movement of plant parts is away from the stimuli then it shows negative tropic movement.

Chapter 7. The Circulatory System

1. The diagram shows different types of blood cells. Name them.

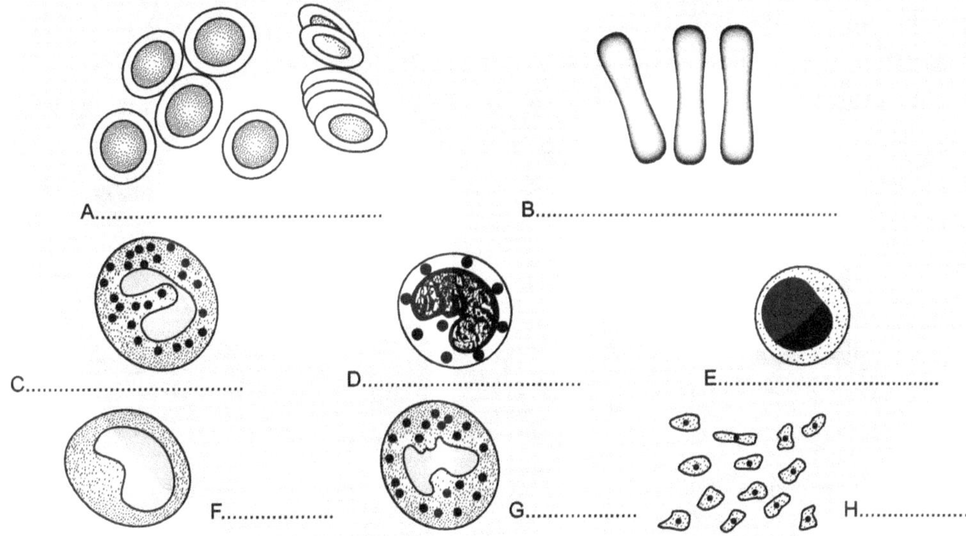

Ans. (A) Red blood cells   (D) Neutrophil   (G) Eosinophil

(B) RBCs side view   (E) Lymphocyte   (H) Platelets.

(C) Basophil   (F) Monocyte

2. Study the following diagram carefully and then answer the questions that follow.

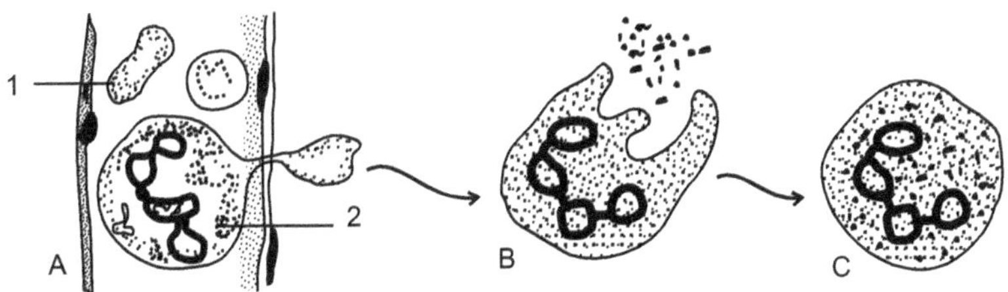

(i) Name the cell labelled 1.

(ii) Identify the phenomenon occurring in A.

(iii) Mention two structural differences between 1 and 2.

(iv) Name the processes occurrring in B and C and state the importance of this process in the human body.

Ans. (i) 1-Red Blood cell [RBC]

(ii) Diapedesis

(iii) RBC is non-nucleated. RBC is round, disc shaped whereas WBC is amoeboid, irregular shaped.

(iv) Phagocytosis process is shown in Fig. B and C and it is the process by which WBCs fight and destroy the germs entering into our body thus providing immunity.

3. Given below is a diagram of a human blood smear.*

Study the diagram and answer the questions that follow :

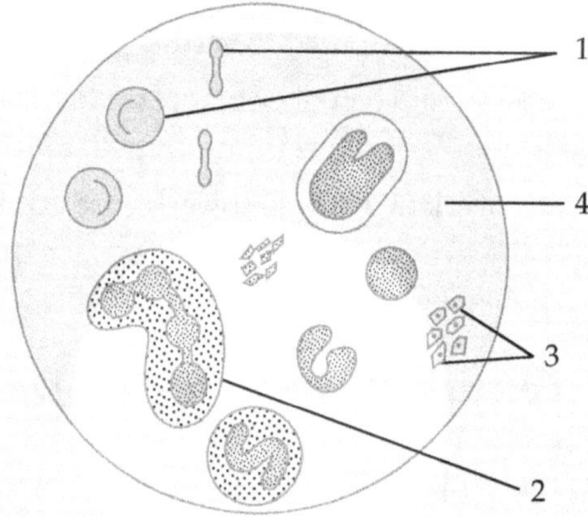

(i) Name the components numbered '1' to '4'.

(ii) Mention two structural differences between the parts '1' and '2'.

(iii) Name the soluble protein found in part '4' which forms insoluble threads during clotting of blood.

(iv) What is the average lifespan of the component numbered '1' ?

(v) Component numbered '1' do not have certain organelles but are very efficient in their function. Explain.

Ans. (i) 1. RBCs,   2. WBC,   3. Platelets,   4. Plasma.

(ii)

RBC	WBC
1. These are biconcave disc shaped.	These are Irregular amoeboid shaped.
2. RBCs do not have the nucleus.	They are characterized by the presence of a large central nucleus.

(iii) Fibrinogen

(iv) About 120 days

(v) Absence of nucleus in RBCs make them biconcave shaped. This increases their surface area for absorbing more oxygen. They do not have mitochondria so they are unable to use oxygen for themselves, so all oxygen is transported and delivered to cells and tissues. Absence of endoplasmic reticulum make them flexible due to which these can easily move through narrow capillaries.

4. The diagrams given below show the cross section of two kinds of blood vessels :

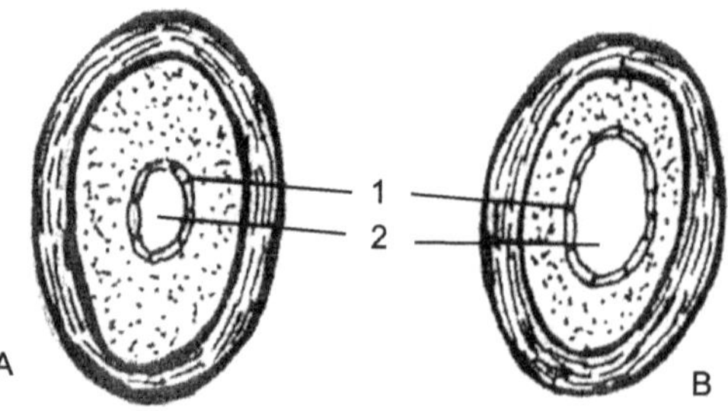

(i)   Identify the blood vessels A and B. In each case give a reason to support your answer.

(ii)   Name the parts numbered 1 and 2.

(iii)   When are the sounds "LUBB" and "DUB" produced during a heartbeat?

(iv)   Name the blood vessel that

    (1) begins and ends in capillaries.

    (2) supplies blood to the walls of the heart.

Ans. (i)   A—Artery, B—Vein, because in A lumen is narrow, in B lumen is wide.

(ii)   1 → Endothelium, 2 → Lumen.

(iii)   Lubb is produced when ventricles contract and atrio-ventricular valves get closed at the beginning of ventricular systole.

    Dub is produced by the closure of semilunar valves at the beginning of ventricular diastole.

(iv)   (1) Hepatic portal vein

    (2) Coronary arteries

5. The figures given alongside are cross-sections of blood vessels.

(i)   Identify the blood vessels A, B and C.

(ii)   Name the parts labelled 1–4.

(iii)   Mention two structural difference between A and B.

(iv)   Name the type of blood that flows :

    (1) through A,   (2) through B.

(v)   In which of the above vessels referred to in (i) above does exchange of gases actually take place?

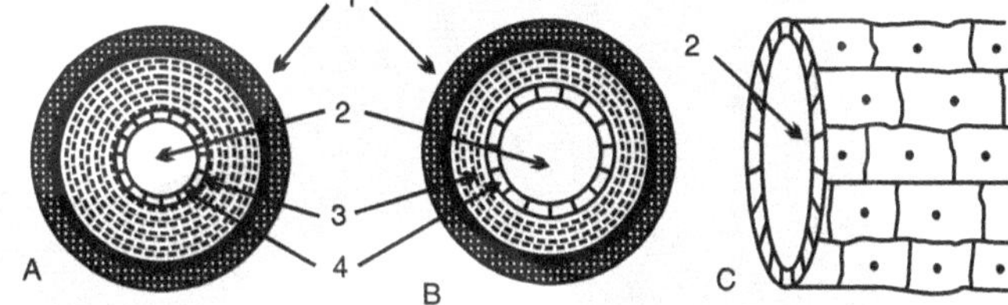

Ans. (i)   (A) Artery,

    (B) Vein,

    (C) Capillary.

(ii)   1. Tunica externa   3. Tunica media

    2. Lumen   4. Tunica intima/Endothelium.

(iii)   Two structural differences between arteries and veins are :

    (1) Arteries are thick-walled and veins are thin-walled.

    (2) There are no valves in arteries while valves are present in veins.

(iv)   (1) Oxygenated blood flows through A.

    (2) Deoxygenated blood flows through B.

(v)   The exchange of gases takes place in C (capillaries).

6. The diagram below represents a certain category of blood vessels showing the role of a special structure in their walls :

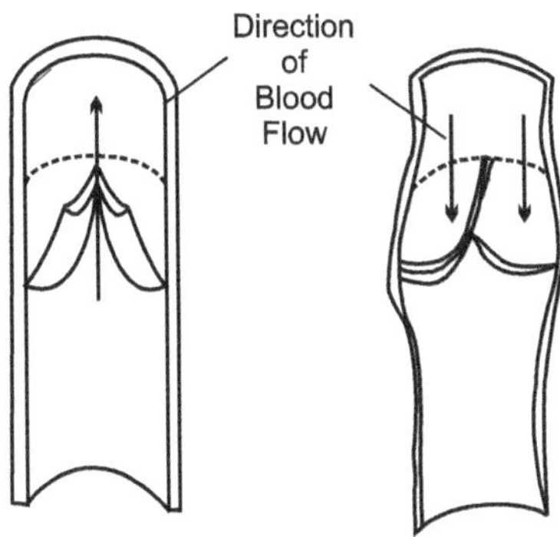

(i)   Name the kind of blood vessels shown.

(ii) What is the structure shown inside the blood vessels?

(iii) What is the role of these structures?

(iv) Are these structures present in any other kind of blood vessel? If so, name it.

(v)   Towards which side of the figure (Top or Bottom) is the heart located?

Ans. (i)   Veins.

(ii) Pocket valves.

(iii) These structures maintain the flow of blood in one direction only by preventing its back-flow.

(iv) Yes. These are present in lymph vessels.

(v)   The heart is located towards the top side of the figure.

7. Given below is a diagram of the external features of the heart.

(i)   Name the parts '1' to '7'.

(ii) What happens if the coronary artery gets an internal clot?

(iii) Which type of blood does part '5' carry?

(iv) Mention one structural difference between part '5' and '4'.

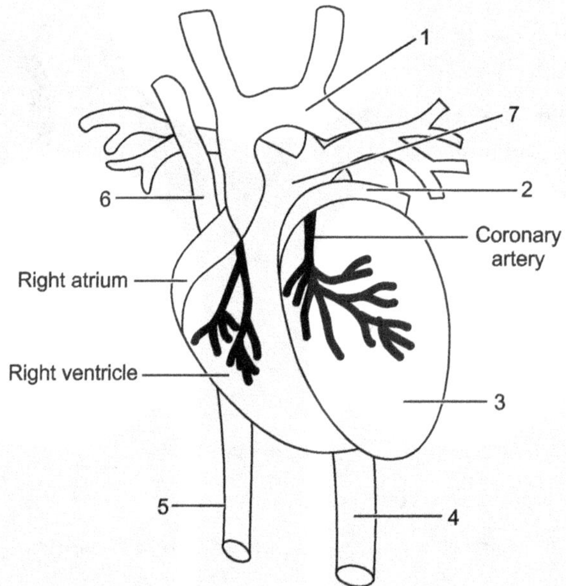

Ans. (i)   1. Aorta, 2. Left atrium, 3. Left ventricle, 4. Dorsal aorta, 5. Inferior vena cava, 6. Superior vena cava, 7. Pulmonary artery.

(ii) If the coronary artery gets an internal clot, the corresponding part of the heart does not get its blood supply. This will result in loss of contraction or even death of the cardiac cells resulting in a heart attack or coronary arrest which may prove to be fatal.

(iii) Part '5' which is the inferior vena cava carries deoxygenated blood which is rich in CO_2 and metabolic wastes.

(iv) Part '4' is more muscular and lumen is narrow while part '5' is less muscular and lumen is wider.

8. The diagram given below represents a section of the human heart. Answer the questions that follow :*

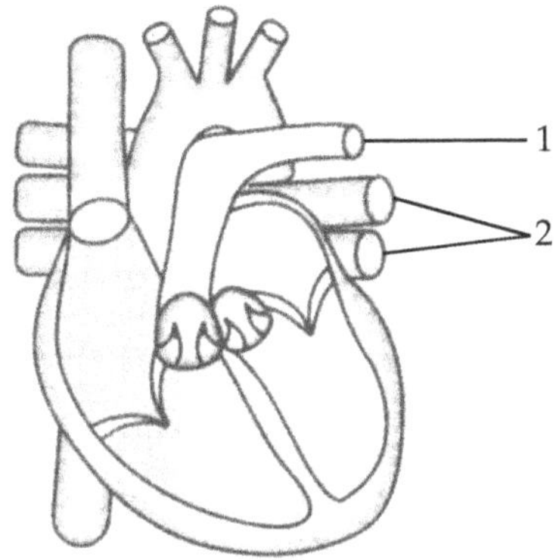

(i)   Which parts of heart are in the diastolic phase ? Give a reason to support your answer.

(ii) Label the parts numbered 1 and 2 in the diagram. What type of blood flows through them ?

(iii) What causes the heart sounds 'LUBB' and 'DUP' ?

(iv) Name the blood vessels that supply oxygenated blood to the heart muscles.

(v)   Draw neat labelled diagrams of a cross section of an artery and a vein.

Ans. (i)   Ventricles are in the diastolic phase as semilunar valves at root of aorta and pulmonary artery are closed and bicuspid and tricuspid valves are open. Blood enters from atria to ventricles through atrio-ventricular valves.

(ii) 1–Pulmonary artery   2–Pulmonary vein

Deoxygenated blood flows through pulmonary artery and oxygenated blood flows through pulmonary veins.

(iii) LUBB sound is caused by the closure of atrio-ventricular valves *i.e.*, tricuspid and bicuspid valves. Due to closure of semilunar valves located at the root of pulmonary artery and aorta, DUP sound is produced.

(iv) Coronary artery supplies oxygenated blood to the heart muscles.

(v)

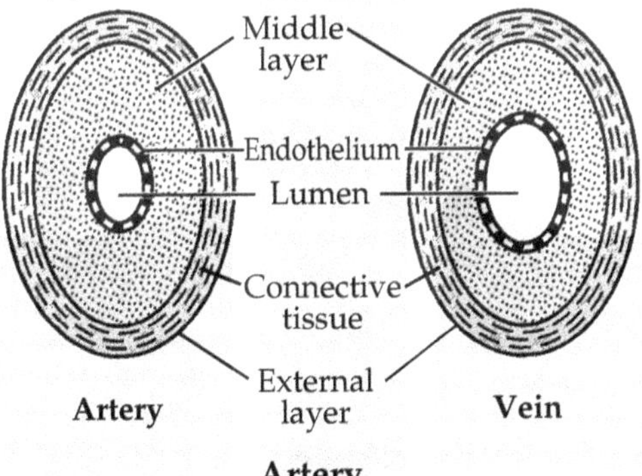

Artery

9. Given alongside is a simple diagram of the circulation of blood in a mammal showing the main blood vessels, the heart, lungs and body tissues. The blood vessel labelled 6 contains deoxygenated blood and the valve leading to it has three semi-lunar pockets.

(i)   Name the blood vessels and organs marked by number 1 to 8.

(ii) What do you mean by the term 'double circulation' of blood in mammals?

(iii) What is diastole?

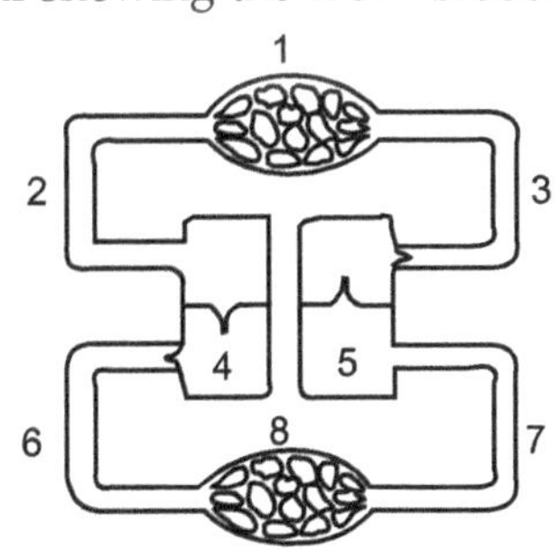

Ans. (i)   1. Veins from upper body tissues.   5. Left auricle

2. Superior vena cava   6. Pulmonary Artery

3. Aorta   7. Pulmonary vein

4. Right ventricle   8. Lungs.

(ii) The heart is said to have double circulation because the blood passes through the heart twice.

(1) It first leaves through the right ventricle, goes to the lungs and then returns to the left auricle of heart (pulmonary circulation).

(2) It leaves through the left ventricle, circulates through the body, and again returns to the right auricle of heart (systemic circulation).

(iii) Diastole is the phase of relaxation of the heart muscles during which the heart chambers fill with blood and the supply of blood to the cardiac muscle is improved.

10. The diagram given alongside represents the human heart in one phase of its activity. Study the same and then answer the questions that follow:

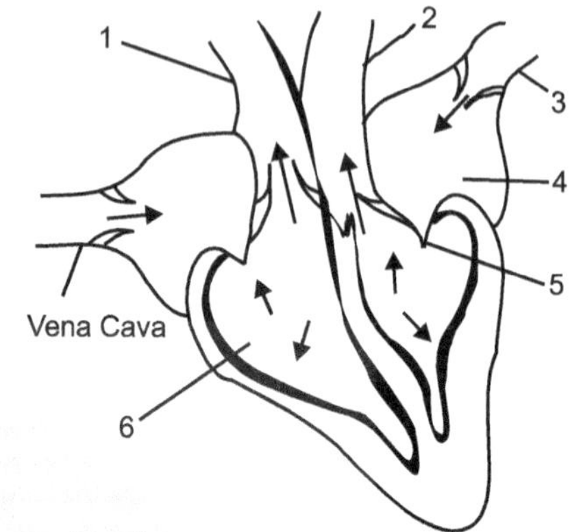

(i) Name the phase.

(ii) Which parts of the heart are contracting in this phase? Give a reason to support your answer.

(iii) Name the part numbered 1 to 6.

(iv) What type of blood flows through the parts marked '1' and '2'?

(v) How many valves are closed in this phase?

Ans. (i) Ventricular systole.

(ii) Both ventricles are contracting in this phase to force blood into the aorta and pulmonary artery. Both bicuspid and tricuspid valves are closed in order to prevent the back flow of blood into auricles and the semilunar valves are open.

(iii) 1. Pulmonary artery   4. Left auricle

     2. Aorta   5. Bicuspid valve (mitral valve)

     3. Pulmonary vein   6. Right ventricle.

(iv) '1'—carries deoxygenated blood.

     '2'—carries oxygenated blood.

(v) Two (Bicuspid and Tricuspid valves).

11. The figure alongside represents the internal structure of a mammalian heart and the associated blood vessels.

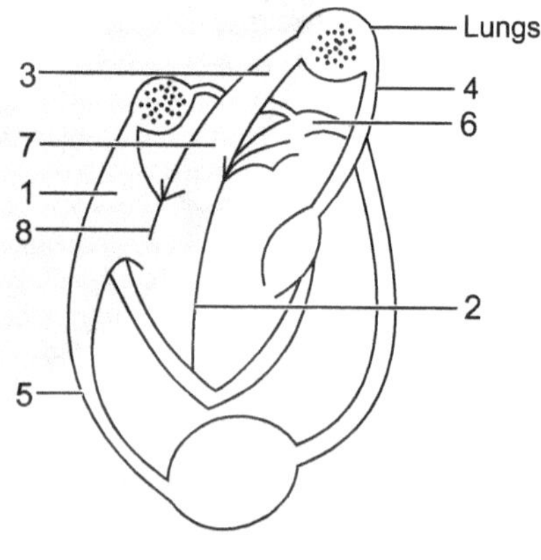

(i) (1) Name each of the structures labelled 1, 2, 3, 4, 5, 6, 7 and 8.

(2) State the function of each of the structures 5, 6, 7 and 8.

(ii) (1) State the function of heart as an entire organ.

(2) Why are the walls of the left ventricle more muscular than the right?

Ans. (i) (1) 1. Right auricle, 2. Left ventricle, 3. Pulmonary artery, 4. Pulmonary vein, 5. Inferior vena cava, 6. Aorta, 7. Pulmonary semilunar valve, 8. Tricuspid valve.

(2) 5 — carry deoxygenated blood from the body parts to the right auricle of the heart.

     6 — distributes oxygenated blood all over the body.

     7 — prevents the back flow of the blood into the ventricles.

     8 — prevents the reverse flow of the blood from right ventricle into the right auricle.

(ii) (1) The heart makes the blood to circulate all over the body.

(2) The walls of left ventricle are more muscular because they have to pump blood to a larger distance than the right ventricle so the walls have to withstand a high pressure.

12. Given alongside is the simplified pathway of the circulatory system :

(i)   Name the blood vessels marked 1 to 8.

(ii) Name the chamber of the heart which :

    (1) Receives blood from '1'.

    (2) Pumps blood into blood vessel '8'.

(iii) Mention two structural differences between blood vessels '7' and '2'.

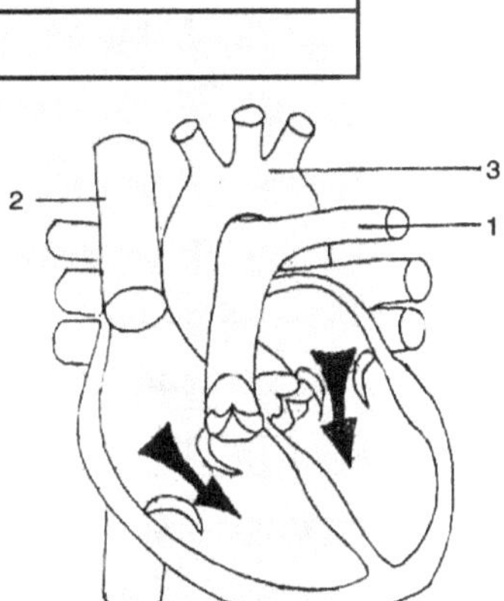

Ans. (i)   1. Pulmonary vein, 2. Dorsal aorta, 3. Hepatic portal vein,   4. Renal artery, 5. Renal vein, 6. Hepatic vein, 7. Inferior venacava , 8. Pulmonary artery.

(ii) (1) Left auricle.

    (2) Right ventricle.

(iii)

Dorsal aorta	Inferior vena cava
(1) It has thick muscular wall.	(1) It has thin muscular wall.
(2) Lumen is narrow.	(2) Lumen is wide.

13. The diagram given below represents the human heart in one phase of its functional activities. Study the same and answer the questions that follow :

(i)   Name the phase.

(ii) Label the parts 1, 2 and 3.

(iii) Which part of the heart is contracting in this phase? Give a reason to support your answer.

Ans. (i)   Atrial systole.

(ii) 1—Pulmonary artery

    2—Superior vena cava

    3—Aorta.

(iii) Simultaneous contraction of both the auricles. Because the cuspid valves are open, allowing blood to flow into ventricles.

14. The diagram given below represents the simplified pathway of the circulation of blood. Answer the questions that follow:*

(i)   Name the blood vessels labelled 1 to 4.

(ii) Which blood vessel supplies oxygenated blood to the muscles of the heart?

(iii) What is the importance of blood vessel labelled 5?

(iv) What is the type of blood circulation that takes place between the heart and the lungs?

(v)   Draw a diagram of the different blood cells as seen in a smear of human blood.

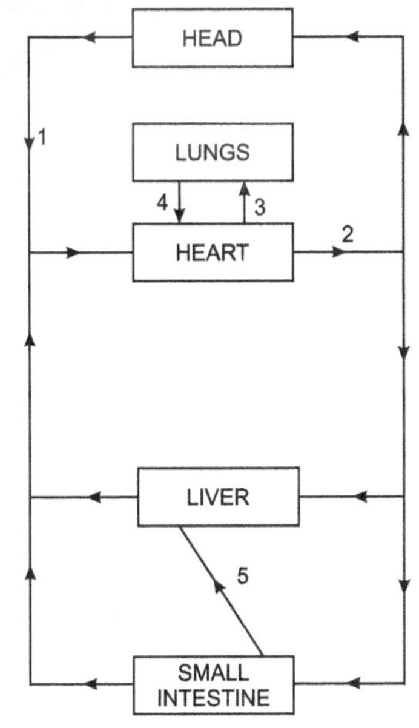

Ans. (i)   1. Superior vena cava; 2. Aorta; 3. Pulmonary artery; 4. Pulmonary vein

(ii) Coronary artery

(iii) Hepatic portal vein carries the blood from stomach and intestine to liver where the excess sugar is stored as glycogen. If any toxins are

---

** Frequently asked previous years Board Exam Questions.*

present in blood, they are detoxified in liver. In this way, the quantity of nutrients flowing in the blood is regulated and circulation of toxic substances in the blood is prohibited.

(iv) Pulmonary circulation

(v)

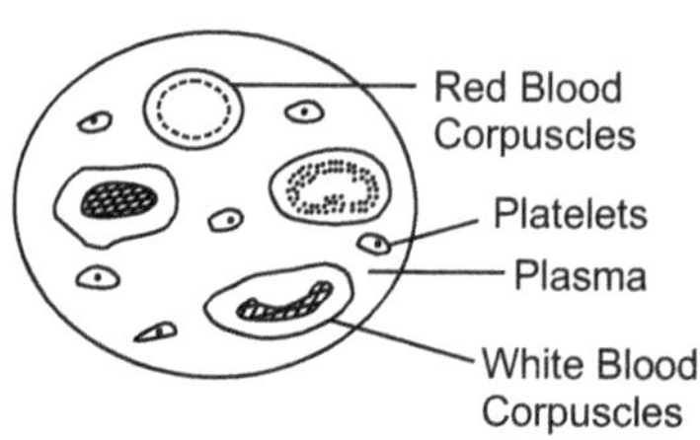

15. Given alongside is a schematic representation of the circulatory system in man. Study the same and answer the questions that follow :
   (i) Label the parts 1 to 4 indicated in the diagram.
   (ii) Give one difference between the parts 1 and 2 based on :
       (1) Their structure.
       (2) The nature of blood flowing through them.
   (iii) What is the specific name of the type of blood circulation that takes place between the heart and the lungs?
   (iv) Name the valve found at the beginning of the part labelled 3.

Ans. (i) 1. Right auricle   3. Aorta
           2. Left ventricle   4. Body parts

   (ii)

Right Auricle	Left Ventricle
(1) The wall of right auricle is thinner and smooth.	(1) The wall of left ventricle is thicker and rough.
(2) The deoxygenated blood flows.	(2) The oxygenated blood flows.

   (iii) Pulmonary circulation.
   (iv) Aortic semilunar valve.

16. Given below is a highly diagrammatic sketch of the internal structure of the human heart :
   (i) Name the parts numbered 1–11.
   (ii) What is the main difference in the quality of blood contained in parts 6 and 7?

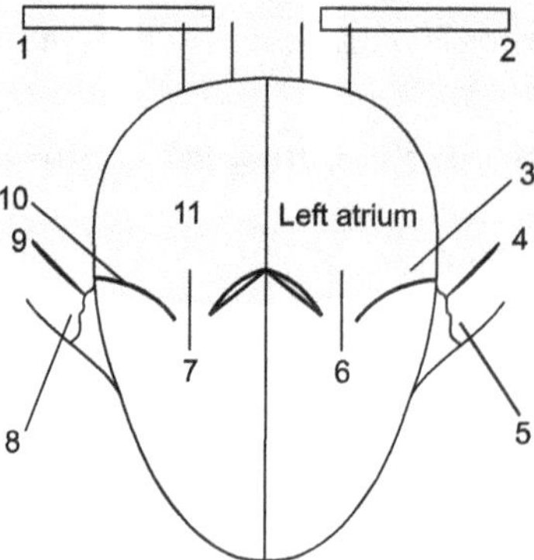

Ans. (i) 1. Anterior or superior vena cava   7. Right ventricle
           2. Pulmonary vein   8. Pulmonary semilunar valve
           3. Mitral or bicuspid valve   9. Pulmonary artery
           4. Dorsal aorta   10. Tricuspid valve
           5. Aortic semilunar valve   11. Right atrium
           6. Left ventricle

(ii) Part 6 contains oxygenated blood whereas part 7 contains deoxygenated blood.

17. (i) The diagram represents the 'closed system' or 'double circulation' of blood in mammals.

Justify the above statement.

(ii) State two structural and two functional differences between the arteries and veins.

(iii) State the changes in the composition of blood as it passes through the following organs :

(1) Lungs, (2) Gut, (3) Liver, (4) Kidneys.

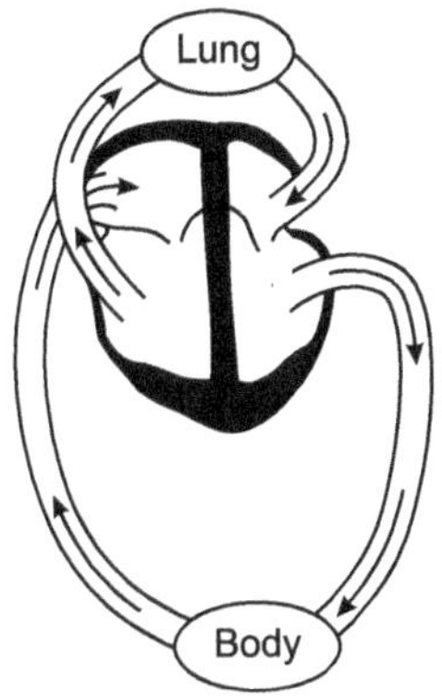

Ans. (i) **Double circulation or closed system :** In human beings, the heart has double circulation as the blood passes through the heart twice.

(1) It first leaves the heart (right ventricle) and goes to lungs and then returns to the heart (left auricle). This circulation is called pulmonary circulation.

(2) From the left ventricle it circulates through the entire body and again returns to the heart (right auricle). This circulation is called systemic circulation.

(ii)

Artery	Vein
Structural :	
(1) Thick-walled.	Thin-walled.
(2) No valves are present.	Valves are present.
Functional :	
(1) Carry oxygenerated blood except pulmonary artery.	Carry deoxygenated blood except pulmonary vein.
(2) Carry blood away from the heart.	Carry blood towards the heart.

(iii) (1) In lungs, the blood releases carbon dioxide and picks up oxygen. Hence before passing through the lungs it contains more carbon dioxide while it contains more oxygen after it has passed through the lungs.

(2) When blood passes through the gut, it absorbs digested food materials *i.e.*, it contains more carbohydrates, proteins, fats, water, ions and vitamins.

(3) As the blood passes through liver, it contains more urea and other waste materials.

(4) As the blood passes through kidneys, it contains less urea and other waste materials.

18. The diagram alongside represents the simplified pathway of the circulation of blood. Study the same and answer the questions that follow :

(i) Name the blood vessels labelled 1 and 2.

(ii) State the function of blood vessels labelled 5 and 8.

(iii) What is the importance of the blood vessel labelled 6?

(iv) Which blood vessel will contain a high amount of glucose and amino acids after a meal?

(v) Draw a diagram of the different blood cells as seen in a smear of human blood.

Ans. (i) 1. Anterior vena cava.

2. Aorta

(ii) Blood vessel 5 supplies oxygenated blood to the liver.

Blood vessel 8 brings deoxygenated blood from lower parts of the body to heart.

(iii) It brings all the digested food and deoxygenated blood from parts of alimentary canal to liver.

(iv) Blood vessel 6.

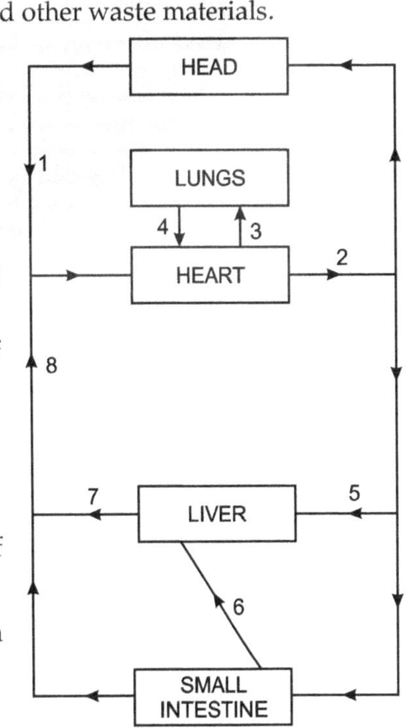

(v)

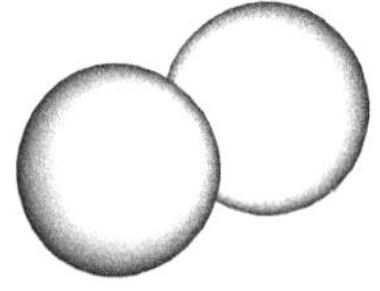

Red blood cells

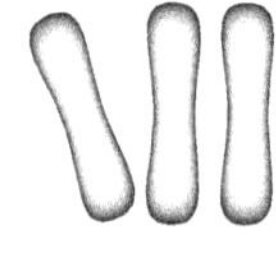

White blood cells

Platelets

Chapter 8. The Excretory System

1. Given alongside is a simple diagram of the human kidney cut open longitudinally. Answer the following questions :

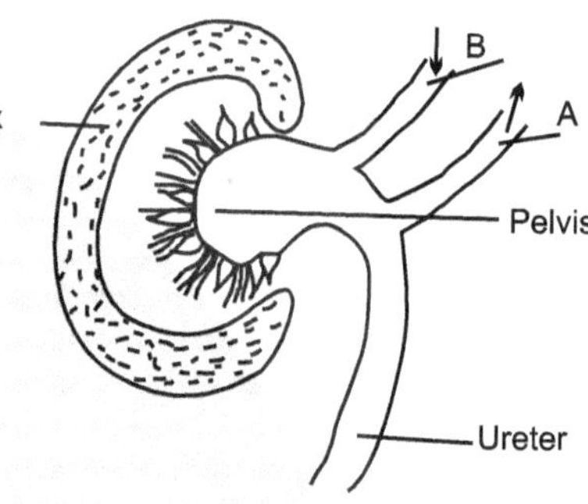

   (i)   Give the definition of excretion.

   (ii) Name the units of the kidney.

   (iii) Why does the cortex of the kidney show a 'dotted' appearance?

   (iv) Mention two functions of the kidney.

   (v)   Write two differences in the composition of the blood flowing through blood vessels A and B.

Ans. (i)   Excretion is the process of removal of all harmful and unwanted products especially nitrogenous products from the body of living beings.

   (ii) The units of the kidney are nephrons.

   (iii) Malpighian capsule lies in the cortex region of kidney and are present in large numbers which gives the cortex of kidney a dotted appearance.

   (iv) Two functions of kidney are :

   (1) It expels out all the nitrogenous products produced in the body.

   (2) It helps in osmoregulation.

   (v)   Two differences in the composition of blood flowing through blood vessels A and B are :

   (1) B contains blood having large amount of water, while blood in A is thicker.

   (2) B carries more O_2 and nitrogenous waste products as it is renal artery.

   A carries CO_2 and no nitrogenous products.

2. The diagram shows the Excretory System of a human being. Study the same and then answer the questions that follow :

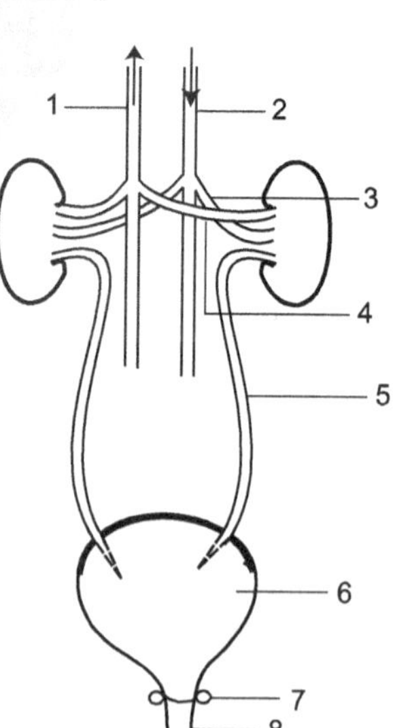

   (i)   Name the parts labelled 1, 2, 3, and 4.

   (ii) Give the main function of the parts labelled 5, 6, 7 and 8.

   (iii) Name the endocrine gland which could be added in the diagram and state its location/position.

Ans. (i)   1—Inferior vena cava

   2—Aorta

   3—Renal artery

   4—Renal vein

   (ii) (5) Ureter—Carry urine to the bladder.

   (6) Urinary bladder—Store urine.

   (7) Sphincter muscle—Control the voiding of urine

   (8) Urethra—Release urine periodically.

(iii) Adrenal gland—At the top of each kidney.

3. Study the diagram given alongside and then answer the questions that follow :

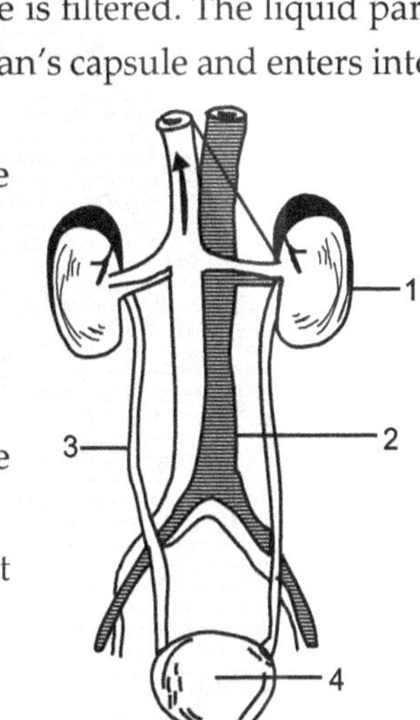

(i) Name the region in the kidney where the given structure is present?

(ii) Name the parts labelled 1, 2 and 3.

(iii) Name the stages involved in the formation of urine.

(iv) What is the technical term given to the process occurring in 2 and 3? Briefly describe the process.

Ans. (i) Renal cortex

(ii) 1. Afferent arteriole

2. Glomerulus

3. Bowman's capsule

(iii) Ultrafiltration, selective reabsorption and tubular secretion.

(iv) **Ultrafiltration :** In it, blood entering the glomerulus under great pressure is filtered. The liquid part of the blood filters through the walls of glomerular capillaries and Bowman's capsule and enters into the nephron where it is called the glomerular filterate.

4. Given alongside is the figure of certain organs and associated parts in the human body, study the same and then answer the questions that follow :

(i) Name all the organ systems shown completely or even partially.

(ii) Name the parts numbered 1 to 5.

(iii) Name the structural and functional unit of the part marked '1'.

(iv) Name the two main organic constituents of the fluid that flows down the part labelled '3'.

(v) Name the two major steps involved in the formation of the fluid that passes down the part labelled '3'.

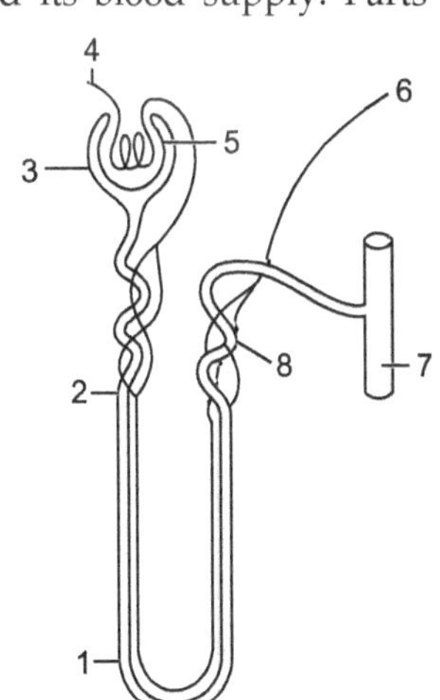

Ans. (i) Excretory system, Circulatory system, Endocrine system.

(ii) 1. Left kidney, 2. Dorsal aorta, 3. Right ureter, 4. Urinary bladder, 5. Urethra.

(iii) Nephron

(iv) (1) Urea, (2) Uric acid.

(v) (1) Ultrafiltration,

(2) Selective reabsorption.

5. The diagram alongside represents a mammalian kidney tubule (nephron) and its blood supply. Parts indicated by the guidelines 1 to 8 are as follows :

1. U-shaped loop of Henle

2. Proximal convoluted tubule with blood capillaries

3. Bowman's capsule

4. Afferent arteriole from renal artery

5. Glomerulus

6. Venule to renal vein

7. Collecting tubule

8. Distal convoluted tubule with blood capillaries

Study the diagram and answer the following questions :

(i) Where does ultrafiltration take place?

(ii) Which structure contains the lowest concentration of urea?

(iii) Which structure contains the highest concentration of urea?

(iv) Which structure contains the lowest concentration of glucose?

(v) Where is the most water reabsorbed?

Ans. (i) 3. Bowman's capsule Glomerulus.

(ii) 6. Renal vein.

(iii) 8. Distal convoluted tubule with blood capillaries.

(iv) 7. Collecting tubule.

(v) 2. Proximal convoluted tubule with blood capillaries.

6. The diagram given below is that of a structure present in a human kidney.*
Study the same and answer the questions that follow :

(i)   Name the structure represented in the diagram.

(ii) What is the liquid entering part '1' called ?
Name two substances present in this liquid that are reabsorbed in the tubule.

(iii) What is the fluid that comes to part '2' called ?
Name the main nitrogenous waste in it.

(iv) Mention the three main steps involved in the formation of the fluid mentioned in **(iii)** above.

(v) Name the substance which may be present in the fluid in part '2' if a person suffers from Diabetes mellitus.

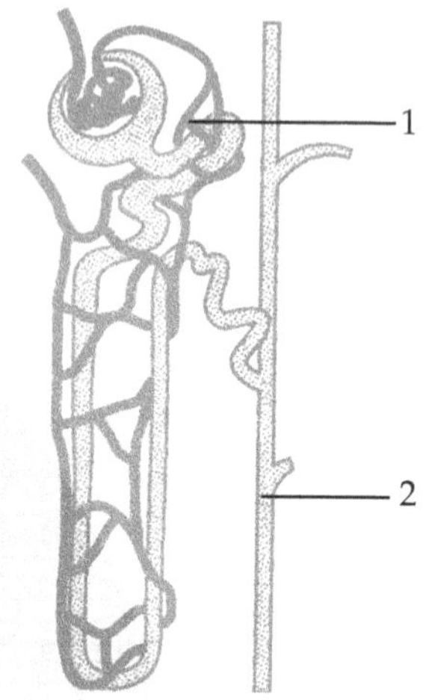

Ans. (i)   Nephron/uriniferous tubule/renal tubule.

(ii) Glomerular filtrate

Two substances present in glomerular filtrate are water and glucose.

(iii) Urine

Urea is the main nitrogenous waste in urine.

(iv) Ultrafiltration, selective reabsorption, tubular secretion and Glomerular filtration.

(v) Glucose

7. The given diagram represents a nephron and its blood supply. Study the diagram and answer the following questions :

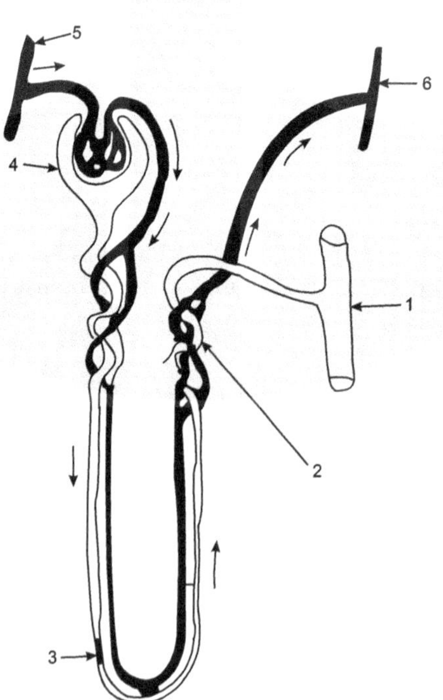

(i)   Label parts 1, 2, 3 and 4.

(ii) State the reason for the high hydrostatic pressure in the glomerulus.

Diagram Based Questions

(iii) Name the blood vessel which contains the least amount of urea in this diagram.

(iv) Name the two main stages of urine formation.

(v) Name the part of the nephron which lies in the renal medulla.

Ans. (i) 1—Collecting tubule   3—Loop of Henle.

         2—Distal convoluted tubule   4—Bowman's capsule.

(ii) The afferent arteriole entering the Bowman capsule is wider than the efferent arteriole which leaves it. So more blood is entering and less blood is moving out of the glomerulus which creates a high hydrostatic pressure in the glomerulus.

(iii) Renal vein.

(iv) Ultrafiltration and Reabsorption.

(v) Loop of Henle.

8. The figure given below shows a part of a nephron.*

Answer the questions that follow:

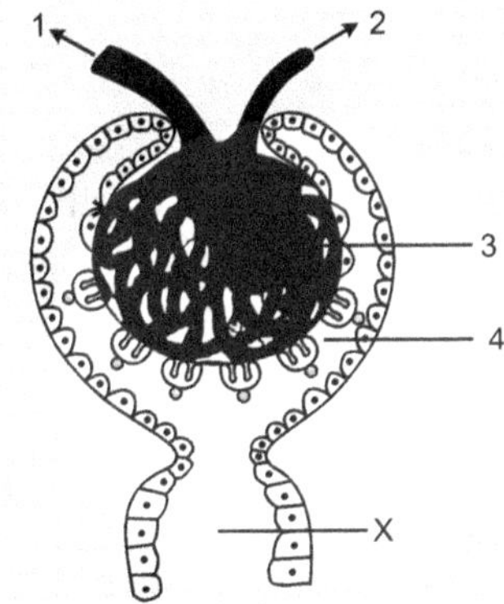

(i) In which region of the kidney is the above structure present?

(ii) Label the parts numbered 1 to 4.

(iii) What is the technical terms for the process that occurs in part 3?

(iv) Why is fluid X not called urine? Justify your answer.

(v) Draw a neat, labelled diagram of the urinary system of man.

Ans. (i) Cortex region of kidney.

(ii) 1. Afferent arteriole; 2. Efferent arteriole; 3. Glomerulus; 4. Bowman's capsule

(iii) Ultrafiltration

(iv) Fluid X is called glomerular filtrate but not urine because it is a very dilute solution that contains not only harmful wastes but also many useful substances like water, salts, glucose etc. which needs to be reabsorbed in the different parts of the nephron.

(v)

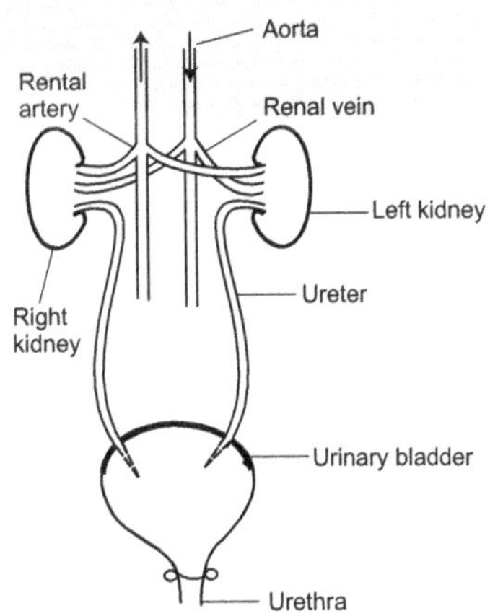

---

* **Frequently asked previous years Board Exam Questions.**

Chapter 9. The Nervous System and Sense Organs

Q. 1. The following diagram is that of a human brain. Guidelines 1 to 5 indicate different parts of the surface of the brain and these are as follows :

1. Frontal lobe of cerebrum
2. Temporal lobe of cerebrum
3. Occipital lobe of cerebrum
4. Cerebellum
5. Medulla oblongata

Study the diagram and answer the following questions :

(i) What handicaps would result from :

  (1) Damage to part numbered 3.

  (2) Damage to part numbered 4.

(ii) Mention one main function of each of the parts numbered 1, 2, and 5.

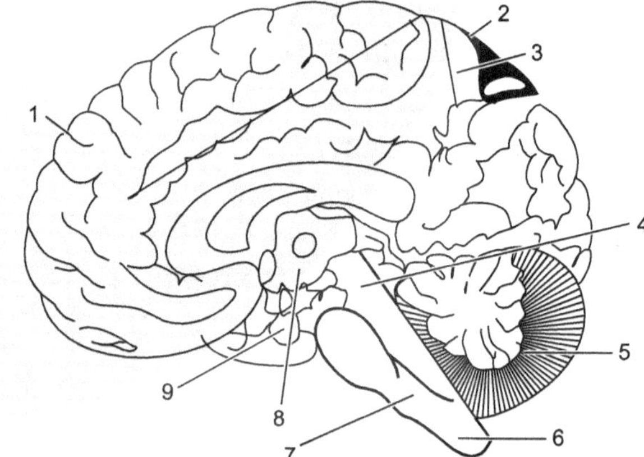

Ans. (i) (1) The part numbered 3 is named as occipital lobe of cerebrum, which is the area of vision. If this part is damaged, the person will be unable to see and will lose his sight/vision..

  (2) The part numbered 4 is named as cerebellum, which is responsible for co-ordinating the muscular activity for body balancing. If this part is damaged, the body balancing during walking and running would be affected.

(ii) **Function of part 1 :** It governs all mental activities (reasoning, will, memory, intelligence, higher feelings and emotions).

  Function of part 2 : It controls all voluntary actions and is responsible for taste and smell. It is responsible for hearing

  Function of part 5 : It controls several involuntary activities, such as heart beat, breathing, peristaltic motion of the alimentary canal, dilation and concentration of blood vessels, etc.

2. The alongside diagram represents longitudinal section of human brain. Label its parts 1-9 as shown with guidelines.

Ans. 1. Cerebrum

  2. Gray matter

  3. White matter

  4. Mid-brain

  5. Cerebellum

  6. Spinal cord

  7. Medulla oblongata

  8. Hypothalamus

  9. Pituitary gland.

3. The alongside simplified diagram shows a section through the brain.

(i) Name the parts labelled A, B and C.

(ii) Give one function of each of the parts A, B and C.

(iii) What is found in region D?

Ans. (i) A—Cerebrum; B—Medulla oblongata; C—Cerebellum.

(ii) A—Controls memory, learning, speech and co-ordinates sensory input and motor output, B—Controls vital processes such as heart rate and breathing, C—Responsible for muscle co–ordination and balance.

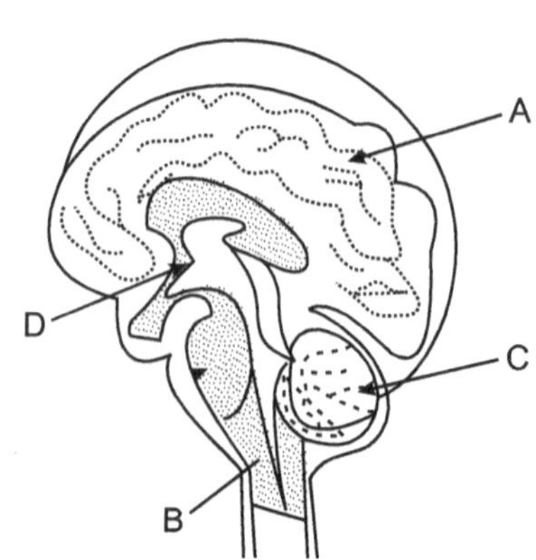

(iii) D—Contains cerebrospinal fluid.

4. The alongside diagram represents the human brain as seen in an external view. Study the same and then answer the questions that follow :

(i) Name the parts labelled 1, 2, 3 and 4.

(ii) Mention the difference in the arrangement of the nerve cells in the parts marked '1' and '4'.

(iii) What are the main function of the parts marked '3' and '4'?

(iv) Name the sheet of nerve fibres that connect the two halves of the part labelled '1'.

Ans. (i) 1. Cerebrum

2. Cerebellum

3. Medulla oblongata

4. Spinal cord.

(ii) 1. Gray matter is outside and white matter is inside.

4. White matter is outside and gray matter is inside.

(iii) 3. Medulla oblongata controls all involuntary movements of internal organs *e.g.*, breathing movements of lungs, beating of heart.

4. Spinal cord performs reflex action below the neck.

(iv) Corpus callosum.

5. The diagram given below shows the internal structure of the spinal cord, depicting a simple reflex. Study the same and then answer the questions that follow :*

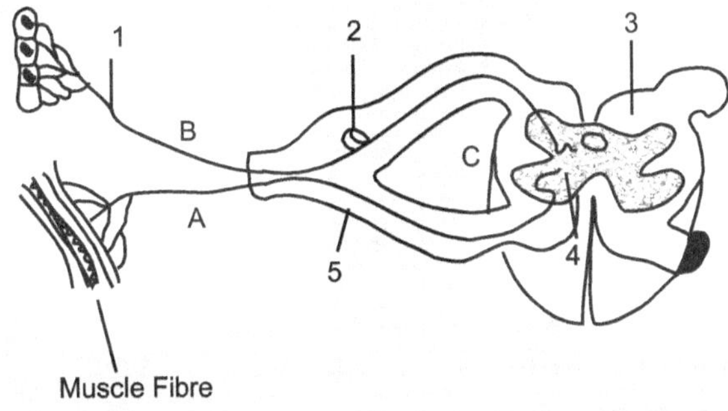

(i) Name the parts numbered 1 to 5.

(ii) Using the letters of the alphabet shown in the figure indicate the direction in which an impulse enters and leaves the spinal cord.

(iii) What is the term given to the point of contact between two nerve cells?

(iv) What is meant by 'simple reflex'? Give two examples of simple reflexes and name the stimuli too.

(v) How does the arrangement of nerve cells in the spinal cord differ from that in the brain?

Ans. (i) 1. Sensory or Afferent fibre.   4. Gray matter.

2. Cell body of sensory neuron.   5. Spinal nerve.

3. White matter.

(ii) B → C → A

(iii) Synapse.

(iv) **Simple reflex** : It is an involuntary, automatic and quick response to a stimulus.

Examples : (1) The closing of the eyelids when a strong beam of light is flashed.

(2) The withdrawal of the hand when it is pricked.

(v) In spinal cord, white matter is outside and gray matter is inside. In brain, white matter is inside and gray matter is outside. *

---

6. The diagram given below represents the spinal cord of a mammal, seen in a transverse section together with the nerves. Study the diagram and then answer the questions given below :

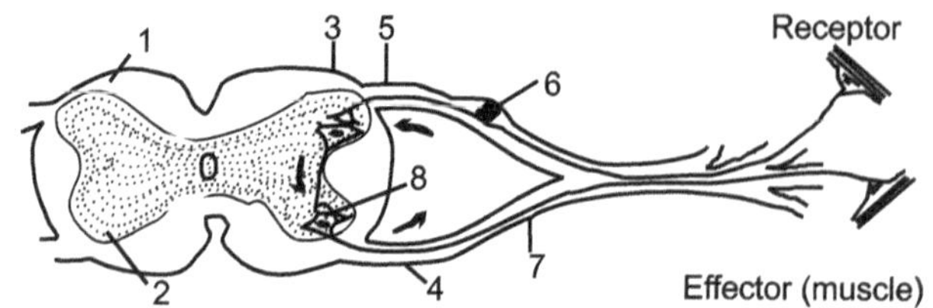

(i) Label the parts 1–8 indicated by guidelines.

(ii) What do the arrows indicate? What is the pathway indicated termed?

(iii) What type of nerve is shown in the diagram?

Ans. (i) 1. White matter   4. Ventral root   7. Spinal nerve

 2. Gray matter   5. Dorsal root ganglion   8. Synapse

 3. Dorsal root   6. Sensory neuron

(ii) The sensory nerve fibre bring sensory impulses from the receptor organ to the central nervous system. The motor nerve fibre relay the motor impulses from the central nervous system to the effector organ. The pathway indicated is termed as reflex arc.

(iii) Sensory or Afferent nerve.

7. The diagram given below shows the internal structure of a spinal cord depicting a phenomenon. Study the diagram and answer the questions :*

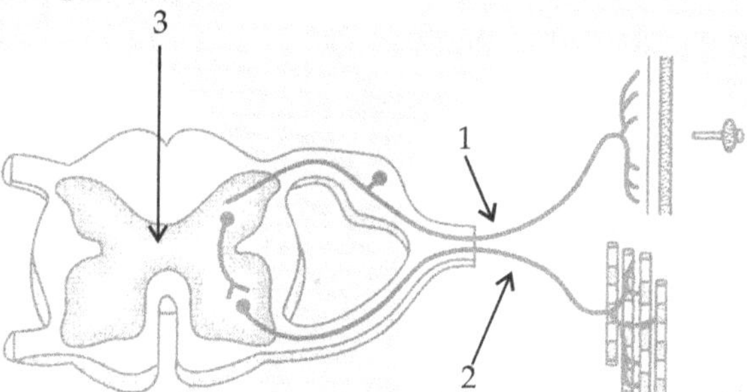

(i) Name the phenomenon that is depicted in the diagram. Define the phenomenon.

(ii) Give the technical term for the point of contact between the two nerve cells.

(iii) Name the parts numbered 1, 2 and 3.

(iv) How does the arrangement of neurons in the spinal cord differ from that of the brain ?

(v) Mention two ways by which the spinal cord is protected in our body.

Ans. (i) Reflex action. It is an automatic, quick and involuntary action in the body brought about by a stimulus.

(ii) Synapse

(iii) **1.** Sensory neuron, **2.** Motor neuron, **3.** Gray matter.

(iv) In spinal cord, the gray matter containing the cell bodies of neurons lies on inner side and white matter containing myelinated axons on outer side, whereas, in the brain, gray matter is outside and white matter lies on inner side.

(v) 1. Spinal cord is covered by three membranous layer of meninges which protects it and also its central canal is filled with cerebrospinal fluid which absorbs shocks.

 2. It is also protected by the vertebrae of backbone.

8. The diagram given below is a representation of a certain phenomenon pertaining to the nervous system. Study the diagram and answer the following questions :

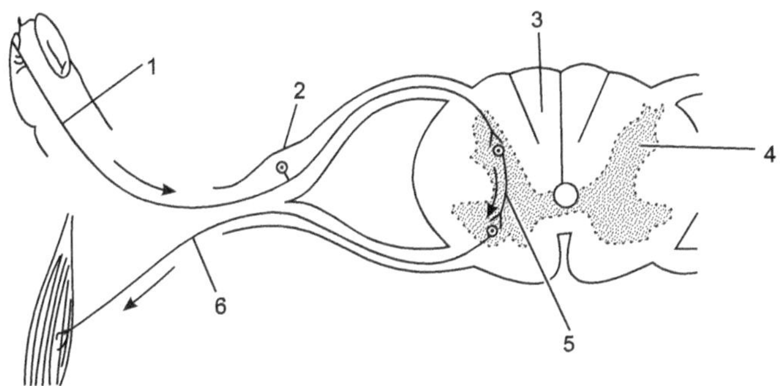

(i)   Name the phenomenon that is being depicted.

(ii) Give the technical term for the point of contact between the two nerve cells.

(iii) Label the parts numbered 1 to 4.

(iv) Write the function of parts 5 and 6.

(v)   How does the arrangement of neurons in the spinal cord differ from that of the brain?

Ans. (i)   Reflex action

(ii) Synapse

(iii) 1—Sensory fibre   3—White matter

2—Sensory ganglion   4—Gray matter

(iv) **Function of part '5' :** Relay Nerve. It receives messages from sensory neuron and passes it to the motor neuron.

Function of part '6' : Motor nerve It passes impulses from the spinal cord to the effector organ.

(v)   In spinal cord the gray matter is inside and white matter is outside around it. In brain gray matter is outside and white matter is inside.

9. The diagram given alongside represents the cross-section of the human eye :

(i)   Name the parts labelled 1–12.

(ii) What is the function of the part marked '10'?

(iii) What would happen if part '5' is damaged or cut?

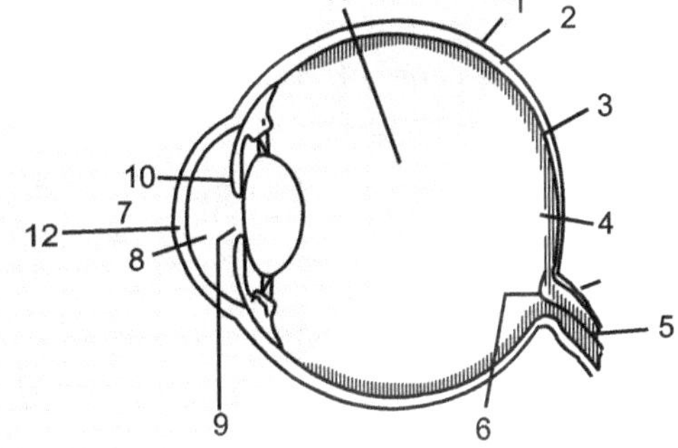

Ans. (i)   1. Sclera 2. Choroid 3. Retina 4. Yellow spot or fovea 5. Optic nerve 6. Blind spot 7. Lens 8. Aqueous humour 9. Pupil 10. Iris 11. Vitreous humour 12. Cornea.

(ii) The function of the part marked '10', the iris, is to regulate the amount of light that enters the eye so that too much light does not damage the delicate cells of the retina.

(iii) The person would not be able to see because the sensations from the eye would not reach the brain.

10. Given alongside is a diagram depicting a defect of the human eye. Study the same and then answer the questions that follow :

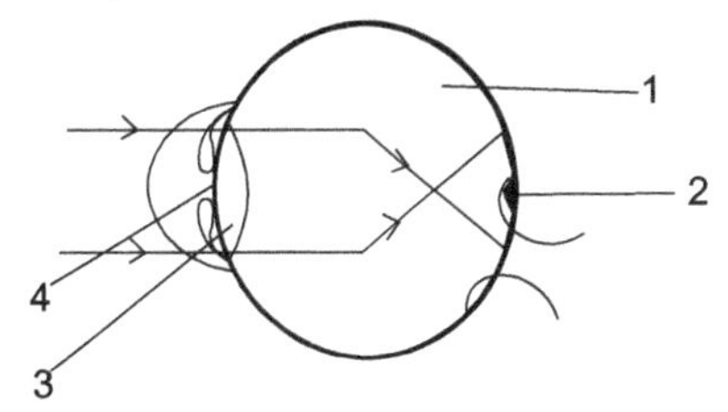

(i)   Name the defect shown in the diagram.

(ii) Give two possible reasons for this defect of the eye in human beings.

(iii) Name the parts labelled 1 to 4.

(iv) Name the type of lens used to correct this eye defect.

Ans. (i)   Myopia or Short-sightedness.

(ii)   The possible reasons for this defect may be :

(1) The eyeball is lengthened from front to back.

(2) The lens is too curved.

(iii) 1. Vitreous chamber.

2. Fovea centralis (yellow spot)

3. Lens

4. Pupil.

(iv)   This defect can be corrected by suitable concave lens.

11. The diagram given below depicts a defect of the human eye which has been corrected by using a suitable lens.*

Answer the following questions:

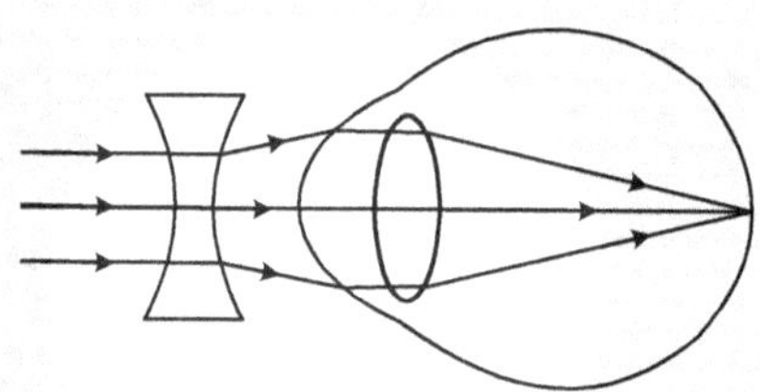

(i)   Name the defect that has been corrected.

Which type of lens has been used for the correction?

(ii)   Mention one cause for the above defect.

(iii) Where would the image have formed if the above lens was not used for correction?

(iv) Name the three concentric layers of the eyeball.

(v)   Draw a neat, labelled diagram of a neuron.

Ans. (i)   Myopia, Concave lens
(ii)   The cause of myopia is lengthening of eyeball from front to back.
(iii) The image would have formed in front of the retina.
(iv) The three concentric layers of the eyeball are sclera, choroid and retina.
(v)

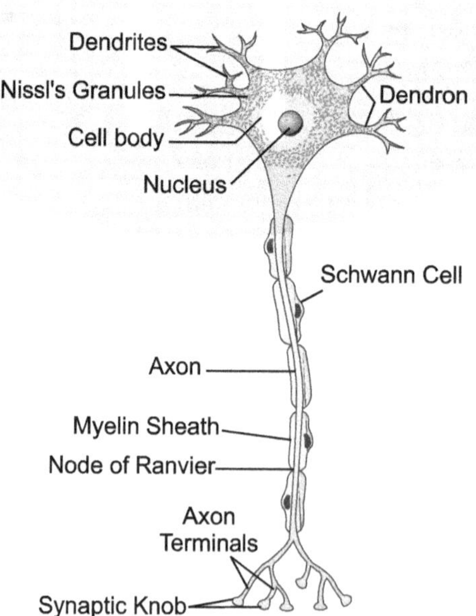

---

* Frequently asked previous years Board Exam Questions.

12. With respect to human eye, explain :

    (i) How is the image formed on the retina?

    (ii) How is the amount of light entering the eye controlled?

    (iii) What type of lens is used for the correction of 'Long sight' defect?

    (iv) With the help of a ray diagram show the defect of the eye and then its correction after use of lens.

Ans. (i) Light from the source when reaches the eye, it gets converged by the lens and an inverted image is formed on the retina.

    (ii) The amount of light entering the eye can be controlled by dilating or constricting the pupil.

    (iii) A convex lens is used to correct long sightedness.

    (iv)

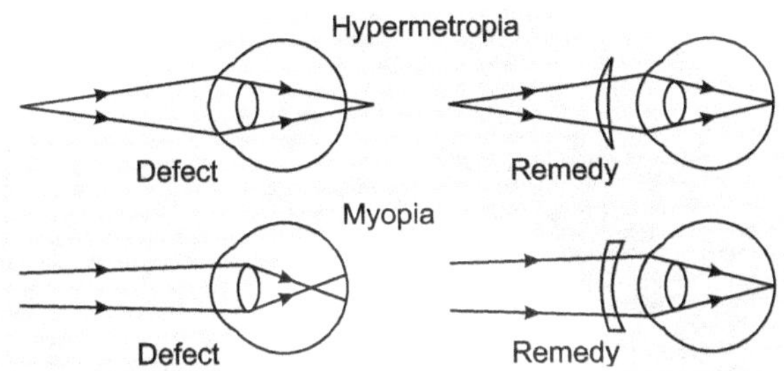

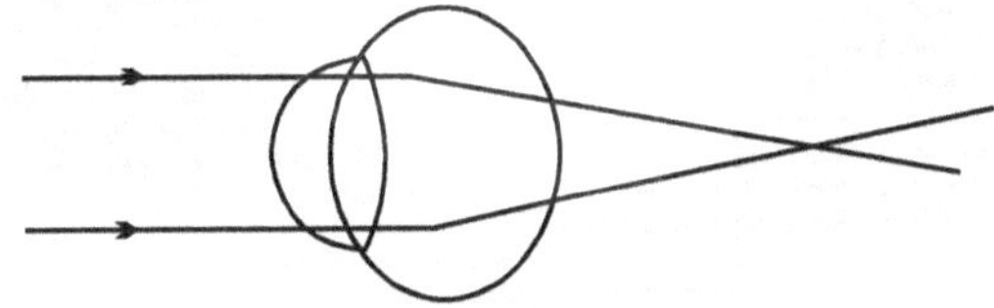

13. Given below is a diagrammatic representation of a defect of the human eye :

    (i) Identify the defect.

    (ii) Mention two reasons for the above defect.

    (iii) State how the defect can be rectified.

    (iv) Name the part of the eye responsible for maintaining the shape of the eyeball.

Ans. (i) Hypermetropia (Far-sightedness) because image is behind the retina.

    (ii) Reasons for hypermetropia are :

       (1) Shortening of eyeball from front to back.

       (2) Lens becomes too flat.

    (iii) It can be rectified by using convex lenses of appropriate power (focal length).

    (iv) Sclerotic (or sclera).

14. Given below is the diagram of a part of the human ear. Study the same and then answer the questions that follows :

   (i)   Give the biological term for Malleus, Incus and Stapes.

   (ii) Name the parts labelled A, B and C in the diagram.

   (iii) State the functions of the parts labelled 'A' and 'B'.

   (iv) Name the audio receptor region present in the part labelled. 'A'.

Ans. (i)   Ear Ossicles

   (ii)   A → Cochlea, B → Semi-circular canal, C → Vestibule.

   (iii) A is concerned with the sense of hearing. B is concerned with the sense of dynamic balance.

   (iv) Organ of corti or spiral organ.

15. The following diagram refers to the ear of a mammal.

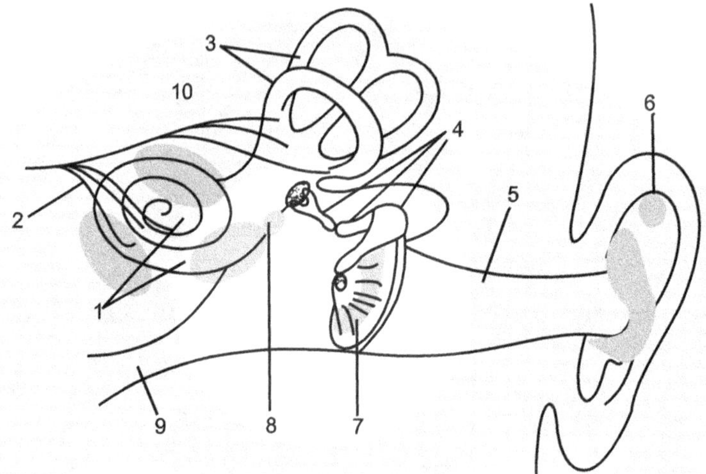

   (i)   Label the parts 1 to 10 to which the guidelines point.

   (ii) Which structure :

      (1) Converts sound waves into mechanical vibrations?

      (2) Converts vibrations into nerve impulses?

      (3) Responds to change in position?

      (4) Transmits impulses to the brain?

      (5) Equalizes atmospheric pressure and pressure in the ear.

Ans. (i)   1. Cochlea   6. Pinna

        2. Auditory nerve   7. Eardrum

        3. Semicircular canals   8. Fenestra rotunda

        4. Ear ossicles   9. Eustachian tube

        5. Auditory meatus   10. Fenestra ovalis

   (ii) (1) Eardrum or tympanum

      (2) Organ of corti   (4) Auditory nerve

      (3) Semicircular canals   (5) Eustachian tube

16. Given below is the diagram of the human ear. Study the same and answer the questions that follow :

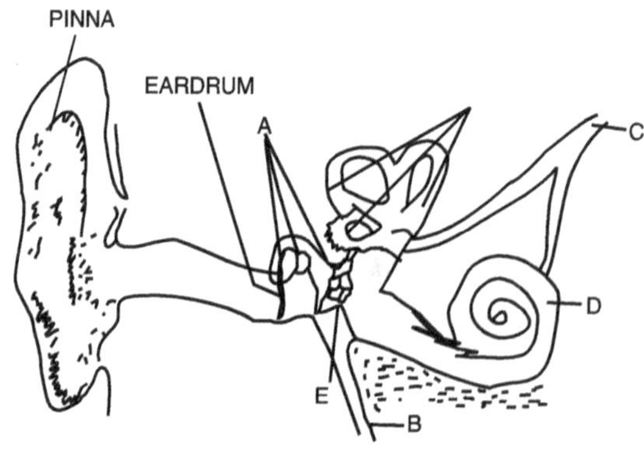

  (i) Give the biological term for the part labelled 'A' and state its function.

  (ii) Name the part labelled 'B' and state its function.

  (iii) Name the part labelled 'C' and state its function.

  (iv) Give the function of ear wax.

Ans. (i) **Ear Ossicles** (Malleus, incus and stapes)—To receive, magnify and transmit the sound vibrations to the membrane of the oval window.

  (ii) **Eustachian tube**—It equalize the air pressure on either side of ear drum allowing it to vibrate freely.

  (iii) **Auditory Nerve**—It transmits the impulses from cochlea to temporal lobe of brain.

  (iv) Ear wax has insect repellent properties hence prevents the entry of insects in the auditory canal. It also checks the entry of dust particles in the ear. Thus, it lubricates and protects the ear drum.

17. Given below is the diagram of the human ear. Study the diagram and then answer the questions that follow :

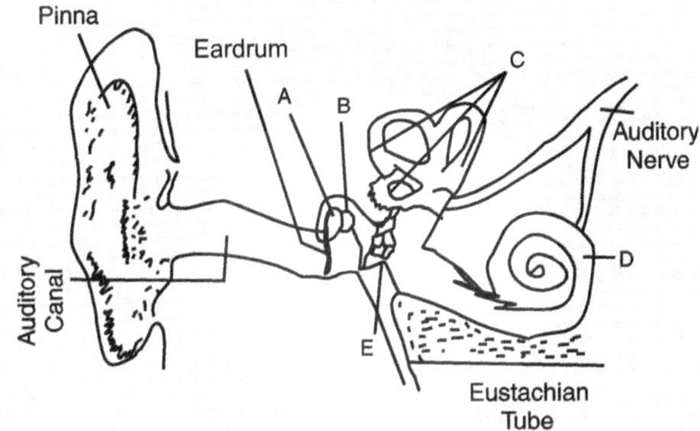

  (i) What role does the eardrum play in hearing?

  (ii) What common term is given to the parts labelled A, B and E?

  (iii) Would there be any difference if these three parts mentioned in (ii) above were replaced by one by one? Why?

  (iv) Give the biological term for the parts labelled C and D.

  (v) Name the fluid which fills the parts mentioned in (iv) above.

  (vi) State the functions of the ear.

Ans. (i) The eardrum is vibrated by sound waves and passes them to internal ear.

  (ii) Ear ossicles.

  (iii) One big ossicle would not be able to produce effective amplification because it would require a greater force of vibration than supplied by the eardrum normally. Moreover, three smaller ossicles with proper distance between them produces multiple amplification and effective transmission.

  (iv) C is semicircular canals and D is cochlea.

  (v) Endolymph.

  (vi) Hearing and balancing of the body.

18. The alongside diagram is the surface of tongue showing taste zone.

  (i) Label the parts 1–4.

  (ii) Where are the receptors for sensations of taste located?

  (iii) Why a person suffering from cold often complains that he cannot taste their food?

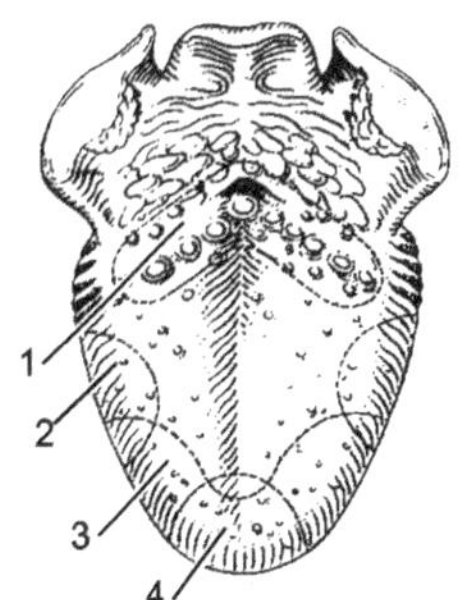

Ans. (i) 1–Bitter Taste Receptors, 2–Sour Taste Receptors, 3–Salt Taste Receptors, 4–Sweet Taste Receptors.

  (ii) The receptors for sensations are located in the taste bud covering the tongue surface.

(iii) A person suffering from cold often complains that he cannot taste his food because his gustatory sensations are not operating well.

Chapter 10. The Endocrine System

1. Place the words at the bottom of the page next to the number that shows the location of the endocrine glands.

(1) ....(2) .... (3) .... (4) .... (5) .... (6) .... (7) .... (8) .... (9) ....

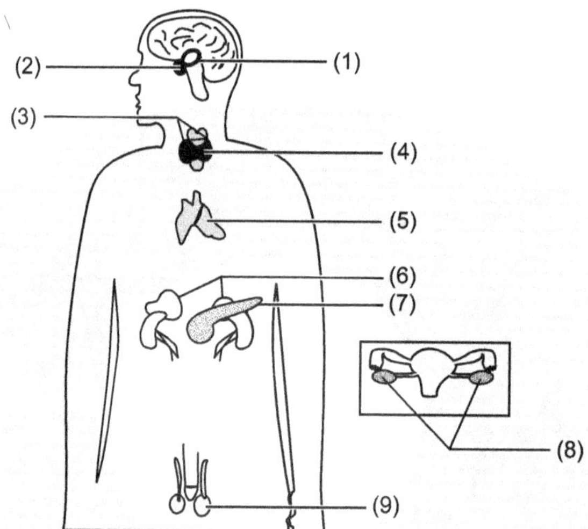

Pancreas, Hypothalamus, Pituitary, Parathyroid, Ovaries, Adrenal, Thyroid, Thymus, Testes

Ans. (1) Pituitary, (2) Hypothalamus, (3) Parathyroid, (4) Thyroid, (5) Thymus, (6) Adrenal, (7) Pancreas, (8) Ovaries, (9) Testes.

2. Given alongside is an outline of the human body showing the important glands.

(i) Name the glands marked 1 to 5.

(ii) Name the hormone secreted by 2.

Give one important function of this hormone.

(iii) Name the endocrine cells present in part 4.

(iv) Name the hormone secreted by part 3.

Give one important function of this hormone.

(v) Name any two endocrine glands which are not shown in the diagram.

(vi) Name one gland which is both exocrine and endocrine.

Ans. (i)

1. Pituitary	4. Pancreas
2. Thyroid	5. Ovaries
3. Adrenal	

(ii) Thyroxine.

It regulates the basal metabolism.

(iii) Islets of Langerhans.

(iv) Adrenaline.

It prepares the body for some emergency situations by causing production of glucose from glycogen in liver and releasing it into blood.

(v) Thymus, Parathyroid.

(vi) Pancreas.

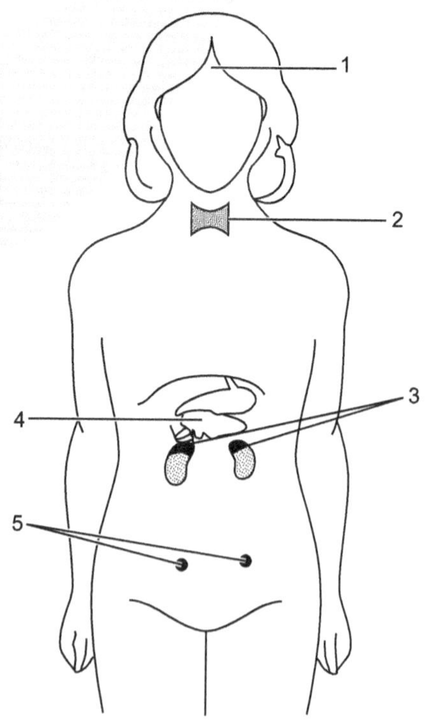

3. Given alongside are the diagrammatic sketches of some endocrine glands. Observe the figures and answer the following questions:

(i) Label the parts numbered 1 to 5.

(ii) Name the hormones secreted by 2 and 5.

(iii) Which chemicals in our body are greatly affected by hormones?

(iv) What is the chemical nature of hormones?

(v) Name the elements related with the functioning of hormones secreted by the structure 2 and 5.

Ans. (i) 1. Larynx   3. Trachea (windpipe)

2. Left lobe of thyroid gland   4. Oesophagus

5. Parathyroid glands.

(ii) Structure 2 secretes thyroxine hormone and structure 5 secretes parathormone.

(iii) Enzymes; which constitute the enzyme system of the body.

(iv) Chemically, hormones may be proteins, amino acids or steroids.

(v) Iodine is related with the functioning of gland 2. While calcium and phosphorus are related with the functioning of gland 5.

4. The diagram given below represents the location and structure of an endocrine gland. Study the same and answer the questions that follow :*

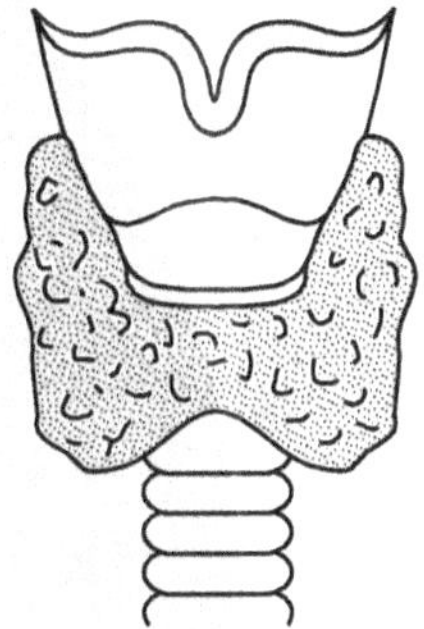

(i) Name the endocrine gland shown in the diagram.

(ii) Name the secretion of the gland which regulates basal metabolism.

(iii) Name the mineral element required for the synthesis of the above mentioned hormone.

(iv) Name the disease caused due to undersecretion of the above mentioned hormone in children.

(v) Name the disease caused due to hypersecretion of the above mentioned hormone.

Ans. (i) The endocrine gland shown in the diagram is thyroid gland.

(ii) The secretion of this gland is thyroxine which regulates basal metabolism.

(iii) The mineral element required for synthesis of thyroxine is iodine.

(iv) Cretinism is caused due to undersecretion of thyroxine in children.

(v) Exophthalmic goitre is caused due to hypersecretion of thyroxine.

5. The sketch aside shows a certain condition in an individual :

(i) Name the condition.

(ii) What is the underlying cause of this condition?

(iii) Name two other conditions that could have resulted due to a similar cause.

(iv) Which hormone is required for iodine synthesis?

(v) Where is thyroid gland located?

(vi) The hormone secreted by thyroid gland is controlled by which hormone?

Ans. (i) Goitre

(ii) The thyroid gland enlarges due to the deficiency of iodine in the diet.

(iii) (1) Cretinism in children

(2) Myxoedema in adults

(iv) Thyroxine

(v) It is located in a mid-ventral position in the posterior part of the pharynx.

(vi) Thyroid stimulating hormone (TSH).

---

6. Study the diagram given below and then answer the questions that follow :

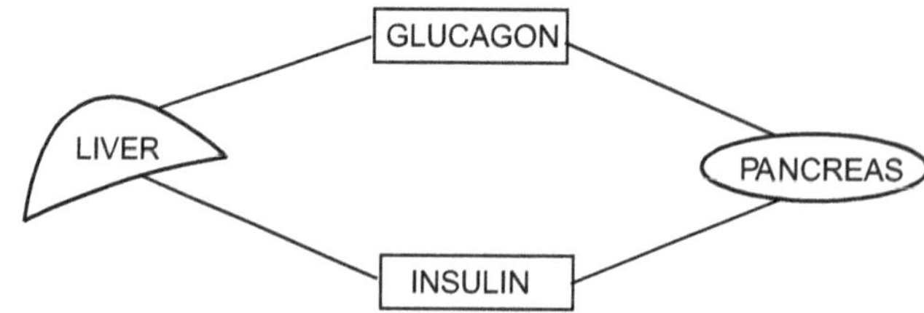

(i) Name the cells of the pancreas that produce (1) glucagon, (2) insulin.

(ii) State the main function of (1) glucagon, (2) insulin.

(iii) Why is the pancreas referred to as an exo-endocrine gland?

(iv) Why is insulin not given orally but is injected into the body?

(v) What is the technical term for the cells of the pancreas that produce endocrine hormones?

(vi) Where in the body is the pancreas located?

Ans. (i) (1) Alpha cells of islet of Langerhans.

(2) Beta cells of islet of Langerhans.

(ii) (1) It increases blood sugar level.

(2) It decreases blood sugar level.

(iii) Pancreas produces pancreatic juice which is carried by pancreatic duct into the duodenum. It also produces hormones which are poured into blood. Because of this dual activity, it is called an exo-endocrine gland.

(iv) If insulin is given orally, it will be digested by the protein digesting enzymes in the stomach. Hence it has to be injected into the body of highly diabetic patient so that it is able to travel into the blood stream, to bring about the required specific effect.

(v) Islets of Langerhans.

(vi) Below the stomach.

7. The diagram given below represent an endocrine gland in the human body. Study the diagram and answer the following question :

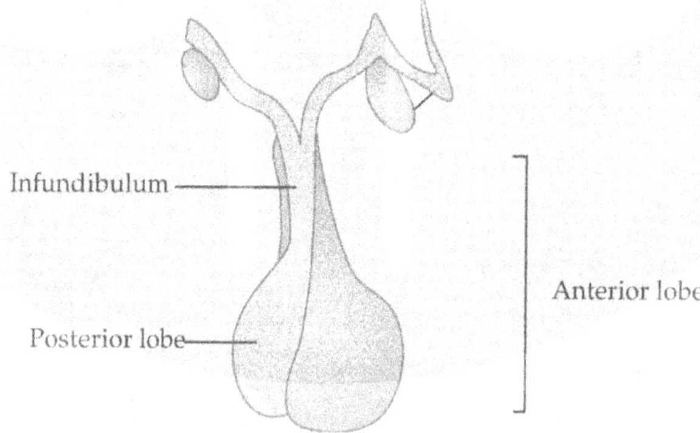

(i) Identify the endocrine gland. Where is it located ?

(ii) Why is the above gland referred to as the 'Master gland' ?

(iii) Name the hormone which in deficiency causes Diabetes Insipidus.

How does this disorder differ from Diabetes Mellitus ?

(iv) Explain the term 'Hormone'.

What is the role of Tropic hormones in the human body ?

(v) Which lobe of the above gland secretes :

1. Oxytocin   2. ACTH   3. Growth hormone

Ans. (i) It is pituitary gland. It is located in the brain between hypothalamus and pineal gland.

(ii) Pituitary gland is called the Master gland as it controls the functions of other endocrine glands and also the main body functions such as growth.

(iii) Hormone is ADH/Vasopressin.

In Diabetes insipidus there is no sugar in urine but it is pale, in Diabetes mellitus sugar is present in urine.

(iv) Hormones are chemical secretions from specific glands which are poured directly into blood stream and produce effect in one or more target organs only.

Tropic hormones stimulate other glands for the production of some other hormones. For example- TSH [Thyroid stimulating hormone] stimulates thyroid gland to secrete thyroxine.

(v) 1. Posterior lobe/neurohypophysis   3. Anterior lobe/adenohypophysis

2. Anterior lobe/adenohypophysis

Chapter 11. The Reproductive System

Q. 1. Given below is a diagram of the lateral section of a testis of a man. Study the same and answer the questions that follow :

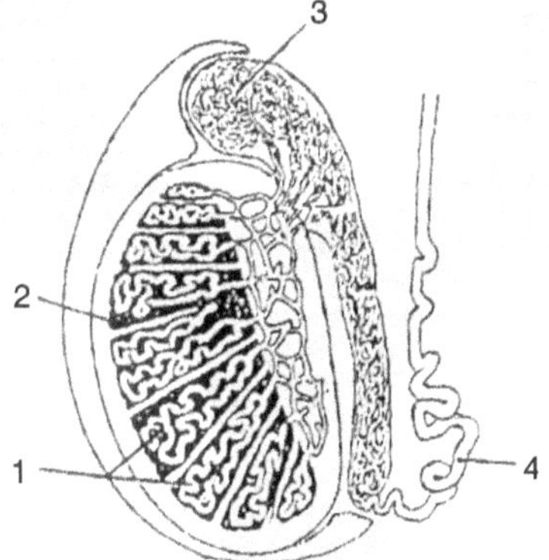

(i) Label the parts numbered 1 to 4 of the diagram.

(ii) State the functions of the parts labelled 1, 3 and 4.

(iii) What is the significance of the testes being located in the scrotal sac outside the abdomen?

(iv) What is the role played by the inguinal canal?

(v) What is semen?

Ans. (i) 1. Seminiferous tubules   3. Epididymis

2. Testicular lobule   4. Vas deferens

(ii) 1. **Seminiferous tubules :** Production, nourishment and protection of sperm.

3. **Epididymis :** Stores and transports the sperm, contributes to seminal fluid.

4. **Sperm duct :** It carries sperms from epididymis to urethra.

(iii) Scrotal sac acts as thermoregulator. The temperature in scrotal sac remains 2–3°C lower than the body temperature which is suitable for maturation of sperm.

(iv) The inguinal canal acts as a passage fro spermatic cord, gonadal vessels and lymphatics.

(v) Semen is a mixture of mature sperm and secretions of the seminal vesicles, prostate gland and cowper's gland. It is a milky fluid which is alkaline in nature.

2. Given alongside is the outline of the male reproductive system:

(i) Name the parts labelled 1 to 5.

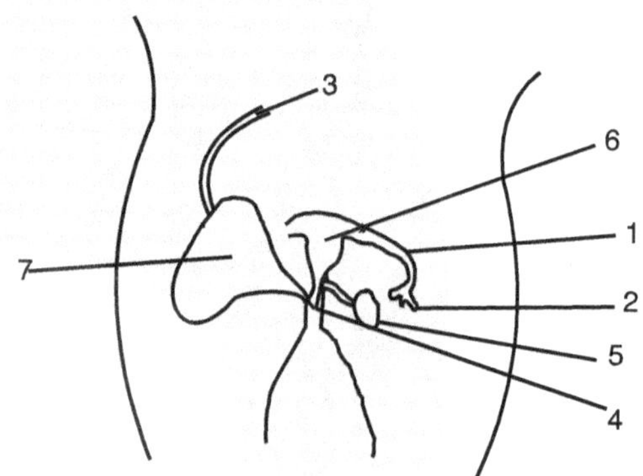

    (ii) State the functions of the parts labelled 1 and 4.

    (iii) Name the cells of part 5 that produce testosterone.

    (iv) Why is the structure 5 present outside the body in the scrotal sacs?

Ans. (i) 1. Prostate gland

      2. Cowper's gland

      3. Urethra

      4. Sperm duct

      5. Testis.

  (ii) 1. **Prostate gland :** It secretes an alkaline matter which neutralizes the acidity of urethra.

      4. **Sperm duct :** It carries sperms from epididymis to the urethra.

 (iii) Cells of Leydig.

 (iv) Testis are located in the scrotal sacs outside the body so that they can maintain a low temperature than the body cavity. This low temperature is necessary for the production and maturation of sperms.

Q. 3. The alongside diagram represents the sectional view of the female reproductive organs of a mammal.

   (i)   Label the parts numbered 1 to 7.

  (ii) What are the main functions of the parts labelled 2, 5, 6?

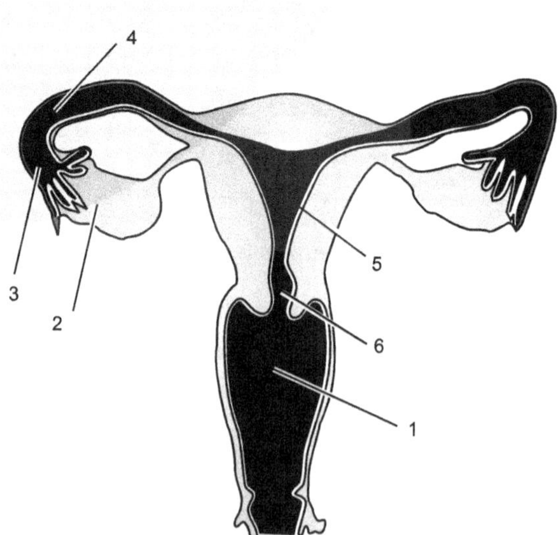

Ans. (i) 1. Fallopian tube   5. Ovary

      2. Fimbriated funnel   6. Uterus

      3. Ureter   7. Urinary bladder

      4. Vagina

  (ii) 2. **Fimbriated funnel :** It collects ovum from the ovary by its ciliary movement.

      5. **Ovary :** It produces ovum.

      6. **Uterus :** It lodges and nourishes fertilized ovum.

4. Given alongside is a diagram of the female reproductive system of a human being :

   (i)   Name the parts numbered 1 to 6.

  (ii) Normally after how many days does an ovary release an egg?

 (iii) Where are the sperms released during coitus?

 (iv) What do the sperms do after being released?

  (v) What is the function of the organ numbered 5?

 (vi) How many days does it normally take from the fertilization of the egg up to the birth of the baby?

Ans. (i) 1. Vagina   4. Oviduct

      2. Right ovary   5. Uterus

      3. Ovarian funnel   6. Cervix.

  (ii) Normally the ovary releases one egg every 28 days by the rupture of the Graafian follicle.

 (iii) The sperms are released by the penis in the vagina near the cervix.

A front view of the female reproductive organs

(iv) The sperms swim up the vagina to enter through the cervix into the uterus and up into the oviduct where it meets the ovum.

(v) The function of the uterus is protection and nourishment of the embryo during the period of gestation.

(vi) The period of gestation is 266–280 days after which the foetus is expelled.

5. The alongside diagram represents the vertical view of the human female reproductive system.

(i) Label the parts indicated by the guidelines 1 to 8.

(ii) How does the uterus prepare for the reception of a zygote?

(iii) What happens to the uterus if fertilization takes place?

(iv) What happens to the uterus if fertilization has failed to take place?

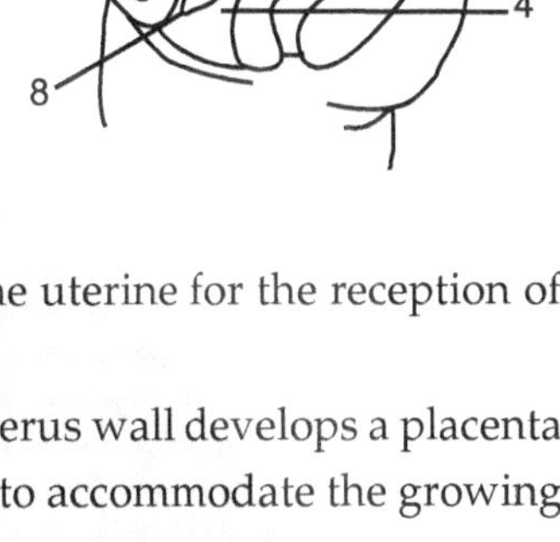

Ans. (i) 1. Oviduct   5. Ovary

2. Funnel of oviduct   6. Uterus

3. Ureter   7. Bladder

4. Vagina   8. Urethra

(ii) The endometrium lining and glands of uterine wall grow to prepare the uterine for the reception of a zygote.

(iii) If fertilization takes place, the embryo is implanted in the uterus. The uterus wall develops a placenta which attaches the embryo to the uterus and the uterine wall expands to accommodate the growing embryo.

(iv) If fertilization fails to take place, menstruation takes place during which endometrium of the uterus is shed off. The capillaries and cells of this layer rupture and disappear.

6. The diagram below represents two reproductive cells A and B. Study the same and then answer the questions that follow :

(i) Identify the reproductive cells A and B.

(ii) Name the specific part of the reproductive system where the above cells are produced.

(iii) Where in the female reproductive system do these cells unite?

(iv) Name the main hormones secreted by the (1) ovary, (2) testes.

(v) Name an accessory gland found in the male reproductive system and state the function of its secretion.

Ans. (i) A—Ovum   B—Sperm

(ii) A is produced in ovary.

B is produced in testes.

(iii) Oviduct (Fallopian tube).

(iv) (1) Progesterone.   (2) Testosterone.

(v) Seminal vesicles.

They produce secretion which activates the sperms.

7. Given below are diagrams showing the different stages in the process of fertilisation of an egg in the human female reproductive tract.*

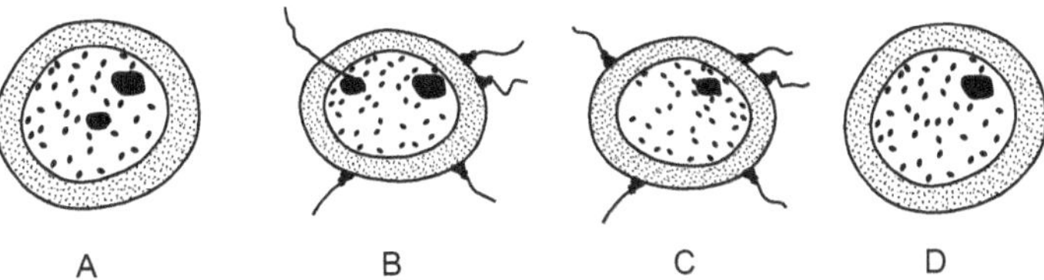

Study the diagrams and answer the questions :

(i) Arrange the letters given below each diagram in a logical sequence to show the correct order in the process of fertilisation.

---

* Frequently asked previous years Board Exam Questions.

(ii)   Where does fertilisation normally take place? What is implantation that follows fertilisation?

(iii) Mention the chromosome number of the zygote and egg in humans.

(v)   Draw a neat, labelled diagram of a mature human sperm.

Ans. (i)   D, C, B, A

(ii)   Fertilization normally takes place in oviduct. Implantation is the process of fixing of blastocyst to the wall of uterus.

(iii) In egg chromosome number is 23 but in zygote it is 46.

(iv)

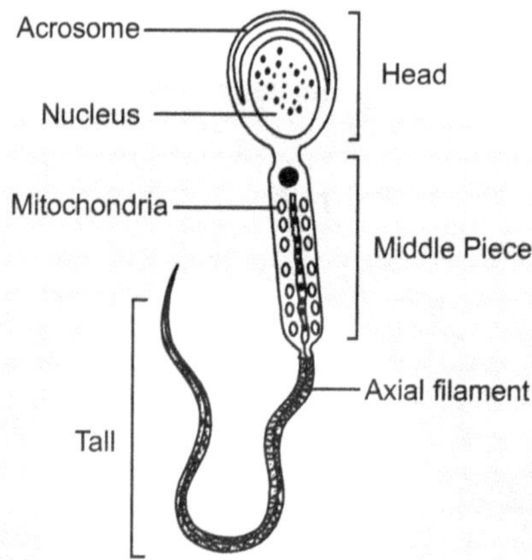

8. The diagram given alongside is that of a developing human foetus in the womb. Study the same and then answer the questions that follow :

(i)   Name the parts '1' to '5' indicated by guidelines.

(ii)   What term is given to the period of development of the foetus in the womb?

(iii) How many days does the foetus take to be fully developed?

(iv)   Mention two functions of the parts labelled '2' other than its endocrine function.

(v)   Name the hormone (any one) produced by the part labelled '2'.

(vi)   What is the function of the part marked '3'?

Ans. (i)   1. Umbilical cord   3. Amniotic fluid
              2. Placenta   4. Cervix   5. Uterine wall

(ii)   Gestation period.

(iii) 280 days.

(iv)   Provides nutrition and exchange of respiratory gases by diffusion.

(v)   Progesterone.

(vi)   Protects foetus from jerks and shocks. Also prevents foetus from sticking to the uterine wall.

9. The diagram given below shows an embryo in the uterus of mammal. Label the parts indicated.

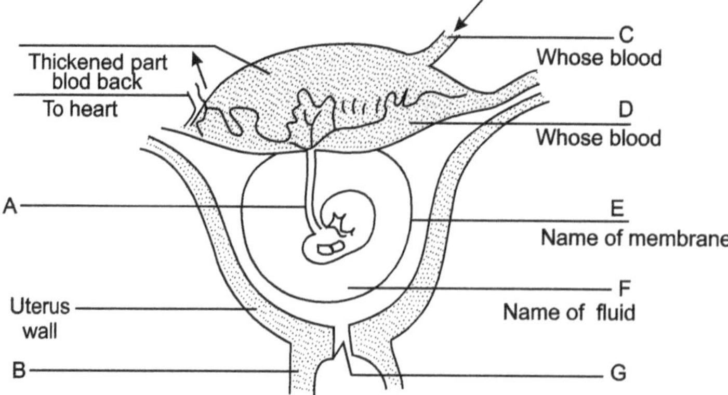

Ans. A– Umbilical cord

B– Vagina

C– Blood of mother flows into placenta

D– Blood of foetus flows into placenta

E– Amnion

F– Amniotic fluid

G– Opening of the cervix

10. Study the diagram given below and then answer the questions that follow :

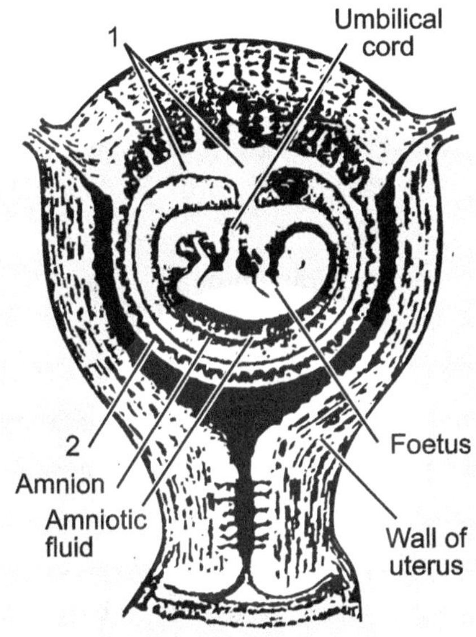

(i) Name the parts labelled 1 and 2. State the function of each part.

(ii) State any one function of the amniotic fluid.

(iii) What is the role of the umbilical cord in the development of the foetus?

(iv) Name the part in the diagram which is endocrine in nature.

Ans. (i) 1. **Placenta**—It helps in the nutrition, excretion and respiration of the embryo.

2. **Chorion**—It forms the placenta.

(ii) Amniotic fluid, present in amniotic cavity, acts as shock absorber and prevents desiccation of embryo.

(iii) Umbilical cord makes the connection between placenta and foetus. It supplies the nutrients and O_2 with maternal blood to foetus and removes CO_2 and excretory wastes from foetus blood into maternal blood. Thus it acts as a transport channel between foetus and mother blood.

(iv) Placenta—It secretes hCG (Human Chorionic Gonadotropin) hormone.

11.

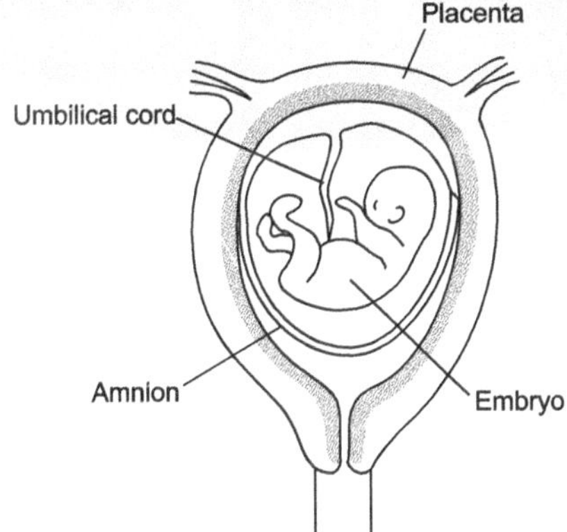

The above diagram is of a developing embryo in a mother's womb :

(i) Write the functions of placenta, amnion and umbilical cord.

(ii) How are the waste products of foetus removed?

(iii) What is gestation period?

Ans. (i) **Functions of Placenta :**

1. It supplies oxygen, water, nutrients and hormones from the mother's blood to the embryo.

2. It transfers carbon dioxide and other waste materials from the embryo to the mother's blood.

3. It shields the embryo from infections as it is impermeable to most of the micro organisms present in the mother's blood.

4. It produces certain hormones like oestrogen and progesterone which are essential for the reproductive process.

The amnion or amniotic sac is made up of protective membranes that are formed around the embryo. It encloses a fluid-filled space which acts as a water-bath and an excellent shock absorber for the young embryo.

The embryo that develops in the placenta is maintained at a constant temperature, well protected and nourished by the umbilical cord.

(ii) Waste products of the foetus are removed through umbilical cord.

(iii) The interval of time between fertilization and birth is called the gestation period. It is about 280 days in human beings.

12. The diagram given below is that of a developing human foetus.*

Answer the questions that follow:

(i) Label the parts numbered 1 to 3 in the diagram.

(ii) Mention any two functions of the part labelled 2 in the diagram.

(iii) Explain the significance of the part numbered 3 in the diagram.

(iv) Define the term 'Gestation'.

What is the normal gestational period of the developing embryo?

(v) Mention the sex chromosomes in a male and female embryo.

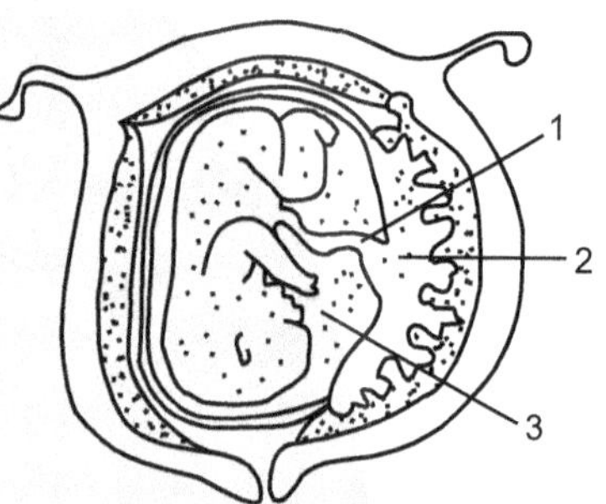

Ans. (i) 1. Umbilical cord; 2. Placenta; 3. Amniotic fluid

(ii) Two functions of placenta are:

1. It allows diffusion of substances like nutrients and oxygen from mother to foetus; and carbon dioxide and waste products from foetus to mother.

2. It acts as an endocrine gland and produces hormones like oestrogen and progesterone.

(iii) Amniotic fluid acts as a shock absorber, protecting the embryo from physical damage by jerks or mechanical shocks. It also prevents sticking of foetus to amnion.

(iv) Gestation is the full term of the development of the embryo in the uterus. In humans, the normal gestation period is about 280 days.

(v) In female embryo, XX sex chromosome is present whereas in male, XY is present.

Chapter 12. Human Population

1. Observe the diagram A and B given below :

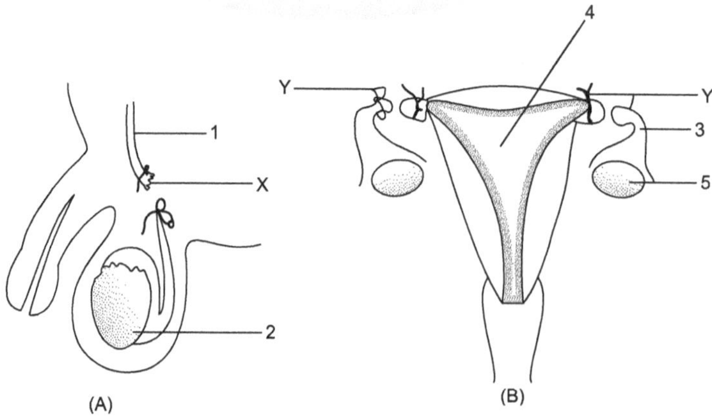

(i)   Label parts 1 – 5.

(ii)   What does diagram A depict?

(iii)   What does diagram B depict?

(iv)   Write comment on X and Y.

(v)   State one function each of part 2 and 4.

Ans. (i)   1. Vas deferens, 2. Testis, 3. Oviduct, 4. Uterus, 5. Ovary.

(ii)   Diagram A depicts vasectomy in males (*i.e.,* cutting and tying the vas deferens).

(iii)   Diagram B depicts tubectomy in females (*i.e.,* cutting and tying the oviducts).

(iv)   'X' represents the cut and tied end of vas deferens in male. Cutting and tying of vas deferens prevents the passage of sperms and avoids pregnancy. 'Y' represents the cut and tied ends of oviducts of female. Cutting and tying of oviducts prevents the passage of ovum and avoids pregnancy.

(v)   Part 2 (Testis) produces sperms (male gametes).

Part 4 (Uterus) carries and protects the foetus till its birth.

Chapter 13. Human Evolution

1. Given below are two stages in the evolution of man.*

Study them and answer the questions than follow :

(i)   Identify Australopithecius and Neanderthal man from the above pictures.

(ii)   Mention two characteristic features each for the two stages.

(iii)   Who proposed the theory of 'Natural Selection'?

(iv)   Name the organism used as an example to explain 'Industrial Melanism'.

(v)   Give two examples of Vestigial organs in humans.

Ans. (i)   A- Neanderthal man, B- Australopithecus

(ii)   Characteristics features of Neanderthal man (A)—

1. Less hair on body, Large head.

2. Large cranial capacity 1500 cm^3.

Characteristics features of Australopithecus (B)—

1. Chin absent, prominent eyebraws ridges..

2. Cranial capacity of 450-600 cm^3.

(iii)   Charles Darwin.

(iv)   Peppered moth- Biston betularia

(v)   Wisdom teeth, Vermiform appendix.

Chapter 14. Pollution

1. Given below is a representation of kind of pollution. Study the same and answer the questions that follow :*

   (i)   Name the kind of pollution.

   (ii) List any three common sources of this pollution.

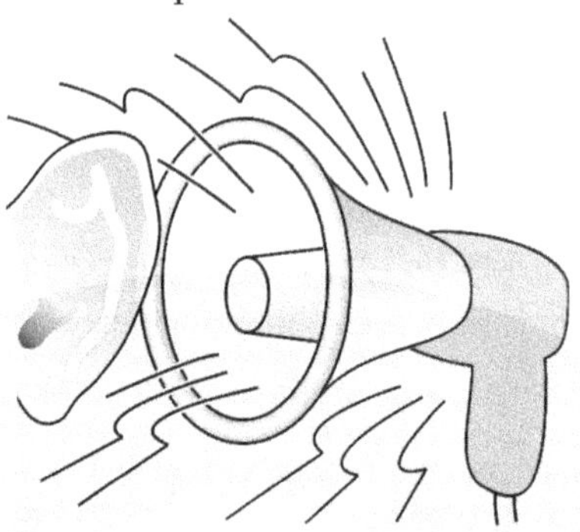

   (iii) Mention three harmful effects of this pollution on human health.

   (iv) Explain the term 'Pollutant'.

   (v)   Name two soil pollutants.

Ans. (i)   The diagram shown represents noise pollution.

   (ii) The three common sources of noise pollution are :

   (1) Industrial machines and workshops

   (2) Loudspeakers and musical bands

   (3) Trains and automobiles on street

   (iii) The three harmful effects of noise pollution on human health are :

   (1) Interrupts concentration of thought and disturbs peace of mind.

   (2) Disturbs sleep and leads to nervous irritability.

   (3) A sudden loud sound can damage ear drum and prolonged noise leads to deafness.

   (iv) Pollutant is any such constituent which causes pollution.

   OR

   A pollutant is a substance or energy introduced into the environment that has undesired effects, or adversely affects the usefulness of a resource.

   (v)   The two soil pollutants are :

   (1) Industrial waste like chemical residues, metallic ash, fly ash etc.

   (2) Chemical fertilizers and pesticides like DDT.

2. Study the picture given below and answer the following questions :*

   (i)   Identify the type of pollution.

   (ii) Name one pollutant that causes the above pollution.

   (iii) Mention the impact of this pollution on human health.

   (iv) State one measure to control this pollution.

   (v)   What is a 'Pollutant' ? Explain the term.

Ans. (i)   Water Pollution

   (ii) Detergents, Sewage, Domestic waste causes water pollution.

   (iii) Water pollution can cause various health hazards in human beings like jaundice, typhoid, cholera and diarrhoea.

   (iv) Industrial effluents should be treated before disposing them into water bodies. Sewage treatment plants should be set up to treat sewage as well recycling plastic, metal.

(v) Pollutant is any constituent which when added to water or soil or air brings about undesirable effect on environment affecting the life of living organisms. In other words, any element or constituent that pollutes either soil, water or air is called pollutant.

3. Given below is a representation of a type of pollution.*

Study the picture and answer the questions :

(i) Name the type of pollution shown in the picture.

(ii) Name one source of this pollution.

(iii) How does this pollution affect human health ?

(iv) Write one measure to reduce this pollution.

(v) State one gaseous compound that leads to the depletion of the ozone layer and creates 'Ozone holes'.

Ans. (i) Air pollution

(ii) Gases emitted from factories, industries and automobile exhausts.

(iii) Air pollution causes respiratory problems and lung disorders like bronchitis. It also leads to poor visibility and asthma.

(iv) Installation of tall chimneys in factories and chimneys should be fitted with filters and electrostatic precipitators. Also, use of efficient engines, unleaded petrol and CNG in automobiles help to reduce air pollution.

(v) CFCs (chlorofluorocarbons)

ICSE Solved Paper 2020

(Two Hours)

Answer to this paper must be written on the paper provided separately.

*You will **not** be allowed to write during the first **15** minutes.*

This time is to be spent in reading the Question paper.

The time given at the head of this Paper is the time allowed for writing the answers.

*Attempt **all** questions from **Section I** and **any four** question from **Section II**.*

The intended marks for questions or parts of questions are given in brackets [].

SECTION-I (40 Marks)

*Attempt **all** questions from this Section.*

Question 1.

(a) *Name the following :* [5]

(i) The process of transformation of several glucose molecules into one molecule of starch.

(ii) The point of attachment of two chromatids.

(iii) The iron containing pigment in erythrocytes.

(iv) The duct which transports urine from the kidney to the urinary bladder.

(v) The part of the brain which is concerned with memory.

(b) *Explain the following terms:* [5]

(i) Allele

(ii) Diffusion

(iii) Photolysis

(iv) Phenotype

(v) Population density

(c) *Given below are certain groups of terms. In each group the first pair indicates a relationship between the two terms. Rewrite and complete the second pair on a similar basis.* [5]

Example: *Cytoplasm: Cytokinesis :: Nucleus: Karyokinesis.*

(i) Widening of hips: Oestrogen :: Deepening of voice in males: __________

(ii) Brain : Meninges :: Heart : __________

(iii) Insulin : Beta-cells :: Glucagon : __________

(iv) Kidney : Renal artery :: Liver : __________

(v) Uterus : Implantation :: Fallopian tube : __________

(d) *Given below are sets of five terms each. Rewrite the terms in correct order in a logical sequence beginning with the first word that is underlined:* [5]

(i) <u>Stimulus,</u> Response, Receptor, Effector, Spinal cord.

(ii) <u>Root hair,</u> Endodermis, Epidermis, Xylem, Cortex.

(iii) <u>Conjunctiva,</u> Yellow spot, Pupil, Vitreous Humour, Aqueous Humour.

(iv) <u>Australopithecus,</u> Cro-Magnon Man, Homo erectus, Neanderthal Man, Homo sapiens.

(v) <u>Artery,</u> Capillaries, Venule, Vein, Arteriole.

(e) *Choose the correct answer from the four options given below :* [5]

(i) The fusion of the sperm and ovum is termed as:

(A) Reproduction   (B) Development

(C) Fertilization   (D) Embryo

(ii) Agranulocytes are:

(A) Lymphocytes, Monocytes

(B) Lymphocytes, Basophils

(C) Eosinophils, Basophils

(D) Eosinophils, Monocytes

(iii) Which of the following is not a natural reflex action?

(A) Knee-jerk

(B) Blinking of eyes due to strong light

(C) Salivation at the sight of food

(D) Sneezing when any irritant enters the nose

(iv) The structural and functional units of excretion in the human kidney is the:

(A) Ureter   (B) Bowman's capsule

(C) Renal pelvis   (D) Nephron

(v) In a human female, ovum consists of:

(A) 23 pair of autosomes

(B) 22 pairs of autosomes and 1 pair of sex chromosomes

(C) 22 autosomes and 1 Y-chromosome

(D) 22 autosomes and 1 X-chromosome

(f) *Identify the **ODD** term in each set and name the **CATEGORY** to which the remaining three belong:* [5]

(i) *Auxin, Ethylene, Adrenaline, Cytokinin*

(ii) *Tympanum, Ear ossicles, Auditory canal, Pinna*

(iii) *Syringes, Soiled dressings, Discarded needles, Houshold detergents*

(iv) *Exophthalmic Goitre, Simple Goitre, Cretinism, Myxoedema*

(v) *Adenine, Guanine, Creatinine, Cytosine*

(g) *Match the items given in column A with the most appropriate ones in Column B and* **Rewrite** *the correct matching pairs:* **[5]**

Column A		Column B
(i) *Biston betularia*	-	*Calcium*
(ii) *Testes*	-	*balance of the body*
(iii) *Clotting of blood*	-	*Light independent reaction*
(iv) *Stroma*	-	*diffusion of gases*
(v) *Stomata*	-	*gonad*
	-	*Peppered moth*
	-	*Light dependent reaction*
	-	*Chlorophyll*

(h) *The diagram given below represents a plant movement.* **[5]**

Answer the following questions.

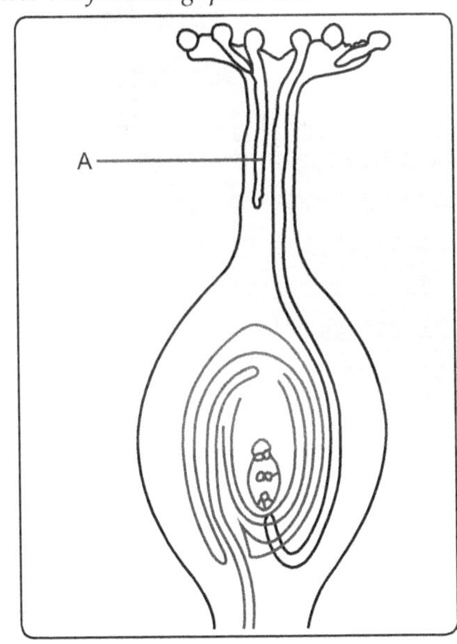

(i) *Name the tropic movement shown in the diagram.*
(ii) *Explain the troic movement mentioned in (i).*
(iii) *Label the part marked 'A'.*
(iv) *What is part A attracted to?*
(v) *Give an example of a plant which shows Thigmotropism.*

Answer 1.

(a) (i) Polymerisation

(ii) Centromere

(iii) Haemoglobin

(iv) Ureter

(v) Cerebrum

(b) (i) Allele is the alternative forms of a gene occupying the same position on the homologous chromosomes, affecting the same characteristic but in different ways.

(ii) Diffusion is the free movement of molecules of a substance from the region of their higher concentration to the region of their lower concentration when two are in direct contact.

(iii) Photolysis is the process of splitting of water molecules into hydrogen ions and oxygen in presence of sunlight inside grana.

(iv) Phenotype refers to the observable characteristics which are controlled genetically.

(v) Population density is defined as the number of individuals per square kilometre at any given time.

(c) (i) Testosterone
(ii) Pericardium
(iii) Alpha cells
(iv) Hepatic artery
(v) Fertilization

(d) (i) Stimulus, receptor, spinal cord, effector, response
(ii) Root hair, epidermis, cortex, endodermis, xylem
(iii) Conjunctiva, aqueous humour, pupil, vitreous humour, yellow spot
(iv) Australopithecus, *Homo erectus*, Neanderthal man, Cro-Magnon man, *Homo sapiens*
(v) Artery, arteriole, capillaries, venule, vein

(e) (i) C. Fertilization
(ii) A. Lymphocytes, Monocytes
(iii) C. Salivation at the sight of food
(iv) D. Nephron
(v) D. 22 autosomes and 1 X chromosome

(f) (i) Odd- Adrenaline;
   Category- Plant hormones
(ii) Odd- Ear ossicles
   Category- Parts of outer ear
(iii) Odd- Household detergents
   Category- Biomedical wastes
(iv) Odd- Exophthalmic goitre
   Category- Conditions due to Hypothyroidism
(v) Odd- Creatinine
   Category- Nitrogenous bases

(g)   **Column A**   **Column B**

(i) *Biston betularia*   - Peppered moth

(ii) Testes   - Gonad

(iii) Clotting of - Calcium
blood

(iv) Stroma   - Light independent reaction

(v) Stomata   - diffusion of gases

(h) **(i)** Chemotropism

(ii) Chemotropism is the phenomenon of growth of plant organs in response to chemicals.

(iii) Pollen tube

(iv) Sugars and peptones

(v) Tendrils of Cuscuta that coils around other plants is an example of thigmotropism.

SECTION-II (40 Marks)

*Attempt any **four** questions from this Section.*

Question 2.

(a) *The diagram given below represents an experiment to prove the importance of a factor in photosynthesis. Answer the questions that follow:*   **[5]**

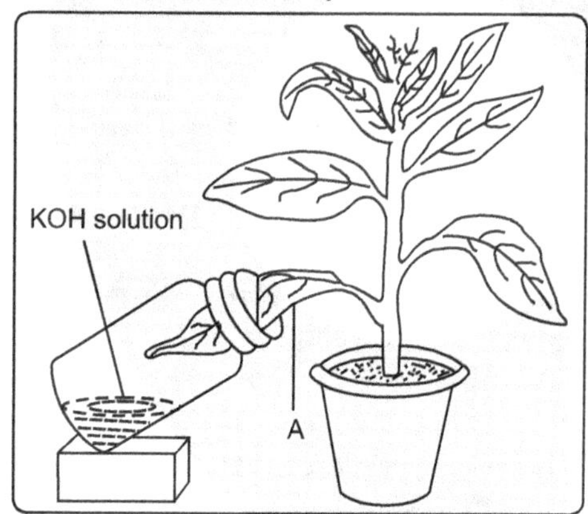

(i) *Which factor is being studied here?*

(ii) *What is the purpose of keeping KOH in the flask?*

(iii) *Explain the term Photosynthesis.*

(iv) *What will you observe when the leaf A is tested for starch?*

(v) *Write a well balanced chemical equation for the process of photosynthesis.*

(b) *The diagram given below represents the simplified pathway of the circulation of blood. Answer the questions that follow:*   **[5]**

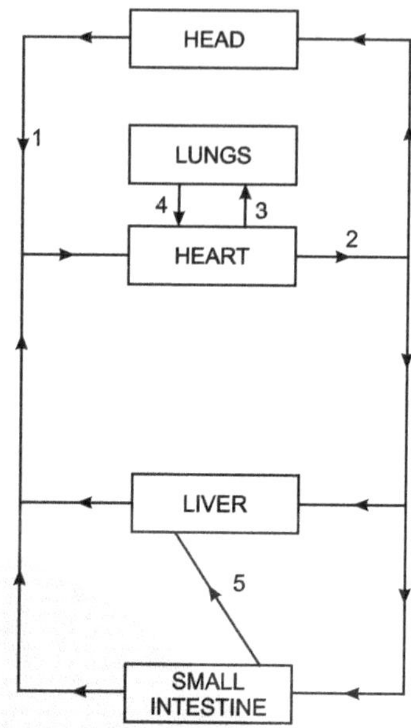

(i) *Name the blood vessels labelled 1 to 4.*

(ii) *Which blood vessel supplies oxygenated blood to the muscles of the heart?*

(iii) *What is the importance of blood vessel labelled 5?*

(iv) *What is the type of blood circulation that takes place between the heart and the lungs?*

(v) *Draw a diagram of the different blood cells as seen in a smear of human blood.*

Answer 2.

(a) **(i)** Carbon dioxide is necessary for photosynthesis.

(ii) KOH absorbs carbon dioxide.

(iii) Photosynthesis is the process by which cells containing chlorophyll using carbon dioxide and water in presence of light energy produce glucose and release oxygen as by-product.

(iv) When leaf A is tested for starch for the portion inside the flask, it does not show blue-black colour indicating absence of starch whereas the portion that is outside will show blue-black colour.

(v) $6CO_2 + 12H_2O \xrightarrow[\text{Sunlight}]{\text{Chlorophyll}} C_6H_{12}O_6 + 6H_2O + 6O_2$

(b) **(i)** 1. Superior vena cava; 2. Aorta; 3. Pulmonary artery; 4. Pulmonary vein

(ii) Coronary artery

(iii) Hepatic portal vein carries the blood from stomach and intestine to liver where the excess sugar is stored as glycogen. If any toxins are present in blood, they are detoxified in liver. In this way, the quantity of nutrients flowing in the blood is regulated and circulation of toxic substances in the blood is prohibited.

(iv) Pulmonary circulation

(v)

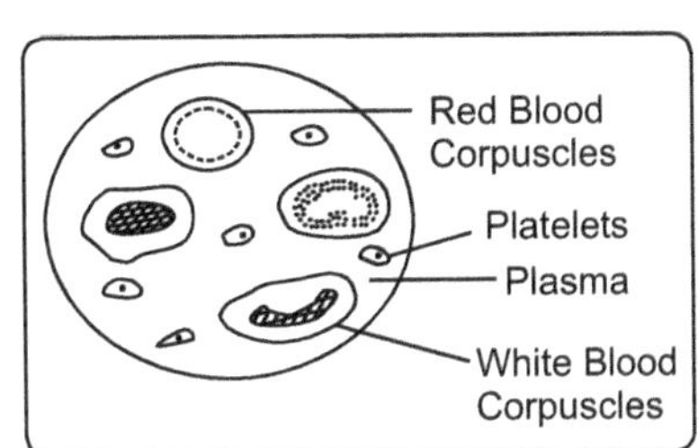

Question 3.

(a) *The diagram given below depicts a defect of the human eye which has been corrected by using a suitable lens.* **[5]**

Answer the following questions:

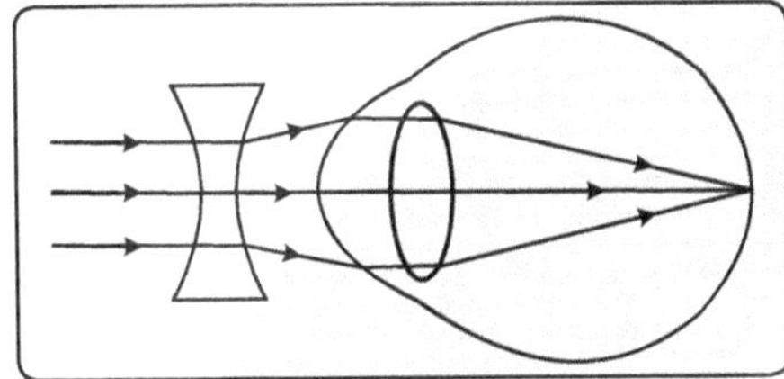

(i) *Name the defect that has been corrected.*

Which type of lens has been used for the correction?

(ii) *Mention one cause for the above defect.*

(iii) *Where would the image have formed if the above lens was not used for correction?*

(iv) *Name the three concentric layers of the eyeball.*

(v) *Draw a neat, labelled diagram of a neuron.*

(b) *Give the biological reasons for the following statements:* **[5]**

(i) *It is advisable to keep green plants in an aquarium.*

(ii) *Water pollution is a major cause of concern in our country.*

(iii) *We cannot distinguish colours in dim light.*

(iv) *Medical discoveries such as antibiotics and vaccinations have indirectly contributed to the sharp rise in human population.*

(v) *Homo sapiens sapiens is the most highly evolved form of man.*

Answer 3.

(a) (i) Myopia, Concave lens

(ii) The cause of myopia is lengthening of eyeball from front to back.

(iii) The image would have formed in front of the retina.

(iv) The three concentric layers of the eyeball are sclera, choroid and retina.

(v)

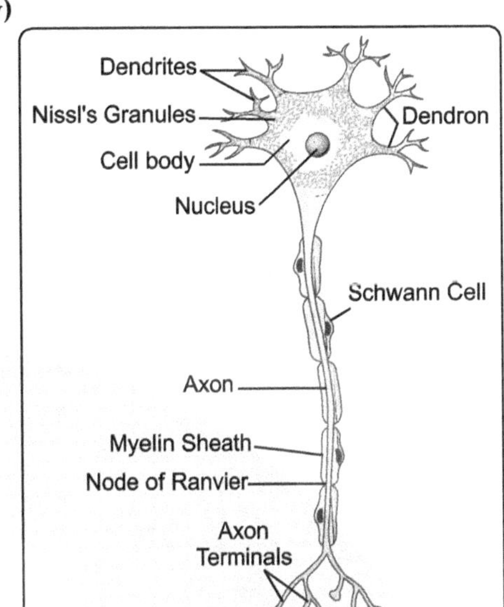

(b) (i) Green plants undergo photosynthesis by which oxygen gas is released which can be utilised by fishes for respiration. So, it is advisable to keep green plants in an aquarium.

(ii) Water pollution is the major cause of concern in our country because most of the wastes from households, industries, power plants etc. are dumped into water bodies without prior treatment. Agricultural activities, oil spills, untreated sewage water also contribute to water pollution. This leads to degradation in water quality, making it unfit for human consumption and other uses and lead to several infectious diseases. Further, decrease in oxygen level in the polluted water harm the aquatic life, leading to loss of biodiversity. All the factors results in water scarcity and making it difficult to sustain the basic needs of the large population of the country.

(iii) In dim light, only rod cells of our eyes function, which do not respond to colour. So we cannot distinguish colours in dim light.

(iv) Due to medical discoveries of vaccine and antibiotics, many diseases have been controlled, increasing the lifespan of the inviduals and decrease in the mortality rate. Thus, they have indirectly contributed to sharp rise in human population.

(v) *Homo sapiens sapiens* is the most highly evolved form of man because they developed a logical and syllabic speech in order to communicate, can cultivate plants and domesticated animals, prepared tools, ornaments, used advanced agricultural techniques. They developed cities; create new survival challenges for themselves as well as other species.

Question 4.

(a) *The figure given below shows a part of a nephron.* **[5]** *Answer the questions that follow:*

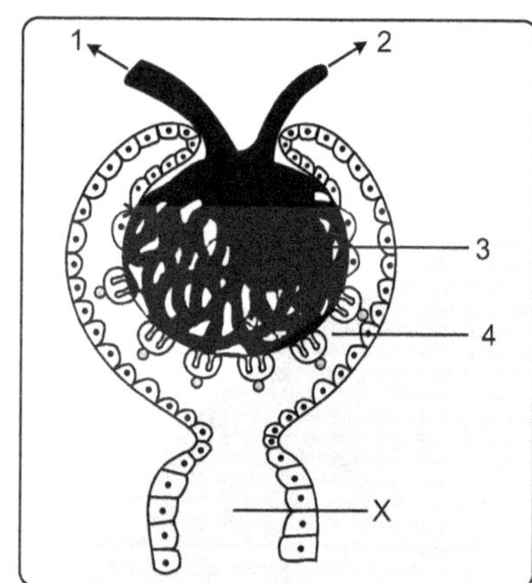

(i) *In which region of the kidney is the above structure present?*

(ii) *Label the parts numbered 1 to 4.*

(iii) *What is the technical terms for the process that occurs in part 3?*

(iv) *Why is fluid X not called urine? Justify your answer.*

(v) *Draw a neat, labelled diagram of the urinary system of man.*

(b) *Differentiate between the following pairs on the basis of what is mentioned in the brackets:* **[5]**

(i) *Transpiration and Guttation (place of occurrence)*

(ii) *Biodegradable waste and Non-biodegradable waste (One example)*

(iii) *Population control and Swachh Bharat Abhiyan (One objective)*

(iv) *Osmosis and Active Transport (Substances undergoing movement)*

(v) *Metaphase and Anaphase (Position of chromosomes)*

Answer 4.

(a) (i) Cortex region of kidney.

(ii) 1. Afferent arteriole; **2.** Efferent arteriole; **3.** Glomerulus; **4.** Bowman's capsule

(iii) Ultrafiltration

(iv) Fluid X is called glomerular filtrate but not urine because it is a very dilute solution that contains not only harmful wastes but also many useful substances like water, salts, glucose etc. which needs to be reabsorbed in the different parts of the nephron.

(v)

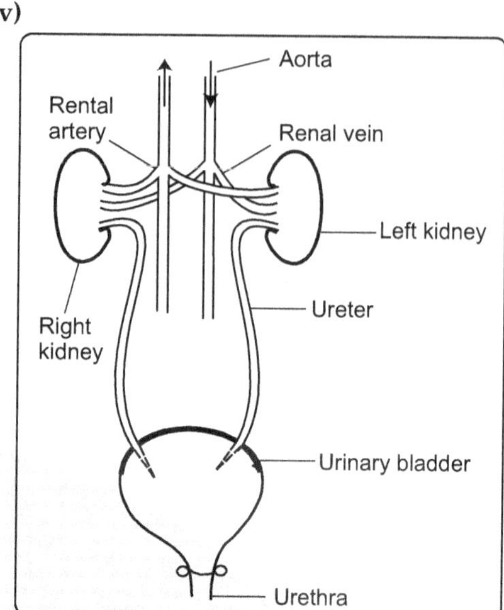

(b) (i) Transpiration occurs mainly through the stomata of the leaves.

Guttation occurs through hydathodes present along the margins of the leaves.

(ii) Example of biodegradable waste is kitchen left overs like peels of vegetables and fruits. Example of non-biodegradable waste is plastics.

(iii) One objective of population control is to make people aware of the advantages of having small family so that they can get proper food, clothing, education, medical facilities.

One objective of Swachh Bharat Abhiyan is to clean streets, roads, infrastructure of country's cities and towns.

(iv) Osmosis is the movement of water molecules. Active transport is the movement of salts or ions.

(v) In metaphase, chromosomes are lined up in one plane at equator of the cell.

In Anaphase, chromosomes move towards opposite poles of the cell.

Question 5.

(a) *The diagram below represents an experiment to demonstrate a certain phenomenon in a green plant:* **[5]**

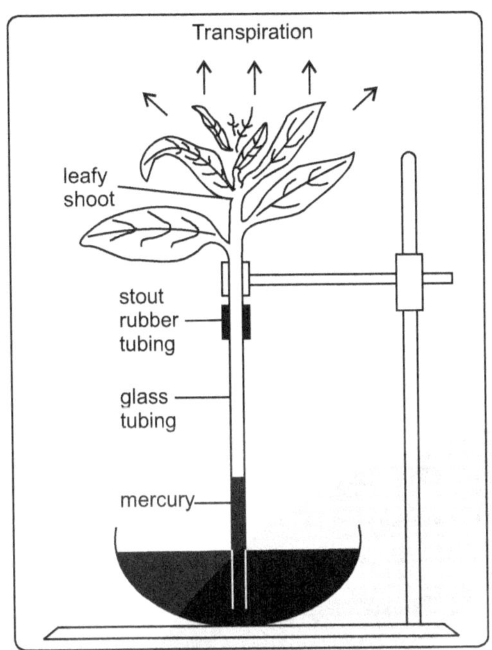

(i) *Will the level of mercury in the glass tubing rise or fall?*

Which conducting tissue of the plant does the glass-tubing represent?

(ii) *Define Transpiration.*

(iii) *How will the rate of the above process differ if the environment of the plant has:*

1. Less humidity

2. High temperature?

(iv) *State any two advantages of transpiration to the plant.*

(v) *Draw a neat labelled diagram of a Plasmolysed cell.*

(b) *Give appropriate biological/technical terms for the following:* **[5]**

(i) *The sensory organ in Cochlea.*

(ii) *Number of live births per 1000 people per year.*

(iii) *The point of contract between two neurons.*

(iv) *The accessory gland in human males whose secretion neutralises the acid in the vagina.*

(v) *Condition when blood sugar level is lowered in the blood.*

(vi) *Structure which helps in the adjustment of the size of the pupil.*

(vii) *A surgical method of fertility control in human males.*

(viii) *Process by which leucocytes migrate through the walls of capillaries.*

(ix) *A sudden inheritable change in one or more genes.*

(x) *A non-dividing phase of the cell cycle where more DNA is synthesised.*

Answer 5.

(a) (i) Mercury in the glass tube will rise.
Xylem

(ii) Transpiration is the loss of water in the form of water vapours from the leaves and other aerial parts of the plant.

(iii) 1. Less humidity increases the rate of transpiration.

2. High temperature increases the rate of transpiration.

(iv) Two advantages of transpiration are:

1. It provides cooling effect to the plant.

2. It provides a suction force which helps in ascent of sap.

(v)

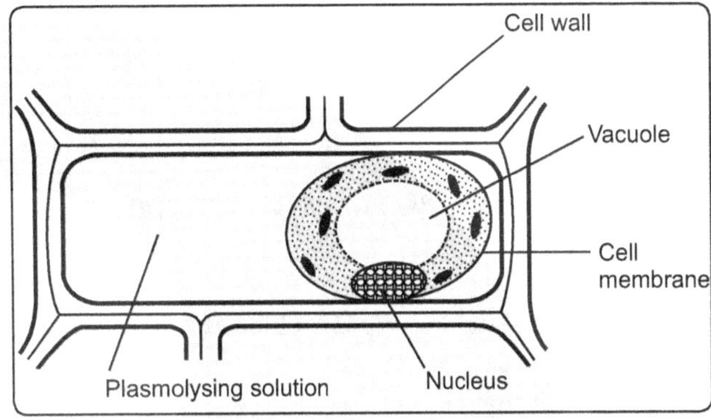

(b) (i) Organ of Corti

(ii) Natality

(iii) Synapse

(iv) Prostate gland

(v) Hypoglycemia

(vi) Iris

(vii) Vasectomy

(viii) Diapedesis

(ix) Mutation

(x) Synthesis phase of Interphase

Question 6.

(a) *State two functions of:* **[5]**

(i) *Ear*   **(ii)** *Ethylene*

(iii) *Tears*   **(iv)** *Testis*

(v) *Cerebellum*

(b) *Complete the table:* **[5]**

Name of the Hormone	*Endocrine Gland*	*Function*
(i)	**(ii)**	*Deposits extra glucose of blood as glycogen*
Growth Hormone	**(iii)**	**(iv)**
(v)	*Thyroid*	**(vi)**
(vii)	**(viii)**	*Prepare body for any emergency*
Oxytocin	**(ix)**	**(x)**

Answer 6.

(a) (i) Ear- **1.** It acts as a hearing organ.

2. It helps in maintaining the dynamic as well as static balance the body.

(ii) Ethylene- **1.** It helps in ripening of fruits.

2. It accelerates senescence.

(iii) Tears- **1.** It serves as a lubricant for the surface of eye.

2. It contains an enzyme lysozyme which kills germs.

(iv) Testis- **1.** They produce sperms.

2. They produce male hormone testosterone.

(v) Cerebellum- **1.** It maintains balance of the body.

2. It coordinates muscular activity.

(b) (i) Insulin

(ii) Pancreas

(iii) Anterior Pituitary gland

(iv) It promotes the normal growth of the whole body.

(v) Thyroxine

(vi) It regulates the basal metabolism of the body.

(vii) Adrenaline

(viii) Adrenal gland

(ix) Posterior Pituitary gland

(x) It stimulates contraction of uterus during child birth and stimulates milk ejection.

Question 7.

(a) *A homozygous dominant tall pea plant bearing red flowers (TTRR) is crossed with a hormozygous recessive dwarf pea plant bearing white flowers (ttrr).* **[5]**

(i) *What is the phenotype and genotype of F_1 individuals?*

(ii) *Write the possible combination of gametes that are obtained when two F_1 hybrid plants are crossed.*

(iii) *Mention the phenotypic ratio of the F_2 generation.*

(iv) *State Mendel's Law of Independent Assortment.*

(v) *Name two X-linked disorders found in humans.*

(b) *The diagram given below is that of a developing human foetus.* **[5]**

Answer the questions that follow:

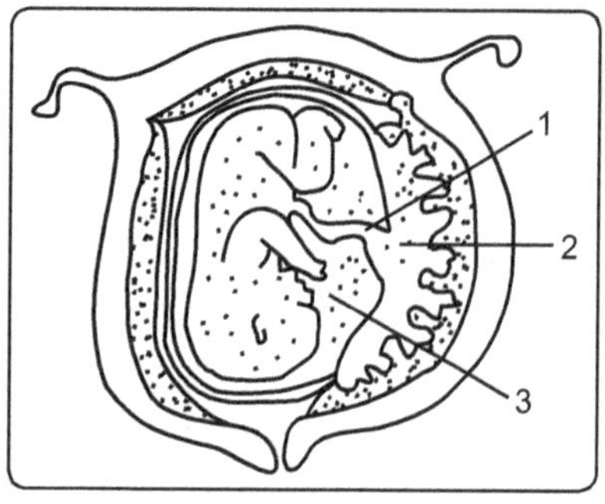

(i) *Label the parts numbered 1 to 3 in the diagram.*

(ii) *Mention any two functions of the part labelled 2 in the diagram.*

(iii) *Explain the significance of the part numbered 3 in the diagram.*

(iv) *Define the term 'Gestation'.*

What is the normal gestational period of the developing embryo?

(v) *Mention the sex chromosomes in a male and female embryo.*

Answer 7.

(a) (i) Phenotype is tall pea plants bearing red flowers.

Genotype is TtRr

(ii) Possible combination of gametes is TR, tR, Tr, tr.

(iii) Phenotypic ratio is 9:3:3:1

(iv) Law of Independent Assortment states that the two pairs of factors in a dihybrid cross are segregated independently during gamete formation and are randomly combined in F_2 generation. Inheritance of factors controlling a particular trait in an organism is independent of the other.

(v) Colour blindness, Haemophilia

(b) (i) 1. Umbilical cord; **2.** Placenta; **3.** Amniotic fluid

(ii) Two functions of placenta are:

1. It allows diffusion of substances like nutrients and oxygen from mother to foetus; and carbon dioxide and waste products from foetus to mother.

2. It acts as an endocrine gland and produces hormones like oestrogen and progesterone.

(iii) Amniotic fluid acts as a shock absorber, protecting the embryo from physical damage by jerks or mechanical shocks. It also prevents sticking of foetus to amnion.

(iv) Gestation is the full term of the development of the embryo in the uterus. In humans, the normal gestation period is about 280 days.

(v) In female embryo, XX sex chromosome is present whereas in male, XY is present.

●●